NATIONAL SECESSION

National Secession

Persuasion and Violence in Independence Campaigns

Philip G. Roeder

CORNELL UNIVERSITY PRESS   ITHACA AND LONDON

First published 2018 by Cornell University Press

Printed in the United States of America

Library of Congress Cataloging-in-Publication Data

Names: Roeder, Philip G., author.
Title: National secession : persuasion and violence in independence campaigns / Philip G. Roeder.
Description: Ithaca : Cornell University Press, 2018. | Includes bibliographical references and index.
Identifiers: LCCN 2018015839 (print) | LCCN 2018017755 (ebook) | ISBN 9781501725999 (pdf) | ISBN 9781501726002 (epub/mobi) | ISBN 9781501725982 | ISBN 9781501725982 (cloth ; alk. paper)
Subjects: LCSH: Secession. | Separatist movements. | Autonomy and independence movements. | Political violence. | Self-determination, National.
Classification: LCC JC327 (ebook) | LCC JC327 .R64 2018 (print) | DDC 320.1/5—dc23
LC record available at https://lccn.loc.gov/2018015839

Contents

Figures

Tables

Acknowledgments

This book would not have been possible without the opportunity to build on the accomplishments of so many distinguished scholars who have gone before and tackled so many of the really difficult issues addressed here. I can only hope that I have done justice to these fine scholars by at least citing their works, even if I have misused some of their contributions.

On a more personal note, once again I learned how much I rely on truly good friends to take a look at an unpolished manuscript. I want to extend special thanks for the many hours and careful comments they provided. Gershon Shafir offered strong encouragement after reading a very early draft of the manuscript, and this kept me going. Valerie Bunce, Caroline Hartzell, and Matthew Hoddie read a slightly improved version and offered extensive and thoughtful suggestions for still more work. Roger Haydon and the two anonymous reviewers at Cornell University Press offered strong encouragement and advice that moved the manuscript to its final draft. I thank each of these wonderful colleagues.

A delight that comes with working at a research university is the presence of outstanding students and research assistants. The University of California at San Diego has been a very special place in this regard. This book began as ill-focused questions that my students and I explored. I think Karthik Vaidyanathan had serious doubts that I knew where I was going in my research (he was right), and his questions challenged me to find focus. In my seminars the students who explored case studies with me introduced me to a wider world. Dotan Haim, Sean Morgan, and Deborah Seligsohn closely read and carefully annotated the first half of the manuscript and thus helped me clarify the theory in this book. Konstantin Ash and Luke Sanford generated GIS-based data and presentations; I would still be puzzling over the diabolically opaque software if I had continued with my original plan to do it all myself. And Brian Engelsma read every last word of the manuscript; his insightful comments helped me clarify the logic and polish my presentation. To all of these students I owe a very special thank-you for their hard work and for making the process of writing this book more enjoyable.

NATIONAL SECESSION

THREE QUESTIONS ABOUT NATIONAL SECESSION

In recent decades the challenge confronting many countries around the world has not been communist revolution or Islamic transformation but national secession. Among the political agendas that have convulsed the world, campaigns to achieve independence through secession have been among the most momentous. These national-secession campaigns promise a transformation every bit as profound and deep as class revolution or religious transformation—not only in the lives of those they claim to liberate but often in the lives of those whom they claim to be their oppressors and even their neighbors. This book asks why some programs for national secession give rise to such significant campaigns and lead to intractable disputes, and even to protracted intense conflicts.

National-secession campaigns are akin to revolutionary activity. In the name of "popular sovereignty," they promise to liberate their people by creating new, independent, sovereign states such as Georgia, Quebec, Scotland, or South Sudan. They promise that these new states will empower their citizens and turn old power relationships on their head: levers of government will be controlled by Eritreans rather than Ethiopians, Latvians rather than Russians, East Timorese rather than Indonesians. Independence will purportedly transform not only the institutions of government but also wealth and property rights, social and cultural patterns: the privileges of oppressors will be stripped away. "Foreigners" and their fellow travelers who enriched themselves under the unjust old regime will be divested. The natural wealth of the homeland, including its land, forests, and resources, will be returned to its rightful owner: the nation. Campaigns for independence promise that the speakers of a national language and the faithful of a national church will be freed from humiliation and oppression. The symbols of the nation will be elevated to a revered place on the national flag, its heroes recognized in monuments, and its history taught in public schools.[1]

The consequences of these changes do not stop at the borders of the new imagined state. For the **common-state** government—the jurisdiction that is currently recognized as the sovereign authority over the secessionists' nation and homeland—the campaign's promises are threats.[2] Secession of Crimea, the Donetsk Republic, and Novorossiia (New Russia) threatened to divide Ukraine almost in half and leave it as a landlocked rump. Secession by East Pakistan threatened to shrink Pakistan's territory by more than an eighth, its economy by almost two-fifths, and its population by more than half.[3] Secession by Slovenia and Croatia threatened to upset a delicate balance among republics within Yugoslavia and initiate an unraveling that would dissolve the federation. Secession by the Baltic states similarly threatened to initiate the unraveling of the Soviet Union. For their neighbors these secessions promised and threatened to change power relations in South Asia, transform the politics of the Balkans and Europe, topple a superpower, and replace global bipolarity with a new world order. Since 1991 great-power confrontations over secessionist crises in Crimea, Kosovo, and South Ossetia have raised fears of a new global cold war.

Yet most attempts to initiate a campaign for independence never get off the ground. Most national-secession projects, such as the Mountain Republic, Transcarpathia, and Turkestan, never get on the international public agenda. Most of their **platform population**—the population that the campaign claims to constitute a nation with a right to a state of its own—is "bought off," in the secessionists' worldview, by the false consciousness, intimidation, and bribes of the status quo. The world may be populated by thousands of nation-state projects, yet most of these have remained the pipe dreams of lone intellectuals or the cherished possessions of small circles that never attract followers beyond the walls of their clandestine meetings. Ernest Gellner is noted for his speculative estimates that the world may contain as many as 800 "reasonably effective nationalisms" and another 7,200 "potential nationalisms." Subtracting the roughly 200 independent nation-states, he estimates that 7,800 potential nation-states have yet to gain independence.[4] Still, only a few of these projects—as is shown in chapter 2, only about 2 percent of these—have become what I label "significant" national-secession campaigns by attracting international attention.

Campaigns for independence can become unusually persistent, and their disputes with existing states may become intractable—with secessionists unwilling to concede or compromise. Victory in a secessionist dispute typically does not come easily or quickly—if at all. The campaign to establish an independent Euskadi for the Basques, which has sometimes been visible and public, but oftentimes invisible and clandestine, has continued for more than a century. The campaign for an independent Ukraine—often small, clandestine, and ignored by most of its platform population, but episodically boisterous and violent—persisted for over seven decades before independence.[5] The campaign for an independent Eritrea—usually violent, but sometimes not—continued for over four decades.[6] Negotiations over independence for Abkhazia, Karabakh, South Ossetia, and Transdniestria—what have come to be known as the "frozen conflicts" of the post-Soviet space—have dragged on with little apparent progress more than two decades after their initial declarations of independence. Negotiations over independence for the Turkish Republic of Northern Cyprus have failed to reach agreement for more than three decades.

Campaigns for independence can become intense—for example, by provoking deadlock in common-state politics or destruction through violence—yet it is only a few that account for the mayhem associated with national secessionism. Still, those few campaigns that do become intense can upset the politics of the common-state, the region, and the world.[7] The conflicts over such national-secession projects as Republika Srpska, South Sudan, and Tamil Eelam unleashed broad destruction, leaving victims dead, wounded, homeless, displaced, or orphaned. In just twenty-three years of national-secession insurgencies from 1989 to 2011, over a quarter-million lives were lost in battle-related deaths alone, and the highest estimates put this closer to 400,000 deaths. In these same years more than 28,000 lives were lost in terrorist acts attributable to groups associated with these national-secession campaigns.[8] To cite just one of these conflicts: in the thirty-year-long armed struggle for Eritrean independence, according to the estimation of David Pool, "around 65,000 fighters had died, 10,000 were disabled, an estimated 40,000 civilian deaths were directly associated with the fighting and around 90,000 children were left without parents."[9] Wars associated with national secessionism have tended to last longer, to be more resistant to negotiated settlement, and to recur more frequently than other civil wars.[10]

The intensity of these campaigns for independence often touches lives well beyond the borders of the common-state from which they seek to secede. Secessionist projects in Kashmir (from India), Tamil Eelam (Sri Lanka), and Air and Azawad (Mali) have brought neighboring countries into conflict with one another. The conflicts for independence within Yugoslavia dragged in participants not just from the Balkans and Europe but also from around the world. Campaigns for independence have spilled over national borders with spectacular terrorist attacks, so even countries with no significant indigenous national secessionism, such as Austria, Germany, Greece, Norway, Sweden, and Switzerland, have become targets of terrorist attacks attributed to national secessionists with grievances against other common-states.

Nevertheless, even among campaigns that drew international attention, most struggles do not resort to violence. Indeed, as will be documented in succeeding chapters, the relationship of campaigns to violence needs to be specified far more carefully, for national-secession campaigns seldom initially emerge in wartime, subsequently engage in violence, or achieve their objectives on the battlefield.

The central question of this book can be stated very simply: how and under what conditions do national-secession projects (1) become significant campaigns, (2) give rise to intractable disputes with their common-state governments over independence, and (3) sustain protracted intense struggles? As will be explained more precisely in later chapters, **significance** refers to getting a claim on the international public agenda; **intractability** refers to the inability to reach agreement with the common-state on the issue of independence; **intensity** refers to the means or public acts mounted by the campaign, such as forcing deadlock within the government, mounting demonstrations on the streets, or launching terrorist attacks; and **protraction** refers to the length of time that this situation persists.

The answer developed in this book can be summarized in an equally simple formulation: the key is coordination of expectations in a platform population—such that other members will see the national-secession program as authentic and realistic. This coordination of expectations concerning the response to the campaign's goals is something broadly overlooked in the literature. As explained more fully in later chapters, **authenticity** refers to the expectation that members of the platform population actually see themselves as a nation; **realism** refers to expectations that statehood is a practical possibility. In this context, authenticity and realism are not issues of one's belief but rather of one's expectations about others in the platform population. Coordination of these expectations can have profound consequences: national-secession projects become significant campaigns only if the leaders coordinate expectations within the platform population around a program for independence. Intractability is a natural consequence of successfully coordinating the platform population's expectations around this program. Protracted intensity in a national-secession campaign is possible only when there is already substantial coordination of expectations and is typically a tactic used to build and maintain this coordination and therefore to reinforce intractability.

This analysis builds on the strategy most commonly used by national-secessionist campaigns—the **strategy of programmatic coordination**—and argues that this strategy should guide the ways in which we analyze national secessionism: our primary focus shifts to the choices made by campaign leaders and their platform populations. The primary loci of their activities are not battlefields but meeting places where programs are drafted and explained, campaign strategies to achieve programmatic goals are designed, cadres are inducted, tactics are selected and taught, and the platform population is persuaded. Our primary analytic attention shifts from sensational acts, such as terrorism and battlefield violence—although these can be important tactical choices made by some campaigns—to seemingly prosaic acts to persuade populations.

Constraints: Bold Ambitions, Weak Forces

The analysis in this book begins from the observation that most national-secession campaigns pursue lofty strategic objectives without the operational capabilities to achieve them. The popular mythology, and the story that secessionists often tell about themselves once they gain independence, constructs images of a bold, direct challenge to the common-state that brings victory over oppressors. During particularly intense periods of a struggle, campaign leaders will inspire the platform population with exhortations that they are about to deliver a decisive blow against the enemy. Yet this is seldom true. And few strategically minded campaign leaders who calculate the likely responses of the common-state government can reasonably expect armed victory. Most national-secession campaigns are far too weak to challenge the common-state directly—a constraint that I label **operational weakness.** Indeed, even among the 171 significant secessionist campaigns tracked here, the median platform population constituted just over 3 percent of the common-state's population. With such limited capabilities, attempts to achieve spectacular victories would spell disaster for most campaigns. Instead, they must await opportunities to receive or pick up independence rather than seize it; that is, they must engage in **strategic opportunism.**[11] Moreover, because they are so weak, most campaigns cannot influence the timing of these opportunities, nor can the campaigns forecast the nature of those opportunities with certainty—a constraint labeled **forecast uncertainty.** Instead, campaigns must await a fortuitous development such as collapse of the central government brought on by its other domestic opponents or international intervention. These opportunities typically come as exogenous shocks to which the campaign must respond rapidly.

Even the few secessionist successes give campaign leaders little evidence that planning for armed victory on the battlefield is a prudent strategy. The reality of strategic opportunism and forecast uncertainty is revealed by the twenty-six national-secession campaigns that actually did achieve independence between

1946 and 2016. None achieved independence by marching to the stronghold of the common-state government and imposing victory. Instead, since World War II, and as described more fully in chapter 2, only two states (Croatia and Slovenia) come close to the myth of armed victory. Over half of the secessionist states achieved independence by simply walking away from a collapsing central government. Another quarter achieved independence after international intervention imposed or guaranteed independence from a resistant or reluctant common-state government.

Indeed, in the face of overwhelming central governments and their own strategic weakness, national-secession campaigns are often open about their objectives of influencing international intervention or waiting for collapse.[12] For example, in China's two most substantial campaigns, many secessionists expect that outside intervention or collapse of the central government in Beijing is the only way that they can achieve independence. In Tibet, Warren Smith reports that when it embraced the goal of independence, the Tibetan government-in-exile focused its campaign on building international political support.[13] In Xinjiang, Gardner Bovingdon reports that when attacking the Public Security Bureau in Lop County, "the protestors are reported to have shouted, 'We'll invite the U.S. and NATO to come, and we'll blow up Xinjiang.'"[14] Bovingdon also recounts a conversation with an unusually outspoken Uyghur editor in 1995: "Minutes later, he mentioned what would happen when China 'disintegrated' (*jieti*), using the very term that had been applied to the Soviet breakup. Taking my lack of expression for skepticism, he assured me that China would follow the Soviet example."[15] For weak campaigns, preparing for intervention or collapse is typically the only prudent strategy.

When operating under these constraints, campaign leaders must prepare a capacity not to force independence on a resistant central government but to demonstrate to leaders of major foreign powers that the campaign's platform population is coordinated around the program of independence, that the proposed nation in control of its homeland will be able to fulfill the obligations of a sovereign state, and that alternative programs offered by the common-state or other campaigns are not viable options. That is, their objective must be to build the capacity to demonstrate **programmatic preemption.** For example, in more than two-thirds of the successful campaigns, referenda on independence demonstrated programmatic preemption by delivering strong support for independence—and in most votes more than 90 percent support.[16] These victories at the ballot box came after long groundwork to coordinate the platform population behind the programmatic goal. A campaign may seek to wear down the common-state government, to influence third parties to create an opportunity to walk away with independence, or simply to await collapse at the center, but in each of these scenarios the campaign must be ready to demonstrate programmatic preemption. Preparing for these opportunities, the campaign must coordinate its platform population around the goal of independence so that local players, whatever remains of the common-state, and the international community conclude that independence is the only viable solution.

The Strategy of Programmatic Coordination

In order to achieve programmatic preemption, national-secession campaigns typically employ a strategy that I label *programmatic coordination*. That is, national secessionists undertake a broad campaign of persuasion, choosing words and deeds for their persuasive power in order to create programmatic preemption. Arguably the foremost theoretician and practitioner of this type of campaigning was Vladimir I. Lenin. Even though he was not a secessionist, Lenin had enormous impact on secessionist campaigns around the world. Prior to the October Revolution, in 1917, Lenin linked his revolutionary cause to the demand for national self-determination within the "prison house of nations" and after the revolution established support for national-secession campaigns as a prominent thesis of Leninism. In the 1920s and later, the Comintern reaffirmed the proclamation of its Fifth Congress on the "nationality question" that "one of the basic principles of Leninism" requires "the resolute and constant advocacy by communists of the right of self-determination (secession and the formation of an independent State)."[17] The Leninist strategy was propagated among national secessionists by the *Short Course* (an instructional manual commissioned by Joseph Stalin), by formal institutions such as the Communist University of the Toilers of the East and the Communist University of the National Minorities of the West, by clandestine schools for insurgents, by sympathetic university classes and discussion groups, and later by the Internet.[18] Mao Zedong, Vo Nguyen Giap, Fidel Castro, Che Guevara, and others developed and elaborated variants of this strategy. This strategy was employed by national secessionists in such exemplary campaigns as Northern Ireland, the Basque country, Turkish Kurdistan, Eritrea, and Tamil Eelam.[19] The retelling of this strategy had global impact, so even campaigns that are seemingly remote from global influences have adopted key elements of this common strategy of programmatic coordination.[20]

Lenin stressed that the critical tasks in building and sustaining a campaign are fostering and maintaining identification with the goal, linking the individual demands of parochial audiences such as peasants or students to the broader cause, sustaining an organization of professional revolutionaries (leaders and cadres) through the hard and often dull times by continuing political education, and developing a surge capacity that can bring a sudden expansion in participation in order to strike at the right moment with demonstrations of broad support for the common goal. In order to fulfill these operational objectives, it is necessary to "give the 'worker in a given field' of revolutionary activity the consciousness that he is marching with the 'rank and file,' the consciousness that his work is directly essential to the Party, that he is one of the links in the chain that will form a noose to strangle the most evil enemy. . . ."[21] As an anonymous Algerian nationalist noted, "strength exists when the masses are mobilized and penetrated by ideas. . . ."[22]

In national-secession campaigns the main operational objective for campaign leaders is convincing members of the platform population that independence is their objective, will serve their individual purposes, has a significant possibility of achieving success, and is likely to be embraced by many other members of the platform population. That is, the strategy of programmatic coordination stresses propagation of this program in order to build the capacity to demonstrate to the platform population and international community that the core claim of nationalism is empirically accurate—that the platform population does, in fact, think of itself as a nation with a right to a sovereign state of its own. As explained in later chapters, arguments to the public on the basis of its self-image (identity) or self-interest (material reward) will vary with the audience, and the importance of adding different audiences will vary with the developmental stage of the campaign. The campaign leaders must not only explain to these diverse audiences how the demand for independence is the logical extension of being a member of the nation. Leaders must also take control of other political issues dear to special interests, link these to the nation-state project, and explain to the platform population how independence will fulfill these diverse and often parochial concerns. To create this programmatic coordination and the surge capacity to demonstrate programmatic preemption requires many organizational developments commonly noted in studies of mobilization, particularly a cadre corps that can disseminate the program, explain its implications to different parts of the platform population, and manage the auxiliaries that will keep the participatory reserve ever ready for mobilization but not continuously mobilized. The hardest tasks confronting leaders of a national-secession campaign may be maintaining this staff, programmatic coordination, and surge capacity during the **longueur**—the long, dull periods when there are few opportunities for heroic public acts and victory is not within sight. The propagation of the program breathes life into these organizational tasks.

The strategy of programmatic coordination stresses that the key to survival and ultimate programmatic preemption is a compelling goal and a credible plan to achieve it that are brought together in a political **program**.[23] With an authentic and realistic program, leaders can sustain a staff through the longueur and mobilize widespread surges of participation in coherent activities at particular moments to press forward to independence. The goal within a *national-secession program* is formulated as a *nation-state project* for a specific population (purportedly a nation) to become self-governing within a sovereign state of its own.[24] Typically this includes an elaborate justification for why this population does, in fact, constitute a nation and does, indeed, have a legitimate claim to its homeland, but elaborate ethnographies and histories are not necessary elements of a national-secession program. The program pairs the project with an **action plan** outlining concrete steps to bring about the proposed outcome of independence.

National-secession programs concern the foundations of the ultimate political community and the proper boundaries of this state within which programs for social, economic, and political institutions typically must compete. National-secession programs seek to create new states—the meta-institutions within which more-mundane constitutional changes, such as the transition from authoritarianism to democracy, or presidentialism to parliamentarism, or socialism to capitalism, are negotiated and implemented. Yet, as Valerie Bunce poignantly observes, "Nationalism is wanton. It can couple with a wide variety of regimes."[25] Nationalist doctrine does not itself present an answer to the question of the proper social, economic, or political institutions within the new nation-state other than that they should be "of, by, and for" the nation.

Consequences of Programmatic Coordination

This strategy has profound consequences for the campaign: an immediate concern becomes uniting individuals with diverse public, parochial, and personal motives behind a common goal. Using the vocabulary of military science and business, while the campaign must constantly keep in sight the **strategic goal** of independence, the **operational objective** in the strategy of programmatic coordination must be to establish programmatic preemption, and this operational objective will in turn shape the choice of **tactics** such as violence.[26] And as this programmatic coordination deepens and broadens, the campaign is more likely to draw the attention of the global community (significance), to produce a deadlock with the common-state government over the issue of independence (intractability), and to find the means and reasons to conduct a broader, more costly, and longer struggle (protracted intensity).

Coordinating Motivational Heterogeneity

The strategy of programmatic coordination brings into the campaign individuals who represent very different *types* with diverse personal motivations, and this motivational heterogeneity makes the operational tasks of campaign coordination even more important. The founders of national-secession campaigns are typically **enthusiasts** who fervently believe that their platform population constitutes a nation with a right to a sovereign state of its own—even when most members of that platform population have not (yet) realized this. Enthusiasts derive satisfaction from contributing to the cause of independence but, particularly in the early stages of a campaign, are usually rare. They may attract a few **expressionists,** who derive satisfaction from engaging in a struggle of protesting, organizing, and even violence. Yet much of the platform population typically comes to the campaign not on the basis of some romantic belief or revelry through action, but on the expectation that independence will address their most pressing needs. That is, with respect to the campaign's claim, they are **pragmatists.** It is the common goal of independence and not the multiplicity of private purposes that gives rise to campaign unity, so programmatic coordination is a continuing concern for campaign leaders: as seen more fully in later chapters, campaign leaders must link these different types, energized by different motivations, to a campaign for a common goal that offers one solution to their diverse purposes.

Choices of Tactics

This operational objective will shape the national secessionists' choice of tactics or means. National-secession campaign leaders have little control over the timing or nature of the opportunities that will permit their campaigns to move closer to their strategic goal of independence. Therefore, national-secession campaigns must persuade different members of the platform population to prepare themselves to demonstrate coordination around the goal of independence in whatever opportunities arise in the future, such as voting for a candidate or party, joining in a demonstration or armed action to sway foreign governments, or ratifying independence in a referendum. The tactical options may include conspiratorial organizing, parliamentary struggle, street protests, terrorism, guerilla warfare, or broad military operations. The choice of one of these tactics will vary with the opportunity created by others, with the developmental stage of the campaign, with the mix of types within the campaign at that moment, and with the anticipated response of their platform population at that stage. Except during the penultimate moment leading to independence, a key operational objective in the choice of any tactic is to achieve still greater programmatic coordination.

In particular, the operational objective influences the use of violence: a national-secession campaign employing the strategy of programmatic coordination typically uses increasing intensity such as violence to build towards programmatic preemption. That is, violence most often is propaganda (that is, persuasion) by other means. The contribution of violence to programmatic pre-emption can be substantial: it may awaken support for independence in a plat-form population by showing that others are willing to make costly commitments on its behalf; raise expectations among potential recruits that independence is a possibility; make the campaign organization appear competent, energetic, and state-like by defending or avenging the nation; maintain discipline among members of the nation and deter "traitorous" defections to other causes or to the common-state; or provoke countermeasures from the government that will reinforce solidarity within the platform population. Campaign leaders sustain intense struggles to make it more difficult for members of the platform pop-ulation to collaborate with the common-state, for other members of the plat-form population to develop competing campaigns for alternative nation-state projects, and for the international community to hope that holding together the common-state is a viable option.[27] Yet the choice of violence—just like the choice of any tactic—must be subject to the stricture, articulated by Lenin, that a campaign at different periods "applies different methods, *always* qualifying the choice of them by *strictly* defined ideological and organizational conditions."[28]

Significance, Intractability, and Protracted Intensity

The strategy of programmatic coordination, as it gets closer to achieving pro-grammatic preemption, increases the likelihood of significance, intractability, and protracted intensity. In order to get the attention of the international com-munity and particularly the attention of the governments of the major powers that control admission to the community (significance), a national-secession campaign must offer a program that has coordinated, or is likely to coordinate, the platform population around the goal of independence. Foreign governments are likely to dismiss any campaign that they deem has little prospect of such coordination. The campaign is more likely to get on the international agenda as it approaches programmatic preemption and demonstrates that the platform population supports the claim that no viable alternative to independence exists.

Deadlock on the substantive issue of sovereignty between national-secession campaigns and common-state governments (intractability) is a consequence of programmatic coordination: when expectations in the platform population align around the program for independence, campaign leaders are less likely to compromise with the common-state government. More members of the platform population see little gain from defection to or collaboration with the common-state. They come to see the enticements offered by the common-state government as less attractive when they suspect that potential collaborators will be attacked by their neighbors as traitors to the nation and possibly stripped of their gains. Successful coordination behind a national-secession program can also have important blowback for the campaign leaders: by making compromise with the central government unacceptable, secessionist leaders tie their own hands because compromise has become too costly for them as well. In sum, disputes with the common-state government become intractable as a consequence of a strategy designed to maintain unity within the campaign's leadership and staff, to develop a following within the platform population so that it conceives of itself as a nation seeking a sovereign state, and to deter defectors and compromisers from within the leadership, staff, or platform population. Intractability is often seen outside the campaign as an undesired deadlock, but for campaign leaders who seek independence, intractability can sustain second-best outcomes such as de facto statehood.

Protracted intense struggles require the capacity that comes from substantial programmatic coordination but typically are sensible undertakings only when campaign leaders expect protracted intensity to move the campaign closer to programmatic preemption. That is, programmatic coordination is both a constraint on and an operational objective of violence. Strategically minded campaign leaders are less likely to attempt a protracted intense struggle if they expect that doing so will reveal opposition to the goal of independence within their own platform population. It is possible only when the leaders can rely on a platform population tightly coordinated on the goal of independence as the solution to their own particular concerns. At the same time, strategically minded campaign leaders are more likely to use violence when they expect that this propaganda by deeds will deepen and broaden programmatic coordination.

Programmatic Theory

The next chapters introduce an analytic approach that complements earlier approaches but in no way seeks to displace them. Still, programmatic theory places at the center of analysis the publically articulated goals of political actors and their strategies to achieve these goals. And this leads the analysis in the following chapters to diverge from earlier approaches in some very significant details.

Bringing Political Goals Back In

National-secession conflicts have been described as battles for hearts, bellies, and more-private parts of human anatomies.[29] Instead, the programmatic theory emphasizes battles for people's minds. To use Eric Hoffer's words, campaigns promise platform populations "sudden and spectacular change in their conditions of life." This promise offers a bold and visionary goal: "Those who would transform a nation or the world . . . must know how to kindle and fan an extravagant hope."[30] This requires a credible program, and it requires the labors of many propagandists and agitators to link individuals with diverse and often narrow, personal concerns to a campaign for a common public goal. Indeed, Lenin stressed that the constant task for campaigns seeking to transform states is to link belly concerns to the campaign's goal. If the campaign permits these material concerns to take precedence and transforms the campaign into a war for bellies, then the campaign is at risk of becoming merely reformist. Similarly, the battle for minds trumps the battle to grab more-private parts. Mao, in the heat of the war against Japan and the Kuomintang, lambasted "the so-called theory that 'weapons decide everything'" and underscored that "it is people, not things, that are decisive." And even in a "contest of strength," such as war, a strategist must look to the "contest of human power and morale."[31] In short, an analytic subtext in programmatic theory is a claim that analysis should take seriously the public demands of political actors, the goals around which they coordinate their members, and the substantive disputes to which these give rise. This diverges from both the raw behaviorism of some studies of movements, protest, and violence and the presumption of unconscious or hidden motivations of much of the micro-motivational literature on greed and grievances. The programmatic approach stresses that even though individuals may bring deeper, disparate, and parochial motivations to a national-secession campaign, what ties them together and shapes their behavior in common patterns is the pursuit of the common public goal of independence.

The focus on political goals and the persuasive efforts on behalf of these goals requires a precisely defined unit of analysis, and here this is a **campaign.** In this usage a campaign is constituted by the persuasive efforts on behalf of a specific goal. It is the programmatic goal that gives the campaign integrity and continuity. A campaign typically exists independently—prior to and after—specific organizations, movements, episodes of mobilization, or civil wars. Studies of these other phenomena follow campaigns only through phases of their development or activism and entirely ignore most campaigns because they do not exhibit the features studied. A campaign survives if persuasive efforts on behalf of its goal continue, even as the personnel, organization, alliances, and tactics of the campaign vary over time. Although the other, more commonly used concepts, such as social movements, may describe phenomena characterized by diverse and changing goals, campaigns are defined by the consistent pursuit of a specific goal.[32] A campaign may form alliances in order to forge movements which embrace groupings that pursue complementary operational objectives but do not share programmatic goals; in other words, movements may embrace multiple campaigns. For example, large parts of the Basque independence campaign coexisted within the Basque movement alongside competing campaigns for Basque autonomy within the Spanish state and for cultural preservation without explicit statehood goals. Within these movements or alliances of campaigns, an independence campaign may become hegemonic—even if only temporarily—but may also find itself subordinate to, marginalized by, or abandoned by co-nationals whom the independence campaign leaders see as compromisers, collaborators, and/or traitors to the cause of independence. Nevertheless, the campaign has a life of its own. Survival of the campaign is measured by the efforts to persuade members of the platform population that independence is the only viable option. Extreme marginalization of national-secession campaigns is common, but death of a national-secession campaign is far rarer, except when a campaign achieves its goal of independence.[33]

In the analysis of campaigns, programmatic theory gives special attention to the role of propagation to achieve programmatic coordination, distinguishing this from the focus on organization and mobilization that is central to the study of social movements. As chapters 3 and 4 elaborate, the "ideological" in Lenin's formulation is at least the equal to the "organizational" in "ideological-organizational work." Although the tangibility of formal organizations makes these attractive objects of study, their coherence and ability to work together towards a common goal such as independence depend on the persuasive efforts to propagate a campaign's goal and action plan. Thus, in the analysis that follows it is the tasks of propagation to further programmatic coordination that define the developmental stages of a campaign and the engagement of different types within the platform population. These serve the prime operational objective of building towards programmatic preemption: campaigns achieve success by persuading members of one or many organizations that they have a common goal which will reward them all.

Rational Use of Limited Information and Emotions

This book takes a rationalist political-cultural approach. The analysis focuses on the relative power of different goals to coordinate expectations about the responses of others. It directs analysis to the power of persuasion and the processes of argumentation through appeals to what are believed to be, on the evidence of observable cues, common knowledge. It privileges the rational process of human calculation, assessment, and choice in linking the private to the public and coordinating on a common goal, but recognizes the power of diverse emotions, private catharsis, and self-expression to energize individuals. Thus, programmatic theory does not jump into the old debate on whether national secessionism is either rational or irrational; it must use the former to harness the latter, and it needs both. Emotions in a population are likely to be heterogeneous, short-term, and evolving within individuals at different rates.[34] The success of a campaign's appeals depends on the ability of its program to persuade potential recruits that the goals of the campaign are authentic and realistic in the assessments of many others who have diverse personal motivations but who are in some essential way "just like one another." Only in this way can the program bring together the energies of diverse motivations behind a common goal.

This model does not assume that either leaders or members have superhuman powers: its strategically minded actors are simply reasoning problem solvers. The analytic model assumes that both campaign leaders and members of the platform population assess the authenticity and realism of the program for independence with what Samuel L. Popkin calls "practical reasoning about government and politics" based on low information. For both leaders and members, the program for independence offered by a national-secession campaign must ring true with the evidence that is available to them. The analytic model begins with abstract, ideal-type reasoning problem solvers who have limited information: both the leaders and members of the platform populations know well their own worlds but have limited information about the others'. Leaders know more about high politics and the complex concept of a nation-state, but the platform population knows more about the interface of the state with the nation's lives—at least in their small parts of the nation. The campaign seeks to link these two worlds in the name of the whole nation. When campaigns introduce a new idea to the platform population about nation-states, members of the platform population weigh this imagined community, the political project for independence, and the claims about its consequences by reality tests based on information shortcuts drawn from what they do know. As elaborated in chapters 5 and 7, they look for *cues* that other members of the platform population are likely to see as corroboration of the authenticity of the program's nation-state project and the realism of its action plan. It is by surviving such reality tests that, as Popkin explains, "campaigns attempt to achieve a common focus, to make one question and one cleavage paramount. . . ."[35] Campaigns need not try to change worldviews but to draw out the connections between the program and individual worldviews. Campaigns gather new adherents through persuasion—argumentation about logical connections and cause-and-effect relationships.[36]

The focus of programmatic coordination is not on individual belief and behavior but on the convergence of expectations among many individuals that supports collective action. For reasoning problem solvers, national independence is a prudent goal only if others can be expected to support it. Thus, this analysis stresses the processes of coordination of actors' expectations about the assessments and behaviors of others, and particularly of the platform population at large. On this coordination within the platform population hinges the expectations of campaign leaders, staffers, reservists, potential recruits, and the international community about the prospects that a campaign will achieve programmatic preemption. The programmatic account brings together elite and popular expectations. Thus, to the earlier debate whether nationalism is an elite or popular ("mass") phenomenon, this says that it must be both.[37] Although intellectuals and campaign leaders write programs for independence and constitute the vanguard of struggles for independence, they are unlikely to initiate, let alone sustain, a campaign for nation-statehood unless they expect to enlist the support of the platform population. Throughout the process of programmatic coordination, both campaign leaders and members of the platform population try to assess the extent to which other members of the platform population will see a particular nation-state project as both authentic and realistic.

Common Goals but Diverse Motivations

The programmatic approach begins with an assumption of motivational heterogeneity. This premise and the focus on political goals as the way to build coalitions among individuals with diverse particularistic, parochial, and sometimes personal concerns represent a return to an earlier understanding of politics: a central problem confronting national-secession campaign leaders as political leaders is building a coalition among participants who are diverse in the extent to which identity, grievances, and greed (micro-motivations) take precedence in their assessment of a political project. They are also diverse in their orientations to the campaign's goal as an end in itself or as a means to other ends: as elaborated in chapter 4, enthusiasts see the campaign's goal as an end in itself and derive satisfaction from working towards this goal, expressionists see the campaign as an occasion for a struggle that is an end in itself, and pragmatists see independence as a means to achieve other, often material rewards.

Recently in the social sciences, for the sake of rigor, empirical theories often make simplifying and homogenizing assumptions about the motivation or type of actors. Rather than jump into the stale debate among realists, positive political economists, political sociologists (or culturalists), and political psychologists who ascribe some single static motivation to secessionists, the programmatic approach begins from an assumption that coordination in the context of motivational heterogeneity is a central problem confronting campaign leaders. Successful secessionist campaigns typically must build a coalition of true believers (a focus of sociological approaches), expressionists (a focus of psychological approaches), the aggrieved (a focus of social psychological approaches), politicians (the focus of realist approaches), and *homines economici* (the focus of political economic approaches). This coalition building is at the core of programmatic coordination.

The coalition process influences the way in which programmatic theory conceptualizes the relationship of agency to structure. The analysis in the following chapters stresses the role of strategically minded actors who make strategic, operational, and tactical choices under the constraints (both obstacles and opportunities) that nature deals to them. Agency does not constitute structure, but it can be artful in the use of those conditions. For example, campaign leaders link the national identity defined by the nation-state project to a variety of ethnic identities or link the campaign goal of independence to the solution of a variety of private or parochial sources of grievance or ambition. Even when confronting obstacles and opportunities that are immutable, campaign leaders can manipulate the ways that the campaign links its goal to these. Not all obstacles and opportunities create equally strong constraints on programmatic coordination by the campaign, so a central analytic task of programmatic theory is to distinguish those elements of structure that are more remote and less constraining from the more proximate and constraining structural obstacles and opportunities.

Thus, this analysis diverges from the many studies of national secessionism in recent years that emphasize the role of exogenously determined identities, grievances, and greed by giving more credit to agents who can make artful use of these in linking them to a campaign goal. None of the commonly identified structural factors force the conclusion that a platform population should have a sovereign state of its own; these are no more than cues to the authenticity and realism of that claim. That is, the link from structure to programmatic preemption is indeterminate. Alternative identities can be linked to a specific nation-state project, different motivations can energize a campaign for independence and be solved by the goal of independence, and so campaign leaders pick which parochial concerns to activate on behalf of the cause of independence. That is, the most commonly cited motivations are typically substitutable for one another in different circumstances in building toward programmatic preemption. The programmatic theory developed in this book privileges the central role of the agency of campaign leaders and propagandists in linking these specific structural features to the campaign's goal.

The End of Bargaining

Programmatic coordination that creates intractability in exchanges between a common-state and an operationally weak party gives rise to situations that are not best characterized as variable-sum games. The parties define the issues that divide them as a nondivisible, nonfungible goal. This diverges from the currently hegemonic metaphor that sees national-secession conflicts and civil wars as bargaining.[38] Yet with successful programmatic coordination, exchanges between leaders of national-secession campaigns and common-state governments cease to be bargaining relationships and evolve into championships. As a consequence of advancing programmatic coordination, exchanges of substantive offers and escalation of means increasingly come to be propaganda by other means addressed not to the party "across the negotiation table" but to an audience of one's platform population and the international community.

This particularly applies to the use of the bargaining metaphor to analyze the use of violence. In the programmatic account, violence is a tactic that strategically minded campaign leaders use when it contributes to the campaign's operational objectives and strategic goals. For national-secession campaigns, most of which operate under the constraint of strategic weakness, using violence to prevail in a contest of arms with the common-state government is seldom a prudent tactical choice. Alternatively, violence can be a valuable continuation of propaganda by other means targeted at the audience observing the exchanges between secessionists and central governments. In these campaigns, violence is designed to persuade the audience, and in particular to reinforce programmatic coordination, rather than to induce the common-state government to cry uncle. The constraints that determine the likelihood of victory in a contest of arms, which have been the focus of a lively literature on civil wars, tend to be remote from the calculations of most national-secession campaign leaders most of the time. Similarly, for these situations, bargaining models of violence, which have been so fruitful in the analysis of contests of violence among sovereign states, are often inappropriate starting points in the analysis of internal wars involving operationally weak national-secession campaigns.

This book offers an explanation for which national-secession campaigns become significant by getting their claims on the international public agenda, give rise to intractable disputes with their common-state governments over the issue of independence, and engage in protracted intense struggles. Its answer is campaigns that are more successful at programmatic coordination—that is, campaigns that foster the expectation that their platform populations will rally behind national independence. The structural conditions that favor this are cues to the authenticity and realism of the campaign's nation-state project and action plan.

In these conflicts, supporters of a national-secession project challenge an existing state by demanding the right to take "their" part of its population and territory out of the jurisdiction of the current government and into another, usually newly independent sovereign state. This book presents an analytic model of national-secession campaigning drawn from the prescriptive strategic advice offered by some of the most-successful leaders of major revolutions and independence campaigns. Whatever their many differences, these leaders knew their craft, were masters of campaigning, and distilled their insights in a vibrant strategy of programmatic coordination that has guided many nationalists in their pursuit of independence. Although this micro-model focuses on the problems of building a successful national-secession campaign, this book does not take sides between secessionists and common-state governments. This book's purpose is to offer a general theory and to explain patterns of significance, intractability, and protracted intensity.

This book is self-consciously "social scientific" but spares the reader many of the lengthy methodological discussions in the main text and places these in the appendices. Hypotheses in chapters 5 and 7 describing macro-level empirical patterns of significance, intractability, and protracted intensity are derived from the micro-model. And my claim throughout is that these follow logically from the main premises and processes described in the abstract theory elaborated in chapters 3 and 4. Empirical corroboration of hypotheses in chapters 5 and 7 rests on macro-level evidence from a multitude of cases compiled in statistical data sets. These data sets permit assessments of the generalizability of claims through global coverage from 1945 to 2010.

STRATEGIC CONSTRAINTS
Goals and Means

National-secession campaigns may recruit through promises of bold actions to snatch independence from the hands of a determined enemy and even visions of armed victories over the forces of the common-state government in order to impose separation. Yet independence seldom comes in this way. And strategically minded campaign leaders who look for guidance from the experience of others who have gone before can gather little evidence from the successful secessions to conclude otherwise. Certainly, founding myths of heroic struggles that seized independence abound. When strategically minded campaign leaders look closely at the successful secessions, however, they see that most national-secession campaign leaders operated under very tight constraints that prevented any direct seizure of independence. And in many cases, when independence came, it did not even come as a direct result of actions by the national-secession campaign. (See the map of successful and unsuccessful national-secession campaigns in figure 2.1.)

Yet few campaign leaders will want just to sit by and hope for a fortuitous outcome. So what does the evidence from the twenty-six successful secessions from 1945 to 2016 suggest that national-secession campaign leaders should do? If they take the time to look for hard evidence from these successes, campaign leaders are likely to see that even the successful secessions highlight the strategic constraints under which national-secession campaign leaders typically operate: these underscore the operational weakness (when compared to the common-state) of even the successful campaigns for independence. These successes show the need for

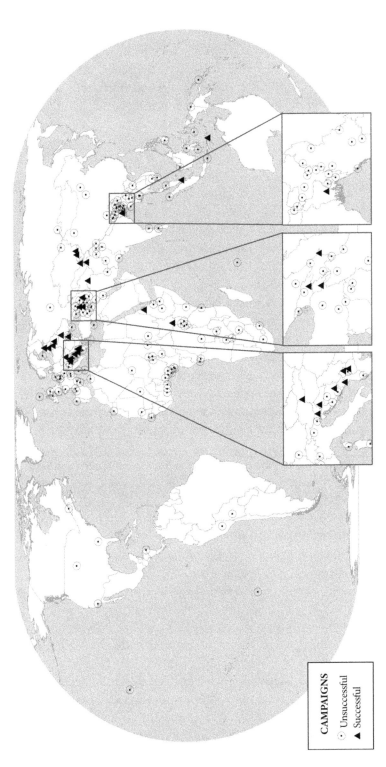

FIGURE 2.1. Significant national-secession campaigns, 1945–2010. Symbols for successful campaigns that achieved independence and unsuccessful campaigns that did not are centered on the capital or largest cities within the territories claimed by the nation-state projects.

CAMPAIGNS
⊙ Unsuccessful
▲ Successful

campaigns to prepare to seize opportunities that are typically created by others (strategic opportunism) and that are difficult to forecast (forecast uncertainty).

A humbling consequence of these strategic constraints is that even the successful secessions give campaign leaders little reason to expect to achieve independence through their own armed victory over the common-state government. Only two of the twenty-six successful cases (Croatia and Slovenia) approached this, but, as explained below, even there the causal link from violence to independence is ambiguous. Violence was more commonly a tactic to influence foreign powers to intervene and impose independence on reluctant common-states (for example, in Bangladesh, Eritrea, Kosovo, South Sudan, and Timor Leste). A second humbling lesson for national-secession campaign leaders from these successful secessions is that in many cases, campaign leaders were not the prime movers to independence. In nine of the twenty-six successful secessions (Azerbaijan, Belarus, Kazakhstan, Kyrgyzstan, Singapore, Tajikistan, Turkmenistan, Ukraine, and Uzbekistan), the national-secession campaigns were excluded from power and in some cases thoroughly marginalized when leaders who were not parts of those campaigns achieved the campaigns' goal of independence.

Instead, these twenty-six successful secessions suggest that the key operational objective of a national-secession campaign should be to develop a capacity to demonstrate programmatic preemption at critical moments: campaigns made their most important contributions by creating a capacity to demonstrate to the international community that independence is the only viable option at a decisive moment—even though the campaign may not create the moment. In pursuit of this operational objective of programmatic coordination, campaign leaders should use every cue and tool available to coordinate expectations in the platform population and international community—expectations that the platform population sees the project for independence as the only viable option. Although the tactics of greater intensity in a struggle with the common-state government are unlikely to bring direct victory over the common-state, the tactic was effective in deepening programmatic coordination and demonstrating programmatic preemption. A segment-state designated for the campaign's platform population could be a particularly valuable tool in this coordination, if used to propagate the nation-state project and the case for independence.[1] Ten national-secession campaigns used common-state elections to win de jure control of governments in the segment-states of Armenia, Bosnia, Croatia, Estonia, Georgia, Latvia, Lithuania, Montenegro, Slovakia, and Slovenia. Another four campaigns achieved de facto control of all or parts of Eritrea, Kosovo, South Sudan, and Timor Leste through armed struggle and campaigning. Control of a segment-state did not bring independence, but it did improve the coordination of expectations and position the campaign to prepare its platform population to onstrate programmatic preemption.

These inferences about strategic constraints, operational objectives, and tactics are the starting points for the strategy of programmatic coordination, which is discussed in chapters 3 and 4.

Identifying National-Secession Campaigns

Before turning to the task of identifying these lessons from successful campaigns, it is important to define the concept of national secession more precisely. On this basis we can also define the universe of cases we will be examining in this and later chapters. This also means identifying closely related types of campaigns that are excluded from this study. (The appendix to this chapter describes the data set for significant national-secession campaigns on which much of the analysis in this and succeeding chapters is based.)

What Distinguishes National-Secession Campaigns?

National secessionism is a political program claiming that a population residing inside another sovereign state constitutes a nation that has a right to its own sovereign state within the part of the common-state's territory that the nation considers its homeland. National-secession campaigns share many qualities with closely related types of campaigns but represent a distinctive combination of peoplehood, statehood, and secession claims. (Figure 2.2 illustrates this idea.) **Peoplehood campaigns** claim that a specific population constitutes an identifiable "people." **Statehood campaigns** claim that a territory should be constituted as a state. **Secession campaigns** are a subset of these statehood campaigns that seek sovereign independence. So national-secession campaigns claim that the identified people should control their homeland as a sovereign state of their own.

National-secession campaigns differ from **regional-secession campaigns** (a different type of secessionist statehood campaign) in that the nationalists claim that their populations such as Abkhazians, Bugandans, Quebecois, or Timorese are not simply agglomerations of individuals but constitute distinct nations and that the territory they claim is not simply a tract but the nation's homeland. Alternatively, the claim of California or Western Canada secessionists that their regions should be sovereign states is not predicated on the claim that the Californians—no matter how special we might be—or Western Canadians constitute nations or that their territories are homelands. Often, such secession campaigns acknowledge a common ethnicity with many from whom they would secede, but hold to different political views. Indeed, in many US cases secessionists claim that their populations are a truer expression of Americanism than the fallen community they would leave behind. For example, the petition

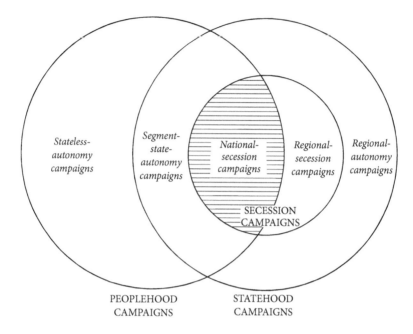

FIGURE 2.2. Types of peoplehood and statehood campaigns

signed by more than 81,000 Texans calling for their state "to withdraw from the union" following the 2012 reelection victory of President Barack Obama maintained that their purpose in seeking independence was "to re-secure their rights and liberties in accordance with the original ideas and beliefs of our founding fathers which are no longer being reflected by the federal government."[2] Thus, J. Paul Goode argues that regionalism is a distinct phenomenon and not just "a diminished form of nationalism." Regionalist campaigns are defined by "their boundaries rather than content," are "concerned with regional boundaries rather than self-determination," and differ from nationalist campaigns "in the fundamental respect that the territorial component is the foundation of community and political identification rather than the reverse."[3]

Not all statehood campaigns on behalf of distinct peoples pursue the goal of secession. **Autonomy campaigns** constitute a type of both peoplehood and statehood campaigns but not secession campaigns, for they seek only a new autonomous state (frequently a **segment-state**) or expanded powers for it within the existing common-state rather than independence. For example, the Volga German campaign sought but failed to secure restoration of the Volga German Republic within the Soviet Union, the Cordillera campaign sought and secured the Cordillera Administrative Region to give greater autonomy to the indigenous peoples of northern Philippines, and more than a half-dozen campaigns have sought creation of new states within India. Other autonomy campaigns have sought expanded autonomy for an already existing segment-state within its current common-state. For example, the Ticino (Italian-Swiss) campaign in Switzerland, the Vojvodina (Magyar) campaign in Serbia, and more than a dozen campaigns in Russia (e.g., Bashkortostan and Sakha) engaged in intergovernmental politics to expand the powers of homeland governments relative to the central government but did not press the goal of independence. In the historical period analyzed in this book (1945 to 2010), many autonomy campaigns did not go on to demand independence. Inclusion of these cases would make our analysis of national secession less precise.[4] Campaigns that did not make public claims to independence that came to the attention of international media in the period under investigation are excluded from the list of significant secession campaigns.

Some peoplehood campaigns seek **stateless autonomy.** As Charles W. Anderson, Fred R. von der Mehden, and Crawford Young note, "In extreme cases autonomist aspirations can be achieved by the simple expedient of internal withdrawal from the political system. Remote areas satisfied with a near-subsistence level of economic activity can simply cease obeying central authority."[5] Even some modern campaigns, such as the Haida Gawaii campaign in British Columbia, the Chiapas Mayan campaign in Mexico, and the Coptic Republic campaign in Egypt, have not sought a modern territorial state but have sought some form of state-less autonomy from central and regional governments. These peoplehood campaigns that do not seek statehood and secession are also excluded from the analysis here.

The national-secession campaigns examined here differ from decolonization campaigns in that they concern separation of a population residing within the metropole rather than in an external territory.[6] Thus, the campaigns for independence of Puerto Rico or Guam from the United States, Nigeria or India from the United Kingdom, Indonesia or Suriname from the Netherlands, and many others are not treated as secessions. The distinction between metropole and colonies is made by international law. For example, the United Nations Declaration on Friendly Relations stipulates that "the territory of a colony or other Non-Self-Governing Territory has, under the Charter, a status separate and distinct from the territory of the State administering it. . . ."[7] International declarations, such as the 1960 Declaration on the Granting of Independence to Colonial Countries and Peoples, draw a bright line between the right to self-determination of colonial and occupied territories that creates an obligation to aid their transition to sovereignty, on the one hand, and the territorial integrity of existing sovereign states that precludes support for secessionist groups that would carve out new states from the metropolitan territory, on the other.[8] In this context, explaining why colonial peoples become the platforms for independence campaigns is just too easy. Indeed, reflecting the very different conditions necessary for each to achieve independence, 87 percent of the 128 colonies that existed in 1945 had become sovereign states by 2016, but 85 percent of the 171 national-secession campaigns that became significant in that period did not achieve independence. Including decolonization cases would provide strong predictors of what distinguishes decolonization from secession, for many independent variables (such as geographic distance, cultural and social differences, or representation in the common-state executive and legislature) correlate with this internal-external distinction.[9] This would not identify the constraints under which some but not other secessionist projects are likely to give rise to significant campaigns, intractable disputes, and protracted intense struggles.

Significant National-Secession Campaigns since 1945

The world is dotted with hopeful nation-state projects—perhaps thousands of projects—although there is no way to count them all because most fall on deaf ears and their brief lives go unrecorded unless a journalist or an ethnographer preserves them as curios. Most remain the pet projects of solitary dreamers; some attract a narrow circle of followers around a dinner table or in a classroom. Few attempts to mount a campaign in pursuit of a nation-state project successfully establish a permanent presence with a corps of cadres carrying the word and activists mobilizing to reinforce this message. Still fewer develop a sustained capacity to stage surge events—for example, to mount mass demonstrations that paralyze the center of a provincial capital such as Catalonia's Barcelona, to get out the vote to capture control of regional governments such as Quebec, to create deadlock in the politics of a common-state such as Belgium, or to unleash mayhem such as in Eritrea. A search of the *Times* of London, the *New York Times,* and *Keesing's Contemporary Archives* between January 1945 and December 2010, checked against printed and Internet sources, identified 171 national-secession campaigns that have been able to sufficiently publicize their programs by word or deed to draw international press attention. This is the operationalization that I will use to identify a "significant national-secession campaign" (see figure 2.1). This convenient operationalization is also a theoretically appropriate indicator of significance: as will become clear in the cases discussed in this chapter, a central operational objective of campaigns is to get the attention of the international community (particularly in Western capitals) in order to convince foreign governments and international organizations that independence is the only viable option. These are the entities that must ratify admission to the community of sovereign states.

STRATEGIC CONSTRAINTS   27

Significant national-secession campaigns were most common in Asia and Europe. The highest number and greatest frequency were in South and East Asia, followed by Central Eurasia and Eastern Europe, and Western Europe (see table 2.1). South and East Asia was the site of forty-seven significant national-secession campaigns. These include such prominent campaigns for independence as Balochistan (Balochis) in Pakistan, Kawthoolei (Karens) in Myanmar, and Bangsamoro (Moros) in the Philippines.[10] The average South and East Asian state faced 1.88 campaigns. Central Eurasia (the Soviet Union and successor states) and Eastern Europe faced thirty-eight significant national-secession campaigns. These included the successful campaigns that broke up Czechoslovakia, the Soviet Union, and Yugoslavia as well as ongoing campaigns for such projects as Crimea (until 2014), Ichkeria (Chechens), and South Ossetia. On average, common-states in this region faced 1.36 campaigns. Western Europe's common-states faced twenty-three significant campaigns that included Euskadi (Basques), Scotland, and Corsica. Western Europe faced more challenges per common-state (1.15) than the global average.

Alternatively, Africa, the Middle East, the Western Hemisphere, and Oceania faced fewer challenges. The sub-Saharan African common-states were somewhat below the global average. Africa's thirty-nine national-secession campaigns included Air and Azawad (Tuaregs), Cabinda, and Eritrea. The Middle East (North Africa and Southwest Asia) at 0.67 campaigns per common-state had far fewer national-secession campaigns than the global average, but these included the successful campaign for South Sudan and costly struggles over the future

TABLE 2.1.   National-secession campaigns by region, 1945–2010

REGION	NUMBER OF NATIONAL-SECESSION CAMPAIGNS	NUMBER OF COMMON-STATES	RATIO
South and East Asia	47	25	1.88
Central Eurasia/ Eastern Europe	38	28	1.36
Western Europe	23	20	1.15
Sub-Saharan Africa	39	45	0.87
North Africa/South-west Asia	14	21	0.67
Western Hemisphere	9	28	0.32
Australia/Oceania	1	5	0.20
Global	171	172	0.99

Notes: Rump-states and post-amalgamation states are counted as continuous with pre-breakup. Campaigns that recur in successor states are counted only once.

TABLE 2.2. Number of common-states facing one or more national-secession campaigns, 1945–2010

NUMBER OF NATIONAL-SECESSION CAMPAIGNS PER COMMON-STATE	NUMBER OF COMMON-STATES
Ten or more campaigns	3
Five to nine campaigns	5
Two to four campaigns	21
One campaign	41
No campaigns	102
Total	172

Note: Rump-successor state (e.g., Serbia) totals are added to original common-state (e.g., Yugoslavia) totals.

of Darfur, Kurdistan, and Western Sahara. The common-states of the Western Hemisphere and Oceania were least likely to face such campaigns.

The common-state challenged by the most national-secession campaigns was the Soviet Union, with fourteen significant national-secession campaigns. If Russia is counted as the successor state to the USSR (and so its crises added), this total reaches seventeen. The USSR was followed by India, with twelve significant national-secession campaigns and Myanmar with ten. Other common-states facing five or more significant national-secession campaigns included Indonesia (seven), France (six), Yugoslavia plus Serbia (six), Nigeria (six), and Iran (five). Table 2.2 shows the number of countries facing one or more significant national-secession campaigns.

Lessons from the Successful Secessions

In designing a national-secession campaign, but unable to foresee the future, campaign leaders must turn to the evidence from successful secessions. The seventy years after World War II offer these campaign leaders twenty-six important examples—states that achieved independence through secession. And these suggest four alternative paths to independence—intervention, expulsion, abandonment, and collapse (see table 2.3). (The four paths are ideal-types, so individual cases, placed in one category or the other, may also display some features of other ideal-types.) These four types of successes are good beginning points for strategists in drafting a strategy, selecting operational objectives, and choosing tactics.

Intervention

Seven campaigns inspired outside powers to intervene and to impose the conditions that made independence possible. These are the cases in which

TABLE 2.3. Successful secessions, 1945–2016

	REFERENDUM ON INDEPENDENCE	RESULTS	TURNOUT	CAMPAIGN IN SEGMENT-STATE[a]	VIOLENCE[b]
INTERVENTION					
Bangladesh	—			Eleventh-hour	High intensity
Bosnia	29 February–1 March 1992	99.7	63.4	De jure control	[High]/None[c]
Eritrea	23–25 April 1993	99.8	93.9	De facto control	High intensity
Kosovo	26–30 Sept 1991	100	87.0	De facto control	High intensity
Montenegro	21 May 2006	55.5	86.5	De jure control	None
South Sudan	9–15 January 2011	98.8	97.6	De facto control	High intensity
Timor Leste	30 August 1999	78.5	98.6	De facto control	High intensity
EXPULSION					
Singapore	—			Marginalized	None
Slovakia	—			De jure control	None
ABANDONMENT					
Croatia	19 May 1991	93.2	83.6	De jure control	High intensity
Estonia	3 March 1991	78.4	82.9	De jure control	None
Latvia	3 March 1991	74.9	87.6	De jure control	None
Lithuania	9 February 1991	93.2	84.7	De jure control	None
Macedonia	8 September 1991	96.4	75.7	Eleventh-hour	None
Slovenia	23 December 1990	94.8	93.5	De jure control	Intense
COLLAPSE					
Armenia	21 September 1991	99.5	95.1	Eleventh-hour	Intense
Azerbaijan	29 December 1991	99.8	95.3	Marginalized	Intense
Belarus	—			Marginalized	None
Georgia	31 March 1991	99.5	90.6	De jure control	Low intensity
Kazakhstan	—			Marginalized	None
Kyrgyzstan	—			Marginalized	None
Moldova	[6 March 1994][d]	97.9	75.1	Eleventh-hour	None
Tajikistan	—			Marginalized	None
Turkmenistan	26 October 1991	94.1	97.4	Marginalized	None
Ukraine	1 December 1991	92.3	84.2	Marginalized	None
Uzbekistan	29 December 1991	98.3	94.1	Marginalized	None

[a] National-secession campaign's control over segment-state: de jure government of segment-state gained through common-state elections, eleventh-hour shift of de jure segment-state leaders, de facto control established over all or parts of the segment-state, or marginalized campaign exercising no control.

[b] High-intensity violence (>1,000 deaths in one or more years); intense violence (25–1,000 deaths in one or more years); low-intensity violence (1–24 deaths in one or more years); nonlethal violence (0 deaths).

[c] Bosnia did not have a war with Serbia (its common-state) but with the internal secession of the Serbians. Yet this intersects with Bosnia's assertion of sovereign statehood vis-à-vis Serbia.

[d] A referendum on independence against the possibility of unification with Romania.

national-secession campaigns actually had greatest influence, but the campaigns for Bangladesh, Bosnia, Eritrea, Kosovo, Montenegro, South Sudan, and Timor Leste exerted influence on the outcome only indirectly—through their influence on the actions of the international community, particularly Western governments. In six of these cases the national-secession campaign constituted the de jure government of the segment-state or had established de facto control over substantial parts of the disputed homeland. Four of these campaigns engaged in intense violence prior to establishing this control. In all but Montenegro, the violence was a major reason for international intervention. In all but Bangladesh, the interveners initially resisted independence, but by the actions of the campaign, such as mobilizing votes in referenda or keeping the violent conflict alive, the interveners came to accept that the program for independence was the only viable solution and imposed this on the common-state government.

Bangladesh's secession depended on the intervention of India to create the decisive moment for independence. The victory of the Awami League in Pakistan's December 1970 parliamentary election had intensified the divide between the Awami League leaders from East Pakistan and Pakistan's president over the shape of center-east relations. The president postponed the opening of Pakistan's Assembly and then imposed martial law rather than see the Awami League become the government of all Pakistan. The swift arrest of the Awami League leader Sheikh Mujibir Rahman (Mujib) and the takeover of the Eastern provincial administration in Dhaka gave the central Pakistani government only tenuous control in the East, as guerrilla activities along the East's borders and near Dhaka rapidly gained in intensity.[11] Still, the guerrilla resistance could not bring victory. This depended on the Indian forces in all stages of the resistance: India conducted relentless air attacks on Dhaka and ground assaults against Pakistani forces. India provided a safe haven for the government-in-exile and transportation back to Bangladesh once the war had ended. And in the dangerous period after the war, India served as the nominal governing authority between the surrender of Pakistani forces on December 16, 1971, the arrival of the interim government six days later, the return of President Mujib nineteen days after that, and the reestablishment of law and order in the capital.[12]

The Kosovo independence campaign recognized its weakness against Serbia and made appeals for international intervention central to its strategy, but this would be a difficult task because there was little initial support in European capitals or in Washington for the idea of an independent Kosovo state. The Kosovo Liberation Army (KLA), consisting of members of the campaign preferring armed resistance, launched its struggle in February 1996. Its operational objective became convincing the West and compromisers within Kosovo, such as Ibrahim Rugova, that independence was the only option.[13] When Serbian

President Slobodan Milošević began his counteroffensive in spring 1998, the KLA quickly discovered the reality of its own operational weakness. According to David L. Phillips, "the KLA tried to defend the civilian population, but it was overmatched," and a humanitarian disaster soon threatened. Even though it was classified as a terrorist organization, "the KLA adopted a basic, but effective communication strategy, using mobile phones to contact journalists and tell them what was happening in the field."[14] The parliament of the self-proclaimed Republic of Kosovo petitioned NATO to intervene, and the republic's leaders arrived in Washington on May 28 to appeal for support.

The first UN involvement on the ground began in fall 1998 with the Kosovo Verification Mission, but the United Nations did not at this time endorse independence. According to James Ker-Lindsay, "unhappy with the continued adherence to autonomy as a model for a solution, the KLA continued its attacks in the hope that this would provoke a heavy handed Serbian response, which in turn would force Western leaders to act decisively on behalf of the Kosovo Albanians."[15] Nonetheless, the initial diplomatic effort, finalized at Rambouillet on February 23, 1999, would have denied the national secessionists' aspirations for independence by keeping Kosovo within Serbia. Fortunately for the Kosovo national-secession campaign, Milošević was unwilling to sign.

The return of war brought Western military intervention on March 24, 1999, as the pro-independence Kosovars had strategized. On June 3 Milošević agreed to the terms set down for an end to the war. The establishment of a separate administration under European guidance (UNMIK) ensured diverging development of Kosovar and Serbian polities that precluded the project for Serbia-Kosovo unity. As Ker-Lindsay observes, "having managed to secure NATO intervention to support their armed campaign against Serbia, [Kosovo's leaders] accepted that a limited period of time as an international protectorate was now going to be a necessary prelude to independence. There could be no return to discussions over autonomy. Independence was now the only acceptable goal."[16] The next years were spent convincing Washington and Europe of this by demonstrating that unity was not viable and that Kosovar Albanians were solidly behind the program of independence.

The Bosnian project became a reality only through direct US intervention. The platform population of the Bosnia program was not solidly behind a unified, independent Bosnia and Herzegovina. Elections to the republic's parliament in November-December 1990 gave Alija Izetbegović's Party of Democratic Action (SDA), which championed this project, only 35.8 percent of the seats. Parties with very different national-secession programs for territories and populations within Bosnia won the remainder, including the Serbian Democratic Party (SDS), which won 30 percent, and the Croatian Democratic Alliance (HDZ),

which won 18.3 percent. The February 29-March 1, 1992, referendum for independence from Yugoslavia confirmed strong support only in the Bosniak and
Croat communities. With civil war and the introduction of Serbia's armed forces,
the survival of the campaign for a unified Bosnia was in question—unless the
Bosnia campaign could enlist support from European, North American, and
Islamic governments. Izetbegović and his foreign minister, Haris Silajdžić, took
their campaign to world capitals, and this worked remarkably well. The Bush
and Clinton administrations coordinated UN economic sanctions to pressure
Serbia to withdraw its challenge, led NATO military actions to pressure Bosnian
Serbs to agree to a negotiated settlement, and authored plans for a Bosnian state
that combined a federation of Muslim and Croat areas with a Serbian "entity." By
shepherding the parties through the Dayton peace process, American diplomats
handed independence to the Bosnian campaign led by Izetbegović. As Steven L.
Burg and Paul S. Shoup note, rather than a victory of Bosnians over Serbia, "the
Dayton agreement reflected the interest of the U.S. administration in bringing
the fighting to a halt. . . ."[17]

The Timor Leste campaign that received independence in 2002 had not posed
a serious threat to Indonesia's control over East Timor. The opportunity for independence arose in a crisis that the campaign did not foresee and for reasons
to which the campaign made only an indirect contribution: the campaign conducted by the Revolutionary Front for an Independent Timor Leste (Fretilin)
made Indonesia's control of East Timor costlier, so in the financial crisis of 1997
both Indonesia and foreign lenders wanted this drain on the economy ended. The
Indonesian economy, along with that of the East Asian tigers, began to slide in
1997, and its currency, the rupiah, went into free fall. Desperate for international
assistance, Indonesia's leadership was suddenly vulnerable to pressure from the
IMF to resolve the costly conflict over the future of East Timor.[18] Preparing for
this opportunity, Fretilin had engaged in a clandestine campaign to coordinate
its platform population around the goal of independence. In a referendum that
the Indonesian president thought would show support for continued unity, an
overwhelming majority of the East Timorese voters (78.5 percent) instead supported independence. Although foreign powers, including Australia, had initially
opposed independence, they acquiesced and ensured that a reluctant Indonesia
would abide by the outcome of the referendum.

The campaign for a South Sudan received the opportunity to walk away with
independence in 2011 as a consequence of international intervention that established peace and ensured that a referendum on independence would be held.
The national-secession campaign had been marginalized within the Sudan People's Liberation Army/Movement (SPLA/M) under Dr. John Garang de Mabior,
who rejected secession in favor of revolutionary transformation of Sudan. After

a stalemate on the battlefield that emerged by the end of the 1990s, mounting international pressure (particularly from the George W. Bush administration after September 11, 2001) led to the Comprehensive Peace Accord (CPA) of January 9, 2005. This contained a promise of a referendum after a six-year interim peace process. The death of Garang in July 2005 and the inability to reach agreement on a path forward within a unified Sudan created the opportunity for the leaders of the national-secession campaign to emerge hegemonic within the SPLA/M. With resistance from Khartoum and limited administrative capacity in the South, the referendum might not have taken place, except for the continuing pressure from Western governments and the United Nations to ensure that the referendum was held on schedule. In January 2011, with a choice between Sudanese unity or separation of the South and strong endorsement of the latter by the new (post-Garang) SPLA/M leadership, 98.83 percent of the voters endorsed independence. This was never the preferred outcome of most foreign powers, including the United Kingdom, the United States, and Norway, yet having staked so much on the guarantee of a referendum, they were bound to accept the reality of programmatic preemption by the national-secession campaign.[19] They then ensured that Khartoum acquiesced in the South's decision to secede.

In Eritrea the opportunity for a surge that would convince the international community to impose independence was created by developments that the Eritreans did not control—the end of Soviet-bloc assistance to Ethiopia, the common-state's draining war with Somali secessionists, and growing opposition to Ethiopia's Derg government from the Tigray People's Liberation Front and the Ethiopian People's Revolutionary Party. The weakening of the Ethiopian military's control over Eritrea, created by these conditions, permitted the Eritrean People's Liberation Front (EPLF) to expel Ethiopian forces from district capitals within Eritrea, the port city of Massawa in 1990, and the Eritrean capital (Asmara) in 1991. Still, the immediate outcome of the Eritrean struggle was not a direct victory over the Ethiopian government but the (possibly temporary) establishment of the independence campaign as the rulers of Eritrea. This had happened a decade and a half earlier, but then the Eritreans had to retreat before the superior forces of the central government once order was reestablished at the center. The different outcome came about by influencing key Western powers. When the Ethiopian opposition took power in Addis Ababa, the EPLF emerged at the right moment as "the sole representative of Eritrean nationalism."[20] There were no credible alternative claimants. The foreign powers initially resisted its demands for independence but had to negotiate with the EPLF and ultimately recognized independence as the only viable option. The referendum on April 23–25, 1993, delivered a 99.8 percent vote for independence. This could not be denied even by foreign powers, including the United States, which had wanted to establish a federal Ethiopia that would include Eritrea.[21] Finally recognizing the EPLF's programmatic preemption in Eritrea, the United States aided Eritrea's exit.

Montenegro's success represents a unique twist in a campaign to persuade Western powers to support independence. After the end of the Milošević presidency in Serbia in October 2000, Montenegro's campaign for independence gathered strength. Campaign leaders gained control of Montenegro's government after they were joined by the republic's most prominent political leader, Milo Đukanović. Under the mounting pressure of Yugoslavia's constitutional and economic crises, Đukanović's Democratic Party of Socialists (DPS) adopted a pro-independence program at its 2001 Congress and pressed for a referendum to resolve the issue of the republic's status. The major obstacle was the international community, which had to be convinced that the federation and even a loose confederation with Serbia were not viable alternatives to independence. Pressure from the European Union induced the DPS government to call off the referendum and to accept the Belgrade Agreement of March 2002—one more attempt to keep the Serbia-Montenegro union together. Nevertheless, the national-secession campaign used this period of an increasingly dysfunctional constitutional arrangement to persuade Montenegrin pragmatists to accept the program of independence. The secessionists confronted an equally well-organized campaign to remind people of the unity of Serbs and Montenegrins and the benefits of a larger state. The European Union relented in its opposition to a referendum on independence but demanded a high threshold of more than 50 percent turnout and at least 55 percent favoring independence. With this scheduled moment, when a surge of support had to be mobilized to demonstrate programmatic preemption, the media campaign intensified.[22] With 86 percent turnout and 55.53 percent favoring independence, the campaign demonstrated its edge over the alternative campaign for a "joint state of Serbia and Montenegro." The European Union acquiesced, Montenegro declared its independence on June 3, 2006, and the international community ensured that Serbia honored Montenegro's decision.[23]

Expulsion

The second pattern, the rarest of the four, is expulsion. For Singapore and Slovakia, independence came because the leaders of the respective regions managed to become such a nuisance that the common-state expelled them. Only in the latter case did the national-secession campaign play a major role in creating this nuisance. In neither case did the national-secession campaign engage in intense violence.

Following the creation of Malaysia in 1963, the efforts of Singapore's leader, Lee Kuan Yew, to mobilize the Chinese vote and to transform Malaysia from a Malay to a multiracial "Malaysian" state threatened the hegemony of the federation's leadership in the governing alliance party. In the summer of 1965 the Tunku Abdul Rahman reached his decision to eject Singapore. (Indeed, the memoir of one of the participants in these events is titled *Ousted!*[24]) On August 7 a separation agreement was signed.[25] Ironically, the leaders of the campaign for Singapore independence had been marginalized, their following had dwindled to very few, and Lee had not even sought independence.

Alternatively, the Slovak leaders who drove Prague to eject Slovakia from Czechoslovakia were backed by fiery nationalist rhetoric and protests in Bratislava, much of it mobilized by the national-secession campaign. Yet the Slovak government and a majority of the Slovak people had not been persuaded that independence was the only option.[26] Independence came because the Czech government in Prague found the price of compromise with the Slovak leaders too high: continued unity would slow Czech plans to move ahead rapidly with reforms at home and integration with Western Europe. Tiring of fruitless negotiations that dragged on from the summer of 1990 through late 1992, the Czech government chose simply to let Slovakia go. Jan Rychlik writes that after the summer elections of 1992, "the Czech side . . . had lost its interest in Slovakia. It was afraid that slowing the dissolution process at this point in time would only create economic chaos and financial losses. . . . Therefore, the Czech side insisted on a speedy and complete division."[27] The Velvet Divorce, the formal separation of Slovakia from Czechoslovakia, came on January 1, 1993.

Abandonment

In the third pattern, the common-state government walked away from the dispute with the secessionists because it had other, more pressing concerns. The national-secession campaigns in Estonia, Croatia, Latvia, Lithuania, Macedonia, and Slovenia simply "picked up the sovereignty" that the common-state left behind. In all six cases the segment-state governments were under control of national-secession campaigns. In all six the international community played a strong supporting role for the secessionists at the final moment. Only in the Croatian and Slovenian cases, however, was deadlock on the battlefield a contributing factor in the decision of the central government to walk away—and even this is a contested interpretation.

The Slovenian election in April 1990 gave the Demos coalition a majority in parliament and control of the government, so secessionist parties, particularly the Slovenian Democratic Union, gained a prominent voice in the governing coalition. Nonetheless, the Slovenian presidency remained in the hands of the Communist leader Milan Kučan, who favored a confederal Yugoslav project over independence. In the next months, a mounting economic crisis led many pragmatists to shift their support from the confederal project to the cause of independence in order to separate Slovenia's economy from the deadweight of Yugoslavia. A deadlock in negotiations over the institutional design of a future Yugoslav confederation effectively removed this alternative from contention with the program for independence. Additionally, the growing risk that Milošević might attempt one more of the "'anti-bureaucratic revolutions' that had already toppled the governments of Vojvodina and Montenegro" brought even the Slovenian president to shift his support to independence. The European Community pressed Slovenia (and Croatia) to keep Yugoslavia whole, and US Secretary of State James Baker even made a sudden visit to Belgrade just before the scheduled declarations of independence to underscore that his government would not recognize either Slovenia or Croatia "under any circumstances." Nevertheless, Slovenia declared its independence on June 25, 1991. In the military showdown with Serbia, which began two days later, Slovenia offered stiff resistance, and the Yugoslav army performed poorly. Yet whether this violence contributed to independence remains a contested issue: some experts contend that the battle was more symbolic than real and that the agreement to let Slovenia go had already been reached before the battle.[28] The Western powers quickly shifted their position on independence and brokered the Brioni Accord on July 7. The Yugoslav National Army (JNA) preferred to redeploy its forces to the conflict over Serbian-inhabited regions inside Croatia.[29] Faced with the fait accompli of independence and the dangers associated with trying to keep Slovenia (and Croatia) inside Yugoslavia, the European Community stepped in to aid Slovenia's exit.

The initial success of Croatia's campaign for independence intersected and progressed apace with Slovenia's, except that in the parliamentary elections of April-May 1990 the pro-independence Croatian Democratic Alliance (HDZ) took fifty-four of eighty seats, and that body elected the party leader Franjo Tuđman as president. Although he had previously expressed his commitment to the goal of independence and despite strong pressure from within his government encouraging swift action to seize it, once in the presidency Tuđman was cautious and initially worked to draft an alternative, confederal Yugoslavia project. Nevertheless, the same factors that led the major Slovenian actors to join the national-secession campaign shaped the June 25 Croatian announcement that it would declare independence on October 8, 1991. War with the Yugoslav National Army (JNA) ensued. The European Community announcement on December 16, 1991, that it would "recognize the independence of all the Yugoslav republics" in one month's time and the swift action by Germany on December 23 to recognize Croatia pressured Serbia to agree to a cease-fire on January 3, 1992, to be supervised by a peacekeeping force that guaranteed the existence of an independent Croatia.[30] Facing this international opposition and confronted by what it saw as more-pressing disputes over the control of Serb-inhabited areas, the central government in Belgrade walked away from the dispute over Croatian independence.

In Macedonia, despite the strong showing in the November-December 1990 parliamentary elections by the nationalist coalition (the Internal Macedonian Revolutionary Organization and the Democratic Party for Macedonian National Unity [VRMO-DPNME]), the parliamentary majority did not immediately adopt the program of the campaign for independence from Yugoslavia and elected the Communist Party leader, Kiro Gligorov, as Macedonia's president. As Serbia's dispute with Croatia and Slovenia grew even after the latter two had declared independence, Gligorov sought to mediate the dispute and find a way to hold the Yugoslav federation together. Only two and a half months after the declarations by Slovenia and Croatia did Macedonia hold a referendum of its own (on September 8, 1991), and this revealed the failure of the campaign to bring on board significant parts of the republic's population—particularly its Albanian minority. Although 96 percent of voters endorsed independence, leaders of the Albanian community mobilized a boycott, keeping turnout to 71 percent of the electorate. Pragmatic Macedonians rapidly shifted to the national-secession campaign as the Yugoslav federation crumbled following the secession of Slovenia and Croatia, as conflict grew within the remaining parts of the federation, and as Macedonians realized that in federation councils their government's representatives were becoming a minority of one republic facing two other republic governments (Serbia and Montenegro) and two provincial governments (Kosovo and Vojvodina) dominated by Serbia. Parliament adopted a new constitution proclaiming independence on November 17, 1991.[31] By this time, as the disputes over the Serb-inhabited areas in Bosnia and Croatia were becoming more urgent for the central government in Belgrade, it walked away from the dispute over Macedonian independence as well.

The Baltic states (Estonia, Latvia, and Lithuania) were among the first to press for independence from the Soviet Union. In February and March 1990 the supreme soviets of all three Baltic states adopted resolutions on preparatory acts to restore state independence. In a series of subsequent acts they declared the annexation of their states by the USSR to be unlawful. In early March 1991 they held referenda on independence, with 77.8 percent in favor in Estonia, 73.7 percent in Latvia, and 90.5 percent in Lithuania. Yet it was not until the August 19–21, 1991, coup (putsch) against Mikhail Gorbachev weakened the central government that the Baltic states had the opportunity for independence with substantial international backing. In the aftermath of the August coup the Soviet government became preoccupied with trying to create a new political order in Moscow, had little time or resources to devote to keeping the Baltic states inside the Soviet Union, and decided to walk away from the dispute over Baltic independence to concentrate on its more-pressing concerns.

Collapse

The fourth pattern—walking away after collapse at the center—was the most common, representing half of all successful secessions. Yet these cases emerged from just one collapsed common-state (the Soviet Union). In these cases, independence came when the central government ceased to function because of the slow-motion coup by the government of the Russian Federation that seized most Soviet assets in the months after the failed August coup, but the national-secession campaigns had only limited roles in creating the opportunity to walk away with independence. In two of these eleven cases (Armenia and Georgia), leaders of the national-secession campaigns had come to leadership positions within the homeland but were unable to induce the central government to grant independence. In only three of these cases (Armenia, Azerbaijan, and Georgia) was there violence, but the most intense violence (Armenia and Azerbaijan) was directed at one another rather than the common-state.

Even where the national-secession campaigns were stronger, they were unable to hasten independence. In Georgia the multiparty independence campaign spearheaded by Zviad Gamsakhurdia won 64 percent of the vote for seats in the republic's Supreme Soviet on October 28, 1990. That body elected Gamsakhurdia as its chairman (and so as Georgia's chief of state) in November. Despite a March 1991 referendum on independence that reported 90 percent support and a formal declaration of independence on April 9, independence did not become a reality until the USSR ceased to exist in December 1991. Armenia represents a slightly different variant on this pattern. Despite a majority won in the August 1989 Supreme Soviet elections, the Pan-Armenian National Movement did not press for immediate independence and did not formally declare its independence until two days after the failure of the August putsch in Moscow. And this did not become a reality until December 1991. In Moldova the leadership of the homeland came over to the national-secession campaign only in the eleventh hour. Despite the growth of the campaign for secession led by the Moldovan Popular Front, the republic's president and parliament were slow to join the campaign—coming over on the eve of the August putsch in Moscow.[32] It was not until six days later that Moldova declared its independence and not until December that independence was realized.

In the other successful secessions, the national-secession campaigns remained thoroughly marginalized and far from the levers of power. Even though Belarus and Ukraine along with Russia were the prime movers in the collapse of the Soviet Union, the campaigns for independence in Belarus and Ukraine had little direct role. They saw their objectives realized on December 8, 1991, when Belarus's Supreme Soviet Chairman Stanislau Shushkevich and Ukraine's President Leonid Kravchuk signed the Belovezhskii Accords with Russia's President Boris Yeltsin. By that time the USSR government under Gorbachev had ceased to function except as a legal fiction. The inability to identify a viable alternative constitutional arrangement that would keep the Soviet Union whole and growing concern that any reformed union would be dominated by the Russian government left the Belarusian and Ukrainian leaders with no viable alternatives and led them to embrace the projects of the independence campaigns in their union republics. Ironically, within both countries the most vocal proponents of independence, such as the Belarusan Popular Front and Ukraine's Rukh, had been marginalized. As Andrew Wilson observes, "Rukh did not have the strength to win independence on its own. This required two more elements—the support of the so-called 'national Communists' like Leonid Kravchuk and the collapse of central authority in Moscow."[33] A similar assessment describes the outcome in Belarus.

In the five Central Asian states (Kazakhstan, Kyrgyzstan, Tajikistan, Turkmenistan, and Uzbekistan), leadership remained in the hands of the Communist Party first secretaries, and the independence campaigns remained small and marginalized. Azerbaijan's story is only slightly different, except that the Azerbaijan Popular Front, infuriated by the central government's handling of the Karabakh issue, put pressure on the Azerbaijan government to secede from the Soviet Union. Independence was thrust upon these states when Belarus, Russia, and Ukraine decided to withdraw from the Soviet Union in December 1991. The national-secession campaigns found themselves with an outcome that they desired but had no role in producing.

Specific Lessons for the Choice of Tactics

Many campaigns engage in substantial escalation of means. Indeed, as noted in chapter 1, national-secession campaigns have been among the most common sources of insurgencies and terrorism in the world. Yet the successful secessions provide campaign leaders little evidence to support the conclusion that this escalating intensity of a struggle will directly bring independence. Escalating intensity has had a more indirect relationship with independence by advancing the operational objectives of building and demonstrating programmatic preemption.

Patterns of Intensity

An expansive definition of violence that includes civil wars, terrorism, and violent protest, involving both lethal and nonlethal violence, sees just over half of the 170 campaigns as mounting some domestic violence between 1970 and 2006.[34] Yet only a third were associated with **intense violence**—claiming twenty-five or more battle- or terrorism-related deaths in one or more years. And just a sixth of all significant national-secession campaigns were parties to **high-intensity violence**—claiming one thousand or more battle- or terrorism-related deaths in one or more years.[35]

The most-intense campaigns were located in South and East Asia. Table 2.4 shows two lists of the ten most-intense campaigns as measured by the proportion

TABLE 2.4.   Most intense and protracted campaigns, 1970–2006

CAMPAIGN	COMMON-STATE	HIGH-INTENSITY STRUGGLE (ANNUAL DEATHS > 1,000)		INTENSE STRUGGLE (ANNUAL DEATHS > 25)		YEARS[a]
		RANK	PERCENTAGE OF YEARS	RANK	PERCENTAGE OF YEARS	
South Sudan	Sudan	1	62.2	9.5	67.6	37
Eritrea	Ethiopia	2	58.3	3	91.7	24
Tamil Eelam	Sri Lanka	3	37.8			37
Ichkeria/ Chechnya	Russia	4	33.3	7	73.3	15
Kashmir	India	5	29.7			37
Republika Srpska	Bosnia	6	26.7			15
Kurdistan	Turkey	7	21.6			37
Nagornyi Karabakh	Azerbaijan	8	20.0			15
Timor Leste	Indonesia	9	14.3	8	67.9	28
Kawthoolei	Myanmar	10.5	13.5	4	89.2	37
Khalistan	India	10.5	13.5			37
Bangsamoro	Philippines			1	100.0	37
Oromiyaa/ Oromia	Ethiopia			1	100.0	37
Ogaadeen/ Ogaden	Ethiopia			5	79.2	37
Shan States	Myanmar			6	75.7	37
Kurdistan	Iraq			9.5	67.6	37

[a] Years for denominator of percentages in previous columns. These are years that the campaign was part of the independent common-state—thus, following the campaign's annexation and prior to its secession—if either occurred.

of years in which they were associated with high-intensity violence and with intense violence.[36] South and East Asia account for seven of the sixteen campaigns that appear on these two lists: Tamil Eelam (Sri Lanka), Kashmir (India), Timor-Leste (Indonesia), Kawthoolei (Myanmar), Khalistan (India), Bangsamoro (Philippines), and the Shan States (Myanmar). The Middle East, Africa, and Central Eurasia plus Eastern Europe follow with three apiece: South Sudan (Sudan), Kurdistan (Turkey), and Kurdistan (Iraq); Eritrea (Ethiopia), Oromiyaa (Ethiopia), and Ogaadeen (Ethiopia); Ichkeria (Russia), Republika Srpska (Bosnia), and Nagornyi Karabakh (Azerbaijan).

Regarding the likelihood that any campaign will employ more-intense means, campaigns in the Middle East and Asia were the most likely to engage in lethal violence (see table 2.5). In these two regions more than half of the significant national-secession campaigns were parties to intense violence associated with at least twenty-five battle- or terrorism-related deaths in one or more years. The Middle East also reported the greatest likelihood of high-intensity violence: more than two-fifths of the campaigns in the Middle East were associated with one or more years of such intensity. As well, the Middle East reported the most protracted high-intensity violence: almost one in twelve years were marred by high-intensity violence. Alternatively, campaigns in South and East Asia were

TABLE 2.5. Maximum intensity of lethal violence per campaign, grouped by region, 1970–2006

REGION (NUMBER OF CAMPAIGNS)	REACHED INTENSE STRUGGLE (≥25 DEATHS IN ONE OR MORE YEARS)		REACHED HIGH INTENSITY (≥1,000 DEATHS IN ONE OR MORE YEARS)	
	PERCENTAGE OF PROJECTS	AVERAGE PERCENTAGE OF CAMPAIGN YEARS	PERCENTAGE OF PROJECTS	AVERAGE PERCENTAGE OF CAMPAIGN YEARS
North Africa/Southwest Asia (14)	57.1	21.2	42.9	7.8
South and East Asia (45)[a]	53.3	20.8	22.2	3.3
Central Eurasia/ Eastern Europe (38)	36.8	6.0	18.4	2.7
Sub-Saharan Africa (39)	25.6	9.0	10.3	1.9
Western Europe (23)	8.7	4.2	4.3	0.1
Western Hemisphere (9)	11.1	0.6	0.0	0.0
Australia/Oceania (1)	100.0	18.9	0.0	0.0
Global (169)[a]	35.5	11.4	16.6	2.6

[a] Singapore was dropped because it achieved independence prior to this period; Bangladesh was dropped because the denominator is only two years.

associated with substantial intense violence but not as much high-intensity violence as the Middle East and North Africa.

The Central Eurasian and East European states were much closer to global averages in the likelihood, intensity, and protractedness of lethal violence. On average, more than a third of all campaigns in these states were associated with intense violence (with at least twenty-five deaths). Yet when these conflicts became violent, they tended to reach highest intensity—such as the conflicts in Yugoslavia and the Caucasus. Still, this high-intensity violence was not unusually protracted: the percentage of campaign years reporting high-intensity violence in these states was just above the global average.

In sub-Saharan Africa, Western Europe, and the Western Hemisphere, national-secession campaigns were less likely to be associated with lethal violence. Campaigns in sub-Saharan Africa were more likely to involve lethal violence than campaigns in Western Europe, but sub-Saharan Africa trailed the Middle East, Asia, and the Central Eurasian and East European states. In the Western Hemisphere the limited violence typically involved isolated acts with few casualties.

The Contribution of Violence to Independence

To the extent that they are constrained by the empirical evidence from other countries, strategically minded national-secession campaign leaders have little reason to anticipate that protracted intense struggle can directly induce common-state governments to grant independence. Few campaigns have commanded the surge capacity to create that outcome (operational weakness). This is reflected in the relatively smaller war effort they can mount: although all other civil wars topped one thousand battlefield deaths in 34.4 percent of the years at war, national-secession wars reached this intensity in only 21.8 percent of such years.[37] Bethany Lacina's findings corroborate this: "wars of secession do seem to induce far fewer deaths per capita than other conflicts."[38] Smaller wars are less likely to push common-states toward conceding independence. And looking more closely at the successful secessions, the most practical operational objective for violence in national-secession campaigns is to build toward and to demonstrate programmatic preemption. One consequence of this is to induce intervention by third parties and to convince them that they should accept the secessionists' demand for independence.

The twenty-six cases of successful secession show that in only six or eight cases (Bangladesh, Bosnia, Eritrea, Kosovo, East Timor, South Sudan, and possibly Croatia and Slovenia as well) did violence bring independence, and then only by influencing foreign interventions against the common-state.[39] In four of the first six cases, violence enabled the campaigns to establish de facto control over at least parts of the secessionist homeland in preparation for the opportunity to pick up or receive independence. In the other eighteen successful secessions there was no substantial violence associated with the national-secession campaign: middle-level insurgencies in Armenia and Azerbaijan were directed at one another rather than the Soviet Union. Georgia's violence was directed at the Soviet Union, but at a very low level, and it did not directly contribute to the Soviet collapse.

This lesson is reinforced by the results of a simple statistical test of the relationship of violence and intervention to independence. (See appendix table 2A.2.) Recent high-intensity war shows no direct statistically significant effect on the likelihood of independence, but multilateral peacekeeping against the status quo is a powerful predictor of independence. These interventions may not have begun on behalf of secession and independence, but they began in opposition to the policies of the common-state government, such as the violence of the Serbian government against Bosnia and Kosovo. Nonetheless, the policies of the interveners evolved toward support for independence, whatever their initial intentions.[40] During an intense civil war and after no more than one year of peace, the "peacekeeping against the status quo" variable increased the probability of independence from 0.7 percent to 18.7 percent. Alternatively, in every instance in which multilateral intervention supported the existing common-state, such as the UN peacekeeping operations on behalf of Croatia (against Krajina) and Bosnia (against Republika Srpska and Herzeg-Bosna), the secessionists failed to achieve independence. In addition, only one of the eleven unilateral interventions on behalf of secessionists succeeded in securing broad international recognition of independent statehood—this was Bangladesh. At most the others achieved de facto separation for Abkhazia, Nagornyi Karabakh, Northern Cyprus, South Ossetia, and Transdniestria, and more briefly for Azerbaijan (Iran) and Kurdistan (Iran), but not formal independence that was widely recognized. (This also underscores the importance of securing attention and support in Western capitals.)

Yet gambling that violence will bring multilateral peacekeeping against the status quo is risky: national-secession wars were only about a sixth as likely as other civil wars to bring significant foreign involvement. The proportion of years at war in which there was significant foreign involvement was 18.5 percent for all other civil wars but only 3.1 percent for national-secession wars.[41]

What Information Was Available to Campaign Leaders about Violence?

Evidence from the period 1945 to 2010 supports the tactical lesson that increased intensity, and specifically violence, is best used as a means to operational objectives rather than a direct means of imposing victory over a common-state government. But we cannot assume that campaign leaders had their research assistants run the logit estimates. What information or common knowledge was available to national-secession leaders who actually lived in this period?

Even the most casual observation about secession struggles prior to the 1990s did not give much reason for strategists to conclude that violence was a prudent choice to achieve the strategic objective of independence directly through armed victory over the common-state government. Throughout most of the period, they did not know that in the 1990s some campaigns would achieve independence after violence. Throughout most of these years, a national-secession strategist trying to calculate whether armed struggle was likely to bring a common-state around to granting independence would have to look back to the Irish struggle that culminated in 1921 for evidence that this strategy could be successful. In the forty-four years until 1965, no states successfully seceded except for the wartime puppet states such as Slovakia. Moreover, Singapore achieved independence in 1965 without violence. It was a full half century after Ireland (until 1971 and Bangladesh) before violence brought independence.

Conversely, in the years from 1945 to 1971, twenty-six significant national-secession campaigns became parties to civil wars but did not achieve independence. The attempts of Biafra and Katanga to secede demonstrated the high barriers to independence even for a movement that could mount an intense armed struggle with foreign support against a weak central government. The grinding wars in Burma that engaged six national-secession campaigns made clear that even the capacity to conduct a protracted struggle was unlikely to bring independence. Bangladesh's independence in 1971 sent the message that the ability to fight could be critical to buy time until the superior force of an external ally could be engaged, but there was nothing in the Bangladesh story to support the view that secessionists could seize independence by themselves or that a protracted civil war without overwhelming outside support could induce a central government to grant independence.

The lessons that could be drawn from the cases that followed 1990 did not substantially alter this: the first use of violence reinforcing claims to independence that were actually realized came in 1991 in Croatia and Slovenia. Yet these cases once again also sent the message that violence may be most effective when it brings international intervention on behalf of independence. This was reaffirmed in Eritrea at about this same time: local armed victory in 1991 over the provincial administration was possible only because other armed opponents defeated the central government, the Derg, in Addis Ababa. And the decisive step to Eritrean independence required convincing the international community in 1993 by argumentation rather than arms—during the postwar peace talks—that independence was the only viable option. In that same half decade (1991–1995), however, more than a dozen secessionist campaigns achieved independence without violence. Although the later successful secessions from 2000 to 2011, including Timor Leste, Kosovo, and South Sudan, involved violence, they provided little evidence that should lead secessionist strategists to see violence as a means for directly seizing independence: all successful secessions used violence to attract outside imposition.

In short, throughout most years under investigation in this book, there was little evidence to lead national-secession campaign leaders to conclude that protracted use of intense means, particularly violence, would bring direct victory over the common-state. Most successful national-secession campaigns have lacked the capacity to force their common-state governments to concede independence. Most campaigns that saw their programs for independence realized did not achieve this directly through a violent struggle.

So What Should Campaign Leaders Do?

Few strategists leading national-secession campaigns were likely to draw the conclusion from this evidence that they should sit on their hands and wait to be gifted with independence. In particular, they did not want to see independence gifted to a competing national-secession campaign when the ultimate moment arrived. The inferences to be drawn from the pattern of successful and unsuccessful secessions since 1945 speak to the need for proper design of operational objectives and choice of tactics under the constraint of operational weakness. If campaigns made a substantial contribution to the achievement of independence, it was by creating programmatic preemption within their platform populations so that the international community recognized that independence for the campaign's proposed nation-state was the only viable option. The next chapter turns to the model of campaigning that for most significant national-secession campaigns answered the question "What is to be done when a campaign has bold ambitions but is limited by its operational weakness?"

ORGANIZATION AND MOBILIZATION IN CAMPAIGN DEVELOPMENT

The successful secessions discussed in chapter 2 provide little evidence for leaders of national-secession campaigns to expect that they will be able to impose separation on their resistant common-state governments. These success stories provide substantial evidence that most leaders should expect to have to wait for foreign interventions to hand sovereignty to their campaigns or for the common-state to collapse under the weight of its other problems. Their own campaign's operational weakness should give campaign leaders little reason to expect to be exceptions. So what are national-secession campaign leaders to do in order to increase the likelihood that the international community will gift them with independence and the campaign will be ready to receive or pick up sovereignty when it is left to be picked up?

This and the next chapter describe the strategy of programmatic coordination that addresses these circumstances. This strategy responds to the strategic constraints identified in the first two chapters: because of operational weakness, campaigns typically cannot seize independence but must engage in strategic opportunism, waiting for opportunities to walk away from a collapsing common-state or to influence third parties to impose independence on a resistant common-state government. The timing of these opportunities is often uncertain, the nature of the opportunities cannot be forecast with certainty, and the campaign has little influence over either the timing or the nature of the opportunities. Constrained by this forecast uncertainty, the immediate focus of the campaign must be to prepare a surge capacity within the platform population that in a variety of circumstances can demonstrate to this population and the international community—and in rare circumstances to the common-state government—that independence is the only viable option.

Subsequent chapters extend this strategy to its implications: when a campaign successfully addresses the operational objectives identified in the strategy of programmatic coordination, it is better able to get its claim to independence on the public agenda (significance). When a campaign can coordinate and maintain support for its nation-state project among its members and prevent collaboration with the common-state, the campaign creates conditions for deadlock between the secessionists and common-state government on the issue of independence (intractability). Independence is the objective of the campaign's coordination efforts; deadlock is often an unintended consequence but is also a second-best outcome that is preferable to the alternatives (except independence). A campaign uses tactics such as violence to build and sustain coordination in the larger population and to reinforce the message that independence is the only viable option to end this deadlock. Nonetheless, only a campaign that is already well along in its efforts at programmatic coordination is able to conduct a broad long-term struggle against the common-state (protracted intensity). Only a campaign that expects to maintain this coordination even in harsh conditions and expects a protracted intense struggle to further coordination within the larger platform population is likely to see this as a prudent tactic.

The revolutionary strategy on which this action plan is based, as noted in chapter 1, is common knowledge—having achieved the status of folk wisdom—in the world of practitioners and analysts. In this strategy, campaign leaders position their program of independence to be the only viable option through careful and often tedious preparation that Vladimir I. Lenin calls "ideological-organizational" work.[1] Three key elements of Lenin's strategy, according to Alfred G. Meyer, are a cohesive elite of professional revolutionaries, propaganda to raise the level of consciousness of the platform population and link its diverse interests to the cause, and a network of auxiliary organizations to direct the participation of the population in public life toward achievement of this goal.[2] These three elements are organization, propagation, and mobilization. Borrowing many elements of Lenin's strategy, and particularly as elaborated by latter-day Marxist-Leninists such as Mao Zedong, leaders of national-secession campaigns know they must coordinate efforts of diverse constituent parts, including leaders, intellectuals, cadres, activists, auxiliaries, and surge-time participants. Throughout most of a successful campaign's history, success depends on the ability of the leaders to hold together and to keep on board the inner core of leaders, intellectuals, and cadres. Yet at key surge moments the activists, auxiliaries, and reservists come to play critical roles.

The programmatic approach developed in this book diverges from and complements the usual treatment of this strategy in three important ways. Other analyses typically focus on the elements of organization and mobilization in the Leninist strategy, but programmatic analysis focuses on the element of propagation, which gives a campaign coordination. Studies of the "organizational weapon" or the cellular structure of revolutionary and terrorist organizations, and analyses of protests, demonstrations, terrorism, guerrilla warfare, and insurgencies, give us deep understanding of the elements of organization and mobilization in campaigns.[3] Yet at the core of Lenin's strategy is programmatic coordination achieved through propagation: this is the "ideological" in "ideological-organizational" work. Achievement of Lenin's revolutionary goal required bringing consciousness to a platform population and guiding it in the achievement of its role. For Lenin, this consciousness was Marxism, and the platform was the proletariat; for secessionists, these are nationalism and the nation. In the life of a campaign, the elements of organization and mobilization may vary and are contingent; alternatively, propagation to achieve programmatic coordination is a constant of primary importance.

By focusing on common goals as the basis of coordination, the programmatic approach highlights a fundamental difference between the constraints within which national-secession and revolutionary campaign leaders operate. The Leninist model for making revolution posits a strategic objective and constraints that are quite different in at least three important ways from the goal and constraints of secessionists. And these require secessionists to make important adaptations in the Leninist strategy for making revolutions. One difference concerns goals: unlike revolutionaries such as Lenin, Mao, or Fidel Castro, secessionists do not seek to conquer the center of power within the common-state but to tear the common-state apart. For example, Che Guevara describes his revolution's "final objective" as "to annihilate the enemy."[4] Few, if any, national-secession campaign leaders aspire to this. Another difference concerns means: even with full mobilization of their platform populations, secessionists typically cannot aspire to mobilize a force capable of overwhelming the common-state government. As noted in chapter 1, their platform populations constitute not the overwhelming majority of the common-state's "people" but only a small fraction. A third difference concerns divisions within the platform population: revolutionary classes, such as the toiling class, may be challenged by national divides. Alternatively, nations are typically socioeconomically diverse, giving rise to competing status- or class-based ideologies within the cause of independence.[5] National-secessionist leaders often must coordinate traditionalists, liberals, socialists, and communists behind the common goal of independence. Because of these differences, national-secessionists must go about programmatic coordination in somewhat different ways than revolutionaries do.

And, as noted in chapter 1, the prescriptive revolutionary theory developed by Lenin and his followers is used by programmatic theory as a micro- and meso-level model for social science analysis. This is refined by drawing on the work of analysts of strategic organizing such as Chester I. Barnard and James Q. Wilson.[6] This model focuses on the operational choices of the secessionist leaders.[7] Miroslav Hroch labels these key actors the "patriots" and argues that "between the manifestations of scholarly interest, on the one hand, and the mass diffusion of patriotic attitudes, on the other, . . . the driving force in this era of national agitation was a group of patriots who . . . saw their mission as the spreading of national consciousness among the people."[8] The analytic model emphasizes the element of calculating choice by these campaign leaders, but it is a choice constrained by the expected and actual responses of the platform population at large.[9] In this model the choices of the actors at all levels are conscious, deliberate, and purposeful.[10] The micro-level model establishes a premise from which specific hypotheses are deduced to identify the macro-level conditions under which secessionist campaigns become significant, give rise to intractable disputes with their common-state governments over the issue of independence, and engage in protracted intense struggles.

The discussion of strategy is divided between two chapters. This chapter rounds up the usual suspects, identifying elements of organization and mobilization that structure the operational tasks of programmatic coordination. Specifically, it presents an overview of the chief constituent parts of a national-secession campaign (leadership, staff, and participatory reserve), the phases of activism, and the developmental stages of a campaign. These are the most commonly studied elements. Chapter 4 turns to elements of the strategy emphasized by programmatic analysis: the central role of a common program in coordinating among these constituent parts. The campaign leaders' common goal constrains them in their choices among incentives to recruit members of the platform population to the campaign. The common goal shapes their choices in deploying differently motivated recruits at different stages of campaign development and in different phases of campaign activism. This model of agency provides the foundation for hypotheses that identify the chief structural opportunities and obstacles that increase the likelihood that a national-secession campaign will achieve significance, intractability, and protracted intensity in later chapters.

Campaign Development

In politics a campaign is "an organized course of action designed to arouse public opinion throughout the country for or against some political object. . . ."[11] It combines the elements of organization, propagation, and mobilization, but what gives it unity is its "political object" (goal). As noted previously, the strategy to achieve programmatic preemption was initially taught by clandestine agents and advisors but has since achieved the status of common knowledge or folk wisdom.[12] Many secessionist campaigns in their activist periods were led by men and women who were well schooled in Leninist and Maoist organizing principles, including the Basque ETA,[13] the East Timorese Fretilin,[14] the Eritrean EPLF,[15] the Irish IRA,[16] the Kurdish PKK,[17] the Sahawari POLISARIO,[18] the Tamil LTTE,[19] and, of course, the leaders of many Yugoslav and Soviet republics.[20] Edgar O'Ballance writes that in 1986 the Tamil Tiger commander of Jaffna invited journalists to his office "adorned . . . with books by famous authors on guerrilla warfare, including the *Memoirs of Che Guevara*, left half-open, no doubt to impress visitors."[21] Secessionists, such as the Irish Republican Army, have been eager to share their knowledge with others.

A national-secession campaign champions the claim that the project for an independent nation-state is a better way to draw international boundaries than alternatives. Like many other campaigns, a national-secession campaign may be organizationally unified or divided. It may engage in extensive or little mobilization of political action. Yet in order to make its point, a campaign must keep unwavering coordination on a single goal (independence) among leaders, cadres promoting the program for independence, and activists and reservists who can be mobilized to vote, protest, build barricades, destroy enemy targets, or take posts within the government when opportunities present themselves. And this requires successful propagation.

In the strategy of programmatic coordination, alignment of the platform population behind the program for independence begins with a long-term process of recruiting leaders and cadres, and this typically targets members of the platform population who see intrinsic value in pursuing independence. But then the campaign must reach beyond the core of preexisting true believers in independence. The campaign must persuade members of the larger platform population that the program's proposed nation complements existing identities, that statehood is actually a desirable goal, and that the program's action plan provides a practical means to independence.

In reaching outward, leaders often find that the intrinsic value of independence alone is not enough to inspire participation in the campaign beyond the few true believers who are not numerous enough to mount a significant surge event. Leaders may recruit individuals who revel in activism and seek expressive opportunities for demonstrative action, but seldom can campaign leaders provide a continuous stream of such opportunities, and only rarely do they have the monitoring and sanctioning capacity to direct a broad and long-term series of such acts. The campaign can expand beyond its core of true believers and activists only by bringing in members with more instrumental valuation of the project. This presents the leaders of national-secession campaigns with the task of building, managing, and sustaining a coalition among participants with diverse economic and power interests. Yet before they achieve some form of statehood, campaigns usually lack the resources to provide a continuous stream of economic and power rewards and to maintain the monitoring and sanctioning capacity to dispense and withhold material rewards effectively.

As explained more fully in the next chapter, the leaders must create and allocate incentives for each of these participants in the campaign in a way that optimizes recruitment, loyalty, and strategic availability so that the campaign can demonstrate to the homeland population, the common-state government, and the international community at critical moments that independence is the only viable solution. Campaign leaders must coordinate among all these different types of actors and deploy them as assets under conditions that change over time—at the right stages of campaign development and phases of activism. The key to coordination is the program itself and particularly its capacity to focus expectations that members of the platform population will see the national-secession program as authentic and realistic.

Illustration: The Timor Leste Campaign

The Timor Leste national-secession campaign provides an illustration of artful persuasion despite shifting organization and mobilization tactics to align a platform population behind a program for independence in the face of overwhelming odds. Like most projects for independence that attract a following, the initial Timor Leste campaign was small, atomized, and ephemeral. Prior to 1975, educated East Timorese tended to be concentrated in the colonial civil service of Portugal, in schools in Portugal, or in exile, but in the preceding two decades they did not coalesce around a common independence program.[22] Reports of small cells operating in isolation were difficult to verify, and their programs remained unclear. Even as late as August 1973, reports of a Timor Liberation Front could not be verified, but in the words of one informant who claimed to be at the center of this organizing, "the group was miniscule, disorganized, and unarmed."[23] Another anticolonial conspiracy comprising office workers and students in the capital, Díli, reportedly met for discussions in the park in full view of the governor's office to dispel any suspicions that they were planning something illegal.[24]

Even on the eve of the Indonesian incorporation of East Timor, most people in the multiethnic population outside the capital "did not think of themselves as Timorese but rather as belonging to a particular linguistic group and . . . treated people from other linguistic groups as foreigners."[25] In the fall of 1975 the East Timorese intelligentsia was divided among supporters of greater autonomy in association with Portugal, integration with Indonesia, and independence.[26] The Revolutionary Front for an Independent East Timor (Fretilin), which played a central role in the campaign for independence, had been formed only a year and a half earlier (May 1974) as the Social Democratic Association of Timor (ASDT), with the initial goal of bringing Portugal's Carnation Revolution to the colony. Fretilin organized a central committee, a National Union of Timorese Students (UNETIM), and a National Union of Timorese Workers in its first year, and then turned to the task of creating rural bases through revolutionary brigades established in many villages. On the eve of an Indonesian invasion of the Portuguese colony, hoping to preclude Indonesian annexation, campaign leaders declared the Democratic Republic of East Timor on November 28, 1975. Following the Indonesian annexation, the leaders of Fretilin pursued two different strategies over the next two and a half decades: a failed military operation that divided the campaign for independence until 1979 and an ultimately successful, more inclusive national front campaign beginning in the early 1980s.

Indonesia invaded Díli on December 7, 1975, and Fretilin retreated into the hills to conduct an armed struggle on a Maoist model. Adopting a Marxist-Leninist ideology, the leadership developed separate political (Fretilin) and armed (Falintil) organizations under a united leadership. The leadership moved decisively against any members who diverged from the program, purging, arresting, and even executing many who questioned Fretilin's program that tied independence to Marxism. As Fretilin devoured the national-secession campaign, its Falintil armed forces steadily lost ground against the overwhelming Indonesian armed forces. The failure to resupply and reequip the forces and "starvation, sickness, and capture" soon took their toll. As Damien Kingsbury observes, "by the end of the 1970s . . . a good part of its strategy thereafter was as much to survive as to inflict casualties on the occupying Indonesians."[27] The Indonesian "encirclement and annihilation campaign" destroyed the organizational structure of Fretilin, the armed forces of Falintil, and the last remaining base area.

From this low point in 1979 the campaign began to rebuild from isolated remnants in the villages and the Indonesian resettlement camps. This time, under Xanana Gusmão the campaign expanded into a broad front of national unity that shifted its emphasis to propagation of a common nation-state project rather than revolutionary armed struggle. It placed Fretilin and Falintil under the authority of a new National Council of the Common-People's (Maubere) Resistance (CNRM), which would serve as a united front for all Timorese parties and organizations supporting independence. According to Kingsbury, "the purpose of this bid for national unity was to be able to present the international community with a broadly based demand for independence, rather than what could have been portrayed as the factional demand of a single political party."[28] Marginalizing but not eliminating Falintil, Gusmão emphasized political organizing and propagation through a new clandestine internal political front in the cities and a new international support network under the direction of Jose Ramos-Horta. Even with Gusmão's capture and imprisonment in November 1992, his earlier shift to inclusive organizing and propagation had set the trajectory of the Timor Leste campaign.

The campaign's opportunity came in 1999, when under international pressure the Indonesian government agreed to put independence to a vote in a "popular consultation." In February, Gusmão was moved from jail to participate in negotiations as the representative of the East Timorese independence cause. So successful was the campaign's coordination that it reportedly mobilized a vote in parliamentary elections that was designed to convince the Indonesian government that it would be safe to proceed with the popular consultation, which the campaign saw as a referendum on independence. And then at that decisive moment the campaign demonstrated programmatic preemption with a 78.5 percent vote for independence on August 30, 1999. Gusmão was elected president of the independent Timor Leste, with Ramos-Horta as his vice president. Since the early 1980s, the Timor Leste campaign had prepared for an opportunity that presented itself unexpectedly, delivering a surge of supporters by activating its participatory reserve on short notice and so making a credible demonstration that a strong majority of East Timorese supported Fretilin's claim that an independent Timor Leste was the only viable option. Despite resistance within the homeland, inside the common-state, and in the broader international community, the campaign for Timor Leste confronted all with programmatic preemption—most of the platform population appeared to reject the alternatives to independence.

The Timor Leste campaign in the 1970s had implemented best revolutionary practices in organizing and mobilizing, but these did not bring independence and actually fragmented the platform population. After the early 1980s, by propagating a nation-state project around which the platform population could coordinate, the campaign positioned itself to persuade the international community that independence was the only option.

Organizational Tasks and Mobilization Phases

Typically, a nation-state project begins as a gleam in the eyes of a dreamer, and most end there. The dreamer may share this project with others in a hut, at an inn, in a classroom, in a conference room, or even on a park bench, but to get this project on the public agenda the dreamer must secure broader subscription through a larger national-secession campaign. Even skilled orators with access to broad audiences may find that their call initially falls on deaf ears. In 1956, when C. Suntharalingam called for secession from Ceylon (renamed Sri Lanka in 1972) and creation of "an independent Tamil Illankai [state]," most Tamil intellectuals and political leaders rejected secession and proposed instead greater linguistic rights for Tamils or perhaps a federal Ceylonese state. A year later a former member of Ceylon's Parliament, V. Kumarasamy, wrote a fiery appeal that Tamils "must secede from the Sinhalese, whether it means even a war of independence."[29] This also produced no immediate rally around the cause of independence. It took two decades of persuasion before many Tamils rallied around independence as the best solution to their mounting problems. To move from isolated events of fiery oratory to a broader campaign, founders of a campaign must fulfill three major operational tasks: recruiting and coordinating a leadership committed to the program of independence and limiting defections from this leadership to other causes; recruiting and educating a staff of cadres and activists also committed to this program, maintaining this staff and its energies though the long dry periods when independence is seemingly remote, and guarding it against defections from the cause; and tying a coalition of diverse interests to the campaign and preparing them as a participatory reserve to surge into action when opportunities arise. Table 3.1 depicts the constituent elements of a campaign as seen from a typical organizational analysis.

This structure defines three **developmental stages** of a campaign—establishment, capacitation, and association—in which one or the other of these tasks is the prime operational goal. At any stage, the campaign may mobilize more or less activity, defining two **activation phases**—the longueur and surges (see table 3.2).

TABLE 3.1.   Organization: Constituent parts of a national-secession campaign

UNORGANIZED POPULATION	ORGANIZED POPULATION	
Independent intellectuals	Leaders	*LEADERSHIP*
	Cadres	*STAFF*
	Activists	
Reserve participants	Reserve participants	*SUPPORTERS*
Passive platform population		

TABLE 3.2. Organization and mobilization: Developmental stages and activation phases of national-secession campaigns

DEVELOPMENTAL STAGE/TASK	ACTIVATION PHASE	
	LONGUEUR	SURGE
ESTABLISHMENT	Defining the program Recruiting leadership	Deterring leader defections Awakening public
CAPACITATION	Recruiting cadres Training activists	Recruiting activists Dress rehearsals
ASSOCIATION	Linking to parochial interests Building auxiliaries	Creating expectation of realism Activating reserve

Note: Table cells show exemplary operational tasks in each activation phase at a particular developmental stage.

These distinctions among developmental stages and between activation phases are only heuristic devices. They emphasize how choices of both appeals and means are constrained by the conditions of the campaign itself. Referring to these as phases and stages does not mean that a campaign for independence must move in a linear progression through them. Indeed, although the longueur is preparation for the surge, the surge capacity requires that the campaign develop a billows-like ability to expand and contract, moving backward and forward between phases of activism, surging and retreating. Smaller surges early on (such as protests or isolated acts of violence) can be investments in campaign developmental stages that make possible still larger surges. Similarly, each developmental stage is in part preparation for the next. Each stage builds on the accomplishments of the previous stage, so leadership coordination is critical to building capacity, which in turn is necessary for the development of an associational network. Yet campaigns may need to retreat from association to capacitation and even back to establishment. And once a campaign moves from one to the next stage, it does not put the issues of the previous stage behind. The tasks and problems of each stage persist into the next; these tasks and problems accumulate and interact with one another. Thus, even in the association stage campaign leaders must continue to attend to the unity of the leaders and intellectuals and the cultivation of cadres and activists.

Stage/Task 1: Establishment—Recruiting Leadership

Stage or Task 1 is the **establishment** of the campaign. Intellectuals coordinate on a common nation-state project and identify leaders among themselves or attract others with organizational skills. They develop one or more groups that are defined by and, in turn, sustain a commitment to the cause of independence. According to a US Joint Chiefs of Staff manual, "a latent insurgency usually begins with a group of like-minded individuals discussing core grievances. . . . During this period the insurgency establishes an identity, cause, narrative, and a firm ideological or political base. . . . [I]t can be a period of frequent fracturing and splintering due to ideological or other internal disputes."[30] This is true of the establishment stage whether the campaign expects to launch an insurgency or not.

In establishing a campaign and sustaining it, founding leaders must reach out to both intellectuals and current or would-be politicians within the platform population. The nation-state project is typically the invention of historians, linguists, artists, and literati. Campaigns often begin with themes of language, culture, and history and "the present and future condition of the nation and of the territory it inhabited." In Lithuania, Alfred Erich Senn writes, "This meant questions of preserving national culture, national traditions, and even the environment."[31] Yet transformation of this into a program that includes an action plan and development of a campaign to propagate it is usually the work of enthusiasts with a keen organizational sense. As Eric Hoffer writes, "A movement is pioneered by men of words, materialized by fanatics and consolidated by men of action." Further, "It is usually an advantage to a movement, and perhaps a prerequisite for its endurance, that these roles should be played by different men succeeding each other as conditions require."[32] Thus, as Anatol Lieven points out, the Lithuanian independence campaign in the late 1980s brought together "intellectuals from the arts and humanities, intellectuals from technical and scientific fields, and junior members of the Communist establishment."[33] Still, a campaign cannot abandon the intellectuals once women and men of action are in control because the intellectuals' ability to conjure new projects poses a constant threat of programmatic competition that could weaken the campaign.

Coordination among the intellectuals who create nation-state projects is a daunting task because the natural tendencies of intellectuals often resist coordination. Even before propagation among other constituencies can commence, most projects fall victim to alternative projects offered by other intellectuals appealing to at least some members of the same platform population. For example, in the Basque community of Spain, Navarrese intellectuals have defined competing projects that claim the Navarrese and their homeland as parts of a Basque, Spanish, or distinct Navarre nation-state; leftist Basque intellectuals have offered competing projects that see Basque workers as parts of the Basque nation or a multinational working class.[34] Sustained coordination among creative intellectuals may be difficult: individual members of the intelligentsia may value their own intellectual independence, and their measure of creativity can be the originality and thus the difference of their formulations, including nation-state projects. Based on his own experience in the Marxist movement, Lenin lamented that "no one will undertake to deny that it is precisely its individualism and incapacity for discipline and organization that in general distinguish the intelligentsia. . . ."[35] As Hoffer stresses, "Men of thought seldom work well together. . . . Teamwork is rare in intellectual or artistic undertakings. . . ."[36] So there is a high probability that unless this tendency is constrained in some way, any national-secession project will face multiple alternative projects.[37]

A few campaigns are fortunate to find early, widespread participation by politicians. In the Baltic states of Estonia, Latvia, and Lithuania, for example, once the Gorbachev reforms permitted open expression of dissent in the Soviet Union, large numbers of Communist Party and state leaders joined the campaigns. As Lieven writes, the Estonian Popular Front was "essentially founded by the liberal wing of the Communist establishment" in April 1988, and this even included the former head of the powerful Estonian State Planning Commission (Gosplan).[38]

In most campaigns, however, the process of winning over political leaders to the goal of independence can be a long process that hinges on unexpected changes of the circumstances confronting those leaders. For example, the South Sudan campaign for independence was marginalized within the regional leadership until after 2005. The voices for separation in the mid-1950s were few as the United Kingdom prepared Sudan for independence. The emergence of the Anya-Nya linked an insurgency that had begun in the 1950s to the cause of independence, but a majority of southern politicians still favored unity and reform of Sudan rather than secession. The Addis Ababa Agreement (February 27, 1972) ended the first civil war but granted only limited autonomy to the South.[39] When war again erupted in 1983, the campaign for independence was marginalized once again—now by the program for a New Sudan. As described in chapter 2, the Sudan People's Liberation Army/Movement (SPLA/M), led by Dr. John Garang de Mabior, rejected secession and focused instead on revolutionary transformation of Sudan. Despite growing divisions within the leadership, an attempted coup in August 1991, and perhaps majority support for independence within the movement by the 1990s, Garang remained in control, and the voices for independence were overruled. Garang's death, just twenty-one days after the Comprehensive Peace Accord of January 9, 2005, gave proponents of independence the unexpected opportunity to rise to leadership within the SPLA/M and to shift its goal to secession. As the interim arrangement proved increasingly unproductive, even the strongest believers in the program for a New Sudan shifted to the program for independence: as Matthew LeRiche and Matthew Arnold observe, "During the final years of the CPA peace process, it was evident even to the

SPLM's Secretary General Pagan Amun . . . that its revolutionary struggle for a united New Sudan was no longer viable."[40]

In many campaigns, practical politicians come over to the cause only in an eleventh-hour switch to save their own careers. For example, the campaign for Bangladesh had emerged among intellectuals and students at Dhaka University as early as 1962 but remained a minority voice within the Awami League, whose leadership campaigned for a confederal Pakistan. The electoral victory of the Awami League in the December 1970 elections to Pakistan's Assembly and the decision of Pakistan's president to postpone the opening of Parliament set the stage for a crisis. Anticipating such a crisis, the Awami League leadership under Sheikh Mujibir Rahman (Mujib) had developed contingency plans for a declaration of independence and a mass liberation uprising, but apparently actually switched to this plan only as the prospect of martial law approached or once it was actually imposed.[41] Similarly, in most union republics of the USSR, such as Belarus or Ukraine, and in Yugoslav republics such as Slovenia and Macedonia, political leaders switched to the cause of independence only as the federations collapsed or the central governments became a threat to their own political survival.

The operational task of recruiting and coordinating among practical politicians with shallower commitment to the goal of the campaign carries a risk of capture that displaces the campaign leaders and their original goals. For example, as described more fully at the end of this chapter, recruitment of Basque politicians to the campaign for Euskadi has attracted to leadership positions many pragmatists who appear content to compromise with Spain, to work within the Spanish system of autonomous communities, and to temper the campaign's independence demands.

Thus, a first operational task of campaign leaders is building a leadership, which includes recruiting intellectuals and current or would-be politicians to the cause of independence. Even in the establishment stage a divergence in motivations between true believers and practical politicians may begin to emerge. Over the longer term the establishment task comes to include greater need to deter defections to other causes, a task that becomes more difficult as the number of pragmatists in the leadership increases. Containing the centrifugal forces and keeping the leadership focused on the cause of independence are essential to campaign coordination.

Stage/Task 2: Capacitation—Building a Staff

The linkage of women and men of ideas who advance a nation-state project to the broader platform population requires a staff with skills that may not be found among intellectuals and politicians. In preparing for opportunities for independence, campaign leaders typically must build a staff that can be sustained over a long period and particularly through the long, dull periods when there are few opportunities for heroic acts and success is not likely soon. In these periods the staff prepares an ever-larger **surge** capacity within the platform population to deliver, when opportunities arise, an appropriate, rapid mobilization of participation by members of the participatory reserve behind the program of independence.

Thus, Stage or Task 2 is **capacitation,** in which the leaders recruit and educate a campaign staff that includes cadres and activists to carry out the tasks identified by the leaders. These may be centralized in a single organization or distributed among multiple organizations. Drawing heavily on the Timor Leste struggle for independence from Indonesia, David Kilcullen describes how an organization such as Fretilin

> establishes a presence with . . . local cells, support systems, intelligence and information-gathering networks, and local alliances.
>
> The group may establish its own businesses, run front companies, or operate in partnership (or competition) with local criminal or business syndicates. It may establish training camps, education or ideological indoctrination centers, recruiting and logistics bases, transportation systems, centers for the production of counterfeit documentation, headquarters camps, media production facilities, and caches of equipment and supplies.[42]

Different organizations may specialize in legal or illegal activities, peaceful or violent action, but the shared commitment to independence unites them in a common campaign. The establishment and running of such networks are the work of the staff.

The staff consists of cadres and activists. Labels may vary among actual campaigns, and the distinction between cadres and activists may be blurry in some campaigns, but the tasks of the staff, influenced by the example of the Russian and Chinese communists, are typically the same. The staff implements activities, decided by the leadership, to prepare the platform population. Much of the workaday activity of cadres includes building, training, and keeping engaged a network of activists whose public acts may recruit, maintain, and mobilize a still larger participatory reserve. The cadres keep these focused on the cause of independence. Cadre-directed activities may be dress rehearsals for surge events. For example, distributing a newspaper is important not simply because it propagates the program—it is more than a low-tech version of a blog or a website—the activities surrounding the creation and dissemination of the newspaper also create the cooperative behaviors or habits necessary for later mobilization. In Lenin's expansion on this operation,

> This network of agents will form the skeleton of precisely the kind of organisation we need—one that is sufficiently large to embrace the whole country; sufficiently broad and many-sided to effect a strict and detailed division of labour; sufficiently well tempered to be able to conduct steadily *its own* work under any circumstances, at all "sudden turns," and in face of all contingencies; sufficiently flexible to be able, on the one hand, to avoid an open battle against an overwhelming enemy, when the enemy has concentrated all his forces at one spot, and yet, on the other, to take advantage of his unwieldiness and to attack him when and where he least expects it.[43]

Even in circumstances where a national-secession campaign turns to insurgency, the cadres remain critical. Thus, Nathan Leites and Charles Wolf, Jr., underscore the importance of a rebellion's cadres to any counterinsurgent war effort: "as long as [the rebellion's] organization core remains intact, so do its strength and stamina. Depleting the core of the organization—acquiring the cadres—should therefore be [the central government's] aim."[44] In engaging the broader platform population (Stage/Task 3, discussed below), the cadres are key to developing a surge capacity.

Activists provide much of the muscle that distributes pamphlets, protests, leads auxiliary organizations, and commits violence.[45] Although guerrillas and terrorists are the activists who have drawn the most attention, in many national-secession campaigns the most important activists are not armed militants. For example, in the very restrictive political environment of the Franco regime, the "subversive actions" that kept the platform population aware of the campaign's program "included graffiti, the distribution of propaganda, public display of the Basque flag ('Ikurriña'), the destruction of Francoist architectural symbols, celebration of the Basque national day (Aberri Eguna), and illegal transmissions of radio messages by the president of the Basque government."[46] In many contexts the most important activists can be unarmed civilian practitioners such as journalists, teachers, and nurses, who print and distribute newspapers, teach literacy courses, or provide medical and veterinary care. In Eritrea, David Pool reports that health care for peasants and pastoralists and veterinary care for their animals were popular ways for the EPLF to introduce its program to the platform population.[47]

Recruiting and maintaining a commitment to independence among these staffers are a key operational task of campaign leaders. Keeping these staffers engaged even when independence is not close at hand and deterring them from "rogue" activities that subvert the message of independence are essential to the success of the campaign. Yet as the Eritrean campaign discovered, professional revolutionaries require not only more intensive political education by more specialized personnel with appropriate materials, but also a more complex logistical support capacity and a more complex communication, monitoring, and sanctioning capacity.[48] Full-time workers must be fed and housed. They require more intensive training, so expert trainers with advanced training materials are needed. They necessitate a network of monitors and self-monitoring (criticism/self-criticism) mechanisms. Because the staff is so costly, the size and internal structure of the staff must often be limited.

Stage/Task 3: Association—Preparing Reservists

Stage or Task 3 is **association,** in which the cadres and activists seek to control or create networks that can be used to mobilize support and provide the infrastructure for a still larger and longer-term surge capacity. The campaign recruits a participatory reserve, educates it, and may even institutionalize this reserve in formal organizations, such as trade unions or students' organizations, in order to lock it in for the longer term and prepare it for instant engagement. The campaign seeks to convince other members of the platform population who will not participate in public or private acts supporting independence that they should at least not express support for the common-state or alternative campaigns.

Under the constraints of strategic opportunism and forecast uncertainty, a national-secession campaign must cultivate a participatory reserve that will be available at the right moments to demonstrate that independence is the only viable option. And even before the ultimate moment when the campaign must demonstrate programmatic preemption, it must be ready to seize opportunities for actions that will build and sustain programmatic coordination. As in the Eritrean People's Liberation Front, members of this participatory reserve might be graded according to reliability into "sympathizers, participants, and dedicated members of the mass associations of workers, peasants, women and youth."[49] These reservists may be mobilized in isolated, individualized activities to support the activists, such as securing secret meeting places for the leaders, surreptitiously acquiring medicines and instructional materials for the staff, transporting personnel and materiel, forging passports, collecting funds, running financially profitable enterprises, gathering and reporting intelligence, infiltrating government agencies, and taking positions of power.[50] The reserve is also important as a collectivity at moments when the campaign needs overwhelming turnout in public acts to vote, to march, to erect barricades—that is, to demonstrate its programmatic preemption. Much of the time, however, most reservists are not active and do not take a public stand on behalf of independence. Hence, campaigns confront a major paradox: much of the time most of the participatory reserve is a deadweight to the campaign, yet lengthy preparation times require constant cultivation of the reserve's readiness. Campaign leaders must rehearse the participatory reserve, test their coordination with the campaign staff, and tap their energies in ways that demonstrate to still others that the platform population is coordinating around the goal of independence.

Because both the timing of events and the nature of the opportunities are uncertain, the campaign leaders confront five challenges: first of all, the campaign must keep the reserve constantly mobilizable but not continuously mobilized. Any attempt to keep the reserve constantly "hot" would soon overtax both the staff and the reserve.

The campaign must seize opportunities for low-risk action—such as protests, demonstrations, and plebiscites—even when independence is not near in order to expand the reserve's capacity for mobilization. These actions are vital to the operational objective of drilling the staff, rehearsing the participatory reserve, and perhaps recruiting new members. As one IRA detainee in H-Block exhorted the Irish population in the North, "So, we are depending on you, the people, our people, to stand by us—by supporting us in our struggle, by protesting, by going out on to the streets. Get as many people behind you as possible. March, rally, and petition, agitate. But please, please, in the name of humanity, stand firmly behind us. Remember you are the people."[51] By such exhortations to action, campaign leaders build a capacity to demonstrate programmatic preemption. In their public statements the leaders often must portray these rehearsals as real opportunities to move closer to independence if they are to have the intended operational effects. But this is a risky ploy because failure to achieve independence by these rehearsals can erode the leaders' credibility prior to real opportunities.

The campaign must develop a billows-like capacity to demobilize as well as to mobilize the participatory reserve in order to minimize destruction to the campaign. The capacity to quickly de-escalate and repurpose can ensure survival. For example, the Tamil Tigers in Sri Lanka, after being overwhelmed in 1987–90 by the Indian Peace Keeping Force, withdrew from Jaffna and its jungle camp at Wanni, but according to Edgar O'Ballance, "It was clear that the Tamil Tigers had not been defeated and disbursed but were emulating Mao Tse-tung's Red Army which, after the Long March, retreated to the remote regions of Yenan to recuperate, recruit, indoctrinate and prepare for future battles."[52] Yet this is also risky because getting the reserve to step back can create divisions and lead some reservists to fall away from the campaign.

Campaign leaders must build a diverse and flexible reserve that will be able to respond to multiple likely scenarios—particularly because they cannot predict with great precision the nature of the opportunities to demonstrate programmatic preemption. Campaign leaders may prepare for such varied surge actions as mobilizing referendum votes, staging peaceful protests in the capital, stepping into an administrative vacuum, conducting coordinated terrorist campaigns, participating in rural revolts, and launching a military assault. The objective is to be prepared to use the most-effective means for the types of opportunity that are most likely to arise. Yet flexibility can be costly: not only does this require a larger and more expensive organizational investment, but preparations for more contingencies with specialists for each possible scenario can also make the campaign more heterogeneous.

Campaign leaders must build an oversized participatory reserve. The necessity of strategic opportunism and programmatic preemption, along with uncertainty about the nature and scheduling of opportunities and uncertainty about the availability of the participatory reserve at any one moment, means that national-secession campaigns cannot stop at building a minimal supporting coalition of 50 percent plus one within the platform population but must build oversized support within the platform population to confront the common-state government and international community with the reality that independence is the only viable option. The campaign seeks to build a following of supporters for independence that at the critical moment visibly overwhelms, or at least unambiguously outnumbers, supporters of alternatives. Forecast uncertainty means that campaign leaders cannot predict with certainty what part of this reserve will be available. Thus, the campaign must make still greater efforts to increase the number of reservists to maintain the campaign's surge capacity at a level that, even with only partial turnout, will demonstrate programmatic preemption. Moreover, a campaign cannot leave large parts of the platform population unaffiliated lest these become affiliates of competitors and particularly of the common-state.

But What about Coordination?

Many elements of this description of organization and mobilization should be familiar because they are the elements of the Leninist strategy that have received the greatest attention in scholarly and policy communities. These elements provide the structure within which the critical element of coordination of a campaign must take place. But what actually provides the coordination that sustains leaders, staffs, and participatory reserve in complementary efforts towards a common goal through periods of preparing for mobilization and in surges of collective action?

The poster child for the costs of disunity is the Basque campaign for Euskadi in Spain. The Basque movement developed advanced organizational structures and perfected mobilization tactics, but the campaign lacked programmatic coordination. Among the oldest secessionist campaigns, dating from the seminal work of Sabino Arana in the 1890s, the Basque campaign remains deeply divided among competing visions concerning any future independent state and has been crippled by defections to class-based revolutionary causes. Moreover, many supporters of the campaign for independence (and perhaps most of them) engage the nationalist movement through organizations controlled by collaborators with the Spanish common-state.

Initially, under the slogan of "God and the Old Laws" (JEL), the independence project of the Partido Nacionalista Vasco (PNV) sought to restore autonomous communities inside a decentralized state based on medieval (or early modern) rights and laws (the *Fueros*). In time this was challenged by projects for a centralized bourgeois or socialist Basque state. In 1930 the Basque Nationalist Action (ANV) left the PNV to campaign for an independent, nonconfessional, centralized Basque state based on modern statutory laws.[53] The call for more militant opposition to Spain emerged within youth groups in the early 1950s and was institutionalized in 1959 in Freedom for the Basque Country (ETA). With the adoption of the strategic vision initially articulated by Federico Krutwig in 1962, ETA embraced an armed struggle based on the model of revolutionary anticolonial war that had been successful in Algeria and Vietnam. By 1965, ETA had adopted the ideology of Marxism-Leninism, but these "third worldists," following Krutwig's intellectual leadership, threatened to tear apart the Basque nation: "the only way to liberate the Basques was to wage a war of national liberation, a revolutionary war that would target as enemies all non-Basques and all members of the Basque bourgeoisie who would not cooperate in the struggle."[54] This ideological embrace of Marxism inspired further fragmentation as Maoists, Fidelistas, and others diverged. Still more importantly, it inspired defections to Españolista campaigns, such as Kommunistak (the Communists) and the Revolutionary Communist League (LCR), which pursued worker solidarity that transcended narrow nationalist appeals.[55]

The greatest obstacle to the campaign for independence, however, has been the collaborationism of many leaders within major Basque nationalist organizations. After the return to democracy in Spain, the best organized effort within the Basque nationalist community came from the PNV, which positioned itself on the center-right of the Basque political spectrum and emerged as the predominant political force in the Basque country. This came through careful organizational efforts that reached down to the grass roots. As John Sullivan notes,

"Throughout 1977 and 1978 the PNV established *Batzokis* (PNV headquarters) in towns and villages all over Euskadi. Some were little more than bars, others were the local administrative headquarters of the party, with an extensive network of cultural activities consisting of dancing, folklore and music."[56] This organizing positioned the PNV to win most elections within the autonomous region. Yet it also weakened the campaign for independence. Although the PNV included the largest part of the Basque community committed to independence, the PNV leadership was balanced between those committed to independence and those content to collaborate with Spain as long as the Basque country enjoyed broadening autonomy. As Sullivan summarizes, "In practice, the ambiguity of whether the PNV was committed to complete separation from Spain was to persist throughout the party's existence. . . ."[57] After creation of the Basque autonomous community within Spain in 1978, "the question of whether autonomy was a step towards independence, or on the contrary, whether its acceptance presupposed Basque loyalty to the Spanish state and its king, was never settled."[58]

Illustrative of this continuing ambiguity was the Plan Ibarretxe, proposed by the Basque President Juan José Ibarretxe (PNV) in 2003 and endorsed by the Basque Parliament in 2004. André Lecours observes that this plan, "while somewhat vague on specifics, rested on the idea that the Basques want to renegotiate sovereignty and their partnership with Spain. The notion of 'self-determination' also features prominently in former President Ibarretxe's subsequent referendum projects."[59] Yet, using the rhetoric of "self-determination," the moderate PNV leadership advanced such plans in order to reform Spain rather than to achieve sovereign independence. In reaching out to more-practical politicians, leaders of the campaign for independence had lost control of the PNV and had become subordinate to politicians eager to succeed within the institutions of the Spanish democracy—at least for the foreseeable future.

This failure of programmatic coordination has been costly for the Basque campaign for independence. Basque nationalists disagree about the shape of the proposed state as either traditionalist, liberal, socialist, or communist; about whether independence should be an immediate objective; and about the action plan to achieve immediate and long-term goals.[60] This lack of coordination has meant that national-secessionist activists often work at cross-purposes to one another: the violent campaign of ETA subverted rather than complemented the parliamentary strategies of most Basque nationalists. Fragmentation, collaboration, and defections to Spanish (*Españolista*) parties of the right and left weakened the campaign. The Basque left continued to bleed supporters from the nationalist cause to communist, socialist, and environmentalist parties that muted the demand for independence and, in some cases, merged with Spanish parties. On the right, the majority of supporters of independence remained a muted voice within a PNV led by collaborationists. After more than a century, the Basque independence campaign remains a fragmented, weakened force.

The fate of the Basque campaign for independence is not unique: even with successful organization and mobilization, the failure to coordinate around a program for the common goal of independence takes its toll in many national-secession campaigns. The response to this challenge recommended by the strategy of programmatic coordination is the topic addressed in the next chapter.

4

PROGRAMMATIC COORDINATION IN CAMPAIGNS

In ideological-organizational work the glue that holds together a campaign through developmental stages and shifting phases of activism is the campaign's goal. However, that goal typically means very different things to the many intellectuals, leaders, cadres, activists, and reservists who are drawn to a campaign. Individual participants are often energized by diverse personal motivations, such as expression of their identities, frustration and resentment, lust for power and riches, or a love of the sport of conspiring, protesting, and destroying. Indeed, successful campaigns must build a coalition among many, if not all, of these types of participants. But the key to campaign success is linking these deeper, often disparate, particularistic motivations to the common solution of independence. In order to bring together the constituent elements of a campaign through the developmental stages and activation phases described in chapter 3, campaign leaders must deploy diverse incentives that will respond to the different orientations to the goal of independence.

The analysis in this chapter begins with the micro-level model that was introduced in chapter 3 with its focus on strategic choices by campaign leaders operating under the constraints on choice presented by their platform population. But the chapter concludes by introducing a broad overview of the macro-level consequences of this model. Specifically, although intellectuals propose a variety of projects for national secession, the critical sorting or selection among these comes as each project must survive the assessment of whether many in the proposed platform population will see it as authentic and realistic. Coordination behind a national-secession campaign's program depends on shared expectations about the definition of the nation, its homeland, and the desirability of sovereign independence. These expectations are grounded in empirical corroborations by individual members of the platform population who must make this assessment under the constraint of limited information about one another. This simplified model of micro-level campaigning and meso-level coordination is a useful analytic tool for deducing hypotheses about the macro-level constraints most likely to lead to campaign significance, intractable conflicts, and protracted intense struggles.

Illustration: The Eritrean Campaigns

Comparison of the Eritrean campaign for independence before and after 1980 illustrates the importance of programmatic coordination. The campaign began with an initial failed effort that linked secessionist projects to specific sectarian or class elements but did not define and propagate a project of Eritreanism that embraced all its various ethnic, class, and sectarian groups. The Eritrean Liberation Movement (ELM), created in 1958, was based on secret urban cells of secular and educated activists who failed to make extensive contact with the countryside. Devoted to staging an urban coup to seize power in the name of independence, the ELM withered away because it refused to reach out to traditional Eritrean elites and could not find refuge in the countryside when the Imperial Ethiopian Government cracked down in the cities. In competition with the movement, the Eritrean Liberation Front (ELF), created in 1960, was based on regional small-town and rural elites that were disproportionately Muslim.[1] This front claimed to adopt the model of the Algerian FLN but never actually imposed programmatic unity on its various commands.[2] Moreover, it was unclear whether the ELF's project embraced all Eritreans as one nation, included its largest ethnic groups, or welcomed members of Eritrea's Christian plurality (and possibly majority).

   The critical failure that followed from this disunity came when the Eritrean campaign was not prepared to seize the opportunity for independence that opened in the mid-1970s with the collapse of the imperial government. The campaign failed to present the Eritrean homeland population or the international community with a coherent and overwhelming claim for a unified, independent Eritrea. As Haggai Erlich asks, "How could they lose the war while throughout 1975–1977 they had enjoyed military superiority over the Ethiopians and regional circumstances had been so favorable to the establishment of an independent Eritrea?"[3] The ELF had mastered many of the best practices of guerrilla warfare but not coordination of its platform population behind the goal of national independence. The front captured three-quarters of Eritrea, built base-area governments to administer the liberated territories and populations, and threatened Eritrea's capital city.[4] Yet the secessionists lost the civil war of 1975–77. Erlich attributes the failure to the internal struggles that divided the campaign: "In the moment of truth, the Eritreans failed to pull together in the name of Eritreanism. The reality of ethnic, religious, regional, social, and personal rivalries couched in revolutionary phraseology legitimizing disunity proved stronger than the relatively young sentiment of Eritrean nationalism."[5]

Dissidents within the ELF, urging Eritrean national unity that could transcend linguistic and religious distinctions, survived the civil war and became the foundation of the Eritrean People's Liberation Front (EPLF), created in 1977. John Markakis writes that "to no small measure, the survival of the dissidents was due to the fact that, in the face of common danger, they were able to integrate organizationally and began fashioning a political consensus that ultimately united the majority of them."[6] At its First Congress in 1977 the EPLF established an institutional structure borrowed from the Communist parties.[7] Much of the EPLF success, where the ELF had failed, came from its extensive investments in programmatic coordination: to reinforce programmatic unity, the EPLF leadership maintained a clandestine party organization (the Eritrean People's Socialist Party) that demanded strict ideological discipline among its members, sent cadres to educate all members of the front, and maintained security and intelligence organizations to monitor adherence to the party line.[8] It recast its program to define an inclusive nationalist campaign. According to David Pool, "The lesson learned by those who split [from the ELF] and subsequently formed the EPLF was the necessity to create a disciplined, nationalist liberation army impervious to social, ethnic, regional, tribal, religious, and ideological divisions."[9] Whereas the initial EPLF program had been written in the Maoist language of class struggle, the EPLF shifted its doctrine to a unifying nationalism.[10] As Ruth Iyob notes, "By the mid-1980s the EPLF could boast of an impressive record of mobilizing the various ethnic groups and classes (including Eritrean women) into a single nationalist force around a single goal: liberation."[11] In this way the EPLF positioned itself to seize the next opportunity to demonstrate programmatic preemption on behalf of independence when the central government again fell.

Linking through a Common Objective

The achievement of programmatic preemption, which can convince the international community that independence is the only option acceptable to the platform population, requires broad recruitment within the platform population.

In the original strategy, Lenin advised that "participation in the movement should extend to the greatest possible number of the most diverse and heterogeneous groups of the most varied sections of the proletariat (and other classes of the people)."[12] Substituting "nation" for "proletariat" describes the tasks of national-secession campaign leaders.[13] Based on his studies of European nationalist movements, Miroslav Hroch cautions that "where the national movement . . . was not capable of introducing into national agitation, and articulating in national terms, the interests of the specific classes and groups which constituted the small nation, it was not capable of attaining success."[14] The campaign must link the program of independence to each of these constituencies. Yet broad recruitment makes the task of programmatic coordination all the more essential and complex.

Diverse Incentives and Motivational Heterogeneity

In order to recruit and sustain these diverse groups in a campaign, strategically minded leaders offer incentives that can be purposive, material, or expressive. These incentives are distinguished by their relationship to the campaign's goal of independence. **Purposive incentives,** according to James Q. Wilson, are "intangible rewards that derive from the sense of satisfaction of having contributed to the attainment of a worthwhile cause."[15] **Material incentives,** most commonly the rewards of money and power, are achieved *by means of* the campaign and independence, but the latter is not an end valued in itself.[16] **Expressive incentives** are opportunities created by the campaign for cathartic release of personal emotions such as anger or rage and opportunities to indulge in the sport of protesting and mayhem where the act is an end in itself. A central executive task of campaign leaders is the allocation of these incentives in different activation phases and developmental stages to recruit and to deploy the human assets needed to further programmatic coordination and to demonstrate programmatic preemption. Leaders allocate these incentives under strict resource constraints: the likelihood of attaining independence in the near term is typically small, the money and power to distribute to campaign recruits are limited, and the opportunities for expressive action are usually few.[17]

A successful campaign cannot offer only a single type of incentive. Building a campaign organization of leaders, staffers, and participatory reserve and building the capacity to demonstrate programmatic preemption require making appeals (offering incentives) to different parts of the platform population with diverse motivations and interests. For example, in the run-up to the referendum on independence in 2006, the Montenegro campaign confronted the relatively simple and well-defined task of persuading its supporters to vote and to cast their votes for separation from Serbia. Nonetheless, the campaign had to devise diverse appeals to persuade different audiences of the rewards they would reap from independence. For example, in the more nationalistic region of Cetinje, the campaign appealed "to the pre-existing self-perception of Montenegrins as a brave, honourable and independent people. Contemporary Montenegrins, the speakers argued, were presented with a unique historical mission—to correct the injustices endured by their forefathers who had to bear the loss of Montenegrin independence in 1918. . . due to Serbian aggression. . . ." To this audience the campaign's message stressed that independence was a worthy end in itself. In the more modern capital of Podgorica, however, the message emphasized that independence would be the best means to other worthy ends. Interests would best be served by ending Montenegro's "subservient role within an unequal and unworkable state union." Independence would bring the benefits of democracy, political stability, civil society, economic growth, and membership in the European Union.[18]

The stages of campaign development constrain the use of specific incentives. Purposive incentives may be all that campaign leaders can offer initially in the establishment stage, but these are likely to recruit only a small circle of individuals who value contributing to independence as reward in itself. Expressive opportunities may be used in the capacitation stage to recruit activists and in the association stage to build a participatory reserve. Promises of material rewards attract a larger participatory reserve in the association stage, but this reserve can typically be activated by these incentives only as the prospect of independence draws nearer. The role of these incentives also varies with the different phases of activism. Many material and expressive incentives can be offered for only short periods unless the campaign has established itself as a governing authority and thus may not be available for the longueur and may best be reserved for critical surge moments. Expressive action may serve as propaganda in any state of the campaign, but it can be difficult for leaders to sustain and direct—particularly in early developmental stages.

A mix of appeals, while operationally necessary to build the capacity to demonstrate programmatic preemption, introduces **motivational heterogeneity** into the campaign. Diverse incentives bring together members of the platform population who come to the campaign for independence with very different personal objectives.[19] Each incentive attracts a particular *type* of adherent to the campaign—enthusiasts, pragmatists, and expressionists—who are distinguished by their different orientations to the campaign goal. Enthusiasts enjoy setting the world right; the pursuit of independence is reward in itself. Pragmatists expect to benefit from their involvement; independence is a means to other ends and not always the most-efficient means. Expressionists often act out frustrations, resentments, and anger or just enjoy the action; the campaign's protests and violence are often ends in themselves while independence and a new political order might limit opportunities to act. (Of course, these are ideal-types, and most real people mix these types in varying degrees.) Strategically minded campaign leaders must match each type to a constituent part (leadership, staff, or participatory reserves) within the campaign structure. Leaders must also match each type to specific phases of activism (longueur or surge) and stages of campaign development (establishment, capacitation, or association). In the strategy of programmatic coordination, these leadership responsibilities frame four significant campaign management challenges.

Campaign leaders must look forward to anticipate the campaign's future need for each type recruited now. The choice of incentives and the types attracted to the campaign will limit the leaders' subsequent options for campaign activism. Leaders cannot expect expressionists to perform desk jobs efficiently. Nor can leaders expect pragmatists to accept the privations of the underground—at least not for long.

These leaders must also anticipate the campaign's future ability to continue to generate the incentives that will sustain the involvement of each type. That is, once particular incentives bring a particular type of recruit into the campaign, those types will expect a continued supply of similar incentives.[20] Enthusiasts expect evidence that their contributions are actually moving the campaign closer to independence and often expect more-immediate demonstrations of sovereignty. Pragmatists seek personal rewards and often demand actions to expand the store of appropriable wealth or power. Expressionists seek more opportunities to act. Before bringing a type into the campaign, forward-looking leaders must estimate the campaign's ability to provide this continuous stream of rewards.

Campaign leaders must anticipate the moral hazards associated with recruiting one type or the other. Each type may divert the campaign from successful achievement of independence: enthusiasts may rigidly oppose compromises with the common-state—even compromises that could aid long-term achievement of independence. Pragmatists may transform the campaign into a predatory rent-seeking machine. Expressionists may press for more extreme action that divides the campaign and loses support in the platform population and international community.

These leaders must manage the conflicts that are introduced when diverse incentives recruit these different types into the same campaign. Splits often emerge between enthusiasts in the political wing and expressionists in the military wing. Enthusiasts in the leadership and pragmatists in the broad membership frequently become alienated from one another.

Thus, in the strategy of programmatic coordination, strategically minded campaign leaders must manage purposive, material, and expressive incentives to

TABLE 4.1.   Incentives and types

	INCENTIVE OFFERED		
	PURPOSIVE	**MATERIAL**	**EXPRESSIVE**
Type attracted by incentive	Enthusiast	Pragmatist	Expressionist
Perspective of type on independence	Independence as ends	Independence as means	Independence as risk
Place in structure			
Leadership	X	—	—
Cadres	X	—	—
Activists	—	—	X
Participatory reserve	—	X	—
Development stages			
Establishment	X	—	—
Capacitation	X	—	X
Association	X	X	X
Activation phase			
Longueur	X	—	—
Surge	X	X	X
Moral hazard risk	Impatient action	Predation	Rogue activism

recruit the right types to each constituent part of the campaign. This management must take a long-term perspective to elicit appropriate responses in the different developmental stages, to sustain participation or readiness for action during the longueurs, and to motivate the right types of surges at the right moments. Across parts and periods of the campaign, management of incentives must coordinate actions of leadership, staff, and reserve toward a common goal. (See table 4.1.)

Propagation and Coordination

The strategy of programmatic coordination advises campaign leaders that propagation of the program plays a central role in managing this motivational heterogeneity. In particular, it is the program's goal that recruits enthusiasts in the longueur, motivates them in the face of physical and material privation, and immunizes them from appeals of the common-state government. The program's action plan identifies the role of expressive acts in the achievement of independence. And, with explanations of the gains to be had through independence, the program can link the campaign organization to diverse material interests in the larger platform population that can be mobilized in surges at appropriate times. Thus, the most important task of campaign founders and subsequent leaders is to design and propagate a program that has the potential to coordinate expectations of these members of a campaign with heterogeneous motivations.[21]

In the strategy of programmatic coordination, much of the campaign's energy focuses on explaining the national-secession program to win new adherents through persuasion.[22] As Alfred G. Meyer notes, in this formulation propaganda does not imply "irrational, tricky, or deceptive means of persuasion. On the contrary, in the original Leninist formulation, propaganda denotes the painful and lengthy effort of so educating the proletariat that it understands and absorbs Marxist theory in all its ramifications and complications."[23] Through propagation a national-secession campaign seeks to help members of the platform population to understand the nation-state's project (goal) and action plan and to see independence as right, beneficial, or both. According to the Irish Republican Army's *Manual of Guerrilla Warfare,* in a propaganda campaign, which "must be continuous . . . , information must be factual to build up confidence among the people in the national movement." And it must "give the people tenacity to stand up to the enemy by showing them the struggle is worthwhile and necessary. They must be made aware that the national struggle will be victorious in the end—but that the end depends on them."[24]

This propagation is particularly important in preparing the surge capacity. To paraphrase Mao's description in "On Protracted War," this propagation first explains the objective of the struggle so that every participant sees why the struggle "must be fought and how it concerns him"; second, it describes the steps and means that are necessary to achieve this end and the participant's role in this program of action; third, it blankets the platform population with the message "by word of mouth, by leaflets and bulletins, by newspapers, books and pamphlets, through plays and films, through schools, through the mass organizations and through our cadres"; and fourth, it conducts this not once but continuously. Every engagement of participants in the campaign must be infused with this message, linking the particular to the general cause.[25] According to Chalmers A. Johnson, by linking every action to the cause, "the rural 'common man' learned that his peril was also China's peril" and the campaign "broke the parochialism of peasants and created a sense of 'China' and Chinese nationality."[26]

For strategically minded campaign leaders, the centrality of programmatic coordination to campaign success may justify the costs of propagation, even as budget constraints limit the scope of these persuasive efforts. For example, despite Eritrea's poverty and limited supply of educated personnel, the EPLF created a network of revolution schools for children under age fifteen, vanguard schools for those older than this, and continuous political education for all fighters, members of mass organizations, and secret cells in villages and towns. The compulsory two hours daily of political education (limited to two hours per week for those on the front line) emphasized a history that depicted a common anticolonial struggle by the multinational but united Eritreans. For the EPLF leaders, the payoff in unity warranted the investment. As Pool summarizes, "The coherence of the political education programme combined with the continuity of the leadership at the centre of this democratic centralism was an important component of the survival of organizational unity." And "political education classes were a major instrument of incorporating and organizing the different social groups of Eritrea and connecting Eritrean society to the front."[27] The most significant national-secession campaigns have been vigilant in pursuing propagation. As the Irish poet Paul Duncan noted, "If there was a Nobel Prize for propaganda, Sinn Féin would have long ago won that prize."[28]

With unlimited resources and time, the objective of propagation would be to convert expressionists and pragmatists into enthusiasts who see the intrinsic worth of the goals in the program. Lenin stressed that "every Party cell and workers' committee must . . . try at every step to push the consciousness of the masses in the direction of socialism, to link up every specific question with the general tasks of the proletariat. . . ."[29] For national-secession campaigns, this ideal objective would mean creating ardent nationalists. Nonetheless, few if any campaigns operate under ideal conditions with unlimited resources to commit to propagation.

Thus, campaigns must settle for less than changing worldviews—less than converting pragmatists and expressionists into enthusiasts. They more commonly must simply draw out the logical connections between the program's objective and individual worldviews. With limited resources and time, campaign leaders must typically settle for awakening the audience to the "fact" that their immediate concerns can be realized through the campaign's goal. Thus, existing identities are typically not replaced by national-secession campaigns but are linked to the program's political goal of a nation-state: a new identity, such as being South Sudanese, typically is linked to, but does not supplant or compete with, existing identities, such as being Dinka. In the Philippines the fighters who joined the Moro National Liberation Front, according to analyses of their songs and ballads, apparently fought first of all for their local communities, but the campaign linked these parochial motivations to the goal of a common *bangsa* (nation).[30]

Nor are interests denied; they are linked to the goals of the program with explanations of how individuals with diverse political or economic ambitions will be better able to pursue their right to happiness in an independent nation-state.[31] The common goal connects pragmatists with diverse particular and parochial interests to the campaign. Jack A. Goldstone notes that "as popular groups almost invariably have only local concerns and goals, the task of building a dominant coalition to address these issues falls on members of the elites." And "to form such a coalition, it is critical to take the various particular complaints, and the various elite and popular ideologies, and forge them into an ideology that has broad appeal."[32] When they enter localities such as villages or specific contexts such as trade union meetings or when they approach professionals or businesspeople, cadres explain how local or particularistic concerns will be realized through the common goal of independence and why alternative programs—particularly the nation-state project of the common-state government—are unable to address these.[33] In Turkish Kurdistan, David Romano writes, "The PKK, with only a few hundred cadres, was able to increase the Kurdish population's sympathy and support by coordinating actions that mattered to the local people, most important of which was opposition to the landlords and exploitative tribal chiefs."[34] Similarly, in the 1990 election campaign to Lithuania's parliament—an election that led to victory of the leading pro-independence organization (Sajudis)—the intellectual Laima Andrikiene, educated at Manchester University, confronted voters who had "questions not about paths to independence, but about food prices, taxes, and the provision of machinery. . . . Seeming to respond to the public mood, Andrikiene spent very little time on flights of nationalist rhetoric, and concentrated on arguing that independence was necessary for economic renewal. . . ."[35] In the Québec campaigns of the 1980s and early 1990s, the Parti québécois (PQ) endorsed free trade as "a strategy of mobilization." According to Hudson Meadwell, PQ "assumes that there is a pool of soft supporters of independence who are averse to the economic risks of transition and statehood. Individuals in this subgroup are predisposed to support independence. If they can be assured that independence is viable, their support will harden."[36] Although the US Department of the Army manual on counterinsurgency disparages the diversity of links made by the cadres as a "bait-and-switch" tactic, this process of linking is an integral and necessary part of programmatic coordination.[37]

In short, at the core of the operational tasks of leaders of national-secession campaigns is propagation to create and maintain horizontal programmatic coordination *within* each constituent part of the campaign (leadership, staff, and participatory reserves) and vertical programmatic coordination *among* these different constituents from top to bottom. The key is keeping all constituent parts, despite the diverse personal motivations of the campaign's members, focused on the common goal of independence. Organizational hegemony—such as a monopolistic political machine in a segment-state—may facilitate this coordination around a nation-state project (goal), but more commonly programmatic coordination must be achieved in organizationally complex campaigns. For example, on the eve of independence one observer commented that Latvia's pro-independence movement from 1989 to 1991 was divided among "various groups that, on occasion, have argued among themselves. Nevertheless, they have maintained from the outset, a remarkable ability to continue their alliance, marching separately toward the same major goal—independence."[38] And without this coordination, even monopolistic machines fail. Without this coordination, campaigns risk greater free riding on the activities of a shrinking active core, substitution of private objectives by leaders and staffers, and defection to other causes, particularly collaboration with the common-state. Propagation of this common objective is central to coordination across all three stages of establishment, capacitation, and association, and between the longueur and surges of mobilization.

Coordinating among Diverse Types

Programmatic propagation is particularly important to addressing motivational heterogeneity among enthusiasts, expressionists, and pragmatists and their diverse private and parochial purposes. According to one Algerian nationalist, "It is impossible to win the other battles if the ideological battle with the people has not been won. . . ."[39] By identifying a common objective, propagation of a well-crafted program can serve at least five essential coordinating functions that strategically minded campaign leaders must consider in linking the different types of enthusiasts, expressionists, and pragmatists in a single campaign.

Vertical coordination from top to bottom of a campaign on a common goal (nation-state project)—or at least anticipation of such coordination—is critical to keeping intellectuals on board—including many of the enthusiasts among them.[40] Defections to alternative projects are limited by expectations about how the proposed platform population will respond: in deciding whether to continue to support a particular national-secession campaign (particularly when weighing alternative programs that also claim to speak in the name of the people), all but the truest of true believers are likely to subject all projects to a "reality test" by trying to discern how the public will respond when the projects are explained to them. Competition among intellectuals is likely to be limited when programmatic coordination in the platform population leads them to conclude that other projects are unlikely to be received as positively. Of course, few if any campaigns ever achieve complete programmatic preemption, but as a campaign gets closer to this unchallengeable status, competition and defection among intellectuals decline.

The common goal directs the energy of activists—and particularly the expressionists among them who come prepared for action.[41] For example, in his comparison of the protracted conflicts of the campaigns for Northern Ireland and Kawthoolei (for the Karen in Myanmar), Paul D. Kenny explains differences in "cohesion" by "the extent to which members come to identify the organization's goals as their own over time."[42] According to the Irish Republican Army's

Manual of Guerrilla Warfare, "The Guerrillas are volunteers and are inspired by an ideal. Therefore their loyalty, understanding of what is at stake and discipline, will be—and must be—on a much higher level than that obtaining in a regular army."[43] In the Basque campaign, according to Robert P. Clark, ETA "believes that well-informed or well-indoctrinated members are in the long run more reliable and more competent at their jobs."[44] Accordingly, ETA devoted valuable time to study sessions and discussion groups to raise awareness of its program among its activists. Without constant education of the activists in the strategic and operational objectives outlined by the program, a campaign can be undermined by expressionists who indiscriminately blow up things.

Propagation of the program is critical to preparing pragmatists in the participatory reserve for surges that are linked to advancing programmatic coordination and demonstrating programmatic preemption. Successful propagation creates the expectation that independence would be the best outcome for everyone, *if only it were possible,* and the expectation that everyone in the platform population knows this.[45] The program's promises will not keep the reserve constantly active over a long period, but it will keep them prepared over the long term for briefer surges. When opportunities present themselves for mass action, the campaign must be ready to expand rapidly by calling on reserve members, many of whom are willing to incur the costs of participation only when they believe the action plan has a high likelihood of success and their enjoyment of any benefits from independence will be contingent on (or proportional to) their participation in surges. Well before the surge, the campaign must already have persuaded the participatory reserve of the desirability of independence; there is usually too little time for persuasion at this late date. The campaign must also create expectations that other members of the platform population will join the surge, that members remaining idle during the surge will be left out of the benefits of independence, and that defectors will lose (and possibly be punished as traitors to the nation).[46] Without this programmatic preparation, a call to action is likely to fall on deaf ears.

The common goal also unites pragmatists with diverse personal and parochial interests as a platform population. Although their ethnic or religious identities, occupation, grievances, emotions, and ambitions may divide them, the program makes it possible to talk of themselves also as a platform population with a common identity as a nation and a common interest in statehood. They are no longer just Tigrayans or Afars, Muslims or Christians, businesspeople or pastoralists; for the sake of deciding which nation-state should be their own, they are Eritreans.

And the common goal links the pragmatists to the enthusiasts in the leadership. By demonstrating their own true belief in the program's goal, leaders and cadres make a credible commitment to pragmatists to see the struggle through to the end. In linking pragmatists to the campaign, the program explains how individual interests will be served by independence, but these expectations of payoff are contingent on the pragmatists' expectation that the campaign's leaders and staff will remain loyal to the cause. Thus, ironically, fanatical attachment of the leaders and staff to a nation-state project can be an advantage not only in holding the enthusiasts in the staff together but also in appealing for support from more-pragmatic members of the platform population with the purest instrumental motivations. The enthusiasm of the leaders and staff makes more credible any claims that they are not mercurial and will stick to the objective of independence until they actually deliver a nation-state. Pragmatists expect that still others will gravitate to the enthusiasts for these same reasons. Of course, pragmatists must be cautious: although pragmatic followers may seek enthusiasts as leaders, they cannot always be certain that leaders are actually the true believers they claim to be.[47] In the absence of credible commitments to the goal by the leaders, pragmatic supporters may withhold support from the campaign until they expect that imminent victory has locked in the leaders. This shapes the operational tasks for the leaders, who may seek ways to demonstrate their enthusiasm, tie their hands so that they cannot renege on their commitment to independence, and still hedge against the risks associated with the contingent commitment of pragmatists.

Uses and Limits of Purposive Incentives

Purposive incentives can energize many campaign leaders and staffers through both longueur and surge. The enthusiasts find intrinsic value in contributing to the common objective. As Eric Hoffer notes, "Faith organizes and equips man's soul for action."[48] Psychological studies of "moral values as motivators of political engagement" confirm the power of purpose to motivate political participation. Linda J. Skitka and Christopher W. Bauman find that strong moral convictions that "something is right or wrong . . . are experienced as a unique combination of factual belief, compelling motive, and justification for action." They "are likely to be stronger predictors of behavior than their nonmoral cousins."[49] Purposive incentives awaken and direct energy derived from the reward of setting things right.

Purposive incentives are particularly important for the survival of the leadership and staff through the long, dull periods when the prospects for material or power payoffs from independence are remote and the opportunities for heroic action are few.[50] Lenin identified purpose-driven leaders and staff as the professional revolutionaries "who will devote the whole of their lives, not only their spare evenings, to the revolution. . . ."[51] Emblematic of this type of enthusiast was Yakov Sverdlov, whom Lenin lionized in his memorial speech "as the most perfect type of professional revolutionary, a man who had entirely given up his family and all the comforts and habits of the old bourgeois society, a man who devoted himself heart and soul to the revolution, and who for many years, even decades, passing from prison to exile and from exile to prison, cultivated those characteristics which steeled revolutionaries for many, many years."[52] Such staffers (cadres and activists) are essential to the survival of the movement in the lengthy process of preparing for open struggle: in his memorial for Ivan Babushkin in 1910, Lenin noted that "had it not been for the tireless, heroically persistent work of such militants among the proletarian masses the [party] could not have existed ten months let alone ten years."[53] Not only do these enthusiasts bring energy to the campaign; they also protect its core from defections, compromises, and subversion.[54]

Such enthusiasts who forgo material rewards are essential for the survival of national-secession campaigns operating under severe resource constraints. For example, in their narrative about the Chechen conflict, Carlotta Gall and Thomas de Waal illustrate the willingness of President Dzhokhar Dudaev to accept material deprivation for his cause. They record the experience of Arkadii Volskii, the deputy head of the Russian delegation sent to negotiate with the Chechen leaders in 1995:

> Within a week of his arrival in Grozny [the capital of Chechnya] Volsky went out to talk to Dudayev in person, meeting him at midnight in the mountains. It was the only meeting between a government official and Dudayev during the war. . . . Volsky brought Dudayev the offer of a Jordanian passport, money and a plane, everything to persuade him to leave Chechnya, at which Dudayev took great offence. "He said, 'No, I am a patriot of my country, I will die here.'"

Dudaev's ideologist Zelimkhan Yandarbiev reportedly uttered, "It is better to die than lose your freedom." Both Dudaev and Yandarbiev demonstrated in deeds that this was not just cheap talk and did, indeed, forgo personal wealth, comfort, and their lives in the pursuit of Chechen independence.[55]

The enthusiasts drawn by these incentives are particularly important to rebuilding the campaign after severe setbacks. Writing soon after the rout of Eritrean forces by the Ethiopian forces in 1978, Erlich asked "Is the Ethiopian victory final?" He concluded that "Eritrean victory may realistically be excluded as a future possibility. The chances of those identified with Eritrean nationalism achieving it by military victory over the Ethiopian armed forces seem very remote." But he added that "at the same time, Eritreanism as a nationalist sense of affiliation, and more so as a strong negation of Ethiopianism, seems strong enough to ensure its continued existence and to provide the motivation for a long, guerrilla war."[56] According to the EPLF's own manual on *Creating a Popular, Economic, Political and Military Base,* written in 1982, after its defeat, "Only through intensive ideological training can dedicated members of associations persevere through difficult conditions without losing their bearings. Armed with such knowledge, they will be able to recruit new members, strengthen the link between EPLF and the people and carry the lofty revolutionary qualities demanded by their position."[57] Erlich was right in predicting that Eritrea would not achieve military victory and also in noting how the successful cultivation of Eritreanism allowed the campaign to survive military defeat and await the next opportunity to surge and finally to convince the international community that independence was the only viable option.

Recruitment of enthusiasts to the cadre corps is critical to aligning cadre actions with the goals of the campaign and then entrusting cadres with the task of spreading the program and faithfully adapting it to a variety of contexts. According to the template developed by Mao, "In the final analysis, leadership involves two main responsibilities: to work out ideas, and to use cadres well."[58] In the European nationalist movements, Hroch finds that "patriots" were critical because they "consciously, of their own volition, and over a long period of time, devoted their activities to the support of the national movement, endeavouring in particular to diffuse patriotic attitudes."[59] True belief among the cadres is critical because they typically must be given considerable autonomy to operate in environments outside the immediate control of the campaign leaders and to speak creatively in order to link the program to particular circumstances. For example, in East Timor, Fretilin sent members out into villages each weekend to popularize its program, relying on the members' knowledge of local customs and beliefs to present Fretilin's message of independence in a form that was easily understood. According to Helen M. Hill, "It was better to tell the Timorese animist believers that they needed a new *lulik* [totem], the Fretilin flag, in addition to the symbols they already revered, and to use this as a starting point for explaining what Fretilin was, rather than to ridicule *luliks* as superstitious. . . ."[60] This cadre autonomy creates serious risks of moral hazard, however. Cadres in remote villages, circulating among the closed circles of family and acquaintances, speaking in local languages about local politics, economic conditions, and specific grievances, and expanding on the consequences of the program of independence, are difficult for campaign leaders to monitor and present significant risks of agency loss, such as changing the programmatic appeal or building a personalist following.[61] This autonomy requires purposive coordination with the cadres and continuing leadership attention to the cadres' political education.

Yet strategically minded campaign leaders cannot rely on purposive incentives alone to achieve programmatic preemption. At least three constraints limit the contribution of purposive incentives to the achievement of programmatic preemption. The number recruited by purposive incentives alone is likely to remain small; even in Lenin's original model, few become professional revolutionaries. Political education to create and to sustain enthusiasm is a costly undertaking with high demands on personnel and materials and with opportunity costs of time lost from other tasks. And overly strenuous attempts at conversion can split a campaign: vigorous indoctrination of pragmatic followers can alienate those who find study sessions tedious and a high price to pay for the future, uncertain benefits of independence.[62]

The Specialized Role of Material Incentives in Coordination

National-secession campaigns promise pragmatists economic and political gains to be had by attaining independence, but these campaigns also create opportunities for immediate gain that may bring pragmatists into leadership and staff positions even before independence. The strategy of programmatic coordination cautions campaign leaders that pragmatists can play a critical role but that this should be limited for the most part to augmenting the surge that demonstrates programmatic preemption. Unless they control administrative mechanisms of a segment-state or a base area, campaign leaders typically do not command adequate material incentives to activate pragmatists through the longueur and must be careful to prevent pragmatists from using the campaign for private predatory gains prior to independence.

During the longueur, campaign leaders and cadres prepare for future demonstrations of programmatic preemption by persuading pragmatists that independence will better enable them in their pursuit of power or profit and that failure to support surges now could exclude "unpatriotic" pragmatists from enjoying those benefits in the future. Anticipation of the future economic advantages of independence persuades business leaders to switch to the campaign. These are the professionals and businesspeople, described by Ernest Gellner, who seek the advantages of a "B-land" that restricts market and political entry to members of the nation.[63] The nearness of the promised outcome may figure prominently in these calculations. Last-minute switching of politicians to the campaign for independence in the face of a collapsing central government—as in Moldova—or in response to a threat to their positions—as in Slovenia and Croatia—reflects calculations of power payoff. In European nationalist movements, Hroch finds that major entrepreneurs, small-scale craft producers, and the petty bourgeoisie were not among the patriots who typically led the national movements in the initial period but were relative latecomers and became increasingly prominent only in the final phase.[64] In sum, for these pragmatists, for whom instrumental evaluations play a larger role in decisions to participate, it is not just the expected payoff from independence but also the likelihood of independence and its nearness in time that motivates them to participate in the campaign. And key in their assessment of the likelihood of independence and its nearness in time is the pragmatists' expectation of how other members of the platform population will respond. Although these members are much less likely to be available as participants during the longueur, a key propagation task of the campaign leadership and staff is keeping these pragmatists prepared for public demonstrations of support when independence draws nearer.

The rapid expansion of more visible participation during surges—whether the surge brings independence or not—can appear to support the conclusion that the demand for independence is all about instrumental economic or power motivations. At the time of greatest visible expansion, campaigns typically reach out to add the pragmatists who have held back because independence had seemed so improbable and investments in the cause of independence had seemed too risky. The enthusiasts have been on board from the beginning, but the entrepreneurs and moderate politicians are often the critical swing constituency that must be convinced to demonstrate their support for the campaign at this last critical moment. So the rhetoric at these surge moments—such as the referenda in Catalonia and Scotland in 2014—is pragmatic and often focused on economics. In the summer before the Scottish referendum, the Scots' leader Alex Salmond stressed that independence would "create sustainable prosperity" and "ensure that everyone feels the benefits of that prosperity."[65] Analysts and news media, which may ignore the campaign until these last dramatic moments, often draw the conclusion that the campaign for independence has been about these pragmatic concerns all along.

Certainly, economics and power may be the key issues to win the critical "swing vote." Studies of the Quebec campaign showed that the Parti québécois "combines an activist base centered around intellectuals with additional electoral support that is located outside of the intelligentsia and, indeed, outside the new middle class altogether. The party thus must be able to recruit in the broader group without alienating its activist base."[66] At the time of the Quebec referenda in the 1980s and 1990s, polls estimated that between 29 percent and 39 percent of the voters were firmly committed enthusiasts for independence and 15 percent to 21 percent were firmly committed enthusiasts for Canada, but between these two relatively unwavering camps were perhaps half of the voters who could be persuaded by more-pragmatic arguments to swing in either direction. The campaign for independence tried to mobilize its enthusiasts by appeals that "Quebecers constitute a people, distinct from the rest of Canada" and by reminding them of "past humiliations and oppressions to which the Quebec people had been subjected, beginning with their conquest by the English." Yet for the "swing" voters, the key issues concerned the economic benefits of independence compared to those of federation.[67]

Nonetheless, strategically minded campaign leaders must anticipate that pragmatic swing constituencies are likely to cease to provide activist participants to the campaign as soon as the prospect of independence recedes. These leaders must anticipate that the leadership and staff will need to hold on until the next opportunity but that the leadership and staff are likely to survive only if the campaign binds them with incentives other than promises of economic and political gain.

Campaign leaders following the strategy of programmatic coordination tend to limit the offer of economic and political gain to the association stage of campaign development and to short periods close to surges. During the longueur, targeted material incentives may serve as an opening wedge for propagation. For example, in Timor Leste, according to Hill, "Initially, the literacy classes and lessons in agricultural management attracted villagers to Fretilin. Participation in these activities then often had a politicising or [consciousness-raising] aspect."[68] Yet at least four major constraints limit the campaign leaders when deciding whether to offer material incentives for advancing programmatic coordination.

Campaign leaders have few material incentives to offer in most periods of building and sustaining a campaign staff. Material incentives are typically unavailable when establishing a campaign and are scarce during the longueur. For most staffers, these times offer only material privations, so pragmatists are less likely to be attracted to the rigors of campaign life. Those few pragmatists who do find themselves inside are more likely to fall away or even defect to the more-immediate and more-lucrative offers of the common-state project.

Campaign leaders typically need to exclude pragmatists from staff positions lest they weaken the campaign. Pragmatists are more likely to use positions within the staff to engage in foraging activities to skim personal gain, such as pocketing revolutionary taxes, demanding payoffs for services or protection, and forging client networks. During the longueur, pragmatists in staff positions, all pursuing personal ambitions, create an incoherent campaign that sends contradictory messages and moves in self-defeating directions. And as Hoffer notes, "When a mass movement begins to attract people who are interested in their individual careers, it is a sign that it has passed its vigorous stage, that it is no longer engaged in molding a new world. . . ."[69]

Campaign leaders may limit building the campaign on offers of economic gain because such offers typically put campaign leaders at a competitive disadvantage vis-à-vis the common-state government. Unless the common-state is in severe breakdown, it commands substantially more economic and power resources to reward defectors than the campaign leaders have to retain them. Indeed, the US Department of the Army's *Counterinsurgency Field Manual* makes it clear that counterinsurgents seeking to disrupt insurgencies will find that a campaign staff built on greed or grievance is easier to buy off: pragmatists "might be co-opted by economic or political reforms, while fanatic combatants will most likely have to be killed or captured."[70]

Appeals primarily to the material interests of the platform population can lead potential recruits to conclude that campaign leaders are mere pragmatists and not to be trusted. This cynicism can be fatal to the campaign: potential participants who might be willing to invest time and money in the cause of independence have greater reason to hold back, fearing that pragmatists leading campaigns built on material incentives will abscond with these investments or will be bought off by the common-state government.

In short, according to the strategy of programmatic coordination, expectations of material gain constitute a fragile bond to coordinate and to sustain action through the longueur. Unless the campaign leaders already control a segment-state of their own that can be turned into a patronage machine, they must limit use of material incentives to promises of postindependence gain.[71] In allocating incentives to deploy the constituent parts of the campaign, leaders often must reserve immediate material incentives for opening wedges for propagation or for short-term surge events. In all instances the important programmatic message propagated by the campaign is that long-term enjoyment of these benefits is contingent on success in achieving independence.

Control over Expressive Incentives

Campaigns create opportunities for expressive action, and the expressionists attracted by these incentives can be particularly important in furthering programmatic coordination and demonstrating programmatic preemption. Even so, in the strategy of programmatic coordination, strategically minded campaign leaders must be particularly careful to allocate expressive incentives to direct expressionists' actions towards the campaign's goal. Expressive incentives—the opportunity to engage in action that is an end in itself—attract activists who revel in public actions, such as agitating, protesting, or burning down or blowing up things.[72] As studies of civil wars and terrorism have emphasized, these actions can be valuable in alerting the platform population to an independence campaign, notifying members of the imagined nation that they are not alone in their hopes for independence, demonstrating that others are willing to take bold action to make independence happen, and recruiting new members. In the Basque campaign for Euskadi, John Sullivan observes that the Burgos trial of ETA activists in December 1970 "had the effect of bringing the ideas of ETA-VI before the entire population of the Basque country, and indeed of the world." Moreover, by the conclusion of the trial, the defendants had become heroes: "The really important effect of ETA's actions was to provide heroes and martyrs to whom the people could rally. . . . [C]hildren in the street could recite their names in the same way that they could those of the members of the football teams."[73] Nonetheless, youths attracted to protests, demonstrations, street brawls, and violence may savor the opportunities for action created by the campaign more than independence itself. Strategically minded campaign leaders must consider four risks for campaigns when offering expressive incentives to join the campaign.

Expressionists who resist programmatic coordination create the risk of sending an incoherent or contradictory message about the campaign to the public. For example, ETA-V's militants, who relished the armed struggle, expanded their violence after 1974 so that the message of Basque unity against the Spanish became obscured: "Gradually, the definition of what constituted a justifiable target widened until the victims included alleged informers, all military officers and police, former policemen, families of Civil Guards, political opponents, people alleged to be involved in the drug trade, and anyone who refused to pay the 'revolutionary tax.' A considerable proportion of the Basque population fell into one or other of those categories."[74] ETA-V leaders committed to a Basque nation-state had lost control of their message because programmatic coordination of its expressionist recruits had weakened.

The number of recruits attracted by expressive incentives is typically only a small proportion of the entire platform population, whereas the proportion unwilling to be associated with expressive acts may be far greater. The mainstream of Basque society decisively turned against ETA in the late 1970s. According to Clark, ETA "raised the level of violence to such heights that moderate Basque leaders finally turned against the organization and condemned its resort to armed struggle in a democracy."[75] This even led to repeated division within ETA itself. For example, in 1982 the ETA-PM armed struggle subverted the peaceful organizing by its own Party for the Basque Revolution (EIA), so the EIA members left ETA at its Eighth Assembly.[76] Commenting on the use of violence in Northern Ireland, Richard English notes, "The Provisionals had early on believed that their violence—and after 1981, their violence tinged with electoralism—would bring victory. But, year after year, it became clear that even the nationalist people in the north emphatically preferred their politicians to espouse non-violent methods. People only came to vote for Sinn Féin in dominant numbers once the IRA's war against the British state had effectively ended. . . ."[77]

Expressionists may take actions that expose the campaign to destructive counteraction. For example, in the 1960s the uncontrolled activism of ETA's military front led to the loss of ETA's political, cultural, and workers' fronts under the antiterrorist suppression campaign of the Franco regime. In the 1970s the leadership of ETA-PM was unable "to control a Military Front whose leaders insisted on their own autonomy," and their activism brought a disastrous military suppression response from the central government against the entire organization.[78]

Once leaders have built their campaign on expressionists, leaders may need to keep the expressive acts going even when these are counterproductive. Expressionists demand constant action, may soon tire of inaction, and may move on unless given frequent opportunities to act. For example, after 1970, ETA-VI's decision to abandon armed struggle led to a sharp fall in recruits among young people, who "found ETA-V's effort to continue guerrilla activity more romantic and exciting."[79] Activists who develop a special attachment to the armed struggle may violently resist any shift in policy that minimizes their role. In the Timor Leste campaign in the 1980s, for example, Gusmão's shift to a broad national front strategy reached out to the Catholic Church and youth groups but diminished the role of the armed struggle. This provoked the movement's military commanders to attempt a coup against Gusmão.[80]

Campaign leaders face the daunting task of motivating periodic surges of activism linked to the promise that this will further the cause of independence, knowing full well that independence is only a remote possibility. Expressionists can play a vital role in these surges—particularly when surges take the form of more intense action. Because it is particularly difficult to sustain incentives for expressionists during the longueur and direct their action during surge events, campaign leaders must invest in propagation to link expressionists' action to the common purpose. Hence, campaigns maintain political education for their activists to explain how tactics are subordinate to the operational and strategic goals of the campaign.

From Micro-level to Macro-level Analysis

When used as an analytic model rather than a prescriptive strategy, programmatic coordination supports hypotheses about the conditions under which specific nation-state programs are likely to give rise to significant campaigns that become locked in intractable disputes and engage in protracted intense struggles.

In comparisons among campaigns, this micro-level model places at the center of analysis the program, popular assessments of its authenticity and realism, and the macro-level obstacles and opportunities that serve as "cues" to aid these assessments.

The Multiplication of Projects That Go Nowhere

Even though the strategy of programmatic coordination is common knowledge, intellectuals propose projects that fail to coordinate expectations within the proposed platform population. It is common knowledge that the authors of a national-secession project must define the new nation and state in a way that will be recognized by the platform population as *the* focal point around which they expect still others to rally.[81] Yet intellectuals may design a failed project because they truly believe in the project even though they know few others will agree, because they overestimate their powers of persuasion, or because they think their project is the rare exception that will overcome the odds. They may also fail because designing a nation-state project that will serve as a focal point is easy to imagine but often a daunting task to accomplish. Trial and error may lead to many failed projects. In at least four scenarios the cues to a focal point may be ambiguous, and it is unclear which, if any, projects will lead a proposed platform population to coordinate around the goal of independence.

When the idea of the modern nation-state is not widely known among members of the platform population, leaders may have a difficult task in writing a program that will actually coordinate elites and publics. In Turkish Kurdistan, from World War I until 1938, the authors of different bids for an independent Kurdistan found little recognition of a nation subsuming tribes or transcending religion. The failure of the Kuchgiri revolt in 1921, in Romano's analysis, was caused by "the lack of Kurdish nationalist identification (politicized ethnicity) among the Kurdish masses of the 1920s."[82] The three great nationalist uprisings of 1925 (Shaikh Said), 1925–30 (Ihsan Nari Pasha), and 1937–38 (Shaikh Sayyed Reza) elicited only limited support from members of the traditionalist population. Among indigenous populations of Mesoamerica, including the Ixil of Guatemala, Joseph M. Whitmeyer reports that appeals to indigenous nationalism failed because the idea of a nation-state did not resonate with their own experiences: despite appeals from guerrillas, "the Ixil generally did not evince such nationalism. Rather, their interests remained local."[83] These populations did not think of themselves as belonging to any nation—a people with the right to a sovereign state of its own—and many were altogether unfamiliar with the idea of nationhood and statehood.

Even when the idea of a nation-state is well-known, leaders may have a difficult time propagating a specific project when the platform population does not recognize the label it invokes, when the platform population recognizes the label but does not see it as the basis for a separate nation-state, or when the platform population sees itself as part of the common-state's nation. The Padania project in northern Italy is handicapped because few residents of the Po Valley region see themselves as Padanians or as a nation separate from other Italians. The Northwest Territorial Imperative (or Butler Plan) has failed, even though many Americans recognize the label "white," because few in the platform population see this as the basis of a separate nation that needs a separate sovereign state of its own.[84]

When the dominant cues for nation and state are in conflict, converging expectations in programmatic preemption may not occur. In Xinjiang many members of the indigenous populations (including Uighurs, Kazakhs, and Kyrgyzes) agree that they do not belong to China's nation but find it difficult to coordinate on an alternative. Two focal points are equally conspicuous—the multiethnic Eastern Turkestan project corresponding to the state of Xinjiang and the mono-ethnic Uighurstan project corresponding to the Uighur nation. These competing projects are expressed today in competing campaigns and alternative diaspora organizations. As Gardner Bovingdon notes, this conflict arises from "different visions of the future homeland and . . . the right to define that homeland authoritatively."[85]

When the idea of nation has become infused with specific class, religious, or ethnic content that divides the platform population, coordinating on a focal point can be more difficult.[86] This appears commonly when the initial articulation of a program for independence is linked to traditional values and where traditional elites continue to play a strong role in the platform population. For example, the initial and continuing link of Basque nationalism to "God and the Old Laws" under the Basque Nationalist Party (PNV) failed to appeal to substantial parts of the Basque population, and it set the stage for competing programs for traditionalist, liberal, socialist, and communist Basque nation-states.[87] Similarly, the campaign for Turkish Kurdistan, initially advanced by traditional village elites, led to challenges from the cities so that programs for independence divided among visions of a traditional, "bourgeois," and Marxist Kurdistan.[88] Marxist nationalists such as the Kurdish Workers' Party (PKK), in developing a class-plus-nation-state project, demanded elimination of vestiges of feudalism and thus attacked and alienated traditionalist nationalists, who sought to preserve these distinctive elements of Kurdish society.[89]

Implications for Macro-level Outcomes

This strategy of programmatic coordination gives rise to the indeterminacy, substitutability, and remoteness noted in chapter 1 regarding the relationship of structural constraints to campaign significance, intractable disputes, and protracted intense struggles. Campaign leaders have considerable discretion in linking specific social identities, grievances, and ambitions to the solution called "independence." For them, structural constraints are typically only cues to coordination: campaign leaders and members of the platform population may or may not see these as reasons to expect that other members will assess the national-secession program to be authentic and realistic. Stronger cues facilitate coordination of expectations within the larger platform population around a common program: without the ability to communicate with other members of the platform population and uncertain whether to believe what others say, each member must evaluate the credibility of any national-secession program by a search for visible cues that are likely to be seen by other members of the platform population and bring them to a common expectation that other members will rally around the project for nation-statehood. The most important cues revealed in the empirical estimations in chapters 5 and 7 are whether the national-secession program refers to conventionalized categories of nationhood and statehood and whether the common-state is defined in a way that excludes the platform population from the common-state's titular nation.

Thus, while the programmatic approach appreciates the importance of social identities as cues to aid programmatic coordination, it sees nothing inevitable, natural, or even typical about an ethnic or religious group embracing the claim that its members constitute a nation with the right to a sovereign state of its own.[90] Contrary to Walker Connor's claim, a demand for an independent nation-state is not a "quite natural next step from ethnic self-awareness."[91] Similarly, although a sense of injustice, relative deprivation, or disorientation under existing conditions may in turn give rise to emotions such as anger, hatred, alienation, or resentment and rejection of the status quo, these do not typically culminate in demands for a new state for one's own group.[92] Nor is national secession a normal consequence of opportunities to capture lootable resources or to create "a virtual monopoly of the desirable posts in the newly independent B-land."[93]

Programmatic theory underscores that identities, grievances, and ambition (greed) often energize individual members of a platform population but that this can explain only disorder, not the coordination of this energy behind the common solution of independence for the proposed nation-state rather than one of the many competing proposed solutions. Instead, grievances, emotions, and ambition constitute raw materials with which national-secession strategists work to recruit. Nations (that is, platform populations) in national-secession programs are political "inventions."[94] Thus, the structural "facts" such as a common language are cues suggesting that other members will assess the program for national independence to be authentic and realistic, but, as Elie Kedourie stresses, nationalism is seldom based on indisputable facts of human differences, even though proponents of nationalist doctrines must attempt to make their platform populations believe that such indisputable facts actually exist.[95] No identity, grievance, emotion, or ambition is common to all members of the diverse coalition assembled by national-secession campaigns—not even those associated with the nation-state project. It is not the commonality of identities, grievances, emotions, or ambitions that gives unity to a national-secession campaign, but the coordination of expectations on a common solution to diverse identities, grievances, and ambitions. National-secession leaders must harness education, propaganda, and agitation to link these in pursuit of the common goal.

Mobilization and violence can play critical roles as tactical choices by campaign leaders but should be analyzed within the context of the specific strategic goals and operational objectives that these tactics are supposed to serve.[96] National-secession campaign leaders choose mobilization to achieve the operational objective of linking different constituencies to the program for independence and demonstrating programmatic preemption to the platform population and international community. The choice of violence is seldom driven by the considerations of the "conditions that favor insurgency" against the central government, such as weak states, unstable governments, rough terrain, and large populations.[97] Because of operational weakness, these obstacles and opportunities that predict battlefield victories are typically remote from the calculations of campaign leaders. Instead, surges of mobilization and violence are used to build programmatic coordination and demonstrate programmatic preemption.

The micro-level programmatic analysis of national-secession campaigns has three important macro-level implications for the questions with which this book began. First, the most important constraints determining whether a national-secessionist program becomes the basis of a significant campaign are cues, believed to be visible to all members of the platform population, that lead leaders to coalesce and enable them to attract a staff because they expect that the platform population will, with the aid of propaganda, coordinate around the same goal expressed in the program for independence. The core task of the establishment stage is identifying those cues, selecting the corresponding nation-state project, and writing a program based on this project. Second, intractable conflicts are the consequence of successful coordination among the leaders and staffers around this program so that the campaign can weather the longueur. This is the core of the capacitation stage. Third, the tactic of protracted intensity is an option for campaigns that have successfully coordinated expectations within the leadership and staff and expect that escalation of means will expand the participatory reserve and prepare it for demonstrations of programmatic preemption. This is the core of the association stage. These are the issues addressed in each of the next three chapters.

SIGNIFICANT CAMPAIGNS
Getting on the Global Agenda

At the heart of every national-secession program is a nation-state project claiming that its platform population constitutes a nation with a right to a sovereign state of its own. Many, and perhaps most, ethnic groups—even many majorities such as the English in the United Kingdom or the Russians in the Soviet Union—have at least one dreamer who has imagined an independent nation-state for that group—either alone (such as a Kurdistan) or jointly with others (such as a South Sudan). Yet only a few of these projects have inspired significant national-secession campaigns. We can never measure precisely how small a proportion because most failed projects go unnoticed, evaporating as quickly as the smoke of the pipe dreamer. Even the isolated curios that do get noticed and decorate many humanistic or ethnographic narratives, such as the Moksha and Erzyan projects, are typically of little larger political importance.[1]

Nevertheless, the 171 national-secession campaigns identified in chapter 2 did get their demands for independence onto the international public agenda at some point between 1945 and 2010. For reasons that are theoretically and practically important, this attribute sets these campaigns apart as significant and frames the question for this chapter: what qualities and conditions permit nation-state projects to become significant national-secession campaigns that secure a place on the international public agenda? To anticipate the answer offered in this chapter: nation-state projects are most likely to give rise to significant national-secession campaigns when the international community expects that the program will be received by the platform population as authentic and realistic.

The analysis in this chapter focuses on macro-level comparisons of cues that favor coordination of expectations on one national-secession program over others. The focus is on cross-sectional differences in relatively stable conditions rather than temporal changes that vary significantly over time because it is the former that are more likely to favor coordination of expectations about the future. These conditions, suggested by the micro-level analysis in chapters 3 and 4, are cues that focus expectations within the platform population concerning the views of others about authenticity and realism. The expectation that this coordination of expectations could lead to programmatic preemption in the platform population draws international attention to these campaigns.

Two Attempts at Coordination

The difficulty of building significant campaigns is illustrated by comparing two national-secession projects in the 1990s along the north shore of the Black Sea—Novorossiia and Moldova (see figure 5.1). Both projects, claiming parts of the Soviet Union, emerged into public view in the period of Mikhail

FIGURE 5.1. Moldova, Novorossiia, and Ukraine. The shaded provinces have been mentioned by authors of the national-secession project as possible parts of Novorossiia.

Gorbachev's *glasnost'* ("openness"). Both faced serious competition not only from the project to keep the common-state whole but also from alternative national-secession projects. But the Moldovan project successfully coordinated a broad campaign for secession that got its claims on the international agenda in the 1990s.

Failed Coordination: The Novorossiia Campaign

In pressing the Novorossiia (New Russia) nation-state project in the 1990s, Professor Oleksii Surylov of Odessa State University struggled to build a following behind his claim that the inhabitants of Ukraine's Black Sea littoral constitute a nation deserving a state of its own. He and his collaborators invented a history and ethnography, with some basis in fact, to provide evidence for distinctive cultural and historical experiences that should separate this region and its population from the rest of the Ukrainian nation-state. After 1990, Surylov and the circle of intellectuals advancing this project created a cultural organization and newspaper to propagate their program but rallied only a small following. Few in the public outside the intellectuals' classrooms found the *novorossiiskii* national label authentic and the corresponding state project realistic. The national label referred to a multiethnic aggregation that had not become a widely recognized category prior to the attempt to invoke it as a rallying point, so few in the platform population had reason to expect others to coalesce around this label. The imagined state did not refer to a homeland that had previously enjoyed independence; more realistic contenders for statehood were the very real provinces (oblasts) including Crimea, Donetsk, Lugansk, and Odessa. The project failed to mobilize a substantial campaign.[2] In the 1990s it was largely ignored by Ukraine's common-state leaders, the international media, and even academic analysts. Indeed, we learned of it in the 1990s principally because some Russian nationalists (including the mayor of St. Petersburg, who was a patron of the young Vladimir Putin), seeking to rally their own followers within Russia, briefly championed the cause of independence of this region after the Soviet Union broke up.

Alternatively, in the 1990s the Crimea campaign successfully coordinated much of its platform population of Russians on the peninsula around its program of separation from Ukraine. As early as January 21, 1991, the Crimean provincial (oblast) government conducted a referendum in which reportedly 93 percent voted for elevating the province's status to an autonomous republic of Crimea. Soon after Ukraine's independence, Yurii Meshkov rose to leadership in the Crimean national-secession campaign and on January 30, 1994, won the presidency of Crimea with 73 percent of the vote in the second-round runoff. In elections to the Republic's Supreme Soviet in March of that year, pro-Russia parties won sixty of ninety-eight seats. Although Ukraine reasserted its control over the peninsula in 1995, the Crimea campaign had coordinated expectations in its platform population that could be mobilized quickly in surges when opportunities arose—as happened two decades later in the 2014 Ukraine crisis. Within eighteen days of the deposition of Yurii Yanukovych as president of Ukraine, the Crimean Supreme Soviet had declared independence (March 11), and within twenty-three days the republic had conducted a referendum that delivered a 96.8 percent vote for independence (March 16).[3]

It is a sign of how unsuccessful the campaign for Novorossiia had been in the 1990s that during the Ukrainian crisis two decades later, the population of the Black Sea littoral still did not rally around this project—despite strong endorsement from the Russian president beginning in April 2014.[4] Leaders of secessionist campaigns certainly espoused the doctrine of nation-statehood. As one leader of the Donetsk constitution-drafting project, who had come from Transdniestria, claimed, "The people have a right to live on their land, to speak the language they want. . . . Only a state can defend that right."[5] This logic attracted various types (enthusiasts, expressionists, and pragmatists) to become leaders and staffers in the Donetsk and Lugansk people's republics, but these secessionists seemed more closely attached to their separate projects focused on secession for the provinces and unification with Russia than the broad Novorossiia project. The Confederation of Novorossiia (or Union of People's Republics) seemed to be a dream that even the founders did not take seriously even after it was formally declared by Donetsk and Lugansk in May 2014. Capturing the failure of the rebels to coordinate on any common project, the *New York Times* correspondent Andrew Higgins reported from Donetsk soon after its declaration of independence that "the cluster of fringe pro-Russia political outfits behind the Donetsk People's Republic . . . disagree on their final goal. They cannot decide whether to push to join Russia, to give substance to their chimerical state or to secure more autonomy for the region within Ukraine." Independence, he added, seemed "a quixotic and, to many here, crackpot project."[6] The secessionist campaigns were particularly ineffective at convincing many pragmatists that independence was desirable or likely, and pragmatists collaborated with the common-state government in large numbers.[7] The appeal of the idea of Novorossiia apparently was weakest in the western parts of the proposed nation-state—including Surylov's home province of Odessa—and was trumped in the South and East by the separate projects for Crimea, Donetsk, and Lugansk.[8] A year after the crisis had begun, the platform population, the common-state government in Kiev, and the international community took the threat of secession seriously, but few saw the project for Novorossiia as the form this was likely to take.

Successful Coordination: The Moldova Campaign

Next door, the campaign for an independent Moldova was initially eclipsed by a Greater Romania campaign and at first was junior partner to the latter in a movement for separation from the Soviet Union. Yet with the growing recruitment of pragmatists—including politicians and entrepreneurs—the campaign for an independent Moldova emerged hegemonic.

The Greater Romania campaign kept alive the idea that Moldovans are part of the Romanian nation. Following the Soviet annexation of Moldavia in 1940, the Greater Romania project survived in conversations around dinner tables and in small private circles of trusted acquaintances, but in the 1970s this project became the focal point of a clandestine network of linguists, historians, writers, and artists. With Gorbachev's *glasnost*, all this changed. According to *Izvestiia*, by early 1988 debates about renewal of the Romanian-Moldovan language "took place spontaneously in institutes, schools, and collectives of the people in the creative arts."[9] Later that year the Mateevici Literary and Musical Club, which demanded expanded usage of the Romanian-Moldovan language, drew as many as two thousand people to its spirited meetings; public recitals by nationalist poets and bards drew crowds of the young; and soon elementary school teachers, particularly teachers of Moldovan language, began bringing their pupils to rallies to champion expanded usage of their language. From humble origins in academic departments as a classroom nation, the growing Greater Romania campaign in Moldova reached out to many politicians and voters who shared the operational objective of independence from the Soviet Union and brought together its core of enthusiasts with a more-diverse collection of more-pragmatic followers in the Moldovan Popular Front (MPF). By August 1989, *Pravda* complained that "at the rally on Kishinev's central square tens of thousands of people had succumbed to powerful and prolonged conditioning from the nationalistically-minded ideologists of the Moldavian Popular Front. . . ."[10] Within a day this had grown to hundreds of thousands and had spilled over into adjoining streets. The MPF grew to be Moldova's largest and most influential political organization, eclipsing even the Communist Party, but as it grew it became more diverse, united by a commitment to independence from Moscow but not reunification with Bucharest.

The Greater Romania intellectuals lost control of the larger movement that they had initiated. The united front's shared operational objective initially disguised the divergence in strategic goals of its constituent campaigns. After December 1991, however, once Moldova achieved its independence, the members committed to the campaign for a sovereign Moldova nation-state asserted their programmatic preeminence.[11] These defected from the MPF in 1992. By early 1994, the Moldovan president, Mircea Snegur, decided to force the issue with a referendum that would demonstrate that Moldovans overwhelmingly rejected the Greater Romania nation-state project that would end Moldova's newly gained independence. On March 6, 1994, the referendum on "independence for the republic," as it was styled, reportedly drew three-quarters of the republic's electorate to the polls, and 95 percent of the voters endorsed the Moldovan nation-state project.[12] Pouring salt in the wounds, later that year, on July 28, Moldova's Parliament adopted a new constitution that labeled the official language of the republic as "Moldovan" rather than Romanian. The Greater Romania intelligentsia in Moldova protested that it was only because the political leaders of the new republic had prevented the public from seeing their true Romanianness that the intellectuals had failed to achieve their objective. The Greater Romania project had built a movement united by the common operational objective of separation from the Soviet Union by alliances with intellectuals and leaders within the ruling circles of Soviet Moldavia and by engagement of the larger platform population, but the leaders of the Greater Romania campaign lost control of the united-front movement to the campaign for a sovereign Moldova nation-state. The latter campaign, drawing on the relatively greater resources of the Moldavian SSR and the Republic of Moldova, had been much more successful at recruiting not only enthusiasts but also pragmatists, such as Snegur, who saw their political and economic future in an independent state of their own. At most points beginning in the late 1980s, expectations focused on the Moldova rather than Greater Romania project, and this put the former on the international agenda.

Significance through Programmatic Coordination

A national-secession campaign is much more likely to achieve significance when it offers a program that can convince the international community that this program will coordinate expectations within its platform population and become the basis for programmatic preemption. Foreign governments are likely to dismiss campaigns with little prospect of such coordination as without foundation and to brand even an activist core around an unlikely nation-state project as a lunatic fringe or criminal conspiracy rather than a national-secession campaign representing the aspirations of a platform population.

Coordinating Expectations

Nationalists, much like revolutionaries, have long appreciated the importance of the coordination of expectations to building significant campaigns. The strategy of programmatic coordination that they commonly follow stresses that select-ing (or writing) the right program and then persuading different parts of the platform population of the rightness and prudence of this program are at the core of this coordination. To achieve this coordination, it is not enough to offer a dream. The argument for statehood must ring true in light of the evidence that hearers have about the members of the nation. That is, members of the platform population must be convinced that an independent nation-state in the name of the platform population is an objective that many other members of the platform population (who are beyond their circle of acquaintances but also in some way just like them) will recognize as a goal that speaks to the diverse identities and interests within the platform population (but also unites them in pursuit of a common goal). Most are unable to consult with many other members of the plat-form population, are uncertain whether current declarations by these others are reliable indicators of their future loyalties and actions, and are frequently even uncertain about their own future responses to calls to action. Thus, each looks for stable, visible cues, which other members of the platform population should also see, that suggest this program will, indeed, coordinate them around a com-mon goal. Anticipating the outcome of this process in the future, intellectuals and leaders are more likely to commit their energies to projects that promise this coordination of expectations. Alternatively, if intellectuals and potential leaders are not convinced that the program will be credible in the eyes of the platform population, all but the truest believers in the rightness of a specific nation-state project are likely to dismiss attempts to build a national-secession campaign. This chapter identifies the visible cues that are most likely to increase coordina-tion on a shared nation-state project.

The coordination process in ethnic politics has been represented by David D. Laitin, in a very fruitful adaptation of Thomas C. Schelling's tipping model, as a choice between two well-specified alternatives, such as choosing to educate one's children in either the language of one's own ethnic group or the official language of the common-state.[13] Similar to this tipping model, in the coordination process of national-secession campaigns, individual members of the platform popula-tion seek to anticipate the choices of other members and to choose the same proj-ect, for their own payoff will be maximized by coordinating with others. Yet in many situations coordination can be a vastly more complicated problem: authors of a nation-state project must convince members of the platform population to coordinate on one specific national-secession program among many alternative national-secession, nonnationalist, or nonsecessionist programs. In this coordi-nation, their particular program must somehow stand out among many alterna-tives that may not be clearly defined. In the extreme the problem of coordination can metaphorically resemble the task of identifying without communication a meeting place on a great grassy plain with several partially obscured convergence points, none of which are easy to see or loom above the others. Unless the coordination process is significantly constrained by some shared expectation that emerges from cues about shared knowledge, the many members of a platform population may not converge on a common nation-state goal; any convergence is likely to involve only some members of the platform population and to be brief.

The coordination problem is further complicated by pressures among intellectuals to express their creativity through alternative formulations of identity that suggest still more convergence points. Many intellectuals within the platform population may prefer the purity, art, or originality of a still newer nation-state project or the sport of intellectual contestation rather than programs that bring consensus, conformity, and a real possibility of independence. Hence, competition among projects is common. For example, at the time of the Russian Revolution of 1917, the intelligentsia of what would become the Belarusians was not only politically insignificant but also deeply divided over whether their people should belong in a Polish, Lithuanian, Russian, or independent Belarusian state. In Central Asia, prior to the official national delimitation of peoples and states that began in 1920, intellectuals and politicians were divided among projects for a united state of all Muslims, all Turkic Muslims, existing administrative jurisdictions such as Turkestan and Bukhara, and individual imagined nationalities such as the united Kazakh-Kyrgyzes, separate Kazakhs and Kyrgyzes, and smaller subdivisions of these such as the Greater Horde.[14]

Programmatic Coordination: Authenticity and Realism

In this competitive environment, strategically minded intellectuals and leaders must define their nation-state project to stand out as uniquely credible.[15] The proposed nation must be recognized as authentic and expected to be recognized as such by others. Different projects often seek to coordinate many of the same individuals but in different guises—for example, coordinating the residents around Minsk as Poles, Lithuanians, Belarusians, or Russians. Simply more artful presentation of an argument is not enough: any such ploy used to privilege a project can be matched by other groups and by the common-state government. The hearers must perceive some "evidence" backing the argument. The nation-state project itself must "ring true" for the members of the platform population by appeals to real facts known to them and, they expect, also commonly known to other members of the imagined nation with whom they cannot communicate. Projects on behalf of national neologisms, such as *novorossiiskie*, run the risk of leaving most hearers scratching their heads and uncertain whether they belong and suspecting that many others will respond with disbelief.

The project for a state must also be recognized as realistic and expected to be recognized as such by others. Nation-state projects are more likely to serve as focal points when they can appeal to evidence known to the platform population that independent statehood is feasible. Thus, the "imagined" nation-states that are most likely to serve as focal points are those that require the least imagination; members of the platform population naturally favor projects that appeal to precedents.[16] Realism also means that programs must include action plans that appear practical; in particular, the program must imagine a state with a real capacity to exercise sovereignty. Realism further means expectations that before independence is achieved, the intellectuals and leaders of a national-secession campaign will remain coordinated around the program and stick with the campaign. Realism is particularly important in recruiting pragmatists, who will play a critical role in later phases of campaign development and particularly in surges.

The intellectuals and leaders who write the program, crafting its definition of the nation-state and devising an action plan, must anticipate these responses. In particular, they must position their campaigns to convince pragmatists, who will probably constitute the largest part of the participatory reserve, that the campaign's program will attract the platform population in ways that make possible programmatic preemption; that its goal of independence will continue to coordinate its leaders, staffers, and reservists; and that its action plan will achieve independence. Authors of programs that put forward projects that fail to identify an authentic and realistic focal point for coordination of expectations and are unwilling to adjust their projects closer to such a point—such as the proponents of the Moksha, Erzyan, and Novorossiia states—will be selected out in the competition to coordinate expectations, and their campaigns will fail to achieve significance.

Constraints on Programmatic Credibility

Thus, the chief "structural" constraints essential for a national-secession campaign to achieve significance are cues that suggest to members of the platform population that they should expect other members to perceive the nation-state project as authentic, to assess the goal of independence to be realistic, and to see collaboration with the common-state as an unviable option. These cues shape expectations that members of the platform population will coordinate around the goal of independence and also that the campaign will achieve programmatic preemption. These cues become important from the very start of a campaign in the establishment stage, and they continue to be important in the capacitation and association stages as well. A campaign may grab international attention as early as the establishment stage if international observers expect broadening and deepening coordination in the capacitation and association stages. Without a favorable alignment of the cues to authenticity and realism, foreign governments may doubt that any large-scale, sustained coordination within the platform population will occur at all; they will not see such projects as requiring their attention. The presence of appropriate cues to the authenticity and realism of a nation-state project should be powerful predictors of which national-secession programs give rise to significant campaigns.

Earlier studies of the rise of national-secession movements have focused on identities, grievances or greed, and tactical-logistical opportunities as predictors. The programmatic theory sees these not as rival explanations but as complements to the process of programmatic coordination. Appeals to identities, grievances, and greed are ingredients in building a coalition behind a common goal. Tactical-logistical opportunities are critical to the success of specific types of surges used by the campaign. Yet it is the national-secession campaign guided by its program that provides the common solution to this dissatisfaction, coordinates energies, and exploits opportunities on behalf of a significant campaign. The identities, grievances, ambitions, and tactical-logistical opportunities commonly cited in the earlier studies are comparatively weaker predictors of which nation-state projects become significant campaigns. (These complementary explanations are examined more closely in chapter 8.)

Statistical Estimation

The strength of these relationships can be estimated with statistical evidence. The estimations reported in this chapter ask how different cues and structural constraints affected the likelihood that between 1945 and 2010 an ethnic group (among the 3,741 ethnic groups examined in this study) would be a platform for one of the 171 significant national-secession campaigns identified in chapter 2.[17] The carefully chosen formulation of a "platform population" underscores that this is not a unitary actor; the leaders of the national-secession campaign advance a claim in the name of the platform population, but individual members of that population must evaluate the claim. The population is a platform both in the sense that the campaign seeks to establish a nation-state on this foundation (platform) and that the claim to nation-statehood is the key plank in the campaign's program (platform). Significance is whether a nation-state project gains the attention of the public in the major powers, as measured by attention of the international print media in London and New York. It should be underscored that the question addressed in this chapter is "prior to" the question asked by many earlier studies that have analyzed variation among "politically relevant ethnic groups" or ethno-political groups.[18] The estimates reported in this chapter identify which ethnic groups become politically relevant groups by becoming platforms for an internationally noted claim to sovereign statehood. The statistical estimations reported in this chapter and chapter 8 (and discussed in greater detail in the appendix to this chapter) are not designed to dismiss arguments that focus on identities, grievances, greed, or opportunities, but to estimate the relative impact of each constraint on the probability that a campaign will achieve significance.

From the results reported in the appendix to this chapter (table 5A.2), it is possible to estimate the probabilities of campaign significance in the presence of different cues and constraints. From these can be estimated the change in the probabilities of campaign significance as cues are introduced (or removed) and as constraints vary. These estimates of changes in the probabilities of campaign significance for variables that are found to be statistically significant at the .05 level are shown in table 5.1. (Although thirty independent variables were tested, only the fifteen significant coefficient estimates appear in this table.) These are based on two specifications of the model, the second of which includes GIS-based variables that are available for only some of the cases. The columns labeled "Change in Probability" report the percentage-point changes in the probabilities of campaign significance as the cue or constraint varies from minimum to maximum value. So, for example, if the probability that an ethnic group would be a platform for a significant campaign was 5.0 percent when the cue or constraint was absent but 25.0 percent when it was present, this represents a change of 20.0 percentage points. The numbers in the columns labeled "Percentage Change in Probability" are the quotients from dividing the percentage-point change by the lowest predicted probability. So, for example, the jump in probability from 5.0 percent to 25.0 percent represents a 400 percent change in probability. For most variables, a particularly large percentage change indicates that when that variable is at its lowest level, the probability of campaign significance is low, and an increase in that variable to its highest level is associated with a relatively substantial change in the probability of campaign significance. The results for the programmatic variables (authenticity, realism, and costliness of collaboration with the common-state) are discussed in this chapter. The results for the cultural and economic motivations and tactical-logistical opportunities identified in earlier studies are discussed in chapter 8.

TABLE 5.1. Changes in probabilities of campaign significance with variation in each cue and constraint

CUES AND CONSTRAINTS	CHANGE IN PROBABILITY		PERCENTAGE CHANGE IN PROBABILITY		CORRESPONDING THEORETICAL RELATIONSHIP
	MODEL 1	MODEL 2	MODEL 1	MODEL 2	
Conventionalized nation	—[a]	—[a]	—[a]	—[a]	Programmatic authenticity
Distinct territory	—[a]	—[a]	—[a]	—[a]	Programmatic authenticity
Prior statehood	75.0	54.8	1,400	1,002	Programmatic realism
Platform size[c]	67.3	62.7	47,889	48,753	Programmatic realism
Constitutional exclusion	44.3	36.8	2,700	2,253	Costly inclusion
Ethnolinguistic coalition	12.7	13.1	217	241	Programmatic realism
Geographic exclave	8.7	—[f]	145	—[f]	Tactical opportunity
Christian[d]	7.1	7.4	251	326	Cultural values
Distance to border[b]	—[f]	7.2	—[f]	316	Tactical opportunity
No alternative homeland	5.8	5.2	426	371	Programmatic authenticity
Democracy	—[f]	5.8	—[f]	201	Tactical opportunity
Muslim[e]	5.6	5.6	197	250	Cultural values
Exclusion from governance	5.3	4.9	323	303	Costly inclusion
Largest group[b]	4.9	5.0	215	285	Programmatic realism
Adjacent homeland[b]	—[f]	3.5	—[f]	103	Tactical opportunity

Notes: All estimates are shown for the variables that are significant at the .05 level in models 1 and 2, respectively, in table 5A.2 (see the appendix to this chapter). Each independent variable varies from its minimum to its maximum value unless noted in the following footnotes to this table.

[a] No projects reached campaign significance without this variable.

[b] Variation is from maximum to minimum.

[c] The largest group is set to 0; maximum value is for groups that were not largest groups.

[d] The variables "Muslim," "Muslim in Christian state," and "Christian in Muslim state" are set to 0.

[e] The variables "Christian," "Muslim in Christian state," and "Christian in Muslim state" are set to 0.

[f] This variable was not significant at the .05 level in this model.

Constraints on Programmatic Success

Cues to an authentic and realistic program and obstacles to collaboration with the common-state project stand out as powerful predictors of which ethnic groups became platforms for significant nation-state campaigns between 1945 and 2010. These cues and constraints are publically visible, so members of the platform population and international community (as well as analysts) are likely to draw the inference that members of a platform population will believe these are known to other members of the platform population with whom they cannot communicate. Stronger cues are likely to lead members of the platform population to conclude that these others will also see the claim to nation-statehood as authentic and realistic. These cues and constraints are signals to the international community that a program for independence has substantial potential for programmatic preemption within the platform population and deserves attention.

Authenticity Cues

Authenticity depends on the mutual expectation that a nation-state project speaks on behalf of an actual nation and its homeland. "Nations" (as opposed to collections of individuals) and "homelands" (as opposed to tracts of land) are human artifacts or "inventions," as Eric Hobsbawm has poignantly noted, but nation-state projects that seek to coordinate a platform population in a campaign are at an advantage if they need to do less inventing.[19] Projects that can rely on the evidence of already conventionalized definitions of populations and recognized patterns of settlement are more likely to be seen as authentic by potential proponents and recruits. Paul R. Brass stresses that "the values and institutions of a persisting cultural group will suggest what appeals and symbols will be effective and what will not be. . . ."[20] Yet the cues are not just cultural. In national-secession campaigns the most important cues are those pieces of evidence that suggest which aggregations of people and land are actually nations and homelands. Members of the platform population (and outside observers) have greater reason to expect that a campaign will grow in size and remain stable over time when it builds on "common knowledge," relying on mutually observed cues about the authenticity of the nation and its homeland.[21]

CONVENTIONALIZED NATIONHOOD

A nation-state project involves a claim that the platform population is not simply a number of individuals, but a grouping, and that the grouping is the type which has a right to a state of its own. Because appeals to invented groupings often leave most members of the platform population scratching their heads, campaigns to propagate claims to nationhood based on cultural conventions facilitate the focusing of expectations in the platform population and limit the alternative projects offered by intellectuals. Indeed, the assumption built into the statistical model that uses ethnic groups as the unit of analysis is that this cultural convention is a fundamental building block structuring national secessionism. Hence,

> **The Conventionalized Nation Hypothesis.** *A nation-state project is more likely to give rise to a significant national-secession campaign against a common-state if its platform population is a conventionally recognized ethnic group.*

Indeed, ethnic distinctiveness is an attribute of all significant nation-state projects—it has been the basis of their claims to peoplehood. Wayne Norman observes that "every serious secessionist movement this century has involved ethno-cultural minorities."[22] This is one advantage that most national-secession campaigns have over most regional-secession campaigns: the latter, such as the campaigns for Padania or Cascadia, often speak on behalf of populations that do not recognize their unity and distinctiveness.[23] This may also explain why more than 90 percent of all significant national-secession campaigns proposed a titular state, such as Croatia, Georgia, or Kurdistan, based on a single dominant ethnic group.

It is important to distinguish this argument from the common claim that national secessionism is a normal outcome of ethnic awareness. Walker Connor, like Hans Kohn before him, makes the case that ethnic groups typically become nations and demand statehood once they become self-aware.[24] Andreas Wimmer extends this logic, arguing that "the principle of ethnonational representativity of governments—that like should rule over likes—became de rigueur for any legitimate state."[25] The Connor-Kohn-Wimmer argument has a very important element of truth. And, indeed, the analysis that follows begins from the (unverifiable) assumption that few ethnic groups—probably only the most isolated—do not have at least one intellectual who has dreamed of an independent nation-state in the ethnic group's name. Yet there is no inevitability or determinacy in this relationship between ethnic groups and nations: most ethnic groups have so far not become nations.

Still fewer ethnic groups actually become platforms of significant national-secession campaigns. Indeed, less than 7.2 percent (270 of 3,741) of the ethnic groups studied in this project were platforms for significant nation-state projects between 1945 and 2010, even when each of the ethnic groups in multiethnic projects such as Ambazonia and South Sudan is counted separately. In the terminology used here, ethnic groups are cultural communities; nations are political communities. Whereas ethnic groups look backward to a population's shared past and its present-day cultural manifestations, nations look forward to a political future through creation or preservation of a state for a specific population.[26] This is consistent with Max Weber's definition that "ethnic groups" are "those human groups that entertain a subjective belief in their common descent." Weber stresses that ethnic groups may not actually share common blood kinship but that they still claim this. Alternatively, Weber defines a nation as "a community of sentiment which would adequately manifest itself in a state of its own."[27] Although ethnic distinctiveness can be a strong cue to coordinate expectations about the authenticity of a claim to peoplehood in nation-state projects, awareness of ethnicity is not sufficient for the rise of nationalism. A nation-state project is not an inevitable outcome of awareness of ethnic distinctiveness, and a significant national-secession campaign is a rare result.

IDENTIFIABLE HOMELAND

A second element of authenticity is a homeland recognizable by members of the platform population. Without an actual territory currently settled by the platform population that can be styled as a "homeland," nation-state projects face an enormous cost in convincing members of the platform population and international community that the imagined nation-state will be a focal point for secessionist sentiment. Few will expect many others in the platform population to see such a claim as authentic. For example, without identifiable homelands, the Romastan project for a Gypsy (Roma) state and the Coptic Republic project in Egypt have failed to rally their platform populations. Hence,

> **The Identifiable Homeland Hypothesis.** *An ethnic group is more likely to become the platform of a significant national-secession campaign against a common-state if the platform population inhabits an identifiable territory within the common-state.*

Using the data from ethnographers who plot the geographic settlement of groups, none of the 3,741 potential projects became significant campaigns unless associated with an identifiable area (within the common-state) where the platform population was numerically predominant; none of the 1,622 ethnic groups that lacked such a pattern of territorial settlement within the common-state became the platform population for a significant nation-state campaign. (Indeed, in subsequent tests these cases are automatically dropped from estimations by the statistical procedure.)

Both national secessionists and common-state governments are keenly aware of the importance of settlement patterns to the authenticity of a nation-state project and engage in such practices as ethnic cleansing or resettlement. For example, the People's Republic of China has maintained a program to settle Han Chinese in Xinjiang. By 2013, they constituted about 40 percent of the region's population; Uighurs held on to a small advantage at 46 percent. In May 2014 President Xi Jinping, speaking at a two-day "work forum" on Xinjiang, called for renewed efforts to promote "labor export" of Uighurs to other parts of China "to enhance mutual understanding among different ethnic groups and boost ties between them."[28] Long-term Han in-migration and Uighur "labor export" increasingly obscure the identifiability of the Uighur homeland. Allegedly, this is the objective of the Chinese government. Uighur nationalists see these trends as a growing obstacle to achieving their goal of an independent nation-state.

NO ALTERNATIVE FOCAL POINTS

The authenticity of a national-secession claim can be undermined by the existence of a competing focal point—a homeland for the platform population outside the common-state. The alternative homeland—particularly an independent nation-state elsewhere—makes it more difficult to convince members of a platform population that the territory they currently occupy is their homeland and that they should become the platform for an independent nation-state there. For example, Europeans living in the United States have not coalesced around national-secession projects, and those who have chosen not to assimilate in US society have often returned to their external homelands in substantial proportions.[29] This is even true for contiguous homelands, although this can be complicated by the tactical-logistical value of these as safe havens (an issue to which the discussion returns in chapter 8). This is not to say that most such populations develop strong attachments to the external homeland, but only that this makes identifying any territory within the common-state as a homeland less likely. For example, Lowell Barrington, Erik S. Herron, and Brian D. Silver find that among Russians living in the other Soviet successor states, fewer than 1 percent (except in Crimea) identified the region in which they currently resided as a Russian homeland.[30] Hence,

> **The Unique Focal Point Hypothesis.** *An ethnic group is more likely to become the platform of a significant national-secession campaign against a common-state if the platform population does not have an alternative, external independent nation-state.*

Indeed, among the 1,944 ethnic groups occupying identifiable territories within the common-state for which data are available, the existence of another state in which they constituted a majority was associated with substantially less national secessionism. As table 5.1 shows, those ethnic groups without a nonadjacent homeland were more than five times *as* likely (stated differently, 426 percent *more* likely) to become platforms for significant national-secession campaigns as those with remote homelands.[31]

Realism Cues

Realism includes the assessment that sovereign statehood is a practical possibility. Strong cues that other members of the platform population will see statehood as a realistic goal include precedents as well as current attributes of the proposed nation-state.

PRIOR STATEHOOD

A highly visible cue to the realism of a nation-state project is prior statehood—particularly if it is recent. Few cues are as powerful in making real the idea of a nation-state and shaping expectations of how others will assess the realism of the project. The nearer in time, the stronger this cue is likely to be.

Nation-state projects may appeal to ancient kingdoms now centuries, and perhaps millennia, dead. Anthony D. Smith recounts how the Armenian diaspora "retained an intense attachment to their original [fourth-century] mountain kingdom and its sacred Gregorian centre, Ethmiadzin."[32] The Basque nationalists kept alive a myth of autonomy, under the ancient laws (*Fueros*) that warded off Roman and Moorish occupations and constrained the Spanish kings: "In the privacy of their families many Basques continued to celebrate the nationalist festivals, absorb nationalist sentiments and nourish the memory of their period of autonomy."[33]

Yet national-secession campaigns find it easier to convince platform populations—particularly the pragmatists—of the realism of their projects when they can point to a recent example of statehood that was experienced within the lifetime of one's grandparents: even those who are too young to have experienced the imagined state firsthand are likely to have been regaled around the dinner table with stories of this state that make it seem real. For example, the reality of independence for interwar Latvia was critical for focusing the Latvian independence campaign from 1940 to 1991. The puppet states of Croatia and Slovakia created during World War II gave dreams of statehood in subsequent years tangible evidence that separation was possible. Eritrea is an important example of this coordinating role: its population is multiethnic and deeply divided by the Christian-Muslim sectarian cleft. Through much of history, this population was not identified as a "people," and the land they occupied was not identified as a "homeland." As Haggai Erlich notes, "Eritrea did not exist prior to 1890. It was an artificial creation of the Italians, and every attempt to describe it as an entity existing prior to that date and to base historical claims on this assumption distorts the facts."[34] Nonetheless, the former colony of Eritrea became a prominent focal point; no alternative projects—such as Greater Eritrea—gained wide acceptance, and the proposal to split Eritrea and annex the Muslim west with Sudan and the Christian highlands with Ethiopia was rejected by most Eritrean intellectuals.[35] The Italian colony—even after its demise—continued to coordinate expectations about how others in the platform population would respond to different proposals for statehood. Hence,

---

The Statehood Precedence Hypothesis. *An ethnic group is more likely to become the platform of a significant national-secession campaign against a common-state if the platform population has previously enjoyed independent statehood.*

Indeed, after conventionalized nationhood and identifiable homeland, the single most powerful predictor of a campaign becoming significant is the precedent of prior statehood. In the empirical tests, prior statehood is defined as an independent country, colony, or proto-state that existed recently (at some time since World War I) separated from the rest of the common-state. Among the 1,944 ethnic groups with homelands for which data are available, platform populations with prior statehood were eleven to fifteen times as likely to have significant campaigns in their names (see table 5.1). The probability of a significant campaign jumped by an average of 65 percentage points (55 and 75 percentage points, respectively, in the two models). Of the 101 ethnic groups with prior statehood at some time since World War I, 92 became platforms for significant national-secession campaigns.

Bringing together the effects of homelands and prior statehood highlights the relative importance of the latter: the probability of a significant national-secession campaign between 1945 and 2010 was 0 percent for those ethnic groups without identifiable patterns of territorial settlement. This was just more than 1 percent for those ethnic groups with identifiable territory in the common-state but an identifiable (and nonadjacent) nation-state outside. This rose to almost 6 percent when there was an identifiable territory within the common-state and no alternative nation-state. But this rose to more than 82 percent when this last configuration was coupled with recent statehood.

The loss of statehood is also a source of grievance, greed, and resources for mobilization against the common-state, but it is a grievance and a resource, unlike many others, that points to a very specific national-secession solution. Others have noted the importance of this grievance. For example, Barbara F. Walter lists lost autonomy among major grievances that make groups more likely to raise self-determination challenges to the state.[36] Michael Hechter and Margaret Levi claim that "the prospects for reactive group formation are maximized" in areas where annexation stripped "peripheries of their most important culturally distinctive governmental institutions."[37] Loss of prior statehood is also likely to leave behind "legacy" groups (such as the nobility of Uganda's kingdoms) who greedily expect to benefit by a return of statehood. And the networks of personal associations created during statehood may survive inside current political and social institutions and offer rewards for participation and enforce punishments for defection to alternative nation-state projects. Nonetheless, loss of statehood is a particularistic grievance likely to be felt immediately by only a small elite segment of dispossessed stakeholders in the old state. Campaign leaders must persuade other members of the platform population that restoration of statehood will address their own immediate grievances—the motivations that are most likely to energize the still larger platform population to contribute time, treasure, and lives to the campaign for independence.

VIABLE STATEHOOD

The realism of a nation-state project includes the expectation, particularly among more-pragmatic potential supporters, that the project has a good chance of becoming a viable nation-state and that others will see it as having this potential. One element of this credibility is a platform population large enough to constitute a sovereign state that will gain acceptance by the international community. More immediately important is the expectation that the campaign can actually attract a large enough staff and participatory reserve to sustain a campaign. Intellectuals, potential campaign leaders, and members of the platform population should expect that boutique campaigns on behalf of small platform populations are less able to create intractable disputes with the common-state government and to stage surge events large enough to be taken seriously by the international community. These are more likely to be dismissed as bothersome curiosities. Hence,

> **The Proposed State Viability Hypothesis.** *An ethnic group is more likely to become the platform of a significant national-secession campaign against a common-state if the platform population is comparable in size to the population of existing sovereign states.*

When drafting their programs, intellectuals and leaders who organize a campaign must anticipate these responses in the platform population and international community. For example, the expectation that Dinka or Nuer independence alone was unlikely to gain enough support led to a focus on South Sudan. The intellectuals and leaders must often carefully balance a trade-off between this realism and authenticity. Emphasizing the first half of this, Stephen M. Saideman, Beth K. Dougherty, and Erin K. Jenne give the label "identity layering" to the process by which "collective identities are consciously and strategically added to." They postulate that "secessionist leaders will try to change their identity (or raise the salience of another identity) when they perceive that the mobilizational value of their existing identity is outweighed by that of an alternative."[38] Yet greater size can often be achieved only by creating a more heterogeneous population that is less authentic as a nation or a more dispersed territory that is less authentic as a homeland. Multiethnic coalitions may require neologisms that potential members do not find credible, so these coalitions are particularly dependent on the availability of other focal points such as historical administrative units like South Sudan, Eritrea, or Western Papua.

The size of an ethnic group and the size of its ethnic kin are strong predictors of which national-secession campaigns are likely to achieve significance. Nonetheless, two qualifications need to be introduced. First, the estimates in table 5.1 show that the largest ethnic group in each common-state is about five percentage points *less* likely to become a platform for a significant campaign than ethnic groups of nearly the same size that are not the largest in that common-state. Halvard Buhaug argues that the largest ethnic groups are more likely to become platforms for nationalist projects to seize and redefine the common-state. The second largest, third largest, and so forth are likely to demand secession because wresting control of the current common-state from a larger ethnic group is unlikely to succeed.[39] Second, as the Proposed State Viability Hypothesis predicts, the realism associated with population size does more to handicap the smallest platform populations than to privilege the largest ones. As figure 5.2 displays, among ethnic groups that were not the largest in the common-state, the likelihood of a significant national-secession campaign, according to model 1, rose by more than 67 percentage points, from 0.14 percent for the smallest ethnic group to 67.42 percent for the largest. Yet the difference in probability between ethnic groups with one hundred thousand and ten million members (a 9.9 million difference in population) was almost 38 percentage points, while the difference between groups with ten million and fifty million members (a forty million difference in population) was less than 20 percentage points. Given the shape of this curve, it would be more accurate to say that the probability of campaign significance was substantially lower for the smallest projects.

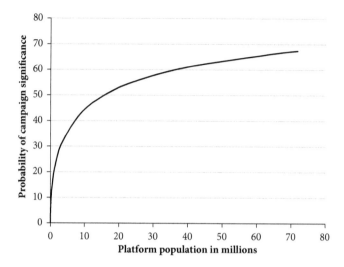

FIGURE 5.2. Platform size and campaign significance. The curve shows the probability that a campaign with a platform population of that size will achieve campaign significance by getting on the global agenda.

Ethnic groups that might expect support from other ethnic groups (for example, among the Papuan-language groups of West Papua or the Turkic-language groups of Xinjiang) were also more likely to become platforms for significant national-secession campaigns. An ethnic group with a population of one million with a potential ethno-linguistic coalition constituting 50 percent of the common-state population was twice as likely to become a platform of a significant campaign as an ethnic group with a potential coalition constituting only 10 percent of the common-state population.[40] Alternatively, potential religious allies appear to have no effect on the likelihood of a national-secession campaign becoming significant.[41]

Costliness of Defection

Affecting both the authenticity and realism of a national-secession program is the expectation that pragmatists will defect from the campaign and either collaborate with the common-state or exit the homeland. Campaigns under serious threat of such defections are less likely to attract the investment of time, treasure, and lives needed to become significant. Leaders and staffers will invest less when they expect pragmatists in the platform population to be lured away. Members of the platform population will be less inclined to invest in a campaign when they expect that more-pragmatic leaders and staffers may defect from the campaign before independence is achieved. The international community has less reason to expect that such national-secession campaigns will achieve programmatic preemption. Barriers to collaboration with the common-state also indirectly increase the authenticity of the national-secession program. These barriers do not directly identify the specific nation-state project of the secessionists as the best alternative, but these barriers are strong cues that fewer members of the secessionists' platform population will see the common-state as their own.

HIGHER COSTS OF COLLABORATION

High costs of collaboration with the common-state increase the likelihood that members of the platform population—particularly, its most-ambitious and energized members—will join the national-secession campaign as leaders, staffers, or reservists. If the only way into full citizenship in the common-state for the platform population is passing or conversion, then the costs to collaboration with the common-state are higher. In these circumstances, full inclusion may require cutting ties to family and friends in one's "cradle" community. Yet even these pathways may be closed if conversion is forbidden or converts are treated as second-class members of the dominant group. Then the costs of inclusion soar. These higher costs increase the likelihood of coordination of expectations around a national-secession project. Hence,

---

The Costly Inclusion Hypothesis. *An ethnic group is more likely to become the platform of a significant national-secession campaign against a common-state if the platform population is excluded from the common-state.*

The most substantial obstacle to inclusion is the definition of the common-state itself in a way that excludes some ethnic groups from the constitutional order.[42] One particularly poignant form of this exclusion (but not the only form) comes with the proclamation of a state religion, such as an Islamic republic, or development of a close working relationship with one religion, such as the special relationship with many national Orthodox Christian churches. The likelihood that an ethnic group will be a platform for a significant national-secession campaign was substantially greater when the ethnic group resides in a common-state that is defined constitutionally as privileging a specific religion (civilization) to which most of the minority does not belong. As the estimates in table 5.1 show, the likelihood of a significant campaign on the platform of that ethnic group was twenty-four to twenty-eight times as high as for other platform populations.

Constitutional exclusion from the common-state is, of course, a source of grievance as well, but it is a grievance that is directly linked to the definition of the common-state and an alternative secessionist state. This grievance may become acute when the state's close association with a specific culture is seen as a threat to the religion, language, or other aspects of cultural life of the platform population. For example, in Thailand the common-state's close association with Thai Theravada Buddhist culture is seen as threatening by the country's Muslim Malay Patani minority. In identifying the sources of the Patani campaign in South Thailand, David Kilcullen argues that "the first is a belief by local people in the South that their unique Patani identity (centered on ethnicity, language, and religion) is under threat from a Bangkok government that unilaterally interferes in their affairs, corrodes their traditional way of life, and is fundamentally illegitimate in their eyes."[43]

Exclusion from the government (even in the absence of constitutional exclusion) has had a significant but less substantial effect on the likelihood that a national-secession project would become a significant campaign. Knowledge that leaders of one's ethnic group have previously been excluded from the common-state government diminishes the expectation that current leaders of the platform population can aspire to high office except through secession. Knowledge of these past practices of the common-state government makes less credible its promises of positions to leaders who collaborate. Indeed, as table 5.1 shows, the likelihood of a significant campaign on behalf of an ethnic group that was consistently excluded from the government (that is, the cabinet or other executive leadership), but not constitutionally excluded, was four times greater than the likelihood of a campaign on behalf of groups consistently included.

Exclusion from governmental office is also, of course, a source of grievance. Like grievances created by constitutional exclusion, grievances associated with exclusion from governmental office go to the very heart of the issue of statehood. Gabriel A. Almond and Sidney Verba argued more than a half-century ago that "the opportunity to participate in political decisions is associated with greater satisfaction with that system and with greater general loyalty to the system."[44] Exclusion from governance may also lead to suspicions of systematic favoritism in distribution of public goods, government jobs, security, and justice, according to Andreas Wimmer, Lars-Erik Cederman, and Brian Min. They find that "it is political exclusion along ethnic lines that breeds ethnic conflict" and that this exclusion from government predicts secessionism.[45] Nonetheless, exclusion from governmental office is a particularistic grievance that is likely to be felt immediately by only narrow elite segments of platform populations. Campaign leaders may find it relatively easy to persuade elites who are energized by this particular grievance that independence is the best path to power. A more difficult task is persuading the larger platform population that independence, which will lead to governance by "their own kind," will also address the parochial concerns of the rest of the platform population.

Constitutional exclusion and governmental exclusion together have a power-ful association with the probability that an ethnic group will become the plat-form for a significant national-secession campaign. Yet constitutional exclusion appears to have the greater effect. For an "otherwise average" ethnic group always included in the government, the probability of a significant campaign was only 1.6 percent. For ethnic groups that never participated in the governing council but were not constitutionally excluded, this probability was 6.9 percent. For eth-nic groups constitutionally excluded as well, this probability was a very substan-tial 45.9 percent.

COSTLY EXIT OPTIONS

Nation-state campaigns should be less likely to face significant defections when exit options are closed to the target population. And yet there does not appear to be a close relationship with achieving campaign significance. Closed common-states like those under communist regimes that prohibited most emi-gration created pressure cookers for national secessionism. Alternatively, where this option of migration to other common-states is open, a national-secession project should find it more difficult to recruit and retain leaders, staffers, and reservists. Hence,

> **The Costly Exit Hypothesis.** *An ethnic group is more likely to become the platform of a significant national-secession campaign against a common-state if the platform population's exit options are costlier.*

The statistical evidence for this is only weak, however. On the one hand, if exit options that permit migrants to live abroad among co-ethnics are measured by the proportion of the ethnic group already living abroad, there is no relationship to campaign significance.[46] On the other hand, if an "adjacent homeland," where the platform population constitutes the majority, indicates an exit option, this does weakly predict lesser likelihood of a significant campaign.[47]

Programmatic theory draws attention to the national-secession program itself and the relationship of the program to common knowledge within the platform population as key predictors of a national-secession campaign's success at coordi-nating expectations and achieving significance. In order for a national-secession campaign to achieve significance, the authors of its program must align the cam-paign's program with the cues that will give its nation-state project and action program credibility when received by members of the platform population and the international community. Most immediately, those cues involve publicly visible "evidence" that suggests to more hearers authenticity and realism that will be recognized by members of the platform population. Conventionalized nationhood and a unique identifiable homeland within the common-state are the strongest cues of the authenticity of a claim to nationhood. A recent prior period of statehood for that same nation-state and a population large enough to sustain a sovereign state are strong cues to the realism of the project for statehood. Realism of the program's action plan and, more indirectly, authenticity of the claims to nation-statehood also entail expectations that members of the platform population will find it difficult to collaborate with the common-state. These are the strongest findings in this chapter's study of campaign significance.

INTRACTABLE DISPUTES
Consequences of Successful Campaigning

In national-secession conflicts, intractability refers to the inability of the secessionists and common-state to reach agreement on the substantive issue of sovereignty. According to programmatic theory, this intractability arises because the stakes have become a zero-sum conflict over an object that each side maintains is nondivisible and nonfungible: because of true belief or concerns for their own political survival, the national-secession and common-state leaders are committed unwaveringly to their respective goals. They narrow the options on the bargaining table to two—unity of the common-state versus independence for the secessionist state. Neither side is willing to accept side payments, such as promises of increased investment or personal wealth, as substitutes for its goal.

Intractability is likely to emerge in national-secession conflicts where national-secession campaigns have been more successful at programmatic coordination. The closer a campaign approaches programmatic preemption, the less likely are its leaders, staff, participatory reserve, and platform population to compromise with the common-state government or otherwise defect from the cause of independence. This affects both the capacity and motivation of campaign leaders to sustain deadlock at the negotiating table. And so, somewhat paradoxically, although the campaign does not seek deadlock (it simply wants the common-state government to concede independence) and deadlock may be a sign of strategic failure, intractability is a consequence of operational success. This success of programmatic coordination transforms the nature of exchanges between the leaders of national-secession campaigns and common-state governments, so what appears to be bargaining is not that at all. Where the stakes are tractable, there is still room for sincere bargaining to find a compromise. In the presence of issue intractability, bargaining becomes fruitless and is replaced by other forms of exchange.[1]

The analysis in this chapter focuses on the contribution of national-secession campaigns to intractability. The analysis treats the campaigns' differential success at programmatic coordination as the important variable that distinguishes one national-secession conflict from another. It takes as a constant that common-state governments resist secession unless, as chapter 2 catalogues, the common-state is too weak to prevent it or the international community imposes it. Only in the exceptional cases of Singapore and Slovakia did a common-state government preclude or end intractability by expulsion.[2]

Programmatic Coordination and Intractability

The more that campaign propaganda fosters the shared expectation that the common goal of independence is the only way to address the many concerns of the diverse platform population, the greater is the likelihood that the campaign can deter compromise with the common-state government. Even among pragmatists in the broader platform population who are attracted by offers from the common-state government, defections will be limited if the campaign leaders have successfully cultivated the expectation that most members of the platform population believe that independence is the best way to secure these benefits. Even the most hard-hearted pragmatist will expect that neighbors will not permit collaborators to enjoy ill-gotten gains in peace. Neighbors in the platform population will loudly denounce any co-national considering such compromises: these are gains wrung by the national-secession leaders from an untrustworthy common-state, worthless ploys intended to buy off the secessionists, and treasonous temptations to subvert the nation's unity.

Most importantly, when programmatic coordination is well advanced, this operational success constrains and motivates campaign leaders to be uncompromising.[3] Enthusiasm in the leadership is reinforced by each leader's expectation that compromise will be seen by others as an act of treason against a nation seeking its independence. Collaboration with the common-state will bring them not power, riches, and prestige but disfranchisement, expropriation, and ostracism. Furthermore, campaign leaders tie their own hands and make compromise more difficult for themselves by the very strategy they employ to build programmatic preemption. The leaders' words bind them: successful propagation to convince the platform population of the campaign leaders' enthusiasm makes it more difficult for campaign leaders to convince the common-state of their willingness to compromise.[4] The leaders' actions to demonstrate their commitment to the cause of independence during the process of programmatic coordination bind their hands still more. Deliberate "unforgivable acts" against the common-state government are credible commitments by national-secession campaign leaders to their platform population precisely because they make later compromises less likely. Blowback may come from the very nature of the leaders' authority within the campaign. Having based their leadership on their enthusiasm for the goal of independence, campaign leaders may risk that authority if they give any hint of compromise. James Q. Wilson notes that "ideological incentives, especially if threat-oriented, tend to constrain and radicalize the leaders of an association. . . ." So ideological "organizations display little flexibility about their objectives or, if the objectives are changed, the transformation exacts a heavy price in associational conflict and personal tensions, often resulting in factionalism and sometimes in fissure."[5]

In addition, the temptation is strong for campaign leaders to use intractability as a means to operational and strategic success. Well-publicized stands that demonstrate and reinforce intractability at the negotiating table constitute potent propaganda that advances programmatic coordination in the platform population. Such stands are also means to demonstrate to the international community that the campaign has achieved programmatic preemption and signal that independence is, indeed, the only viable option.

Exchanges Transformed from Debates to Championships

Where campaign leaders are able and motivated to sustain this uncompromising position on the issue of sovereignty over the platform population and its homeland, exchanges between the campaign and common-state government are transformed. Under the constraints of increasing programmatic coordination in the national-secession campaign (and as long as the common-state government will not concede independence), exchanges that begin as debates can evolve into variable-sum games, zero-sum games, and then championships.

In their interactions the national-secession and common-state leaders may not begin with a presumption of intractability as they explore the openness of the other side to conceding. The exchanges may initially resemble what Anatol Rapoport calls a **debate** in which the objective is "to convince your opponent, to make him see things as you see them." The arguments in the debate are intended first of all to persuade the other side by logic. A secondary objective in this debate is to influence the audience of platform population and international community. As national-secession and common-state leaders discover that the other side is unwilling to concede the issue of sovereignty, their direct exchange may become a **game**—specifically, a variable-sum game in which the purpose of arguments addressed to the other side is to explore whether they will accept side payments for surrendering sovereignty and to change their cost-benefit calculations in this trade-off. As they discover that the other side cannot be manipulated in this way, because the other's attachment to sovereignty over the platform population and homeland is nonfungible (just like their own attachment), this becomes a zero-sum game. In such games of pure conflict, the best that each side can hope for is to "outwit" its opponent with seemingly sincere offers of compromises that actually concede nothing on the issue of sovereignty. When national-secession and common-state leaders discover that the other side cannot be outwitted because it also understands that there is only one zero-sum issue on the table, one that cannot be masked by pseudo-compromises, the exchanges may continue as a **championship**, "in which the objectives are to convince some bystander."[6] What had been a secondary objective, influencing the audience of platform population and international community, becomes primary in a championship.

In championships, even as exchanges continue, even if their representatives continue to sit around the same negotiating table, bargaining has ended. Wilson observes that organizations that rely on highly valued purposive incentives "will attach such importance to their goals that not only will the results of bargaining seem unsatisfactory (a bargain by definition is an agreement in which neither party attains all his goals at zero cost) but the very idea of bargaining, with its inevitable implications of compromise, will appear objectionable."[7] Indeed, championships only superficially resemble the bargaining that has become central to so much analysis of secessionism in the international relations literature because what appears to be bargaining over the issues with the common-state is a means by which cadres-dressed-as-diplomats conduct the propaganda which convinces the platform population and international community that the independence project is the only viable option. Sometimes it may be difficult for the parties at the table to discern what type of exchange they are engaging in, but often (as attested by the statements of participants quoted later in this chapter) they know full well that they are not actually bargaining with the other side but propagating their programs among other audiences.

This is also true of what might appear to be "bargaining with violence." It was Thomas C. Schelling who noted that in conflicts, "two things are being bargained over, the *outcome* of the war, and the *mode* of conducting the war itself."[8] In the bargaining literature on which he built, the mode is chosen to influence the other side's cost-benefit calculations about the outcome.[9] Yet once the parties realize that the outcome is nondivisible and nonfungible for both sides, and so interactions have ceased to be games and become championships, then the costs of conflict (and so the mode of conducting the conflict) cannot be used to affect the value of independence for the national-secession campaign or territorial integrity for the common-state government. Agreements to control the tactics employed by the national-secession campaign and common-state government may have no bearing on the resolution of the substantive disagreement over independence. With this transformation of exchanges, the tactics chosen by national-secession campaign leaders are increasingly selected in order to influence the platform population and international community, not the common-state government (see chapter 7). For the leaders and cadres of national-secession campaigns, what outsiders may see as bargaining by deeds in a game becomes a continuation of propaganda by other means in a championship.

Disputes can reach this level of intractability characterized by championships and pseudo-bargaining when campaigns have achieved an advanced level of programmatic coordination. On the one hand, advanced programmatic coordination gives national-secession campaign leaders the *capacity* to sustain an uncompromising position towards the common-state: they anticipate continuing support as the deadlock drags on. On the other hand, advanced programmatic coordination *motivates* an uncompromising stance: when the platform population is firmly committed to the program for independence, campaign leaders anticipate little gain from compromise with the common-state. When the authority of campaign leaders is based in large part on their demonstrated enthusiasm for independence, any compromise might jeopardize not only the unity of their campaign but also their own authority within it.

Issue Intractability in Frozen Conflicts

This chapter examines the relationship of programmatic coordination to issue intractability in five extreme cases—the "frozen conflicts" of the Soviet successor states from 1990 to 2015. These five cases illustrate in stark terms the dynamics of intractability between national-secession campaigns and common-state governments that emerge when campaigns successfully coordinate platform populations behind the goal of independence. These cases illustrate three important elements of this relationship that bridge the topics in the previous chapter and this one: extensive propagation of claims to nationhood and statehood is key to creating programmatic preemption, which demonstrates that the platform population is unified in the claim that independence is the only viable option. Programmatic coordination makes possible and motivates the uncompromising commitment of campaign leaders to sovereignty at the negotiating table, which creates intractability with the common-state governments. And this intractability transforms negotiations into a championship with pseudo-compromises and pseudo-bargaining. In four of the disputes the issue of sovereignty remained intractable a quarter century after it first became apparent.

Most national-secession campaigns around the world, of course, achieve at best only a fraction of this. The close look at these extreme cases is designed to illustrate starkly the causal links that the large-n statistical studies in chapters 5 and 7 may not document.

These five cases also represent a significant slice of the unrecognized, de facto states of the last half century. Pål Kolstø labels the latter "quasi-states" and in 2006 identified seven surviving "quasi-states," including Abkhazia, Nagornyi Karabakh, South Ossetia, and Transdniestria, which are all discussed here, and six former "quasi-states," including Chechnya, which is discussed here.[10] The purpose of this chapter is not to explain the attainment or maintenance of the status of de facto independence. Nonetheless, this status interacted in important ways with the campaigns for independence and with intractability. De facto statehood reinforced the authenticity and realism of the programs for independence. An important element in the creation and maintenance of the de facto states, as Kolstø notes, was external support. The complex interaction of external support with the operational and strategic objectives of campaigns is an issue to which the discussion will turn in the penultimate section of this chapter.

The discussion that follows first examines the campaigns' efforts to coordinate platform populations behind nationhood, statehood, and independence. The second section discusses how strong programmatic coordination by these national-secession campaigns affected exchanges with the common-state, fostering issue intractability, championships, and a form of pseudo-bargaining. The third section explores the dilemma for campaign leaders created by external support—resolving immediate operational problems but possibly raising obstacles to the achievement of long-term strategic objectives.

Programmatic Coordination in Five Intractable Conflicts, 1988–2016

Although their roots go back decades, five significant campaigns for independence all gave rise to intractable conflicts with their respective common-states in the last four years of the USSR. This followed loosening central governmental control under Mikhail Gorbachev's perestroika. The increasingly independent union-republic governments of Azerbaijan, Georgia, Moldova, and Russia challenged the government of Gorbachev and asserted control within their own borders. Yet the moves of these union-republic governments produced a defensive backlash from the regional administrations in Abkhazia, South Ossetia, Nagornyi Karabakh, and Chechnya and from local authorities in the Transdniestria area, who feared that growing independence for the union republics would diminish the regions' autonomy. The regional administrations sought to end their subordination to their respective union-republic governments through a series of escalating claims—by declaring themselves union republics on a par with Azerbaijan, Georgia, Moldova, and Russia; by petitioning for admission to another union republic (Nagornyi Karabakh to Armenia or Russia; Transdniestria, South Ossetia, and Abkhazia to Russia); or by declaring themselves independent members of the global community of sovereign states.

With the exception of Transdniestria (and Chechnya to a certain extent), the national-secession campaigns began from a solid programmatic base because they built on existing nation-states: each built on the titular nationality of an existing autonomous republic (ASSR) or autonomous oblast (AO). These segment-states had institutionalized the claims to nationhood and statehood for their titular populations even before the conflicts of the campaigns with their union-republic governments became crises. Nonetheless, the five national-secession campaigns varied in the nationhood and statehood constraints they encountered. Nagornyi Karabakh and Abkhazia encountered more-favorable conditions for coordinating their platform populations around the goals of nationhood, statehood, and independence. The South Ossetia campaign had to contend with somewhat greater disagreement within its platform population on the issue of independence. The Transdniestria campaign had to create its platform population and homeland anew. The Chechen project for an independent Ichkeria, which was based on a firmer foundation of nationhood, faced profound disagreements on statehood and independence. Leaders of the national-secession campaigns quickly assumed leadership positions within the regional administrations, enlisted the support of leading politicians, and brought enterprise leaders and new entrepreneurs on board with opportunities to enrich themselves through legal and illegal undertakings.[11] All relied on external support to stand against the overwhelming military capabilities of their respective common-state governments, but that proved to be a double-edged sword: this support preserved all but Chechnya as de facto states, despite the national-secession campaigns' operational weakness. Yet it made more difficult the task of convincing the international community that these independence projects represented the only viable options.

Intractability emerged not only because the national-secession campaigns presented authentic and realistic programs but also because most of the common-state governments raised the costs and risks of collaboration and compromise. In particular, Azerbaijan, Georgia, and Moldova acted in ways that reinforced skepticism among national-secession campaign leaders that compromise could lead to arrangements that would empower the platform population in its homeland and include its representatives in common-state governance. Despite the critical need, the common-state governments did not make their promises to the national-secession campaign leaders more credible. The common-state governments made only ambiguous commitments about the constitutional guarantees or rights they would grant the secessionists once they conceded, demanding instead that the secessionists first concede before any concrete proposals could be made public.[12] The common-state governments were inconsistent, so their words and actions in related policy areas (such as obstacles to resettlement of Azeri and Georgian refugees) and over time subverted the credibility of their promises to empower the platform populations of the national-secession campaigns.[13] The common-state governments were unwilling to take incremental steps that would begin implementing some of their promised concessions, such as decentralization or federalism, before the national-secessionist leaders conceded.[14] And the common-states' treatment of parallel regions and minorities then under central authority (such as Nakhichevan in Azerbaijan, Ajara in Georgia, and Gagauzia in Moldova) magnified for the platform population the perceived risks of compromise.[15] The response in the national-secession campaigns to the perceived risk of collaboration with the common-state in four of the conflicts was even stronger coordination around their programs for independence and fewer defections.

In contrast, the constitutional order and political practices of the Russian Federation in the 1990s made more credible the promise that collaboration would bring political control by the platform population within the homeland and incorporation of its leaders in common-state decision making. Most importantly, the examples of other republics that were governed by homeland ethnic political machines (such as Bashkortostan and Tatarstan) made more credible the Russian promise that Chechen collaborators would be empowered within a Republic of Chechnya if they rejoined the Russian Federation. This made it easier for the common-state government to peel away some layers of support around the Ichkeria campaign's hard-core enthusiasts: for those who were more pragmatic in their attachment to the independence program and even for enthusiasts who began to doubt the realism of the project for independence at this time (but not its authenticity), the lower costs of collaboration became decisive.[16]

All five national-secession conflicts escalated to actual violence in the first half of the 1990s. These civil wars all ended shortly with cease-fires which limited the tactics that each side used to press its case on the substantive disagreement over sovereignty. Nevertheless, the cease-fires did not end the deadlock over the issue of secession. The war over Chechnya resumed at the end of the decade, ending in victory for the common-state government.[17] The wars over Abkhazia and South Ossetia resumed briefly in the next decade, ending in a new deadlock after Russia defeated Georgia on the battlefield. In each instance, the war was initiated by the common-state government, which was dissatisfied with the status quo. Each national-secession regime, acknowledging that it would not achieve formal sovereignty on the battlefield, was willing to accept the frozen conflict as a second-best outcome and to wait for opportunities to achieve independence by convincing the international community that this was the only viable option.

Nagornyi Karabakh

Nagornyi Karabakh's conflict with Azerbaijan became intractable after the Nagorno-Karabakh Autonomous Oblast (NKAO) in 1988 appealed to the Presidium of the USSR Supreme Soviet to transfer the oblast from the jurisdiction of Azerbaijan to Armenia.[18] (See figure 6.1.) Denied official approval from Moscow, the regional council (the AO soviet) unilaterally voted to secede from Azerbaijan and join Armenia on July 12, 1988. A declaration of independence came soon after the failed coup against Gorbachev in August 1991, when an assembly of deputies from all soviets within the oblast and the neighboring district of Shaumianovskii *raion* declared a Nagorno-Karabakh Republic (NKR). On November 26 the Azerbaijan Supreme Soviet voted to revoke the autonomous status of the oblast, but troops from Armenia prevented forceful reintegration: Armenian armed forces invaded Azerbaijan in January 1992 and by mid-1992 controlled Nagornyi Karabakh and the Lachin corridor that links it with Armenia. In the next months the Armenian forces extended their control to neighboring districts of Azerbaijan.

FIGURE 6.1.   Armenia, Azerbaijan, and Nagornyi Karabakh

The Bishkek cease-fire of May 12, 1994, left Armenian armed forces in place and kept Nagornyi Karabakh outside the control of Azerbaijan. The conflict had killed between twenty and thirty thousand and displaced a million. Over the next twenty years, the only significant break of the cease-fire came in the 2008 Mardakert skirmishes and again in 2016, but worries that war could resume remained strong.[19] Underscoring the danger created by this intractability, Azerbaijan's President Ilham Aliev warned, "The war is not over. Only the first stage of it is."[20]

The local Armenian platform population coordinated around the nation-statehood of Nagornyi Karabakh but remained divided over whether the Karabakh should be part of Armenia or an independent state.[21] The conventionalized separation between Armenians and Azeris and the historical occupation of the Stepanakert region by Armenians were "common knowledge" among Armenians, even if the historiography was disputed by Azeri scholars.[22] The out-migration of Azeris during the 1992–94 war and official encouragement of Armenian settlement afterward homogenized the population of the new nation-state even further: whereas Armenians constituted 76.9 percent of the population of the NKAO, according to the Soviet census of 1989, this proportion jumped to 99.7 percent in the territories claimed by the Nagorno-Karabakh Republic, according to its own 2005 census.[23] The NKR sponsored a new history that reinforced the sense of separate nationhood. Analysts at the International Crisis Group (ICG) pointed out that through "selective interpretations of history, myths, symbols and religious imagery . . . Nagorno-Karabakh has become the dominant symbol of nationhood and statehood, capable of harnessing tremendous emotional power."[24] Although beginning from the weaker institutional foundation of an autonomous oblast rather than autonomous republic, sovereign statehood based on the NKR became a more realistic claim with the consolidation of new political institutions. The State Defense Committee under the chairmanship of Robert Kocharyan assumed effective control and transformed itself into the NKR government, with its own president, parliament, bureaucratic administration, police, and armed forces. Direct presidential elections were introduced in 1997 and held again every five years.[25] Elections to the National Assembly were introduced in 1995 and held again every five years. A popular referendum in December 2006 ratified a constitution, codifying the republic's claim to be a sovereign state. Few, if any, prominent Karabakh Armenians publically endorsed the option of return to Azerbaijan—programmatic preemption appeared nearly complete.

Abkhazia

After decades of sporadic crises, the long-standing conflict between Abkhazia and Georgia became intractable soon after March 18, 1989: an assembly of Abkhazian deputies from the autonomous republic's regional and local legislative councils (soviets within the Abkhazian ASSR) appealed to the USSR leadership to elevate Abkhazia to the status of a union republic outside the jurisdiction of Georgia (see figure 6.2). Failing to persuade Moscow, the autonomous republic's government began unilateral action to effect this change. In June 1992, six months after the dissolution of the USSR, Abkhazia proclaimed itself a sovereign state under its 1925 Constitution. The Abkhazian crisis escalated to armed conflict on August 12, 1992, when Georgian troops entered and occupied much of the republic. In response, and with help from volunteers mobilized by the Confederation of Mountain Peoples and from the Russian armed forces, the Abkhaz leaders conducted a coordinated year-long counteroffensive to expel the Georgian army; the Abkhaz army reached the republic's border with Georgia on September 30, 1993. Signature of the Moscow Agreement on May 14, 1994, formalized a cease-fire. The war left more than 2,500 dead and 300,000 Georgian refugees who fled Abkhazia. The United Nations Observer Mission in Georgia (UNOMIG), authorized in 1993, monitored and verified the cease-fire until June-July 2009. Russian peacekeepers along the border between Abkhazia and Georgia prevented further attempts by Georgia to reverse the secession and so sustained it for more than two decades. Yet in the presence of intractability at the negotiating table, resumption of violence was always a threat: indeed, in 2006 and 2008 Georgian and Russian-Abkhaz forces traded control of the Kodori Gorge.

The platform population rallied behind the claims to Abkhaz nationhood and statehood, even though Georgian nationalist historians challenged the claim that present-day Abkhazians are descendants of the settlers on which Abkhazia is based. Establishing the authenticity of their claim to their homeland was at the top of the national-secession campaign's agenda and was apparently successful. Abkhaz intellectuals invested strenuous efforts in search of "glorious ancestors" to compile a history with documentary evidence supporting the claim of the Abkhaz nation to its homeland—a story taught in schools.[26] Capturing the spirit of this effort, the Abkhaz World website adopted as its banner/slogan "Whoever loses homeland loses all." Commenting on the results of their own opinion surveys and interviews, John O'Loughlin, Vladimir Kolossov, and Gerard Toal note that "the Abkhaz believe that their contribution to the victory over Georgia, as well as their sufferings and deprivations, are unique. As a consequence, they believe that they deserve the right to determine the destiny of the republic."[27] By law, instruction in schools had to be conducted in Abkhazian and Russian, although Georgian instruction continued where the authorities had not clamped down. Whatever the disagreements among regional, institutional, and personal alliances that contended in Abkhazian elections, the consensus that Abkhazia should remain independent and maintain a close alliance with Russia was apparently nearly complete. For example, in the 2009 and 2014 presidential

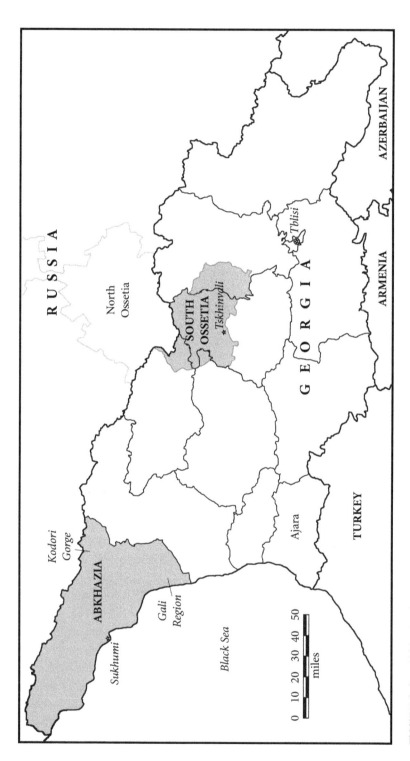

FIGURE 6.2. Abkhazia, Georgia, and South Ossetia

elections, all of the candidates were adamant that they would not negotiate away independence—there were no viable alternatives mentioned in public discussions.

The demographic support for the Abkhaz claim to a homeland was initially precarious. In the 1989 census, Abkhazes constituted only 17.8 percent of the republic's population, while Georgians constituted 45.7 percent. After substantial out-migration by Georgians, the official but contested Abkhazian census of 2011 reported that the proportions had flipped, with 50.7 percent Abkhazes and 19.3 percent Georgians.[28] To solidify their claim to the homeland, Abkhazian officials encouraged the Abkhaz diaspora to return and limited return of Georgian refugees to only the Gali region along the border with Georgia.[29] There was strong public opposition among Abkhazes to the Georgian return or even granting citizenship to Georgian residents.[30] The attempt by President Aleksandr Ankvab to issue passports to tens of thousands of Gali Georgians brought protests that forced his resignation. Immediately after his resignation, around 22,000 Georgians in the Gali region were reportedly stripped of their passports, citizenship, and rights to vote in the upcoming presidential election.[31] Abkhazian law prohibited the sale of land to foreigners and restricted long-term leases; public pressure reinforced this by ostracizing non-Abkhaz residents who had skirted these restrictions.[32]

Using the administrative structure of the ASSR as its foundation, the Abkhazians undertook a vigorous state-building project to establish the realism of statehood and the claim to sovereignty. On November 26, 1994, the Abkhazian Supreme Soviet adopted a new constitution that reaffirmed the republic's sovereignty based on "the people's right to free self-determination" and Abkhazia's claim to be a subject of international law. This was ratified by popular vote on October 3, 1999.[33] The Abkhazian elites were keenly aware of the importance of institution building to make credible their claims to statehood in the eyes of the international community. So they sought to establish the rule of law, a democratically elected government, an army in effective control of its territory, and an economy with sustainable growth.[34] The national-secession campaign leadership institutionalized its position by creating a presidency, a cabinet, a parliament, and its own local district governments. Direct presidential elections were held in 1999, 2004–05, 2009, 2011, and 2014.[35] These created real transitions from Vladislav Ardzinba to Sergei Bagapsh in 2004–05 and then to Raul Khajimba in 2014.[36] In both elections where the incumbent was precluded from running again, the insider candidate failed to win first place (Khajimba in 2004) or resigned under pressure of street protests organized by the opposition (Aleksandr Ankvab in 2014).[37] Popular elections to the People's Assembly were held in 1996, 2002, 2007, and 2012.[38] In 2014 Freedom House evaluated the Abkhazian political system to be "partly free" in its ranking system—a unique accomplishment among these secessionist governments.

South Ossetia

The conflict between South Ossetia and Georgia became intractable while both were still part of the USSR, following failed local moves to elevate the status of the South Ossetian Autonomous Oblast (AO) to an autonomous republic.[39] (See figure 6.2.) Intractability followed the seating of a Georgian nationalist majority in the Georgian Supreme Soviet in November 1990 and its vote to annul all acts of the AO soviet to elevate the region. On November 28, 1990, South Ossetia's soviet unilaterally proclaimed its autonomous oblast to be a union republic—a status equal to that of Georgia—and on December 11 declared that henceforth it would be directly subordinate to the USSR government in Moscow and not the Georgian government in Tbilisi. The Georgian Supreme Soviet and its Presidium countered with legislation that simply dissolved the South Ossetian AO, declared a state of emergency in the South Ossetian capital of Tskhinvali and the adjacent countryside, and ordered troops of the republic's police (MVD and KGB) to establish control over the region.[40] In this escalating crisis, the USSR government stepped in to block Georgians from retaliation against the South Ossetians. Once it became clear that the USSR would dissolve, the AO soviet declared South Ossetia's independence on December 22, 1991, and a referendum the next month affirmed this. On April 17, 1992, the South Ossetian soviet called on Russia to admit the territory to the newly independent Russian Federation. When Georgian forces tried to establish control over South Ossetia, fighting resumed, but Russian armed support tipped the balance in favor of the Ossetians. In the Sochi Agreement on June 24, 1992, the parties agreed to a cease-fire. The war left at least two thousand dead and thirty thousand refugees from South Ossetia.

The failure to reach agreement on the status of South Ossetia left open the prospects of a resumption of violence. Indeed, within months of taking office in Georgia during the Rose Revolution, President Mikheil Saakashvili initiated military operations in July and August 2004, leading to a new but limited conflict between Georgia and South Ossetia in which twenty-two died. In the summer of 2008, Saakashvili turned once again to the option of resolving the dispute by military action, moving Georgian troops into South Ossetia in order to reassert control. The outcome of the August 7–12, 2008, war was a setback for Georgia's ambition to reintegrate South Ossetia after Russian armed forces overwhelmed the Georgians and expelled the Georgian government from the few villages that it still controlled in South Ossetia.

The coordination of the South Ossetian platform population behind a common nationhood program proved somewhat more difficult—complicated by the presence of North Ossetia within the Russian Federation and the willingness of some leading South Ossetians to defect to the Georgian project. South Ossetian campaign leaders worked to strengthen the authenticity of their claim to their homeland by restrictive resettlement policies and intense propaganda. In 1989 Ossetians had accounted for about two-thirds of the region's population and Georgians only 29 percent. The systematic destruction of Georgian villages within the republic during the 2008 war and refusal to permit Georgians to return strengthened Ossetian demographic predominance, which might have otherwise been threatened by large-scale return of Georgians and broad out-migration by Ossetians.[41] Following the 2008 war, official estimates placed the Ossetian proportion at 80 percent—an estimate of uncertain accuracy.[42] Official propaganda to reinforce nationhood was well under way: claims of the historical roots of the Ossetians as the first settlers in the region, claims of a Georgian genocide against Ossetians in 1920, and reminders of recent Georgian aggression, as it was characterized by the South Ossetian campaign, were major themes in history textbooks and on the republic's official websites.[43]

There were some highly visible defections from the national-secession campaign's leadership: the first president, Liudvig Chibirov (1993–2001), began to negotiate for some form of association with Georgia and had to be checked by other campaign leaders. Chibirov was ultimately defeated in the 2001 elections by Eduard Kokoity, who denounced any compromise with Georgia on the issue of independence. Five years later, former Prime Minister Dmitrii Sanakoev joined the Georgians to head an alternative administration that promised development assistance if the region returned to Georgia.

Nonetheless, programmatic coordination in the broader South Ossetian platform population held up against the temptation of collaboration and compromise: in the words of ICG analysts, "for most Ossetians, Sanakoev was a traitor, the aid a bribe and the policy an attempt to divide the Ossetian nation."[44] Alexander Skakov quotes participants in a Carnegie Moscow Center roundtable that after two decades, "there are no 'pro-Georgian' forces in the republic today, no groups or politicians openly expressing sympathy for Georgia and the possibility of returning South Ossetia to the Georgian fold as a full-fledged autonomous entity within Georgia."[45] A new referendum on independence on November 12, 2006, turned out an overwhelming vote in the areas of the republic controlled by the national-secession campaign at the time, confirming the secessionist government's claim to sovereignty.[46]

On the other hand, there was less consensus whether their homeland was the sovereign state of South Ossetia or a united Ossetia (including the North) and, if the latter, whether Ossetia should be inside or outside Russia. On the issue of future ties to the North, President Leonid Tibilov vacillated between promises to strengthen the republic's sovereignty and affirmations that "the Ossetians are one people and should live in a single state within the Russian Federation." President Kokoity was rebuffed by Moscow several times when he proposed unification within Russia.[47] By early 2014, United Ossetia (Edinaia Osetiia), which became the dominant political party in the South Ossetian Parliament after winning 45 percent of the vote, called for an immediate referendum on unification with the North. Polls suggested that support would be overwhelming—perhaps over 90 percent.[48]

Making statehood a reality and any claims to sovereignty realistic in the eyes of South Ossetians was also a more difficult task for the national-secession campaign leaders. The less extensive institutional development common in autonomous oblasts (compared with autonomous republics), incomplete South Ossetian control until 2008 over the region that the campaign claimed as its homeland, and ambiguities regarding whether the national homeland was South Ossetia or united Ossetia conspired to slow coordination around a program of South Ossetian statehood. The republic signaled its renewed intention to institutionalize statehood in 2001 with a referendum finally ratifying its 1993 constitution. Presidential elections were held in 1996, 2001, 2006, 2011–12, and 2017.[49] Parliamentary elections were held in 1999 and every five years after that. But it was not until the 2008 war that the republic's government gained control over all South Ossetia.

Transdniestria

The Transdniestrian (or Transnistrian) crisis began to simmer during the period of perestroika as non-Moldovan economic and administrative elites living on the east bank of the Dniester River grew increasingly concerned with the growing Moldovanization of politics in the Moldavian SSR. It became an intractable conflict soon after Moldova proclaimed its sovereignty (see figure 6.3). On September 2, 1990, the Second Congress of People's Deputies of All Levels of the Transdniestrian Region proclaimed a separate Transdniestrian Moldavian (Soviet Socialist) Republic (PMR), with the intention of removing the region from the jurisdiction of Moldova but keeping it within the USSR. Immediately after dissolution of the USSR in December 1991, the Moldovan government attempted to establish its control by sending police across the Dniester River, but these encountered armed resistance from the PMR, backed by Russia's 14th Army and volunteer Cossack formations. Armed conflict intensified beginning on March 2, 1992. With Russia serving as mediator, both sides agreed to a cease-fire in the Moscow Agreement on July 21, 1992. Casualties were much lighter than in the other conflicts, with perhaps only a thousand dead. Nonetheless, the dispute over the status of Transdniestria remained intractable for a quarter century.

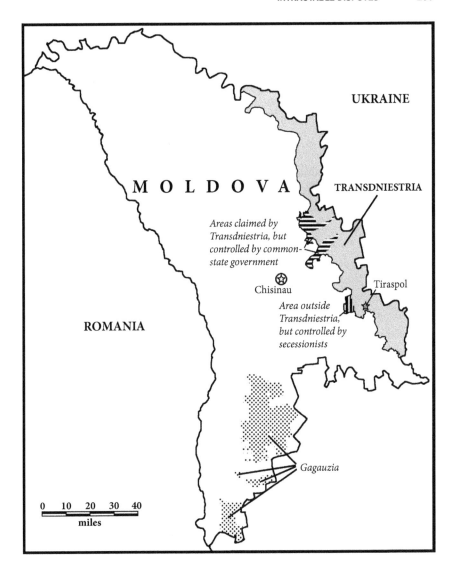

FIGURE 6.3. Moldova and Transdniestria

The claim to nationhood for the Transdniestrian platform population was more difficult to authenticate in the eyes of this population and the international community. The platform majority was initially united only in being not Moldovan, comprising multiple ethnic groups linked to alternative external nation-states. Yet throughout most of its history, the PMR had a Moldovan plurality: in the 1989 Soviet census the population in the districts that became Transdniestria comprised 39.9 percent Moldovans, 28.3 percent Ukrainians, and 25.5 percent Russians. By 2004, according to the census conducted by the

Transdniestrian government, in the areas that it controlled, the Russian share had grown to 30.4 percent, the Ukrainian share held steady at 28.8 percent, and the Moldovan share had shrunk to 31.9 percent.[50] Seen through the PMR's lens, however, non-Moldovans constituted two-thirds of the total. Transdniestria University began to produce histories, atlases, and textbooks to document a separate past as the foundation for claims to a separate future. PMR presidential advisor Anna Volkova summarized this effort: "In Moldova the official ideology is Moldovanism, while in the PMR, it is Transdniestrian internationalism."[51] Despite uncertain authenticity of claims to nationhood, as Stefan Wolff observes, "After two decades of separation and relentless pro-independence (and pro-Russian) propaganda, public opinion in the Transnistrian region is generally oriented eastward and has been almost completely isolated from discussions of any political alternatives to independence."[52] The civil servants in the governing coalition appeared to be the strongest defenders, while the business executives who joined the campaign were more pragmatic on the issue of independence. As Oleh Protsyk observed, "The business community is much more ambivalent about whether continued insistence on achieving independence and the refusal to consider proposals for reintegration with Moldova is the optimal strategy for ensuring growing market capitalization of their businesses and the region's overall economic development."[53] Yet the hegemonic Sheriff business cartel strongly supported independence, and one of its leaders became president in 2011. Compared to the other frozen conflicts, it does not appear that the nationhood project inspired widespread enthusiasm, and pragmatic attachment to independence was contingent on calculations of gain under alternative statehood projects. Sustaining programmatic preemption into the future was a key challenge for the national-secession campaign.

Establishing the reality of statehood and the realism of ambitions for sovereignty was also a difficult task because a state and government had to be created anew; there had been no jurisdiction or unified Transdniestrian administration since 1940.[54] On November 25, 1990, voters elected a Supreme Soviet (later Parliament), which in turn established the new government of Transdniestria. The government proceeded to establish its control over police and judiciary within the region and quickly consolidated many institutional foundations of statehood. A referendum in December 1995 approved a constitution for the PMR. Igor Smirnov was elected president on December 1, 1991, and reelected in 1996, 2001, and 2006, but lost to Yevgenii Shevchuk in 2011.[55] Parliamentary elections were held in 1995 and every five years after that. A referendum conducted in Transdniestria on September 17, 2006, reportedly returned a 97 percent vote for independence from Moldova and free association with Russia. Transdniestrian politics showed significant pluralism, with suggestions that some members of the elite might collaborate with Moldova, but the Transdniestrian government was vigilant in identifying any public hints of collaboration and responded to most attempts to question PMR independence with severe repression.[56]

Chechnya

After the Chechen National Congress (CNC) staged a successful coup in the capital city of Groznyi while Russia was still part of the USSR, a national-secession conflict between the leadership of the Chechen-Ingush Autonomous Soviet Socialist Republic (ASSR) and Boris Yeltsin's reformist government of the Russian Federation (RSFSR) became intractable (see figure 6.4). Elections coordinated by the CNC elected its leader, Dzhokhar Dudaev, as president of the republic, and on October 27, 1991, Dudaev declared the republic's independence. The end of intractability at the negotiating table came not through compromise but on the battlefield with a Russian rout of the Chechen forces. This came only after nine years—on Russia's third attempt. The first attempt to end the intractable conflict came after Yeltsin's declaration of a state of emergency on November 9, 1991, but ended with a bungled attempt to use troops of the Russian Ministry of Internal Affairs (MVD) to secure the airport in Groznyi and other strategic points around Chechnya. Russia's second attempt to regain Chechnya began on December 11, 1994, when Russian armed forces once again entered the region. The indecisive and bloody war continued for two years. Peace talks in the late summer of 1996 led to the Khasavyurt Agreement of August 30, 1996—a compromise permitting the Chechens to claim that their republic was independent and Moscow to claim that Chechnya remained a subject of the Russian Federation.[57] The third and successful Russian attempt to end the intractable conflict began in late September 1999, when Russian air forces resumed bombing of strategic targets within Chechnya. And by the beginning of February 2000, Russian troops had taken control of the last rebel strongholds within Groznyi. Despite continuing terrorist attacks, the Russian government imposed a settlement, creating a new Chechen government and conducting elections for a Chechen president on October 5, 2003.[58] Estimates of the toll from Chechnya's two wars vary widely, with the Chechen State Council Chairman Tau Dzhabrailov claiming in August 2005 that 160,000 civilians and soldiers had died in the two wars, but the Russian human rights group Memorial placed the total closer to 89,000. The number of displaced persons at the peak of fighting in 2000 was estimated variously as 300,000 by Human Rights Watch and 600,000 by the Migration Policy Institute.[59]

The authenticity of the claims that the Chechens are a nation with a right to statehood was complicated in the Soviet period by the continuing dispute whether Chechens and Ingushes constituted one Nakhchuo nation. The realism

FIGURE 6.4. Chechnya and Ingushetia

of an independent Ichkeria was undermined by the establishment of a Joint
Chechen-Ingush ASSR and the interval of Stalinist dispossession between 1944
and 1957, when both populations were deported to Central Asia and their
republic temporarily dissolved. Uncertainties about the realism of the project
for sovereignty, doubts that all Chechens (including those who had been officials
in the Soviet and Russian Federation administrations) would be welcomed in
an independent Ichkeria, and the risk that the campaign could be captured by
others with very different projects led many potential and actual leaders of the
national-secession campaign to collaborate with Moscow.

    Thus, the campaign for an independent Ichkeria was built on a weaker con-
sensus about nationhood and on weak state institutions.[60] The leadership of the
Chechens was divided among fervent nationalists (typified by Dudaev), pragmatic collaborationists who sought to maintain ties to Russia (typified by Ruslan
Khasbulatov), village leaders unwilling to accept strong external guidance from
either of the first two groups, and radical Islamists seeking to subsume Chechnya
within a larger emirate or caliphate. Compromises with the common-state and
defections to other causes were common. The Soviet-era titular establishment
under Doku Zavgaev, the Communist Party first secretary and then Supreme
Soviet chairman, resisted calls for independence in 1990 and 1991, apparently

out of fear that this would unleash divisive forces within the Chechen-Ingush ASSR and create an opening for more-radical elites in Chechen society. Following the deposition of Zavgaev in September 1991, seizure of power by the CNC the following month, and consolidation of control in the hands of Dudaev, the anti-Dudaev forces attempted a coup in March 31, 1992.[61] The anti-Dudaev forces coalesced once again in December 1993 as the Chechen Republic Provisional Council reportedly sought to enlist the former speaker of the Russian Congress of People's Deputies (Khasbulatov) as its head. Although the council officially remained silent on the issue of sovereignty, Khasbulatov appeared to seek a return of Chechnya to the Russian Federation.[62] Still later, remnants of the pro-Russian administration and parliament, under the leadership of Zavgaev, attempted to reconvene the old parliament in the fall of 1995, to hold elections and convene a new parliament in the summer of 1996, and to reconvene the parliament in the fall of 1999. Although the campaign for independence was made in the name of their people, many traditional elites resisted the attempts of the various Chechen governments to control the villages. Some of these traditional elites opposed all statehood projects.

The growing role of radical Islamists from throughout the North Caucasus and from abroad, typified by the native-born field commander Shamil Basaev, further divided the national-secession campaign in its objectives, and even the top campaign leadership was not immune to defections to the Islamist cause: in 2007 the last president of the shadow secessionist government of Ichkeria, Dokka Umarov, declared the republic a province within the Caucasus Emirate. Alternatively, the growing influence of Wahhabis in the campaign for independence reportedly contributed to the decision to collaborate with Moscow by such Chechen nationalists as Akhmad Kadyrov, a Sufi leader appointed by Dudaev to serve as mufti of Chechnya. In 1999 Kadyrov offered to establish a new administration for Chechnya that would remain within the Russian Federation.

The institutionalization of statehood was similarly weak. The official binational nature of Chechen-Ingushetia, inherited from the Soviet era, left a difficult institutional problem to resolve at the very beginning of independence: the separation into two republics. The growing centralization of power in the hands of President Dudaev, the dissolution of parliament in April 1993, and the closing of the constitutional court two months later left Ichkeria without some of the most important institutions of statehood. Dudaev developed a personalist administration, filling positions with members of his own clan. Competing attempts by Khasbulatov, Zavgaev, and Moscow to create alternative administrations that would keep Chechnya within the Russian Federation slowed the institutionalization of statehood. Following the death of Dudaev, the secessionist regime in

January 1997 conducted presidential elections in which three significant contenders competed for office.[63] Parliamentary elections were held at the same time, but the secessionist parliament remained a shadowy body. Alternatively, after Russian victory on the battlefield, the Russian Federation called new presidential and parliamentary elections in October 2003 for a Republic of Chechnya that became a subject (constituent unit) of the federation. This established the first coherent state structure for the Chechen nation.

Consequences of Campaign Coordination for Issue Intractability

The programmatic coordination of platform populations in these frozen conflicts transformed exchanges between the national-secession campaigns and common-state governments into championships where the primary objective was to persuade an international audience rather than the other side. In all five conflicts, negotiations began soon after the cease-fires but then identified the core issue as sovereignty, on which the national-secession campaigns and common-state governments would not compromise or trade. As long as the national-secession leaders could deter defections and collaboration with the common-state, their exchanges with the common-state government ceased to be bargaining. At the same time, they learned that they could not persuade the common-state government to adjust its position or outwit it with proposals that it would misunderstand. For the national-secession campaign leaders, the primary purpose of negotiation became rallying the platform population behind the cause of independence to reinforce programmatic preemption and convincing the international community that the only viable option was independence. Thus, none of the formal negotiations following the cease-fires produced progress towards an agreement on the sovereignty issue, and most became forums to reinforce the propaganda to their platform populations, to demonstrate programmatic preemption, and to impress the international community with state-like behavior. For example, in the Russia-Chechnya negotiations, Taimaz Abubakarov, Dudaev's minister of economics and finance, reportedly observed that on both sides, "negotiations were carried out not in search of compromise but as the latest demonstration of the uncompromising nature of the sides' positions."[64] In the Georgia-Abkhazia negotiations, one "leading Abkhazian government official" reportedly admitted to interviewers that the "only reason we are participating in the Geneva discussions is because every time we sit down at the table, it is another act of recognition of our independence."[65]

The Sovereignty Issue

The national-secession programs, around which platform populations coordinate, make sovereignty the core issue that gives rise to intractability. The campaign and common-state are not simply bargaining over the allocation of decision rights, such as which government may raise taxes or determine the language to be used in classrooms. Instead, they seek an answer to the still more fundamental question of who will allocate (delegate) such decision rights, retain the right to rescind any initial delegation, and reallocate decision rights in the future. Within each sovereign jurisdiction, decision rights may be delegated to smaller or larger jurisdictions, they may be delegated to public or private sectors, but the right to make, rescind, and remake this allocation defines the jurisdiction that is sovereign. And this was the issue at the heart of these five national-secession conflicts: each side in these intractable disputes claimed to be the sovereign jurisdiction that would decide where decisions about the platform population and its homeland would be made. By extension, this question also framed a stark binary choice about their future relationship: would decisions that redefine this relationship in the future be made by domestic processes within the political organs of the common-state or by international bargaining between two sovereign states?[66] For example, at his inauguration in January 2004, President Saakashvili proclaimed, "Georgia's territorial integrity is the goal of my life" and promised to restore Georgia's sovereignty over both South Ossetia and Abkhazia before the next presidential elections in 2009. Yet the leaders of the Abkhazian and South Ossetian national-secession campaigns rejected this claim: they insisted that there could be no "vertical link" between Georgia and their states and that their future relations could be only horizontal.[67] As ICG analysts report, both Georgians and Abkhazians "consider compromise on status a red line not to be crossed."[68]

For enthusiasts, their programs, and their campaigns, sovereignty is a nondivisible value on which there can be no compromises. Proposals at the negotiating tables of the frozen conflicts envisioned that the sovereign prerogative to allocate and reallocate decision rights governing the territory and population of the secessionist region might be assigned in three different ways: (1) to the currently recognized common-states (Azerbaijan, Georgia, Moldova, and Russia), (2) to the secessionist nation-states (Abkhazia, Chechnya, Nagornyi Karabakh, South Ossetia, and Transdniestria), or (3) to new common-states above both (such as a Transcaucasian Federation). For the enthusiasts in the national-secession campaigns, only the second of these options was acceptable without conditions. The third option might be acceptable if the superior entity was not a state but an international organization such as the Commonwealth of Independent States (CIS)—but this was just option 2 with mascara. So-called compromises that national-secession campaign leaders offered on the sovereignty issue simply masked the enthusiasts' unwillingness to concede on the issue of which government would be sovereign. For example, in the Chechen conflict, Dudaev is reported to have offered a conciliatory compromise in autumn 1993: he proposed negotiations to establish "relations on the basis of principles of multilateral cooperation, friendship, and mutual help. Moreover we do not see strategically a place for the Chechen Republic outside the single economic, political and legal space which covers the current Commonwealth of Independent States."[69] Yet his proposal that Chechnya be admitted as a member of the CIS was a claim for sovereign statehood on a par with the Russian Federation; it compromised not one tittle on the issue of sovereignty. Anatol Lieven records an interview with the Chechen official ideologist Zelimkhan Yandarbiev: "When I interviewed him on 16 December 1994, a few days after the start of the war, he showed the true diplomat's skill of sounding ready for compromise on confederation with Russia, while in fact (as I discovered on reading my notes) making no concrete surrender of substance."[70] In later rounds of negotiations, Chechnya's President Aslan Maskhadov rejected Yeltsin's offer of a treaty of mutual delegation of powers, similar to the one signed with Tatarstan, and proposed instead a "full-fledged treaty" with Moscow similar to agreements signed by Russia with foreign powers.[71]

For enthusiasts in the post-Soviet frozen conflicts, sovereignty is not fungible; it cannot be traded for promises of side payments. Indeed, in the eyes of the enthusiasts those who would trade independence for personal gain, such as South Ossetia's Prime Minister Sanakoev, were traitors to the nation. In an interview, Dennis Sammut (of the London-based NGO LINKS) reflected the frustration of many outside observers of the Karabakh crisis, who felt that the parties should give up on the sovereignty issue for the sake of economic gains to cooperation. Sammut complained that Armenian and Azeri politicians failed to approach compromise in an instrumental fashion which looked for solutions that would aid the integration of both countries within Europe-Asian society.[72] Yet the parties fired back that they could not sell sovereignty for promises of economic enrichment: after rejecting the Minsk Group's latest proposal, Armenian President Ter-Petrosyan said that "however badly the people live, there are holy things, there are positions that they will never surrender under any circumstances."[73]

Deadlocked Formal Negotiations

All five conflicts were subjects of formal negotiations, although only four involved direct talks between the leaders of the national-secession campaigns and the common-state governments. As of 2016, direct negotiations between the

Nagorno-Karabakh and Azerbaijan governments had not even begun because the latter refused to recognize the NKR as a legitimate authority. Alternatively, negotiations between Armenia and Azerbaijan sponsored by the OSCE's Minsk Group began in 1992 and were frequent, but they produced no settlement. Most of the appearance of movement came from the international mediators. The Finnish and Russian co-chairs of the OSCE Minsk Group offered formal proposals for a settlement in July 1995, September 1995, and March 1996. In the next ten years, the French, Russian, and US co-chairs offered proposals in June 1997, December 1997, November 1998, and November 2007. In the first six years of the new millennium, under international sponsorship the presidents of Armenia and Azerbaijan met in Paris (March 2001), Key West (April 2001), Astana (October 2002), Prague (November 2002), Warsaw (May 2005), and Rambouillet (February 2006). In the seventeen months from May 2004 to September 2005 alone, the foreign ministers of the two countries met eleven times. Following the 2008 Georgian war, a new sense of urgency in the international community prompted more intense negotiation; the presidents of Armenia and Azerbaijan met five times in the first three quarters of 2009.[74] Yet all negotiations stalled over the issue of sovereignty. As Tony Vaux and Jonathan Goodhand note, "There has been a tendency of both sides to treat the negotiations not as an exercise in pragmatism but an affirmation of ideology. . . . Internal sovereignty therefore appears to be non-negotiable."[75]

In order to resolve the Abkhazian conflict, three years after the May 1994 Moscow Agreement the United Nations opened what came to be labeled as the Geneva Peace Process, with a coordinating council in which the Abkhazian and Georgian sides met to discuss a peace settlement. In November 1994, even before the opening of negotiations, the Abkhazians proclaimed that they would "not accept any settlement based on the idea of Abkhazia as an integral part of Georgia."[76] For the Georgians, however, recognition of the territorial integrity of Georgia within its 1991 borders was a nonnegotiable demand. And these positions defined the deadlock that continued for the next two decades. After the 2008 war the parties met in a new format, the Geneva International Discussions on the conflict in Georgia, and held twenty-eight rounds of talks by June 18, 2014. Towards the end of this series, the Abkhaz Minister of Foreign Affairs, Viacheslav Chirikba, announced that Abkhazia had not moved from its position announced in 1994.[77] After two decades of meetings in Geneva, the international mediators were still pleading with the sides "to move beyond their established positions, to listen and learn from each other."[78] The problem was that they had, in fact, listened, but they had learned that the other side would not concede on sovereignty.

In South Ossetia the 1992 Sochi Agreement established a joint control commission composed of representatives of North and South Ossetia, Russia, and Georgia, with participation by the Organization for Security and Cooperation in Europe (OSCE). The commission supervised compliance with the cease-fire and conducted negotiations over substantive issues in the conflict. Yet there was immediate deadlock on the sovereignty issue, and as a consequence, discussions stalled. Attempts to negotiate a political settlement resumed in earnest in February 1999.[79] Over the next four years, under OSCE sponsorship the parties met in Vienna/Baden (2000), Bucharest (2001), Castelo Branco (2002), and The Hague (2003), but the South Ossetian and Georgian positions hardened in these negotiations: Georgia insisted on recognition of its territorial integrity within its 1991 boundaries, and South Ossetia refused to accept subordination to the government in Tbilisi. After South Ossetia's presidential elections of December 2001 brought Eduard Kokoity to office, the South Ossetians refused even to discuss compromises on sovereignty with the Georgian government.[80]

In the Transdniestrian conflict, negotiations began under sponsorship of the OSCE but also soon deadlocked. In the 5+2 Negotiations, as the process came to be known, the international mediators seemed more interested than the parties in identifying compromises, but repeated initiatives from the international community failed to produce movement between the parties on the status issue. Thus, negotiations went through cycles of intense meetings initiated by the international mediators, followed by stalemate between the Transdniestrian and Moldovan negotiators over the issue of sovereignty. For example, the OSCE offered its first plan for a peace settlement on November 13, 1993, and negotiations followed for the next year or so but stalled in the summer of 1995. This cycle was repeated on June 17, 1996, after initialing of a new memorandum, and once again on May 8, 1997, after the parties signed the Moscow (or "Primakov") Memorandum.[81] In November 1998 and August 2000 mediators tried to reopen talks (the "Primakov Project"), but the parties refused even to negotiate. The international mediators meeting in Kiev drafted an impressive forty-two articles for a final settlement, which they codified on July 2, 2002, in the so-called Kiev Document.[82] Under pressure from the mediators, the parties held eleven rounds of negotiations but did not draw closer in their positions on the status of Transdniestria. The two sides even refused to sign a short memorandum of only a few sentences that established basic principles for a future agreement: Transdniestria rejected the idea of a federal state; Moldova rejected the idea of a state built on a "contractual basis" between two equal partners.[83] In November 2003 Russia submitted the "Kozak Memorandum," but the parties could not even agree on the premises for negotiation. In the course of two decades of deadlocked negotiations, the positions drew no closer as the participants staked their leadership on their side of the table on not losing on the sovereignty issue.[84] The 5+2 Negotiations broke up in February 2006 and did not resume for five years. The Meseberg Memorandum by the German and Russian presidents in June 2010 signaled renewed great-power interest in restarting the negotiations, which resumed in September 2011, but found agreement on further rounds of talks difficult.[85]

In the Russia-Chechnya conflict, the Russian government under Yeltsin and the Chechen government under Dudaev (1991–96) and Maskhadov (1997–99) were able to hold only intermittent meetings to search for a settlement during the periods of relative peace between November 1991 and December 1994 and again between August 1996 and October 1999. Both Dudaev and Yeltsin publicly proclaimed a desire to reach a negotiated settlement with the other side, but each subverted his own credibility as a sincere negotiator by inconsistent and opportunistic deeds and words. As Yeltsin's nationalities advisor Emil Pain reportedly observed about Dudaev, "One moment he seemed ready to make terms, the next he would take a hard line, utterly confusing Moscow policy-makers."[86] In the end it was Russian armed victory and negotiations with defectors from the Ichkeria campaign that hammered out a surrender of sovereignty to Russia, a compromise on self-government by more-pragmatic Chechen nationalists, and a settlement that lasted more than a decade.

Pseudo-bargaining

When national-secession and common-state leaders realize that the issues on the bargaining table are nondivisible and nonfungible for the other side as well as for themselves, the result is likely to be pseudo-bargaining—a mimicry of sincere negotiating. At this point offers from national-secession and common-state leaders may be represented as conciliatory and reasonable compromises but are not actually designed to move the negotiations forward. In the first quarter century of the frozen conflicts, national-secession and common-state leaders had to appear to negotiate in good faith in order to appear state-like and win support from the international community. Both sides were careful to mask their claims to sovereignty with the appearance of a serious search for compromise. (For these very reasons, spotting pseudo-bargaining can be difficult for observers. And even the parties to the negotiation may sometimes be uncertain about the willingness of the other side to concede.) The common-state and campaign leaders examined a range of options that purportedly would soften the harsh edges of the sovereignty issue. Nonetheless, these leaders were quick to look to the issue of sovereignty in any proposal and careful not to make commitments that would actually compromise on this.

In the Transdniestrian negotiations, for example, what were offered as "compromises" or "bold innovations" by each side actually barely disguised an unbending position on the binary issue of sovereignty. At the same time, each side scrutinized all proposals for their impact on sovereignty. Moldova appeared to make a significant compromise when on February 10, 2002, President Voronin outlined his government's proposal for a new Moldova constitution purportedly based on federal principles. Nonetheless, Voronin's plan demanded that Transdniestria first recognize the territorial integrity of and unity of state authority within Moldova, the enforcement of laws and normative acts of the central government throughout Moldova, and a single citizenship. Transdniestria rejected this and demanded recognition of its sovereignty and status as a member of the international community. Transdniestria offered what it also claimed was a compromise: a confederation between equal parties based on a "contractual basis." Yet in the Transdniestrian proposal, the contracting parties were coequal sovereign entities, and decision making in the confederation would be based on mutual vetoes exercised by delegates sent by (and instructed by) the member-states.[87]

In the Karabakh crisis, Azerbaijan offered "the highest degree of self-government" to the Karabakh region and hailed this as a compromise of the interests of the two sides. Yet this offer did not compromise on the fundamental issue of sovereignty because it was premised on recognition of the territorial integrity of Azerbaijan and the status of Karabakh as a constituent unit.[88] Armenia and Nagornyi Karabakh had already rejected this. They proposed, instead, what they characterized as a compromise offer: the population of the Nagorno-Karabakh Republic should decide its fate in a referendum. Azerbaijan's government looked through this seeming compromise and saw the foundational issue of sovereignty. As Azerbaijan President Ilham Aliev responded, "Azerbaijan will never participate in processes, which would envision a mechanism for legal secession of Nagorno-Karabakh from Azerbaijan. This is our unequivocal position."[89]

The governments of Armenia, Azerbaijan, and Nagornyi Karabakh were not at a loss for imaginative proposals on the status of Karabakh that appeared to offer compromises on the status issue. But the parties looked behind each proposal for its implications regarding the stark binary choice concerning sovereignty over the Karabakh platform population and the territory it claimed as its homeland. Indeed, at least seven distinct plans were on the table for the final status of Karabakh: (1) autonomy for Karabakh within Azerbaijan (the Maresca plan), (2) a new union- or common-state (such as a new Transcaucasus federation) above and linking Azerbaijan and Karabakh (the 1998 Minsk plan), (3) an intergovernmental organization (frequently referred to as a "confederation") between the two sovereign states of Azerbaijan and Karabakh, (4) condominium or joint rule over Karabakh by both Armenia and Azerbaijan (the Goble plan), (5) annexation of Karabakh by Armenia, (6) independence of Karabakh as a sovereign member of the international community, and (7) preservation of the ambiguous status quo.[90] There were numerous variants on each of these plans; some were coupled with promises of side payments. Nonetheless, after two decades the parties appeared no closer on the fundamental issue of sovereignty: the government of Azerbaijan still demanded recognition of its sovereignty over Karabakh, so only option 1 was acceptable, but the government of Karabakh still refused to be subordinated to Azerbaijan's sovereign control.

In the Abkhazia crisis several proposals were placed on the negotiating table, including (1) Abkhazian integration within a unitary Georgia, (2) Abkhazian autonomy within a unitary Georgian state, (3) Abkhazian statehood within a Georgian federation, (4) Abkhazian statehood within a new regional federation (such as Transcaucasia), (5) an Abkhaz-Georgian confederation between two sovereign states (actually an international intergovernmental organization), and (6) independence for Abkhazia. The first, second, and third options would make Abkhazia a constituent entity of Georgia, the fifth and sixth would require cooperation between two sovereign states, and the fourth imagined the creation of a new state in which both Georgia and Abkhazia would be coequal members. Georgia endorsed the first two options; Abkhazia endorsed the sixth but indicated that it might consider the fourth or fifth. For example, when direct talks were held between their presidents in 1997, the Georgians proposed broad autonomy for Abkhazia within a unitary Georgian state. Alternatively, a federal model was offered by the UN Security Council, the EU, NATO, OSCE, and the US government and was refined in 1999 in the Boden Paper. Abkhazia saw the implications for sovereignty in these proposals and refused to discuss either autonomy inside Georgia or a federation that would make Abkhazia a constituent of Georgia. Instead, at most the Abkhaz leaders offered to return to the "association agreement" that made Georgia and Abkhazia coequal members of a larger union, like that which had governed relations between March and December 1922: a Transcaucasian federation.[91] Georgia had made it clear that this was an unacceptable arrangement.[92]

Generalization of Deadlock

In these intractable conflicts, because the issue of sovereignty hung over all other issues on the table, both national-secession and common-state leaders resisted agreement on any issues that might set a precedent (even if only a symbolic precedent) for the issue of sovereignty. For example, in negotiations over the status of Karabakh, other issues such as the timing of troop withdrawals became subsumed by the status issue. After taking office in 1998, President Robert Kocharyan insisted that "the withdrawal of troops from . . . occupied territories would only begin after a guarantee had been secured that Nagorno-Karabakh would never be subordinated to Baku." After taking office in 2003, President Ilham Aliev insisted that Karabakh's status could be addressed only after withdrawal of Armenian troops.[93] Similarly, on such procedural issues as whether negotiations should be direct between the governments of Karabakh and Azerbaijan (as if they were coequal parties) and whether negotiations should begin without preconditions, the parties took stances derived from their position on the sovereignty issue.[94] ICG analysts report that "There is a growing understanding that any procedure that would pre-determine final status would by definition be unacceptable to one side or the other."[95]

For the sake of defending their positions on sovereignty, the national-secession campaign leaders were even willing to make costly sacrifices of gains that could come from cooperation on other issues. For example, in the Abkhazian and South Ossetian negotiations, the OSCE representative to the talks complained that the working group on humanitarian issues was "disrupted" because of the intractability over sovereignty.[96] Abkhazia and South Ossetia insisted that international humanitarian assistance teams enter their territories only across their open borders with Russia rather than the closed "international" border with Georgia. Alternatively, Georgia insisted that these teams enter only from Georgia as recognition of its sovereignty over the territories. Discussions of the resettlement of internally displaced persons were off the table for Abkhazia and South Ossetia because the return of Georgians might dilute their claims to nation-statehood prior to formal recognition of their sovereignty. As the Abkhazian representative reportedly told ICG interviewers, "the refugee [IDP] issue is radioactive, impossible."[97] Even the seemingly benign and mutually beneficial issue of reopening the rail lines through Abkhazia was held hostage to the dispute over sovereignty. The Georgians demanded control of the railway through Abkhazia; the Abkhazians, whose economy would benefit enormously from reopening the line, refused to give the common-state government such control within the Abkhazian homeland and added "that the moment Georgia insists on establishing its own customs control posts on Abkhaz territory, [Abkhazia] will break off negotiations immediately."[98]

The Dilemma of External Support

In the frozen conflicts, de facto statehood made an important contribution to programmatic coordination within the platform population, but sustaining de facto statehood depended on external support. This support confronted the national-secession campaign leaders with a dilemma in their attempts to demonstrate programmatic preemption to the international community. Russia's support for Abkhazia, South Ossetia, and Transdniestria and Armenia's support for

Nagornyi Karabakh permitted these national-secession campaigns to attain de facto statehood and prevented rollback by the common-state governments. Azerbaijan, Georgia, and Moldova would otherwise have been in a position to reimpose central rule and force many of the campaigns' enthusiasts underground—as Russia did in Chechnya.

De facto statehood expanded opportunities for campaign leaders to convince more pragmatists within their platform populations that independence was a real possibility and that working for reintegration promised few rewards. De facto statehood, which offered greater control over information and education institutions within the homeland, even provided many more opportunities for the campaign to convert some pragmatic members of the platform population (or their children) into enthusiasts. As the example of Chechnya underscores, without external support and de facto independence, more-pragmatic members of the platform population, including some who mixed pragmatism and enthusiasm, such as Kadyrov, were more likely to defect from the campaign and collaborate with the common-state government. External support and de facto independence did not affect the nature of programmatic coordination and its relationship to intractability but provided campaign leaders with greater resources to propagate their nation-state projects and demonstrate the realism of their action plans.[99]

Despite this operational value of external support, there was an important strategic cost. Russian and Armenian support made it more difficult for these campaigns to convince the European Union and the United States that the projects for independence were based on programmatic coordination within the platform populations and thus were the only viable options. To the consternation of the national-secession campaign leaders, the discourse in most of the international community construed these as interstate conflicts between Georgia and Russia and between Armenia and Azerbaijan rather than struggles for self-determination.[100] For example, in many world capitals there was broad acceptance of Georgia's description of Abkhazia and South Ossetia as "occupied territories," a status that has almost no legitimacy in international law, rather than states seeking self-determination, which grants some claim to legitimacy.[101] In short, for campaign leaders the strategic objective of convincing the international community to accept independence as the only viable option requires careful selection of external allies. Allies that are themselves ostracized or have little ability to induce other states to follow have more limited strategic value for the campaign and may be harmful to the strategic objective. Yet campaign leaders, such as those described in this chapter, often face a dilemma in that short-term operational objectives may be served by such allies, even though this risks the future loss of broader international support.

These close-up views of five conflicts illustrate how issue intractability is possible and more likely when campaigns for independence approach programmatic preemption. Tighter programmatic coordination comes about as a consequence of both the campaigns' persuasion and the common-states' high barriers to collaboration. Programmatic coordination gives campaign leaders both the capacity and the motivation to make no compromises with the common-state governments on the issue of sovereignty. When common-states will not concede independence, the result is transformation of formal negotiations from debates (intended to persuade the other side) into championships (in which the primary purpose of the campaign leaders is to influence an audience comprising the platform population and the international community). The exchanges at the negotiating table become a mimicry of sincere bargaining.

In the social sciences bargaining model, the intractability of conflicts associated with national-secessionism simply does not sit well. In a now standard political-economic theory of bargaining, conflict is costly, and there is always an agreement to avoid war that would leave all parties better off. The obstacles to reaching agreement are a combination of private information about one's own preferences, capabilities, and resolve, which each has an incentive to misrepresent, and difficulty in making credible commitments to implement an agreement. Yet this standard model rests on assumptions that are violated by the most significant national-secession conflicts. For example, in the standard model the prospect of zero-sum conflicts caused by the internal dynamics of the actors is discounted.[102] Yet where the national-secession campaign is well advanced in programmatic coordination, where the issues on the bargaining table have become nondivisible and nonfungible, and where debates and games have given way to championships, bargaining as described in the standard social sciences model has ceased. Disagreements over the issue of sovereignty will continue even when there are clear credible commitments to enforcement of compromises because compromise itself has become unacceptable. In many of the most-intractable national-secession disputes, there has been an abundance of proposals for innovative and creative compromises to guarantee the liberties of national-secession platform populations willing to rejoin their respective common-states. There have also been legions of volunteers who could be used in any number of creative and redundant configurations to offer near fail-safe insurance that every last clause of a compromise settlement is implemented. Yet there has been no progress whatsoever on the issue of independence that divides the national-secession campaign from the common-state. The words around the negotiating table are not designed to influence the progress of negotiations. They are the acts of cadres-dressed-as-diplomats designed to influence the platform population and international community; they have become propaganda by other means.

PROTRACTED INTENSE STRUGGLES
Reinforcing Intractability

National-secession disputes account for a substantial part of all political violence. Of the 367 episodes of civil wars from 1945 to 2010, more than two-fifths (44.7 percent) were associated with national-secession disputes, another 3.3 percent with autonomist disputes, and the remaining 52 percent with all other types of civil conflicts, such as military coups, revolutions, communist insurgencies, communal violence, and drug wars.[1] More than a quarter (27.7 percent) of all attributable acts of domestic and international terrorism between 1970 and 2010 were associated with national-secession disputes—perpetrated either in support of or in opposition to independence.[2] When national-secession campaigns turn to violence, it tends to be more protracted than violence associated with other causes. Between 1945 and 2010, episodes of national-secession civil wars tended to last about 21.9 percent longer than episodes of all other types of civil wars. And national-secessionist civil wars are more likely to recur: the rate of recurrence—that is, the number of subsequent episodes divided by the number of first episodes—was about 24.1 percent higher in national-secession than in other types of conflicts.[3]

Nevertheless, the conditions under which protracted intensity is possible and sensible for a national-secession campaign are uncommon. Fewer than two-fifths of all significant national-secession campaigns (only 66 of 171, or 38.6 percent) were ever parties to civil wars that claimed at least 25 lives in a single year between 1945 and 2010. Only a quarter of the campaigns (43 of 170, or 25.3 percent) were associated with terrorist attacks between 1970 and 2010.

The question examined in this chapter is precisely focused: under what conditions are national-secession campaign leaders more likely to mount protracted intense violence? Intensity can be measured by the growing costs inflicted on others and conceived of as a spectrum of actions, such as peaceful protest and demonstrations, occupations of public spaces, boycotts and embargoes, vetoes or nullification of central-government acts by regional governments, terrorist attacks, guerrilla warfare, or large-scale military operations. These actions may take place in a cabinet meeting, a constitutional assembly, polling stations, the streets of the capital, or a rural battlefield. Intensity is one measure of a campaign's surge capacity, in which leaders call on activists within the staff to expand their action or on the participatory reserve to begin action. It may be manifest in tactics other than violence: even a peaceful campaign can become more intense with the rising costs it inflicts on others, such as boycotts and embargoes. Nonetheless, the most visible and widely studied form of escalating intensity is violence, and that is the focus of this chapter. Violence inflicts outsized costs, attracts broad attention, and has relatively well-established measures.

Protraction refers to the length of time that a campaign is able to sustain activity. For example, the Kawthoolei campaign among the Karens engaged in protracted intense struggle against Burma/Myanmar for more than half a century: between Burma's independence in 1948 and 2010, the campaign sustained a war that claimed at least twenty-five lives in fifty-seven of sixty-three years. Alternatively, the Euskadi campaign among the Basques of Spain is much older but has been only sporadically intense: beginning in the 1890s under Sabino Arana, the Basque campaign survived well over a century. It engaged in a year-long war against the Francoist army of Spain in 1936–37 and a terrorist surge beginning in 1970, but this conflict claimed twenty-five or more lives in only eleven of sixty-six years after World War II.[4] Whereas the Euskadi campaign has been more protracted, the intensity of the Kawthoolei campaign has been more protracted. This chapter explores the latter phenomenon: protracted intense violence.

The empirical analysis in this chapter does not ask why violence happens but why national-secession campaign leaders choose to engage in protracted intense violence. This issue has four important implications. The violence studied in this chapter concerns only that associated with national-secession conflicts, not the broader and more-diffuse categories of "ethnic wars" or "self-determination wars." The campaign must engage in protracted intense struggle: the initiator of an episode may be either the campaign or the common-state, but the campaign must engage in violence to be considered here; one-sided protracted intensity by the common-state, such as a campaign of genocide without resistance, is not included in this analysis. The analysis focuses on the choice of the campaign leaders to undertake protracted intense struggle and offers no explanation for why common-state governments choose to engage in violence. (This requires a very different analysis and another book.) And the analysis is not on the timing of the outbreak of episodes of violence but on the relative capacity and inclination of different campaigns to engage in protracted intense struggle. These constraints are longer-term conditions that affect the expectations about the future rather than short-term changes. In short, the empirical analysis seeks to identify the conditions under which leaders of campaigns focused on national secession choose to engage in a struggle that is both more intense and more protracted.

The empirical analysis once again focuses on structural conditions that serve as cues and constraints (obstacles and opportunities) in the campaign leaders' calculations. As in previous chapters, the hypotheses describing the tactical choice of violence are deduced from extensions of the micro-level model that assumes a strategic decision maker or reasoning problem solver who chooses tactics with limited information and uncertainty about the intentions of the rest of the platform population. The strategically minded decision maker balances the costs and benefits of using violence under the constant strategic and operational constraints identified in chapters 1 and 2 and under the varying constraints of campaign development described in chapter 3. Protracted surges of violence are one of the activation phases described in chapter 3. The chief constraint on the choice to initiate a surge is the state of programmatic coordination, described in chapter 4.

Most of the conditions that predict protracted intensity are quite similar to the conditions that predict campaign significance. That is precisely the point made by programmatic theory. Protracted intensity is less common when programmatic coordination is less advanced. In the establishment or early capacitation stages, campaigns may engage in violence, but this is likely to be small-scale and sporadic. It may include showcase acts designed to recruit more staffers and to begin the association phase. To conduct intense violence over a protracted period, however, requires the coordination of a more developed campaign and the expectation that programmatic coordination will be reinforced rather than destroyed by a protracted intense struggle. This is possible only after a campaign is well along in capacitation and association stages, enabling it to sustain such a struggle, to minimize defections under the mounting costs of the struggle, and to reap and consolidate the propaganda dividend from violence.

Chapter 8 continues this discussion but turns to common alternative explanations for violence. As in the analysis of campaign significance, the programmatic account does not dismiss the findings of earlier studies of ethnic or "self-determination" violence, which have tended to focus on either motivations or opportunities. Programmatic theory treats these as complements to the analysis in the current chapter. Nonetheless, as is explained more fully in chapter 8, these show much weaker relationships with protracted intense struggle by national-secession campaigns.

The Programmatic Account of Violence

Programmatic coordination is both the purpose of protracted intense struggles and the chief constraint on the capacity for a protracted intense struggle. A national-secession campaign employing the strategy of programmatic coordination uses increasing intensity such as violence to achieve programmatic preemption. As a continuation of propaganda by other means, escalating intensity is a tactic to expand and reinforce coordination among members of a platform population, to demonstrate this coordination, and to lead the international community to conclude that independence is the only viable option. Limited by the campaign's operational weakness, strategically minded campaign leaders recognize that protracted intensity is unlikely to achieve armed victory over the common-state government. Instead, campaign leaders sustain intense struggles first and foremost to expand enthusiasm for the goal of independence and expectations of its practicality among members of the platform population and to deprive the international community of any hope that holding the common-state together is a viable option.[5]

Programmatic coordination is also a constraint on the ability to sustain this struggle. Conducting a protracted intense struggle requires a campaign that is already well advanced in its programmatic coordination. Attempting to stage and sustain protracted surges of intensity is prudent only when campaign leaders are reasonably certain that the call to action will not reveal a serious lack of support for the cause but instead will clearly demonstrate the resistance of broad segments of the platform population to compromise with the common-state government on the issue of independence. Sporadic acts of violence are possible in earlier stages of campaign development and can be prudent investments in fuller programmatic coordination. Alternatively, protracted intense struggle is possible and prudent only when campaign leaders can count on the unity of the leadership and staff of the common nation-state project, a following within the platform population that conceives of itself as a nation with a right to a sovereign state, and pragmatic supporters who believe that independence will solve their particular problems and view violence as moving the campaign closer to its strategic goal of independence. Where these elements of programmatic coordination are stronger, violence is more likely to be intense *and* protracted *and* focused on the common goal of national independence.[6]

In the strategy of programmatic coordination, formulated in the seminal work of Vladimir I. Lenin, a campaign must not bind itself "to any one particular form of struggle," such as parliamentary struggle, political demonstrations, mass political strikes, partial military revolts, partial peasant revolts, or insurrection. He rejects any "attempt to answer yes or no to the question whether any particular means of struggle should be used, without making a detailed examination of the concrete situation of the given movement at the given stage of its development. . . ."[7]

Organizational-Mobilizational Constraints on the Use of Violence

For strategically minded national-secession campaign leaders constrained by the campaign's operational weakness, the primary value of violence is campaign health: the most important goal of violence is building and sustaining support from other leaders, staff, participatory reserve, and platform population.[8] The traditional focus in academic and policy analyses (noted in chapter 3) emphasizes that violence can strengthen organization and mobilization: violent bank robberies may appropriate funds, raids on poorly guarded armories may yield weapons, and guerrilla dragoons may intimidate village youths into enlisting. Specific actions may also be training or dress rehearsals for a surge when the opportunity for independence arises. At the same time, emphasizing the organizational half of Lenin's formulation, this traditional focus highlights the resources of a campaign as important constraints on the choice of protracted intense violence. Coordinated, sustained, and large-scale violence, such as long-term terror, rebellion, or civil war, requires extensive organizational capacity (personnel, materiel, and funds). A tightly disciplined staff is required to mobilize and sustain surges of participation, to deter defections by the less resolute, to broadcast the link of the action to the program of independence, to institutionalize the support that the actions inspire, and to counterretaliate against common-state retaliation.

When viewed from this organizational perspective, protracted intense struggle is expensive and thus beyond the organizational resources of most campaigns. For example, ETA's First Assembly created "*liberados,* full-time activists who lived in clandestinity and devoted all their energies to the organization. Such a development substantially increased ETA's need for money."[9] The activists who could not earn a living in the open economy had to be housed and fed and their families provided for; they also had to be trained and armed. ETA was able to appropriate scarce resources for these purposes but lacked the organizational capacity to reap the benefits of its violence, institutionalize these gains, and prevent them from accruing to other groups and causes. Indeed, Jose Maria Escubi, one of the leaders of ETA in the late 1960s, broke with the organization in 1970 when he became "critical not of armed struggle as such, but of continuing a campaign of violence when ETA lacked the political and organizational capacity to benefit from it."[10] In short, using protracted intensity to further programmatic coordination is often beyond the organizational capacity of even relatively strong campaigns, and to attempt such surges would quickly reveal this limited capacity. Even when the campaign has the organizational resources to undertake a protracted intense struggle, the tactic may have high opportunity costs—forgone opportunities for programmatic coordination as personnel, material, and fiscal resources are diverted to violence and its support. And without the additional capacity to institutionalize the support for the campaign created by violence, the campaign gains little lasting benefit.

In the traditional analyses, any campaign leader considering violence must calculate the impact of violence on organizational-mobilizational capacity: more-intense acts, and violence in particular, may unleash common-state retaliation that disrupts the campaign's leadership and staff and sets the campaign back in fulfilling its operational objectives by months or years. The first attempt of ETA at armed struggle occurred in July 1961, when a plot to derail a train carrying Spanish veterans to a memorial celebration of Franco's victory in the civil war brought mass arrests that left ETA's leadership and staff "paralyzed and dismantled." Each subsequent action exposed the support network to retribution, so many auxiliaries had to flee to France. The retribution had "disastrous consequences for those involved in propaganda, cultural, or educational work." Furthermore, "The priority given to armed struggle meant that such people [cadres] were never able to develop the consistent work in the factories to which ETA-V was, in theory, committed."[11] The retribution brought constant turnover in leadership at the top so that ETA was commonly under the leadership of inexperienced revolutionaries. The crackdown after the turn to violence sent established leaders such as Federico Krutwig into exile in 1968 to be replaced by younger and less experienced leaders, but these were arrested in 1969: "The organization went through two entire generations of leaders in less than three years. . . . Thus the new generation that now was forced to take command of the organization in Spain after the arrests of 1968 and 1969 was even younger and more untested and inexperienced than its predecessors."[12]

Nothing is wrong with this traditional analysis, which focuses on organization—as far as it goes. Nonetheless, it misses half—and arguably the more important "ideological" half—of the model of "ideological and organizational" development in the strategy developed by Lenin.

The Contribution of Violence to Programmatic Coordination

In the strategy of programmatic coordination, the chief operational objective of violence is building toward programmatic preemption, and the chief constraint on launching protracted intense struggle is the current and expected state of programmatic coordination before and after that launch. Certainly, strategically minded campaign leaders choose different tactics and choose to initiate surges of activity to fulfill such operational tasks as building and maintaining the unity of the leadership and staff, expanding and sustaining the readiness of the participatory reserve, shifting more of the platform population from latent support to participatory reserve and from reserve to activists, and preparing the passive platform population to accept independence.[13] More fundamentally, they choose tactics to convince each of these constituent parts of the platform population of the authenticity and realism of the campaign's goal. Thus, protracted intensity is a means to establish and maintain the campaign's program as the only viable solution in the eyes of the platform population and international community. Even when choosing a direct attack on the government, as the counterinsurgency manual of the US Joint Chiefs of Staff notes, "insurgent military action is secondary and subordinate to a larger end. . . ."[14] And at the operational level, that end is to create and to reinforce programmatic preemption, positioning the platform population as the undeniable future source of sovereignty in its own nation-state when opportunities for independence arise.

In this strategy, violent acts can be some of the most visible and persuasive cues seen by many members of the platform population and interpreted as common evidence of the authenticity and realism of the program for independence. Demonstrative blows against the common-state may include destruction of its symbols, assassination of its officials, or attacks on its centers of power. These acts seek to create or keep alive the belief among leaders, staffers, participatory reserve, and the larger platform population that the struggle for independence is making progress against the common-state, to keep activists engaged to prevent them from drifting away, and to make a credible commitment to the platform population that the campaign leadership will not compromise with the common-state government. In the context of a campaign, leaders choose greater violence in order to create or reinforce among intellectuals, staff, participatory reserves, and platform population the expectation that the program for independence will offer the only viable option when the opportunity for independence arises. Thus, in choosing a surge of greater violence, campaign leaders must carefully calculate the response of the different constituent parts of the platform population.

Very often the most immediate operational objectives of campaign leaders concern the impact of violence on the programmatic coordination among leaders and staffers. Campaign leaders are more likely to be enthusiasts, but staffers may include some expressionists, so the leaders often use violence in three different ways to influence other leaders and staffers.[15] Violence recruits new leaders and staffers by creating expectations that the campaign offers opportunities for enthusiasts to contribute to a worthy cause and for expressionists to engage in action. Violence can maintain programmatic coordination within the existing leadership and staff by reinforcing enthusiasm and creating expectations of future expressive opportunities.[16] Violence can increase the credibility of the leadership in the eyes of the staff by providing a signal of the leaders' enthusiasm and commitment to the project.

Nonetheless, in the long period of programmatic coordination, interactions between leaders and staffers are constrained by their expectations about the response of the platform population, which may comprise proportionately fewer enthusiasts or expressionists and more pragmatists. In this broader context, campaign leaders may use violence to serve five additional operational objectives in pursuit of programmatic preemption. Violence can be a cue to the platform population of both the authenticity of the claim that a nation is seeking independence and the realism of its action plan to achieve independence. Even sporadic acts of violence can be dramatic cues that can make a particular national-secession program prominent for members of the platform population and stand out from alternatives as a basis for coordination. Visibly violent acts provide the platform population evidence that others beyond one's small circle of intimate confidants are committed to the goal of independence and are willing to take costly actions on behalf of the cause of independence. And they are cues that many will expect other members of the platform population to see in a similar light. For example, for atomized supporters who had been dispersed and isolated from one another in post-occupation East Timor, violent acts provided information that other supporters had survived and remained committed to the cause of independence. In the words of Damien Kingsbury, "Its simple existence was proof enough that its claim existed and was able to continue to exist." And in this way, violent acts became "a beacon and the focal point for all facets of the independence movement, both within East Timor and abroad...."[17] More intense, coordinated, and protracted violence may heighten expectations that independence is a realistic goal that the campaign has the means to achieve. In Turkey, according to David Romano, a series of violent acts "went a long way towards negating a Kurdish psychology of impotence...."[18]

Violence on behalf of the cause, particularly as it becomes more intense and protracted, reinforces the realism of the program by providing evidence that the campaign leaders are able to act like a state—by protecting or at least avenging the population. In East Timor the Revolutionary Front for an Independent Timor Leste (Fretilin) and its associated armed force (Falintil) created safe havens for some of its platform population, and Falintil established its reputation as the defender and avenger of the Timorese against the occupying Indonesians. It deterred Indonesian attacks by threatening retaliation. And when it could not deter Indonesian attacks, Falintil at least demonstrated to the members of the platform population that their suffering had not gone unpunished: "Falintil's attacks against the Indonesian military and its agents were quick and usually brutal, and often carried the message that to harm an East Timorese was to expect revenge."[19] In ETA's struggle against Spain the retaliatory assassination of police chief Melitón Manzanas in August 1968, according to John Sullivan, was "popular among large sections of the population, as it demonstrated ETA's power to strike back at the oppressor of the Basque people."[20] Acting like a state also means punishing spies, subversives, and collaborators as traitors to the nation. After 1985, following Turkey's introduction of the village guard system that offered material incentives to young Kurds, "the PKK reasoned that it had to demonstrate in no uncertain terms the heavy price of supporting the Turkish state."[21] The PKK presented itself as effectively fulfilling the duties of a state that was decisively attacking an illegitimate, foreign, occupying power and those "traitors" who collaborated with the enemy.

Violence can be a tool by which campaign leaders make more credible the promised link between the goal of independence and the resolution of the many specific grievances of individual constituencies. This is particularly important in reassuring the pragmatists, to whom the campaign leaders can send costly signals of their commitment to specific policies once independence is achieved. For example, the Turkish Kurdistan campaign used violence in villages to redistribute land to its followers taken from "certain hated Kurdish landowners, aghas, and tribal chiefs."[22] This was a down payment on the socialist society that the PKK promised to build in an independent Kurdistan.

Violence can also be a costly commitment to the platform population, and particularly its pragmatists, that the leaders and staff will not compromise with the common-state government and abandon supporters who commit to the cause. Acts of violence, particularly if the common-state government labels these as "unforgivable" and swears to prosecute their authors, make more credible the campaign leaders' promise to the platform population that the leaders will see the struggle through to the end. And these acts that tie the leaders' hands give pragmatists evidence that their own investments of time, talents, and treasure are less risky.

Finally, violence can create physical and psychological space necessary to propagate the program and build the campaign. Base areas created in a civil war, such as the proto-states created by the Eritreans and Kachins, are zones for continuous propagation of the national-secession program. Sometimes this creates safe havens only at night, as was the case in many Basque and Kurdish villages. Nevertheless, each night the village becomes a zone in which communities can meet and cadres can explain the cause of independence while the common-state government is absent. In the areas of Turkish Kurdistan where the common-state authorities withdrew from the villages each night, the secessionists created a moonlight secessionist state to fill the gap of authority with nighttime Kurdish schools, people's tribunals, and police.[23] The nighttime propagation by words and deeds continued to bind many in the platform population to the campaign even after the sun arose each morning.

Programmatic Coordination as a Constraint on the Use of Violence

The reciprocal relationship of violence to programmatic coordination as both purpose and constraint influences how strategically minded campaign leaders use violence. National-secession leaders should call for protracted intense struggle only when they expect that the call to arms on behalf of the cause of independence will be seen by the platform population as both proper (on behalf of an authentic goal) and prudent (a realistic step to that goal). This expectation influences the leaders' calculation of whether they can mobilize sufficient participation in violence to make it intense and protracted. Campaign leaders must be able to rely on individual staffers and individual members of the participatory reserve who will risk much in the struggle. According to the strategy of programmatic coordination, this is possible only when staffers and participatory reserve subscribe to the authenticity of the program's goal and realism of its tactics. For example, Peter Paret and John W. Shy stress that guerrillas must be energized "by some powerful idea—love of country, hatred of the foreigner, envy of the rich landowner. . . . [I]t requires an element of individual conviction to compel men to take part in this most punishing kind of combat."[24] The campaign leaders must also be able to rely on the larger platform population's support for independence in the face of mounting losses. As Mao argues, "Guerrilla warfare must fail . . . if its political objectives do not coincide with the aspirations of the people. . . ."[25] An Algerian nationalist leader engaged in the protracted armed struggle with France reportedly observed that "it is impossible to win the other battles if the ideological battle with the people has not been won. . . ."[26]

On the other hand, according to the strategy of programmatic coordination, a protracted intense struggle is prudent only when campaign leaders calculate that it will reinforce, broaden, or deepen programmatic coordination in the platform population. The surge is sensible only if it leaves the campaign and platform population more unified. Strategically minded national-secession campaign leaders must consider at least three ways in which the attempt to conduct a protracted intense struggle may have just the opposite effect.

Where programmatic coordination is weaker, violence can open up sharp divisions within the leadership and staff over the campaign's action plan and alienate members of the participatory reserve and platform population, leading some to defect from the campaign. The impact may be particularly pronounced among the pragmatists, such as entrepreneurs and politicians, who must be brought on board at the critical moment of the surge to demonstrate a united front for independence.[27] Even in the Euskadi and Northern Irish campaigns, where some "respectable" pragmatists in the platform population were willing to condone violence, a protracted campaign brought a backlash. In the larger Euskadi campaign, ETA's use of violence drove other Basque parties further away. By 1988, after two decades of the ETA surge, most major Basque parties came together to condemn ETA violence: the Ajuria-Enea Pact opened a decade in which all Basque parties except ETA's own Herri Batasuna (HB) drew "a line between so-called 'democratic' and 'violent' political actors, evinced by the marginalization of HB from Basque political life." ETA's return to violence yet again in the late 1990s led to a further precipitous fall in HB vote share.[28]

Where programmatic coordination is weaker, violence, once unleashed, may be difficult for campaign leaders to control and may change the character of a campaign as it becomes dominated by expressionists. Violence aids recruitment, but it recruits a particular type (the expressionist described in chapter 4) who demands more violence and may swell the parts of the campaign that seek to transform the campaign into just a violent struggle. For example, "Armed struggle enabled ETA to appeal to young men who would not have committed themselves to study, discussion or routine political work, but responded to ETA's call to arms."[29] These young men demanded more opportunities to engage in violence, which attracted still more of their type. Indeed, the "third worldist" strategy of Krutwig envisioned just this effect on the campaign: ETA's objective was to use terrorism to unleash in Euskadi a guerrilla war similar to what had achieved independence for Algeria. The third worldists attracted to ETA by Krutwig's strategy "were impatient to launch the armed struggle immediately."[30] More terrorism became necessary just to keep these recruits on board. And the expressionists directed this violence against widening circles of the Basques—alienating these members of the platform population from the cause of independence.

And where programmatic coordination is weaker, intense surges can be costly to a campaign's credibility by revealing the hollowness of claims of imminent independence and undermining the perception of programmatic realism. When ETA terrorism turned out not to be "the first steps in a guerrilla war, where the people would themselves take up arms," continued violence revealed this action plan to be unrealistic and fostered skepticism about the entire Euskadi independence program.[31]

Campaign leaders calculating the benefits and risks of launching violence may also include in the equation a more personal consideration: even when more intense action, and particularly violence, benefits the campaign, it may not benefit the leaders who choose violence. For example, should Spain dissolve or tire of the struggle with Basque nationalism and permit Euskadi to go its own way, the likely beneficiary would not be the most militant nationalists in ETA but the moderates in the PNV.

Similarly, in Northern Ireland some leaders in the Irish Republican Army real-ized that the armed struggle for independence was benefiting the more-peaceful parties, such as the Social Democratic and Labour Party (SDLP). As the SDLP presciently observed in the mid-1970s, "The Provisional IRA can achieve nothing by carrying on their campaign of violence but they can achieve almost anything they desire by knocking it off."[32] Indeed, the mounting evidence of these costs of violence came together to persuade many IRA leaders to shift their tactical empha-sis away from persuasion by violence to an "argumentative-electoral" struggle. It had long been clear that the Irish nation in the North, even if fully mobilized, would not defeat the United Kingdom.[33] And the experience of the protracted intense struggle also revealed that violence was actually stiffening British resolve rather than inducing London to retreat from its last toehold in Ireland.[34] But the IRA also learned that electoral support for Sinn Fein—a barometer of progress toward programmatic preemption—was dwindling as a consequence of its asso-ciation with the crises that the IRA was creating. As a tactic to achieve program-matic preemption, violence was proving counterproductive. In the 1990s the IRA did, in fact, "knock it off." By the 2011 elections to the Northern Ireland Assem-bly, after adopting a parliamentary rather than armed struggle, the IRA's Gerry Adams emerged as leader of Northern Ireland's second-largest party (Sinn Fein, behind the Democratic Unionist Party), which eclipsed the previously dominant SDLP within the "Irish" community of the North and emerged as a major par-ticipant in negotiations over the future of its nation and homeland.

Predicting Protracted Intense Struggle

In identifying conditions under which strategically minded national-secession campaign leaders are most likely to undertake a protracted intense struggle, pro-grammatic theory begins from the perspective of the campaign leaders. Yet a leader's assessment that it is prudent to undertake such a struggle must first of all estimate the expected response from other leaders, the staff, and participatory reserve. In turn, the response of each of these constituent parts of the campaign is conditioned on the expected response of the broader platform population. The leaders must gauge not only the willingness of each constituent part to partici-pate, which is an assessment of the current state of programmatic coordination, but also the impact of protracted intense struggle on the continuing coordina-tion of each of these constituents and further coordination of still more constitu-ents behind the goal of independence.

In this operational assessment, campaign leaders must first take stock of the authenticity and realism of the program for independence in the eyes of members of the platform population. Yet the responses of the platform population to calls for violence and reactions to violence itself depend on attitudes that are typically difficult for leaders to measure before the event. Members of the platform population may not even be able to predict accurately their own response to a protracted intense struggle because their future responses may be conditioned on their individual, constantly updated expectations about the responses of others in the platform population. Each may have reasons to disguise her or his true sentiments about a protracted intense struggle and to suspect that other members of the platform population also have reason to keep this information private. Instead, leaders and members of the platform population (as well as analysts) must rely on observable cues that provide low-cost "evidence" of the expected state of programmatic coordination.

Programmatic theory predicts that the more these cues suggest that members of the platform population will see the doctrine's claim to nationhood as authentic and the action plan for statehood as realistic, the more likely it is that a campaign will engage in a protracted violent struggle. The statistical estimations of the strength of these relationships reported in this chapter involve the 171 significant campaigns. These are already distinguished from other campaigns by the cues to authenticity and realism identified in chapter 5. Variation among these significant campaigns on the same variables represents still stronger cues to programmatic coordination. These very strong cues provide the "evidence" on which campaign leaders decide whether violence is likely to further programmatic coordination. They are also the most powerful predictors that analysts should look for in identifying campaigns most likely to engage in protracted intense violence.

Protracted Intensity

The primary index of protracted intensity used in this analysis (and described more fully in the appendix to this chapter) rises as either the intensity or the protraction of violence increases and reaches its maximum value when violence is both most protracted and most intense. Intensity is measured by the annual deaths associated with each secessionist conflict. The index includes battlefield- and terrorism-related deaths. Protraction is measured by the number of years that violence continues. Multiplying intensity by protraction yields an index that ranges from 0, representing no years with violence, and 100, representing violence with the highest level of casualties every year. Between 1970 and 2006 the average score for all 170 national-secession campaigns stood at 9.2. As figure 7.1 and table 7.1 show, almost two-thirds of the twenty campaigns with the most

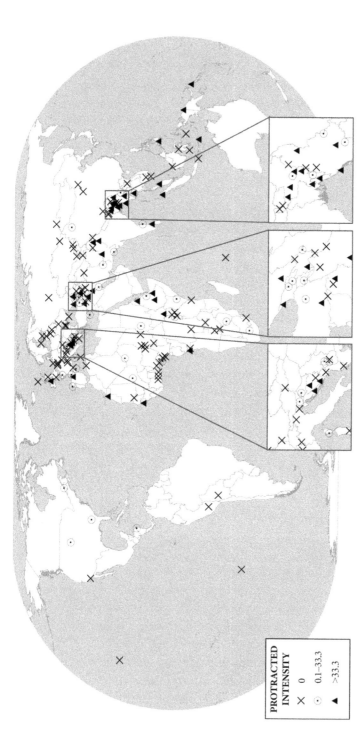

FIGURE 7.1. Protracted intensity in national-secession campaigns, 1970–2006. The symbol for each campaign's index of protracted intensity is centered on the capital or largest city within the territory claimed by the nation-state project.

PROTRACTED
INTENSITY

✕ 0

⊙ 0.1–33.3

▲ >33.3

TABLE 7.1. Twenty most-protracted intense struggles by national-secession campaigns, 1970–2006

CAMPAIGN (COMMON-STATE)	INDEX OF PROTRACTED INTENSITY	CAMPAIGN (COMMON-STATE)	INDEX OF PROTRACTED INTENSITY
Eritrea (Ethiopia)	79.7	Northern Ireland (UK)	47.6
South Sudan (Sudan)	67.2	Kachinland (Myanmar)	42.6
Bangsamoro (Philippines)	65.5	Kashmir (India)	41.9
Kawthoolei (Myanmar)	63.2	Oromiyaa (Ethiopia)	41.6
Ichkeria (Russia)	62.5	Tripura (India)	39.7
Tamil Eelam (Sri Lanka)	55.9	Euskadi (Spain)	38.3
Shan States (Myanmar)	51.9	Bangabhumi (Bangladesh)	36.1
Timor Leste (Indonesia)	50.4	Manipur (India)	34.6
Kurdistan (Iraq)	48.3	Ogaadeen (Ethiopia)	34.1
Kurdistan (Turkey)	47.8	Western Sahara (Morocco)	31.5

protracted intense struggles were located in the East India-Bangladesh-Myanmar area, the northern Middle East and Caucasus, and East Africa.

Two supplementary indicators of intense struggle are also used as dependent variables. These permit a check on the primary estimation with panel data (that is, data with separate observations for each year as well as each campaign). The first is an indicator of at least twenty-five battle- or terrorism-related deaths in a single year from 1970 to 2006. The second is an indicator of at least twenty-five battle-related deaths from 1945 to 2010. Unlike the first index, these two dependent variables indicate intensity in a single year but not its protraction.

Table 7.2 shows the predicted change in the index of protracted intensity under different constraints as each varies from its minimum to its maximum value. Table 7.3 shows changes in the probability of a *new* episode of civil war involving at least twenty-five deaths in any year as each constraint varies from its minimum to its maximum value. (In table 7.3, years of *continuing* violence are dropped.) Although the effects of more than thirty independent variables were estimated in different specifications of the equations, these tables show only constraints found to be statistically significant at the .05 level in tables 7A.3 and 7A.5. The details of the estimation procedures are described in the appendix to this chapter.

TABLE 7.2. Change in index of protracted intensity, 1970–2006, with maximum variation of each independent variable

	PREDICTED CHANGE IN INDEX	PERCENTAGE CHANGE	CUE OR CONSTRAINT
Exclusion from participation	22.365	531.3	Realism
Constitutional exclusion	20.105	952.6	Realism
Platform size	17.818	—[a]	Realism
Governmental exclusion	8.275	392.1	Realism
Statehood	6.872	99.1	Authenticity

Note: Based on the OLS regression results in table 7A.3 (estimation 1).

[a] At minimum value this predicts an index of zero (slightly negative).

TABLE 7.3. Changes in probabilities of new civil war, 1945–2010, with maximum variation in each cue and constraint

	CHANGE IN PROBABILITY	PERCENTAGE CHANGE IN PROBABILITY	CUE OR CONSTRAINT
Constitutional exclusion	5.004	553.99	Realism
Exclusion from participation	2.843	420.33	Realism
Statehood	0.989	132.71	Authenticity
Balance of coercive capacity[a]	0.813	219.10	Tactical
Weak common-state regime	0.777	86.11	Tactical

Notes: Probabilities are estimated from the logit equation in table 7A.5 using the Clarify procedure. Other variables are set to their means as identified variable varies between minimum to maximum values, except:

[a] Identified variable ranges from maximum to minimum value.

Programmatic Authenticity and Realism

The likelihood of protracted intense conflict is greater if there are stronger cues to the authenticity and realism of the program for independence. One powerful cue is an existing titular-state on the national homeland proposed for independence: this may come in the form of a segment-state (such as the Kurdistan Autonomous Region or the Estonian SSR) or a de facto state (such as Northern Cyprus or Abkhazia).[35] Expectations of greater credibility (compared to projects associated with states that exist only in the imagination) make it easier and more prudent for campaign leaders to undertake a protracted intense struggle. Hence, extending the logic of the Statehood Precedence Hypothesis advanced in chapter 5,

> **The Titular-Statehood Hypothesis.** *The likelihood of protracted intense conflict is greater if the nation-state proposed by the national-secessionist program is based on an existing segment-state or de facto state.*

In many cases, these are already nation-states that lack only sovereign independence. Indeed, in the statistical estimations, segment-states and de facto states are associated with substantially more protracted intense struggles: on the index of protracted intense struggle, as shown in table 7.2, national-secession campaigns associated with either form of statehood scored 6.9 points higher than those without statehood. The score for the average campaign without statehood was 6.9, but with statehood the score was double this, at 13.8. From 1945 to 2010, as shown in table 7.3, the probability that a campaign would become party to a new episode of civil war was more than double (133 percent *more* likely) for campaigns with statehood in the previous year.[36]

In the programmatic account of violence, this close relationship between an existing segment-state or de facto state and violence is easy to explain: national-secession campaigns with segment-states or de facto states (compared to campaigns without them) typically achieve and expect greater programmatic coordination. The simple existence of the state, even if the secessionists do not occupy leadership positions within it, is a powerful cue to authenticity and realism and thus typically coordinates and sustains expectations throughout the associated platform population. The existence of the state, its flag, its capital, and its political institutions makes it easier for campaign cadres to persuade the platform population, including its pragmatists, that independence for the nation-state is a practical possibility.[37] Moreover, as illustrated in chapter 6, segment-states and de facto states are able to expend considerable resources in propagating the idea of nationhood for the titular population and its link to the status of the homeland. When secessionists control the segment-state, they wield still more means to sustain the campaign and command greater surge capacity even through the longueur.[38]

Common-state governments are aware of this situation and wary of the threat that it can pose. In China, for example, Warren Smith reports that "the brief experiment with limited autonomy in the early 1980s had convinced the [Chinese Communist Party] that any autonomy, cultural or political, would allow a revival of Tibetan nationalism and Tibetan demands for ever greater autonomy up to and including independence."[39] The resistance of Georgian nationalists to demands for segment-states within Georgia for Abkhazia and South Ossetia reflected their own experience prior to December 1991 in using their own segment-state within the USSR to advance the Georgian national-secession campaign. In the hands of determined secessionists, a segment-state or de facto state can transform membership in the campaign from voluntary to mandatory. The segment-state or de facto state can develop strong sanctioning capacity to mobilize large-scale, coordinated, and sustained or recurrent participation in collective action, including violence. It gives leaders the capacity to compel members of the platform population to break their ties to the common-state government or leave the homeland, so it reduces the threat of collaboration. Thus, segment or de facto statehood is a key cue for leaders deciding whether the use of violence on behalf of a nation-state project would inspire other leaders, staffers, reservists, and even members of the larger platform population to rally around the goal of independence.

Appreciating the importance of statehood, campaigns often try to transform themselves into states within a state—even when the state is informal.[40] Following this model, when the Eritrean secessionists (EPLF) were able to control larger areas, they created the classic base areas with

> an array of administrative departments, workshops and medical facilities. From the front's training establishments came the frontline units, the "barefoot doctors" who would range far and wide, the armed propaganda squads operating in the villages, the guards for Ethiopian prisoners of war, the engineering teams constructing ground roads from Sahel through the highlands, and the mass administration responsible for activities ranging from political education to land reform, agricultural activities and veterinary advice for pastoralists.[41]

Similarly, when the Tamil Tigers (LTTE) controlled the Jaffna Peninsula of Sri Lanka, it created a state to collect taxes, to regulate trade, to police and provide justice, and to maintain public services.[42] Even these informal states within states make more credible the claim to statehood in the eyes of the platform population and move the campaign a giant step closer to programmatic preemption.

Another constraint affecting programmatic realism is the size of the platform population.[43] As noted in chapter 5, smaller platforms make for less realistic nation-state projects. Hence, continuing the logic of the Proposed State Viability Hypothesis introduced in chapter 5,

---

The Independence Viability Hypothesis. *The likelihood of protracted intense conflict is greater if the platform population is comparable in size to the population of existing sovereign states.*

As the results in table 7.2 show, the difference between the smallest and largest platform populations is almost 18 percentage points. Nonetheless, the robustness of the finding on the Independence Viability Hypothesis should not be overstated. (As shown in tables 7A.2 through 7A.5 in the appendix to this chapter, the variable "platform size" is statistically significant in less than half of the estimations.) Moreover, as shown in figure 7.2, the size constraint is most important for campaigns on behalf of boutique nation-states based on very small platform populations: there is a sharp drop-off of protracted intense struggle for platform populations below 830 thousand, where the predicted index falls below 10. Alternatively, compared to platform populations at 830 thousand, this index is only another 7 points higher for platforms at 71 million.[44]

A still more important factor in campaign leaders' expectations of the response of the platform population to protracted intense violence concerns whether constituent parts of the platform population, without incurring great costs, can collaborate with the common-state.[45] Where collaboration is costless, campaign violence may induce many in the platform population to defect from the campaign. Campaign leaders must anticipate this reaction. As discussed in chapter 5, obstacles to collaboration with the common-state not only make more authentic the secessionists' claim that the platform population is a separate nation with a

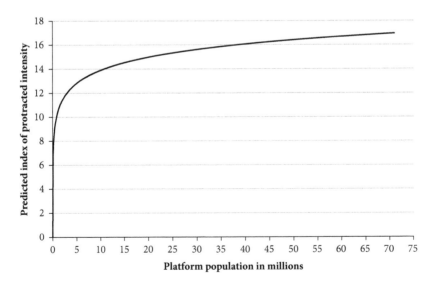

FIGURE 7.2. Platform size and protracted intensity. The curve shows the predicted index of protracted intensity for a campaign with a platform population of that size.

right to a separate sovereign state but also make more realistic the action plan: where collaboration with the common-state is costlier, each member of the campaign's platform population has less reason to expect that others will defect to the common-state. This makes violence a less risky choice for national-secession campaign leaders.

The costs of defection from the campaign and collaboration with the common-state will be substantially higher when the common-state defines itself as the manifestation of the sovereign right of a titular population that excludes the secessionists' platform population, excludes leaders of the platform population from governmental positions, or places obstacles to political participation by members of the platform population. Hence, continuing the logic of the Costly Inclusion Hypothesis introduced in chapter 5,

---

Costly Collaboration Hypothesis. *The likelihood of protracted intense conflict is greater if collaboration with the common-state is costlier.*

Indeed, on the 100-point scale of protracted intensity, as shown in table 7.2, the national-secession campaigns based on platform populations facing obstacles to political participation ("exclusion from participation") scored 22.4 points higher than other campaigns, those based on constitutionally excluded platform populations ("constitutional exclusion") scored about 20.1 points higher, and those based on platform populations consistently excluded from governmental positions ("governmental exclusion") scored 8.3 points higher. The probability that a campaign would become party to a new episode of civil war with at least twenty-five deaths in any year between 1945 and 2010, as shown in table 7.3, was 5.0 percentage points higher for campaigns based on platform populations facing constitutional exclusion from the common-state and 2.8 percentage points higher for platform populations with obstacles to political participation in the common-state.[46]

Bringing together these separate indicators of exclusion shows that compounding barriers to collaboration with the common-state were associated with greater likelihood that campaigns would engage in protracted intense struggle. For campaigns based on a platform population facing fewest obstacles to collaboration—that is, without constitutional or governmental exclusion, and only an average level of obstacles to political participation—the predicted index of protracted intensity was 2.1. For those campaigns based on platform populations facing only average obstacles—that is, with average levels of inclusion in government and average obstacles to political participation—the predicted index stood at 8.3. With complete exclusion from leading government posts but only aver-age obstacles to other political participation, the predicted index was 10.4. With complete governmental exclusion and maximum obstacles to political participa-tion, the predicted index jumped to 27.0. With highest obstacles—that is, with constitutional exclusion and maximum obstacles to political participation—the predicted index of protracted intensity jumped further, to 38.8.

In the logic of the strategy of programmatic coordination, the different prob-abilities reflect the impact of the alternative barriers to collaboration on different constituent parts of the platform population: as noted in chapter 5, governmen-tal exclusion directly affects only a small elite constituency within the campaign. Yet protracted intense violence requires this elite to appeal to concerns of the broader platform population: constitutional exclusion and obstacles to partici-pation directly affect the larger platform population.

The evidence also suggests a relationship between open democratic common-states and violence in national-secession conflicts that is very different from the relationship between democracy and violence when the insurgents have a differ-ent strategic goal. Democratic regimes are no more or less likely to experience protracted intense national-secession struggles than other regimes. There is no "domestic democratic peace" with national-secession campaigns.[47] Indeed, the domestic regime variable is statistically significant only once in tables 7A.2 to 7A.5, and this suggests that national-secession campaigns are more, not less, likely to turn to violence in states governed by more-democratic regimes.[48] Yet, any *positive* relationship between democracy and national-secession violence more plausibly reflects the greater programmatic coordination of national-secession campaigns in societies where the ideas of popular sovereignty and the nation-state infuse public life. The idea of nation-statehood developed, and has had the lon-gest time to become implanted, in the North Atlantic world, where the most stable democracies are located.

This programmatic account of violence in national-secession campaigns began by noting the strategic constraint of weak campaigns with bold ambitions: leaders of a national-secession campaign turn to violence not to achieve vic-tory over the common-state except in rare circumstances. Instead, in the strat-egy of programmatic coordination, the tactic of violence serves an operational objective—coordinating expectations on a secessionist project as the only viable alternative to the currently unacceptable assignment of sovereignty over the nation and its homeland. Nonetheless, the choice of this tactic is constrained by the capacity of the campaign to inspire participation in surges of activity, to sustain this activity, and to reap the programmatic benefits. The tactic of vio-lence provides the essential complement to the cultural identities, economic grievances and ambitions, and tactical-logistical opportunities identified in the broader literatures on rebellion and civil war. These factors, discussed more fully in chapter 8, explain outbursts of violence and contests of violence with the common-state government, but not the linkage of motivations and opportunities to campaigns for national independence. Programmatic theory sees the tactical choice of violence as a continuation of propaganda by other means: it serves an operational objective to position the national-secession campaign to pick up sovereignty and walk away with independence when the common-state collapses or the international community intervenes.

COMPLEMENTARY EXPLANATIONS
Motivations and Opportunities

Earlier studies of nationalism and self-determination conflicts have focused on cultural and economic motivations and on tactical and logistical opportunities that complement the programmatic account of campaign significance and protracted intense struggles. The motivations literature explains how secessionism and associated violence can be the means to fulfill private ends—such as expressing identities, grabbing riches, releasing emotions, or righting wrongs. These studies of cultural identities, economic grievances, and greed (or ambition) reveal sources of the energy that propels individuals into action, but the programmatic account adds that without programmatic coordination, most motivations commonly identified in these earlier studies are unlikely to focus on the common solution of independence: these motivations predict a propensity to act up or act out but do not predict either campaign significance or protracted intense national-secession struggles. Most studies of tactical and logistical opportunities have focused on explaining when rebels choose to engage in contests of violence with the common-state government. In analyses of self-determination conflicts, violence is treated as a means to induce the common-state government to concede independence. Yet, as the programmatic account qualifies, national-secession campaigns are seldom strong enough to accomplish this, and few strategically minded campaign leaders who can look down the game tree should anticipate that independence will come by prevailing over the common-state in a contest of violence.

When applied to the analysis of national-secession campaigns, three qualities characterize the attempt to generalize the causal links proposed by the literature on motivations and opportunities: indeterminacy, substitutability, and remote-ness. Yet programmatic theory does not dismiss the findings of these earlier theories; it sees them as highlighting complements to the core task of program-matic coordination. Where identities are well formed, this may provide a more authentic platform for a national-secession campaign. Where conditions give rise to grievances, this provides more concerns that national-secession campaign cadres can shape into problems that independence will solve. Some tactical and logistical opportunities for a contest of arms may reduce the costs of violence, even though the odds of victory over the common-state in a battlefield engage-ment are low. The statistical estimations reported in this chapter (and explained more fully in the appendices to chapter 5 and chapter 7) are not tests to dismiss these complementary explanations. Rather, these estimations measure the rela-tive contribution of these alternative structural constraints (obstacles and oppor-tunities) to campaign significance and protracted intense struggles. Nonetheless, compared to the cues and constraints on programmatic authenticity and realism, these effects are substantially weaker and often statistically insignificant.

Cultural and Economic Motivations

Micro-motives, such as cultural identities, economic grievance, or greed (ambi-tion), make individuals available for recruitment by national-secession cam-paigns. Yet these micro-motives alone are likely to lead to agendas that are particularistic or parochial, and unlikely to focus on independence as a solu-tion. The emotions associated with identities, grievances, and greed are likely to vary within a population and to evolve for individuals members at differ-ent speeds and along different paths. This is not unique to national-secession campaigns: as Stathis N. Kalyvas notes, civil wars are often "concatenations of multiple and often disparate local cleavages, more or less loosely arrayed around the master cleavage."[1] The motivations to act may not continue once personal or local concerns are addressed, so any activity is more likely to be short-lived. Without propagation to link these micro-motives to an authentic and realistic program of national secession, simple identity, grievance, and greed are likely to produce political action that is scattered, small-scale, and sporadic rather than coordinated, intense, and protracted. Indeed, according to the original strategy of programmatic coordination, the limitations of "spontaneous" movements without proper "consciousness" of the goal must be at the center of the strate-gic concerns of campaign leaders.[2] For Vladimir Lenin and Mao Zedong, and for the national-secession campaigns that follow their strategic advice, arduous programmatic preparation and continuous programmatic propagation focus the energies fueled by the micro-motives on a common solution, coordinate local outbursts into the intense pressure of a common struggle, and tie outbursts at different points in time in a protracted struggle.

The attempt to generalize from individual cases where specific cultural and economic motivations were present to hypotheses describing general patterns encounters two of the problems identified here. Taken together, these mean that there is no sufficient or necessary link from specific types of identities or specific economic grievances and ambitions. First is **indeterminacy.** Specific cultural identities, economic grievances, and greed have certainly been shown to give rise to political discontent, instability, and violence in individual cases, yet they do not necessarily point members of a potential platform population to a common nation-state solution. Many members of ethnic groups with well-formed cultural identities, strong cultural or economic grievances, and ambitions for economic or political advancement do not draw the conclusion that the solution to their own problems or ambitions is independence or at least may not focus on the same imagined nation-state as the solution. Because there is no determinate link from these motivations to national secession or secessionist violence, most identities, grievances, and greed cited in earlier studies are not sufficient to cause national secessionism.

Second is **substitutability.** The same identities, grievances, and ambitions are not present in all cases where national-secession campaigns achieve significance or undertake protracted intense struggles. Instead, in the rise of campaigns to significance and the choice of protracted intense tactics, these motivations are raw materials with which campaign cadres work to fulfill the task of programmatic coordination. Cadres are artful at linking diverse identities, grievances, and ambitions to a common solution; typically, there is an abundance of these motivations that can be linked to the goal of national secession. Thus, the pattern in one national-secession campaign often differs from that in another. For a national-secession campaign to achieve significance and undertake protracted intense struggle, the only identity that is nonsubstitutable is the political identity cultivated by the campaign and associated with its proposed nation-state. The only grievance that is nonsubstitutable is the dissatisfaction fostered by the campaign that sees the current common-state as a prime obstacle to the fulfillment of individual aspirations. Other motivations are substitutable one for another so that—with the exception of identities, grievances, and greed specifically focused on a nation-state that is an alternative to the common-state—none of the other identities, grievances, or ambitions are necessary for a significant campaign.

Still, it is important not to go too far in this argument: Paul Collier's assertion that "conflict is not caused by division, rather it actively needs to create them" misses the more complex relationship of these motivations to campaign significance and protracted intense struggles.³ The national-secession program creates a solution but not the underlying identities, grievances, and greed. Whereas the solution is typically an invention of the campaign and must be propagated, the proposed solution must be authentic and realistic in the assessments of the platform population. And the national-secession campaign must link this invented solution to real identities, grievances, and ambitions. As Edward Aspinall finds in his close study of the Aceh separatist conflict in Indonesia, it takes "hard ideological work by nationalist political entrepreneurs to transform unfocused resentments about natural resources into grievances that would manifest violence."⁴ Because a variety of cultural and socioeconomic grievances can be linked to national-secession campaigns, this may create the illusion that the grievances were invented, but this is simply a superficial appearance. The program may create a common narrative with an explanation of a purported common source of these grievances (the absence of independence) or it may not, but the grievances are not simply created of whole cloth—they are real. The key to programmatic success is defining a solution that can build a coalition among more of these very real but diverse motivations.

In this sense, the debate between those who argue that national secessionism must be *either* rational *or* emotional is misdirected. In the social science analysis of the 1960s and early 1970s, when grievance explanations were the dominant theme in the literature, Douglas P. Bwy summarized the scholarly consensus: "the majority of the participants engaging in such activity are dissatisfied, discontented, and often disaffected individuals."⁵ Subsuming separate analytic emphases of frustration, injustice, and disorientation, the most fully developed theory of grievances borrowed from Leon Festinger's frustration-aggression theory to advance the causal logic of "relative deprivation." In Ted Robert Gurr's formulation, "utilitarian motives" in violence are typically limited to the cathartic payoff of an expression of rage and so "are contingent upon and secondary to 'nonrational' motivation to act violently out of anger."⁶ Stuart J. Kaufman, in a brilliant analysis of the contribution of myth-symbol complexes, stresses that considerable energy comes from "emotions, not rational calculations, [that] motivate people to act."⁷

Yet the focus on motivations has been less successful in explaining the coordination of this anger, rage, and disorientation behind the common objective of independence, the synchronization of local outbursts in intense violence, or the sustenance of this in a protracted struggle. The cause-and-effect logic of the campaign's program is necessary. Without this instrumental "rationality," individual angers are unlikely to sum to a significant campaign for independence, and separate acts of violence—no matter how individually extreme—are less likely to sum to a protracted intense struggle. In short, "emotion" and "rationality"—as this original analytic dichotomy characterized them—cannot be separated in national-secession campaigns. The program is an analysis explaining why the solution to the problems that give rise to energizing emotions is independence, and the program provides a plan of action. Conversely, the arguments for the program may not mobilize much energy without linking to diverse issues that carry profound emotional baggage for some individual members of the platform population. Some members of the platform population may be human calculators without emotions, but these are less likely to bring much energy to the campaign.

Cultural Identities and Divides

As expected, the statistical estimations introduced in chapters 5 and 7 provide little evidence that deeper cultural divides or specific patterns of cultural values and civilizational divides are more likely to give rise to significant national-secession campaigns or to protracted intense violence. (The exception to this is the link of campaign significance and protracted intense struggles to the idea of the nation-state, which spread from the North Atlantic to cultures with the longest and most intense interaction with the original nation-states.[8])

In the stories of the rise of significant campaigns, concern for the culture of the platform population is a motivation among many founders and early enthusiasts: detailed studies of the origins of individual nation-state projects have recorded that the intellectuals who were present in the initial emergence of salon and classroom nations were often concerned with cultural issues such as language preservation in these early stages.[9] Culturalist analyses find that greater identity with the secessionist nation is likely to be associated with heightened sensitivity to wrongs against the nation, a search for scapegoats, a willingness to sacrifice for the nation, and a readiness to act out, so "the intensity of emotional responses to threats or opportunities for the nationalist will be strong and volatile."[10] Gurr extends this analysis to argue that ethno-cultural identity becomes more salient "the greater a people's dissimilarity from groups with which they interact regularly," and this in turn might increase secessionism.[11] This may be a constant that explains why, as noted in chapter 5, all major national secessionist projects have been based on identifiable ethnic groups.

Violence, according to these earlier theories, often accompanies deepening identity within a platform nation and differentiation from the "other" population within the common-state. The best candidate for a general theory explaining the causal link from cultural diversity to national-secessionist violence, building on the pioneering work of Henri Tajfel, is social identity theory, which "suggests that the mere presence of different groups is sufficient to cause conflict and competition."[12] Walker Connor warned of "the formidable threat that ethnic heterogeneity poses to political stability. . . ."[13] Thus, culturalists' theories often predict that deeper ethno-cultural divides should increase the likelihood of violence on behalf of national secession.[14]

Nonetheless, indeterminacy means that ethnic groups do not typically become nations with significant national-secession campaigns or support national-secession violence. Indeed, as noted in chapter 5, fewer than 7.2 percent of the 3,741 ethnic groups in the data set were platforms or parts of platforms for significant campaigns. Between 1970 and 2006, only 4.5 percent of these ethnic groups were parts of platform populations of significant national-secession campaigns that engaged in violence—even nonlethal violence. In addition, substitutability of motivations means that no specific cultural divides are more important than others in achieving campaign significance or sustaining protracted intense struggles. These conclusions are supported by three different subgroups of statistical estimations in the data introduced in chapters 5 and 7.

That evidence does not implicate any single religious tradition in the rise of national-secession campaigns to significance. For example, the evidence does not support Francis Robinson's claim that singles out Islam in the rise of national secessionism.[15] Instead, Christian ethnic minorities are slightly more likely than Muslim ethnic minorities to become platforms for significant national-secession campaigns, both Christians and Muslims are more likely than Buddhist or Hindu ethnic minorities, and groups adhering to ethnic religions are least likely. As table 5.1 shows, Christian ethnic minorities were about four times as likely as other minorities, and Muslim ethnic minorities about three times as likely, to become platforms for significant national-secession campaigns. In model 1 in table 5.1, for example, the probability that an "otherwise average" ethnic group will become a platform for a significant campaign is 2.8 percent when it is neither Christian nor Muslim, but 8.5 percent when it is a Muslim ethnic group and a still higher 10.0 percent when it is a Christian ethnic group.[16] This nationalism may be rooted in the common notion of a nation found in these Abrahamic traditions, as Adrian Hastings suggests.[17] Yet rather than differences among the tenets of the foundational theologies, it is more likely to be differential exposure to the Western European idea of the nation-state (which roughly covaries with distance from the North Atlantic) that accounts for their different probabilities of becoming platforms for significant national-secession campaigns.[18]

Nor is cultural distance between majorities and minorities a culprit in most societies: on average, campaigns based on platform populations with greater linguistic or religious separation from the rest of the common-state population are no more likely to give rise to significant campaigns or to engage in protracted intense struggle for independence than are less dissimilar groups.[19] (See the results for "Muslim minority in Christian state" and "Christian minority in Muslim state" in table 5A.2 and for "linguistic distance" and "religious distance" in table 7A.2.) And no general pattern implicates either ethno-linguistic or religious divisions as more prone to nationalism or violence. In individual instances, language may play a central role in the process of contrastive self-identification and become a powerful motivator, as Joshua A. Fishman argues.[20] In other instances, it may be religious differences that are fundamental to defining "who we are," and beliefs in different gods may give rise to "fault-line wars," as Samuel P. Huntington claims.[21] Yet globally these and other cultural divides are indeterminate and substitutable sources of the energies in national-secession campaigns and secessionist violence. And linguistic or religious differences without a program to give these energies political meaning that can be resolved by independence are not good predictors of protracted intense national-secession struggles.

Cultural unity or divisions *within* platform populations may influence the likelihood of campaign significance but have little general effect on the propensity or capacity of campaigns to engage in protracted intense violence.[22] As noted in chapter 5, significant campaigns on behalf of multiethnic platform populations are less common than campaigns on behalf of a titular ethnic group. Yet as a general pattern, neither ethno-linguistic diversity nor religious (civilizational) diversity within a platform population affects protracted intensity.[23] (See the results for "linguistically divided platform" and "civilization-cleft platform" in table 7A.2.) This is consistent with Miroslav Hroch's study of the patriots in eight nationalist campaigns in Europe, in which he finds that "the level of activity of the national movement did not depend . . . on the linguistic homogeneity of the territory on which it developed."[24] Division of the platform population by international boundaries also does not affect the likelihood of either campaign significance or violence.[25] (See the results for "adjacent homeland" in tables 5A.2 and 7A.2.)

Economic Grievances and Greed

Diverse economic grievances and greed motivate many who support campaigns for independence and engage in violence. In the development of a campaign, pragmatists motivated by their own economic grievances and ambitions become critical participants episodically and particularly during the final steps to independence. When assessing the potential of a program to create programmatic preemption, platform populations and the international community must anticipate the likelihood that grievance or greed will attract such "swing" participants to the campaign in the future. Yet because of indeterminacy and substitutability, no general pattern links specific economic grievances or ambitions to the long process of bringing a campaign to significance or sustaining a protracted intense struggle. Indeed, the attempt to reduce the causes or sources of national secessionism to economics has been criticized for quite some time. As Charles W. Anderson, Fred R. von der Mehden, and Crawford Young observed more than half a century ago, "Economic arguments may be used by separators to rationalize withdrawal but are rarely accepted as persuasive grounds for renouncing fragmentation by determined secessionist movements."[26]

Indeterminacy and substitutability have been reflected in the earlier literature by a variety of suggested relationships and sometimes diametrically opposite relationships between economic conditions and national secessionism, along with inconclusive empirical results. To cite just one example, the economic grievances literature has cited poverty or relative underdevelopment as a source of resentment and anger that feeds secessionism. Michael Hechter hypothesizes that where this economic inequality is reinforced by a cultural division of labor, minorities on the periphery may develop secessionist nationalisms.[27] Alternatively, greed rather than grievance has been used to explain the motivation of economically well-off regions to secede. Wealthier ethnic groups and homelands may bridle at the transfer of resources to bring up less developed regions.[28] In recent studies, economic greed has been linked to the economic opportunities offered by so-called "lootable resources" such as diamonds and petroleum. Michael L. Ross summarizes this claim, which he attributes to Philippe Le Billon, Paul Collier, and Anke Hoeffler, as follows: "resource wealth, if located on a country's periphery or in an area populated by an ethnic minority, will give local residents a financial incentive to establish a separate state."[29]

Each of these relationships may hold in select cases, but because of the indeterminacy and substitutability of the links from any one motivation to national secessionism, specific patterns of economic grievances or greed are not strong predictors of general patterns of campaign significance or protracted intense struggles. Indeed, in the tests reported in chapter 5 all the estimates of the association of economic grievance or greed with campaign significance are statistically insignificant: poverty, underdevelopment, relative inequality of the homeland, and the presence of lootable resources are not predictors of campaign significance. Similarly, the results reported in chapter 7 indicate only weak patterns linking specific economic conditions to protracted intense national-secession struggles. These conclusions are supported by the results of three groups of estimations.

Poverty and underdevelopment may give rise to grievances but are weak predictors of either campaign significance or protracted intense violence. The results for campaign significance are consistent with the earlier finding of Hroch that "we do not find the poor, either urban or rural, among the patriots of any of the nations we have studied. . . ."[30] Protracted intense national-secessionist violence shows no general relationship to poverty or underdevelopment—to neither common-state socioeconomic development nor homeland development. (See the results for "GDP per capita," "common-state urbanization," "homeland development," and "homeland urbanization" in tables 5A.2 and 7A.2.[31])

Economic inequalities may give rise to a sense of injustice that fuels resentment, anger, or rage, but inequalities do not predict national-secession campaign significance or protracted intense struggle.[32] (See the results for "relative homeland development" in tables 5A.2 and 7A.2.) The one economic constraint on campaign significance that even approaches statistical significance at the .05 level (a positive relationship with homeland development in model 2) does not support a grievance hypothesis but may support a greed hypothesis. Perhaps more important still, it is also closely linked to the argument about economic development, social mobilization, and the emergence of a nationalist intelligentsia advanced by Karl W. Deutsch. He defines the term *social mobilization* as the process by which populations move "from traditional to modern ways of life."[33] When these modernized people remain linguistically and culturally different from the assimilated population and are reminded of this difference by their interaction (social communication) with the assimilated population, they are likely to generate a national-secession campaign. Hroch stresses the role of the intelligentsia in this social mobilization process: "In the case of most of the nations investigated, organizational and ideological leadership was concentrated in the towns." Furthermore, "the patriotically active territory lay in all the cases investigated either in part or entirely on the most productive and the most market-oriented part of the territory occupied by an oppressed nationality."[34] Douglas A. Hibbs, Jr., drawing on the work of Deutsch as well as Lucian W. Pye and Clifford Geertz, finds in empirical tests that "the conjunction of a socially mobilized and culturally differentiated population has severe consequences for national unity and domestic stability."[35] This one almost-significant result may be less an indicator of economic greed and more a measure of the availability of a resourced, potentially nationalist intelligentsia within the "homeland." Yet this is only a suggestion to be inferred from the results rather than a "test." Otherwise, the general pattern suggests only a weak link between specific economic grievances or ambition and campaign significance.

And where socioeconomic changes are so rapid and extensive that normal adaptation is difficult, the consequence may be what has been labeled "formlessness," "deinstitutionalization," and "anomie," and the individual members of that society may experience disorientation. In Liah Greenfeld's account of the rise of nationalism, change can bring about *ressentiment*: "a psychological state resulting from suppressed feelings of envy and hatred."[36] Yet the statistical results do not show a general pattern at the macro-level linking rapid change to protracted intense struggles by national-secession campaigns. (See the results for "economic growth" in table 7A.5.[37])

Remoteness of Tactical-Logistical Considerations

The literature on tactical and logistical opportunities such as weakness in the common-state government, availability of external support, or topographical features identifies conditions favoring the secessionists in a future contest of violence with the common-state government. Yet most national-secession campaigns throughout all three developmental stages operate under the constraint of operational weakness, and this has meant that few if any have been in a position to plan armed victories over the common-state government. Therefore, the constraints identified by the opportunities literature are remote from the calculations of strategically minded national-secession campaign leaders or their platform populations—a quality labeled **remoteness.** These only weakly influence whether a national-secession campaign becomes significant and its leader decides to engage in protracted intense violence. Certainly, leaders contemplating contests of violence with the common-state government must think ahead to opportunities such as future regime vulnerability or overburdened state capacity and how topographic features might give the campaign safe havens in a future conflict. Yet most campaigns throughout most of their histories are not immediately focused on such direct decisive contests with the common-state. Most campaign leaders who are particularly astute recognize that they will never engage in such contests and will need some unforeseen event or international intervention to achieve independence.

Opportunities that affect the "feasibility" of conducting an armed struggle against the central government have long been a focus in the literature on rebellion. In recent studies of civil wars, the critique of the grievances approach leveled by political economists has once again become common—that is, there is always enough grievance or greed to motivate violence, so the key variation that explains why violence occurs in some but not other countries is in opportunities to engage in violence. Earlier RAND studies of insurgencies, such as the rebellions by the Hukbalahap in the Philippines and the Vietcong in South Vietnam, had advanced this claim and focused on tactical-logistical opportunities as key constraints on rebellion.[38] More recently, James D. Fearon and David D. Laitin argue that "the factors that explain which countries have been at risk for civil war are not their ethnic or religious characteristics but rather the conditions that favor insurgency."[39] Paul Collier, Anke Hoeffler, and Måns Söderbom stress that in the economic theory of rebellion, "the conditions that determine the feasibility of rebellion are more important than those that influence motivation" and that "the feasibility thesis suggests that where insurrection is feasible, it will occur with the actual agenda of the rebel being indeterminate."[40]

This feasibility thesis builds on the analytic perspective that violence is bargaining by actions designed to influence the resolution of the substantive issues on the table. As T. David Mason, Joseph P. Weingarten, Jr., and Patrick J. Fett explain, at every stage (before, during, and after war) each party is assessing the expected benefits of victory (value of benefit × probability of victory) and expected costs of achieving victory (time to victory × cost per time period) against the expected payoff to settling (value of benefit × certainty of enjoying this benefit).[41] In this model applied to national-secession campaigns, the choice of violence for secessionists should hinge on considerations of the impact this will have on inducing the government to grant independence or at least to compromise and grant other concessions.[42] In these earlier analyses of the opportunities for civil war, the resort to violence poses a puzzle: why are secessionists and common-state governments unable to reach a compromise on the issue of independence that avoids costly violence?[43] The programmatic account stresses that a prior question or puzzle should be addressed: why would rational secessionists even contemplate a contest of arms with the common-state?

The programmatic account of violence highlights four limitations when applying the "feasibility thesis" to national-secession campaigns. First, the opportunities that define the "feasibility of rebellion" refer to constraints that can turn contests of violence with the common-state government into a sensible option with reasonable prospects for victory. This is applicable to many revolutionary groups and coup plotters who seek to seize power in the common-state capital and must weigh the balance of capabilities and weaknesses in the common-state government. For these strategists, as Collier and Hoeffler argue, "The incentive for rebellion is the product of the probability of victory and its consequences," and "the probability of victory depends upon the capacity of the government to defend itself."[44] Yet for most national-secession campaigns, planning to use violence for victory over the common-state government is not prudent. Indeed, among national-secession campaigns that were parties to conflicts that caused at least twenty-five battlefield- or terrorism-related deaths in any year between 1970 and 2006, the median size of the platform population constituted just 2.0 percent of the common-state population. Even if every last woman and man was mobilized under arms, the campaign would be overwhelmed in a battle with the common-state. Constrained by this operational weakness, it is unlikely that tactical opportunities that could enable powerful revolutionary groups to achieve victory in a contest of violence with the common-state government were the factors that led national-secession campaign leaders to employ violence. The programmatic account does not dismiss the importance of these opportunities affecting the feasibility of rebellion—particularly in instances where campaign leaders have based these programs on an atypically large platform population. Yet such favorable instances are rare for national-secession campaigns.

Second, the feasibility thesis criticizes the motivation hypothesis by noting that there are always enough grievances to justify rebellion, but a mirror criticism about overdetermination could be leveled against the tactical-logistical opportunity approach: there are always enough opportunities to engage in many forms of very destructive violence. For example, ETA has never been at a loss for weapons, explosives, and money to create mayhem. According to Robert P. Clark, "Finding weapons and explosives has never seemed to be much of a problem for ETA." An open international market in illegal arms makes available "practically any kind of weapons . . . in almost any quantity needed." ETA can steal what it cannot buy. And "since the mid1960s, ETA has never had any problems securing funds to support their activities."[45] Tactical-logistical opportunities are not the critical variables that constrain the choice of campaign leaders to engage in a protracted intense struggle.

Third, these tactical and logistical opportunities for prevailing over the common-state government are less constraining when the operational objective is programmatic coordination. Where violence is a continuation of propaganda by other means, the most important tactical-logistical constraint on the choice of actions by a campaign throughout its life is programmatic: it is a population primed to resist the temptation of compromise with the common-state and to participate in surge events. To make action more intense and to sustain this require favorable human logistics in the platform population. Arms are easier to come by than support. Arms can flow in quickly; programmatic coordination must build up over time.

And fourth, this bargaining model to explain the use of violence is even less illuminating when bargaining over the substantive issues has given way to issue intractability: once the issue on the table is nondivisible and nonfungible and exchanges become championships (analyzed in chapter 6), the choice of violence is not made to influence the other side.

Thus, this programmatic approach diverges from analyses of insurgency, based on Mao Zedong and elaborated in US counterinsurgency manuals, insofar as these see the unfolding of insurgent violence as driven by the logic of prevailing over the common-state in a contest of arms. This common analysis of insurgent violence distinguishes three phases of a struggle progressing from preparations for combat in a latent period to guerrilla warfare and then to broad military engagements with the common-state government. These are commonly labeled the insurgents' "strategic defense" (Phase I), "preparation for the counter-offensive" (Phase II), and "strategic counteroffensive" (Phase III).[46] In this standard analysis, activities in the latent period are preparation for Phase II, which will in turn lead to Phase III. Yet for most national-secession campaigns most of the time, with little prospect of ultimate armed victory over the common-state government, it makes little sense to move beyond the latent period of Phase I. For most it makes little sense to use violence at all or even to prepare to do so. And even campaigns that employ guerrilla warfare (typically a Phase II activity) have little reason to prepare for or even to expect an opportunity to escalate further to a strategic counteroffensive.

In the programmatic account the logic in the unfolding of insurgent violence is provided by programmatic coordination: violence is typically a surge tactic used in pursuit of the operational objective of furthering coordination or demonstrating programmatic preemption. So, for example, the overwhelming coercive capability of a strong state may be as inviting a target for a small campaign that seeks to further campaign coordination as a weak state is for the largest campaigns that seek victory on the battlefield.[47] As Andreas Wimmer summarizes his own findings, wars conducted by national-secessionists "cannot be interpreted as merely opportunistic reactions to a weakening imperial grip on power, but are driven by the power of nationalist ideologies."[48]

Balance of Capabilities and State Weakness

Although common-state weakness may be critical to a campaign at the moment it walks away with independence, it is unnecessary and unlikely during the long period of building the campaign to prepare for this surge event. Expectations that the common-state will be vulnerable to challenges at some future time may increase the likelihood that intellectuals, leaders, cadres, and followers will coalesce around national-secession projects, but the campaign typically must organize and achieve significance when the state is not yet vulnerable. Thus, measures of current regime weakness or instability are weak predictors of significant national-secession campaigns. Indeed, in the statistical estimations, ethnic groups facing regimes with disproportionately high governing loads (relative to capacity) and common-states with unstable regimes were no more likely to become platforms for significant national-secession campaigns than ethnic groups facing less-burdened and more-stable regimes.[49] (See the results in table 5A.2 for "relative governing load," "democracy," "autocracy," and "regime instability.") In model 2 in table 5.1, just the opposite appears to be the case: when the history of stable democratic rule in the common-state is longer, the campaign is more likely—not less likely—to achieve significance. Yet this may be still another indicator of the close association of nationalism with the North Atlantic experience, where both nationalism and modern democracy were born and have flourished.

The weakness of the link to campaigns' engagement in protracted intense violence is even more striking.[50] When examining just national-secession campaigns, the evidence does not support Laitin's general observation about all civil wars that "indicators of weak states . . . are good predictors of civil war."[51] The results show that state weakness and the balance of coercive capabilities have had only weak influence on decisions of national-secession campaign leaders to engage in protracted intense violence. (See "balance of coercive capacity" in tables 7.3 and 7A.2.[52])

Indeed, it is a buildup of common-state military capability relative to the platform population that is associated with the initial outbreak of civil wars and the continuation of intense violence. (See the results in tables 7A.4 and 7A.5 for "balance of coercive capacity.") But that speaks to the response of the common-state to mounting crises rather than the strategic calculations of campaign leaders. Most campaigns are so weak relative to the common-state that even a central government in turmoil can overmatch secessionists on the battlefield. As the results in table 7.3 show, only in the timing of the initiation of a new episode of civil war does common-state weakness show a significant effect.

Geographic and Topographic Opportunities

Favorable geographic or topographic features for a contest of arms are weak predictors of national-secession campaign significance and even weaker predictors of protracted intense struggles. As table 5.1 shows, the presence of a geographic exclave containing parts of the platform population and proximity of the homeland to an international border appear to increase the likelihood that a national-secession campaign will achieve significance. Alternatively, distance of a homeland from the common-state capital does not appear to have this effect.[53] (See the results in table 5A.2 for "geographic exclave," "distance to border," and "distance to capital.") An exclave or international border may be more than a future tactical advantage when the moment for a surge arises. Well before this, these may also be important cues to the realism of a nation-state project. The physical separation of the Bengalis of East Pakistan contributed to the realism of the project for independence. The rarity of independent sovereign states completely surrounded by another (for example, San Marino) makes it harder to make a credible claim to independence without an international border. This commonsense logic of realism was even reflected in the design of the Soviet model of ethno-federalism, where union republics such as Turkmenistan with a right to secession were distinguished from equally large autonomous republics such as Tatarstan without this right because the latter, deep inside the Russian Federation, lacked an international boundary that would permit it to exercise its right to self-determination.[54]

The safe haven and support of an external but contiguous homeland—factors that are frequently cited as tactical and logistical advantages favoring secessionist activity—actually decrease in a very small way the likelihood of a national-secession campaign achieving significance. The typical argument for the tactical and logistical advantages created by such adjacent areas notes that provision of arms, materiel, and other resources and the availability of safe havens for conspiring, staging, retreating, and regrouping lower the organizing costs of a rebellion. Yet the costs of defection from the national-secession campaign, stressed by the programmatic theory, are also lowered by the availability of easy emigration.[55] As the estimate in table 5.1 shows ("adjacent homeland"), ethnic groups in one state that constitute the majority in a neighboring state are about half as likely on average to become the platforms for major nation-state campaigns as are ethnic groups without such adjacent homelands.[56]

In addition, geographical and topographical features, such as distance from the common-state seat of government and mountainous terrain, are widely cited as tactical opportunities that favor military operations by rebels. Yet while geographic remoteness and mountainous terrain may aid small-scale and sporadic armed actions, they make protracted intense struggle more difficult. Even a protracted intense campaign of terrorism may be more difficult when the homeland is target-poor and its safe havens are more remote from the most valuable targets for highly visible attacks. The difficulty of larger-scale military operations in inaccessible terrain hinders both the national-secession campaign and the common-state government.[57]

Thus, for national-secession conflicts, commonly cited features of geography and topography, while important in individual cases, predict no pattern of protracted intense violence that holds across many campaigns. Distance of the secessionist homeland from the seat of the common-state government, geographical separation of part of the homeland from the common-state territory, proximity of the homeland to an international border, an adjacent homeland, and a homeland in mountainous terrain are not significant predictors of protracted intense struggles by national-secession campaigns.[58] (See the results in table 7A.2 for "distance from capital," "homeland exclave," "distance to international border," "adjacent homeland," and "mountainous terrain," respectively.)

Logistical Support Opportunities

The availability of logistical support either from abroad or from local sources has only a weak relationship with either campaign significance or protracted intense struggles. Diasporas, and particularly resourced expatriates, have been identified in many individual campaigns as an important source of logistical support, yet these do not appear to be part of a general pattern that links larger communities of resourced expatriates with significant national-secession campaigns. Gardner Bovingdon notes that the expatriate communities of Uighurs in Turkey, Western Europe, and North America "by preparing histories and political materials and disseminating them among Uyghurs in Xinjiang and around the world, . . . have played a role in sustaining both Uyghurs' sense of themselves as a distinct people and their belief in the possibility of independence in the future."[59] The co-ethnic expatriates who fled Soviet Ukraine, Estonia, Latvia, and Lithuania for North America or Western Europe kept nation-state projects alive under even the most difficult circumstances of Soviet rule until the Soviet state collapsed. The consulates of the governments-in-exile of the Baltic states, the Ukrainian research institutes at such universities as Harvard and Alberta, and the endowed Armenian history professorships at Harvard, Columbia, UCLA, Berkeley, Michigan, Tufts, and Fresno State propagated the histories and cultures of these nations, contributed to the coalescence around specific nation-state projects, maintained (often covert) ties with the underground campaigns within the Soviet Union, and stepped in after perestroika to assist the building of national-secession campaigns.[60] Yet the measure of substantial and resourced expatriate communities—the population size of co-ethnics living in OECD countries in 1985—does not support a general pattern linking these to significant national-secession campaigns. (See the results in table 5A.2 for "resourced diaspora.") These expatriate communities may also represent a ready exit opportunity that increases the risk of defection from the campaign back home through emigration and makes campaign significance less likely.

In addition, national-secession campaign significance is not as sensitive to the availability of local financial or in-kind support. Indeed, for national-secession campaign leaders the most important logistical constraint is the expected response of the platform population. Thus, national-secession campaigns differ substantially from rebels without a cause, for whom, as Paul Collier argues, "The motivation of conflict is unimportant; what matters is whether the organization can sustain itself financially." For rebels without a cause the key constraints are elements of resource logistics: "It is the conditions for predation which are decisive."[61] Thus, it may be the availability of "lootable resources" at home (that is, high-value assets such as oil fields and diamond mines that cannot be moved outside the reach of the insurgents) that enable the latter types of insurgencies. Yet the results of the statistical estimations do not suggest that lootable resources increase the likelihood of campaign significance. (See the results in table 5A.2 for "petroleum in homeland" and "diamonds in homeland.")

These logistical support opportunities are also remote concerns in the calculation of whether to engage in protracted intense struggle. The statistical estimates show that the presence of lootable resources in the homeland, the proximity of external communities of supporters, and a larger community of resourced expatriates are not systematically related to the likelihood of protracted intense violence. (See the results in table 7A.2 for "petroleum in homeland," "diamonds in homeland," "adjacent homeland," and "resourced expatriates."[62]) Certainly, there are important instances when campaigns have picked the pockets of wealthy expatriate communities or looted local assets that could not be hidden.[63] Nonetheless, the absence of such sources does not preclude finding alternative funding, and their presence still requires programmatic coordination before there is a campaign to tap them.

This absence of a general pattern in national-secession violence is consistent with the findings in other macro-level empirical studies. Michael L. Ross ranks thirty-six civil wars in the 1990s by the proportionate share of primary-commodity exports in the common-state's gross domestic product. The fourteen secessionist civil wars were less than half as likely to be associated with more resource-dependent countries—28.6 percent of separatist civil wars, compared to 63.6 percent of other civil wars, occurred in the eighteen more-resource-dependent countries.[64] Similarly, Monica Duffy Toft finds that ethnic groups living in resource-rich regions were actually less likely to be involved in violence.[65] In assessing the impact of cross-border sanctuaries on the incidence of civil wars, Fearon and Laitin do not find a significant relationship; Tanja Ellingsen and Barbara F. Walter actually find that groups with ethnic brethren in neighboring states were significantly less likely to engage in violence.[66] This is consistent with the programmatic account that for most national-secession campaigns, these logistical constraints on armed victory over the common-state are remote considerations.

The pattern of results confirms the expectation of programmatic theory that in a global analysis of national secessionism, these indeterminate, substitutable, and remote constraints will show only weak relationships with campaign significance and protracted intense struggles. This result does not dispute the findings of others; these motivations and opportunities often do contribute to the outbreak of other types of civil wars and to individual cases of significance and protracted intensity in national-secession campaigns. Nonetheless, in the global patterns of such campaigns, the stronger constraints among those examined in this chapter are the factors that also serve as cues to the authenticity and realism of the program for nation-statehood. Responses to specific national-secession programs are more positive among populations with more direct and more sustained exposure to the idea and practice of nation-states. Ethnic groups in the European and Ottoman realms and the ethnic groups they influenced through colonial and missionary contacts are more likely to become platforms for significant national-secession campaigns, and that likelihood appears to grow with more direct and longer exposure. The credibility of a nation-state project is stronger when its claimed homeland within the common-state is physically separate from the rest of the common-state and shares a border with other independent states. Imaginations focus on these simple cues, and expectations draw the attention of members of the platform population and the international community. These are the foundations of successful programmatic coordination.

9

LOOKING FORWARD
Implications of Programmatic Analysis

The national-secession campaigns analyzed in this book proclaim bold ambitions to redraw international boundaries and transform the lives of those who live within them but typically possess limited means to achieve this. National secessionists seek to create new sovereign states: the meta-institutions within which their citizens make more-mundane changes, such as transitions between authoritarianism and democracy, expansions or restrictions of political freedoms and property rights, reorderings of economic and social statuses among citizens and foreigners, and privileging, fostering, discriminating against, or even suppressing cultures. National-secession campaign leaders have little evidence to support expectations that the common-state government against which they struggle will readily concede independence or that secessionists will be able to seize independence against its resistance without outside help or an unexpected collapse at the center. Looking around at the secessionist campaigns that have achieved independence, they have reason to expect that the international community will accept separation only if the secessionists can make independence appear to be the only viable option.

The strategy of programmatic coordination has been a response by national-secession campaigns to these circumstances. Operating under the constraint of operational weakness, campaigns have invested in long-term programmatic coordination within their platform populations in order to develop the capacity to demonstrate to the international community that the platform population will not accept compromise with the common-state and that independence is the only viable option. The campaign seeks to demonstrate that the platform population is, in fact, a nation with a right to a sovereign state of its own.

This strategy serves as an analytic model that informs our answers to the question with which this book began: how and under what conditions do national-secession projects become significant campaigns that get on the global agenda, give rise to intractable disputes with their common-state governments over independence, and engage in protracted intense struggles? In the programmatic account the advance of programmatic coordination determines the campaigns that are likely to emerge as significant challengers to common-states because only when this claim is credible to the platform population (or is expected to be credible) is it likely to be seen as a challenge requiring attention from the international community. Intractability—deadlock on the issue of sovereignty between national-secession campaigns and common-state governments—is the consequence of successful programmatic coordination within the platform population so that few of its members will compromise with the common-state. Protracted intensity is a tactic to reinforce the programmatic coordination that gives rise to intractability. Protracted intense struggles require the capacity that comes from substantial programmatic coordination but typically are sensible undertakings only when campaign leaders expect protracted intensity to move the campaign closer to programmatic preemption.

The programmatic analysis of national-secession campaigns in this book has only begun a research program that calls for replication and corroboration of its initial findings and further elaboration of its theory and its hypotheses. I conclude this book by mentioning just a few of these extensions, beginning from issues closest to the current analysis.

Implications for Future Analysis

The claims in this study depend in part on the strength of the statistical models reported in chapters 5, 7, and 8. The validity of the empirical dependent variables—campaign significance and protracted intensity—should be scrutinized by future researchers, especially to detect any bias in the measurement of these concepts. And the independent variables should be examined for any missing or misspecified explanations. (For an example of a first attempt to scrutinize my findings, see my analysis in the appendix to this chapter.) Indeed, these are the common tasks of normal science.

Comparing Types of Campaigns and Their Violence

The analysis in this book that begins with the goals of campaigns suggests that campaigns that are not national-secessionist may face some very different constraints. The focus on goals suggests four different ideal-types of campaigns and five different ideal-types of civil wars based on the objectives of their leaders: coup conspirators, revolutionaries, national-secessionists, transformers, and rebels without a cause:[1]

- *Coup conspirators* seek to take control of the central government of an existing state and may hope to change the regime, but they have little ambition to transform society or the economy.[2]
- *Revolutionaries* seek to take control of the central government of an existing state, but they also seek to change the rules by which status and wealth are distributed in society at large.[3]
- *National secessionists* seek to separate from an existing state, create a new sovereign state, and establish new standards for allocating power, status, and wealth in their new state.
- *Transformers* (such as the early communists or the Islamic State) seek not only to replace the existing government within a single state or the boundaries of a single state but also to replace the existing state system with a new order—at least in part of the world.[4]
- *Rebels without a cause,* who create civil wars without campaigns, are bent on predation, foraging, and self-enrichment, but they do not appear to have a significant political or social agenda.[5]

Multidimensional civil wars—such as the 2014–16 war in Iraq—are difficult to analyze because they combine multiple, simultaneous, equipoised campaigns with very different agendas—such as a campaign for revolution within Iraq conducted by some Shia and Sunni leaders, transformation within the Muslim world conducted by ISIS, and national secession conducted by some Kurdish and Assyrian leaders.

Future research should explore the extent to which differences in goals among these campaigns and civil wars have implications for the strategic constraints, operational tasks, and tactical options confronting their leaders. The programmatic approach predicts that the strategic goals of these different campaigns should determine where campaign leaders can expect to find most recruits and allies. The relative ability (or inability) to recruit more widely and to form broader alliances defines the maximum capabilities that campaign leaders can expect to command and therefore constrains their operational objectives. These expectations of maximum capabilities at full mobilization and expectations of the most likely path to achieving the group's goal should constrain the choice of tactics by campaigns—particularly, the ways that each type of campaign uses violence. Campaign goals should also shape how campaign leaders anticipate the response of the international community, including likely governmental and nongovernmental allies, opponents, and veto players. And these goals are likely to influence the types of solutions and compromises that campaign leaders will find acceptable and their exchanges with their common-state governments. Whether these implications of programmatic theory are actually corroborated by evidence is the task for future research.

Analyzing Micro-motivations and Individual Responses

The analysis in this book focuses on macro-level outcomes; it posits many micro- and meso-level processes. In future studies, some of the "givens" at the micro-level in the current analysis, such as individual preferences and types, could be transformed into dependent variables, and the processes of coordination at the individual and campaign level, such as persuasion, could be "unpacked." The explosion of new methods of textual analysis, survey experiments, and opinion research provides scholars with new tools to explore the processes of preference formation and persuasion that constrain campaigns for national secession (as well as revolution and transformation). Modern tools may give us insight into why some members of platform populations are enthusiasts, expressionists, or pragmatists when presented with national-secession programs and whether they assume a similar orientation to other programs and campaigns. Which individual preferences are easier to link to a national-secession program, which nation-state projects are more likely to be seen as authentic, and which action plans are accepted as realistic could all be studied more closely at the micro-level with these tools. The study of individual assessments of national-secession programs and meso-level coordination of expectations is a fertile field for investigation, yet it is surprisingly understudied by modern social science.

Analyzing Common-State and International Decision Making

This book analyzes the strategic choices of campaign leaders. It emphasizes that the outcome of independence also depends on the choices of common-state government leaders and of leaders in major foreign powers in the international community. Understanding the outcome of independence requires two complementary studies of choice: the strategic choices of common-state government leaders and the foreign powers that are veto players in the international community. The analysis of each requires a different model and is likely to identify very different constraints leading to key decisions on the road to significance, intractability, protracted intensity, and independence. Valuable research has already begun to explore these distinct decisions.[6] Similarly, exploratory research has sought to bring these distinct decisions together to identify why some nation-state projects are favored over others, but this area is certainly in need of further study.[7]

Anticipating Future Campaign Challenges

The models of significance and protracted intensity introduced in chapters 5 and 7 imply warnings of future challenges: one obvious prediction is that many of the same campaigns will continue to be in the spotlight.[8] Campaigns may surge and retreat in a billows-like manner, but to the extent that these campaigns have engaged the operational tasks of programmatic coordination, they may be around in the future to worry the international community. The 145 significant campaigns identified in chapter 2 that have not achieved independence should be watched for future surges—even if they are currently in a longueur. Indeed, since I first wrote these words, Crimea became just such an international crisis.

In addition, some campaigns that have not yet achieved significance or engaged in protracted intense struggles are likely to do so in the future. The models identify platform populations for which national-secession campaigns were primed for significance but did not get their claims onto the international agenda between 1945 and 2010. These are possible new challengers in the future. Table 9.1 shows those platform populations for which the estimation model in chapter 5 (table 5A.2, model 1) predicts greater than four-to-one odds of a significant campaign but a national-secession campaign based on that platform

TABLE 9.1. Projects with greatest unrealized potential to achieve significance as national-secession campaigns, 1945–2010

PLATFORM POPULATION	PROJECT	PROBABILITY	COMMON-STATE
Marathi	Maharashtra	98.8	India
Dusun/Kadazan	Sabah	98.0	Malaysia
Murut/Kelabit	Sabah	96.4	Malaysia
Turks	Rumelia	94.1	Bulgaria
Fulani	Unknown	93.6	Senegal
Toucouleur	Unknown	93.6	Senegal
Bajau	Sabah	92.4	Malaysia
Kedayan	Sabah	89.8	Malaysia
Melanau	Sabah	89.0	Malaysia
Sulu-Samal	Sabah	83.9	Malaysia

Note: The list includes projects that in the full estimation equation (see table 5A.2, model 1) were estimated to have greater than 80 percent probability (four-to-one odds) of a significant secession campaign but did not have one in 1945–2010.

TABLE 9.2.   National-secession campaigns with greatest unrealized potential for more protracted intense violence, 1970–2006

NATIONAL-SECESSION CAMPAIGN	PREDICTED ADDITIONAL YEARS[a]	COMMON-STATE
Tibet	4.3	China
Afar	3.9	Ethiopia
Assyria	3.6	Iraq
Monland	3.3	Myanmar
Moldova	3.0	USSR
Chemama	3.0	Mauritania

Note: The list includes projects that the combined estimation equation (see table 7A.2) predicts should have had the equivalent of at least three more years of intense violence than was actually observed.

[a] The number of additional years of intense violence predicted in the estimation.

population failed to get on the international agenda between 1945 and 2010. These include three national-secession campaigns (Maharashtra, Rumelia, and Sabah) that were active at some point in the years from 1945 to 2010 but failed to get on the international agenda and one project that has thus far failed to support a campaign recorded even in close studies (labeled "unknown" in table 9.1). (For more information on these campaigns, see the appendix to this chapter.)

The models also identify significant campaigns that were primed for substantially greater violence between 1970 and 2006. These are likely future hot spots. Table 9.2 shows those national-secession campaigns for which the estimation model in chapter 7 (table 7A.2, combined estimation) predicts the equivalent of at least three more years of intense violence than was actually observed. The Tibet, Afar, Monland, and Chemama campaigns stand out for the potential for more protracted intense violence in the future. Assyria and Moldova are probably no longer at risk of protracted intense national-secession struggles because the Assyrian population is now dispersed after genocidal violence visited on its communities and the Moldovans achieved independence in 1991. (For more information on these campaigns, see the appendix to this chapter.)

Responding to Programmatic Coordination

It is the academic's conceit that scholarship can tell the world how to work better. Certainly, earlier academic theories have profoundly shaped important strategies for development and counterinsurgency that have been employed to address national-secession campaigns. More modesty may be in order when drawing policy implications from this book: policy implications derived here are yet to be tested and so constitute an agenda for future research. Nonetheless, this book may have two key implications for the unenviable task of addressing the reality of national-secession campaigns (and, by extension, revolutionary and transformational campaigns). These implications concern the centrality of common-state narratives and the role of outsiders in such conflicts.[9]

Developing Common-State Narratives

The analysis in this study stresses that in conflicts with national secessionists (and by extension, with revolutionaries and transformers), central governments must elevate the war for minds. The core of the common-state response to national-secession campaigns must be an authentic and realistic program that offers an alternative nation-state project. The common-state program must envision a state built on a platform population that includes the entire citizenry. Inability to offer an inclusive common-state doctrine may be the first sign that trying to sustain an existing central government is an imprudently risky investment.

Drafting such a common-state program may seem a simple undertaking, but it often encounters strong resistance within the common-state and among its domestic supporters. To illustrate, consider the obstacles to Iraq's necessary response to the Kurdistan and Assyria national-secession campaigns, complicated further by the ISIS transformational campaign and Sunni and Shia revolutionary campaigns: the common-state must advance a doctrine of Iraq-ness that envisions a nation-state that is not Arab or Islamic but is rooted in the eight-decade-old common-state based on the platform of the multiethnic, multi-confessional population living within its borders. If the assessment of Iraqi intellectuals is that this common-state narrative is not viable (and they may well be right), this may be evidence that the Iraqi common-state project should be abandoned for partition along lines proposed by more-viable programs for national-secession—to the extent that these exist.

In engaging the war of programs with campaigns for national secession (or revolution or transformation), the effectiveness of the common-state narrative may well depend on the nature of the campaign it confronts and that campaign's progress in programmatic coordination. Rebels without a cause can often be bought off by particularistic rewards such as money or power and may require little programmatic response. National-secession, revolutionary, and transformational campaigns require more-extensive programmatic responses that speak to their respective core claims. Where a campaign has had only limited success at programmatic coordination and at cultivating enthusiasts, the required programmatic response by the government may be more limited. In this circumstance, as Ronald Wintrobe argues, where pragmatists dominate the campaign,

"If one can un-bundle the goal or make the indivisible divisible, then there may be ways to provide these goals in a way which satisfies some of the potential supporters of the group and thus dries up support for the grander ambitions of the leaders of extremist groups."[10] But where a national-secession (or revolutionary or transformational) campaign has made major advances in programmatic coordination and more of its supporters are enthusiasts, the opportunities to peel away supporters in this way will be substantially fewer. Here the war of programs must be fully engaged. Where the campaign has actually achieved programmatic preemption, as appears to be the case in many frozen conflicts, it may be too late for a war of programs; bargaining is over and unlikely to reopen for a generation or more.

Programmatic analysis suggests that development policies, whether standing alone or parts of counterinsurgencies, can counter the process by which campaigns link private motivations to a national-secession program but typically focus on removing indeterminate and substitutable causes of grievance. Development projects may strip away pragmatists from a campaign with offers of solutions to their separate parochial concerns—such as political office, investments in public goods, or land reform. Nevertheless, even if common-state development policies peel away the outer layers of pragmatists in the participatory reserve of a campaign, this does not disrupt the true-believing core of leaders and staff—unless the falling away of pragmatists is so substantial that even enthusiasts come to question the prospects of achieving programmatic preemption and the realism of the action plan for independence. More commonly, peeling away pragmatists only sets back the campaign's programmatic coordination—in a way predicted by its strategy—without limiting its ability to rebuild its surge capacity through its use of further programmatic linking.

Because grievances and ambitions are unlimited and substitutable, a campaign with leadership and staff still coordinated on the campaign goal can reconstitute itself by building on new grievances and ambitions. At the core of their strategy of programmatic coordination is the task of building the billows-like capacity to weather moments of declining expected support from outside the core of the campaign without jeopardizing its core and then to resume recruiting from there. It is very difficult for a common-state to anticipate and respond to all the various grievances and ambitions. In responding to campaigns, development policies buy breathing space, but programmatic analysis suggests that the government must use these short reprieves to engage the war of programs fully. The critical challenge for development policies is the programmatic task of persuading the pragmatists in the platform population that long-term and sustained remedies of current and future problems will come through the solution promised in the common-state program. It is not the fact that people are momentarily richer that drains the campaign's lake of pragmatists but the expectation that future gains will best be secured through the central government's project, if only many other members of the platform population will rally round.

The common-state narrative must offer a bold, ambitious, optimistic vision of the platform population's future under the common-state—and one that is authentic and realistic. Earlier social science theories have attributed national secession and revolution to greed, anger, pride, and envy. Yet the disdainful treatment of national secession (and revolution and transformation) as manifestations of medieval sins (omitting only gluttony, lust, and sloth) misses the source of the appeal of campaigns: an appeal to virtues of faith, charity, and hope. National-secession (as well as revolutionary and transformational) campaigns offer bold visions of a world set right. The optimistic promise for the future gives campaigns their forward momentum. The response from the central government requires a bold vision that competes with the promises of the national secessionists. It requires a just-as-authentic and more-realistic common-state program.

The Need for Outsiders to Be Nearly Invisible

The analysis of the strategy of programmatic coordination suggests that in addressing campaigns, outsiders have a very limited role to play in the war for minds. The very nature of the task of programmatic coordination means that the common-state government bears the primary burden and that too visible a role for outsiders can subvert this. Outside supporters should contemplate intervening only when an existing government can conduct a campaign on behalf of a program that has a good chance of being seen as authentic and realistic by the common-state population. Only in rare and extraordinary circumstances can an out-of-power alternative government successfully achieve such programmatic coordination if it comes to power through outside support.

Although it is widely recognized in counterinsurgency doctrines that the host-country government, such as the government in Baghdad, bears this responsibility, the admonitions about restraint by outsiders may not go far enough. In its understanding of tactics and particularly the use of violence and warfare, the strategy of programmatic coordination has been influenced by the broad vision of Carl von Clausewitz.[11] Vladimir I. Lenin paid homage to the Prussian strategist's triple insight that war is "a true political instrument, a continuation of political intercourse, carried on with other means"; that military operations must be constrained by the balance among the people, the political leaders, and the armed forces; and that political aims are the business of political leaders alone.[12] As Clausewitz observed and strategists of programmatic coordination have stressed, the important triangular balance is among the population, *their* political leaders, and the bureaucracy and armed forces of *their* state—be it the common-state, a secessionist state, a revolutionary state, or a thoroughly transformed new order such as a regional caliphate. The strategy of programmatic coordination carries a warning: in the war for minds, outside powers, by such activities as developmental assistance or military interventions, can create the space for propagation of the central government's program, but any actions by outside powers that make it appear that the central government's program is actually the work of outsiders may make the task of engaging the war for minds even more difficult. In the critical triangular relationship, foreign allies of the common-state play an auxiliary role that is best served by remaining largely invisible or at arm's length lest they stand between any of the parties to the critical triangulation.

The self-control demanded of outside supporters of host-country central governments is often daunting and humbling and is not for the fainthearted or vain. Backing a central government in a war for minds often requires restraint to resist jumping in further when the government stumbles or fails. It requires the strength to accept ingratitude when the host-country central government does not characterize the outsiders as a beloved savior: the host-country central government must be free to distance itself from the outside power, sometimes criticizing it as an illegitimate interventionist (and neocolonial) power, and to claim that programs inspired and financed behind the scenes by outsiders are actually homegrown.[13]

Appendix to Chapter 2

The analysis in this book focuses on 171 national-secession campaigns that by word or deed have been able to draw attention in the United Kingdom or United States to the independence claim in their programs. (See table 2A.1.)[1] These campaigns were identified in searches of issues of the *Times* of London, the *New York Times*, and *Keesing's Contemporary Archives* published between January 1, 1945, and December 31, 2010.[2] These results were compared with lists of nationalist movements compiled by James Minahan, the national self-determination conflicts identified by Monty G. Marshall and Ted Robert Gurr, lists of separatist movements and unrecognized states in Wikipedia, and websites of secessionist organizations and associations.[3] These encyclopedias, lists, and websites helped identify both possible "missing" cases not found in the initial search of news sources and possible "specious" news items not corroborated by a second source. Each of the anomalies was explored through further searches on the group names—and many groups had more than one name—in the three news sources and monographic sources, particularly the Library of Congress country-studies series. In the end this required only minor changes to the list compiled in the initial search of the news sources.

In every case the news item, encyclopedic entry, website, or monographic source was scrutinized to ascertain whether the international media actually recorded a claim to sovereign statehood advanced on behalf of an identified nation. To be included in this study the homeland identified in this claim had to be part of the metropolitan territory of the common-state and the claim had to be directed against that common-state. In addition, the common-state's total

TABLE 2A.1. Significant national-secession campaigns, by region and common-state, 1945–2010

COUNTRY	CAMPAIGN	COUNTRY	CAMPAIGN
Americas		Georgia	South Ossetia
		Kazakhstan	Northern Kazakhstan
Bolivia	Collasuyo	Macedonia	Illyrida
Canada	Quebec	Moldova	Gagauz Yeri
Chile	Rapa Nui	Moldova	Transdniestria
Nicaragua	Miskitia	Russia	Ichkeria/Chechnya
Peru	Collasuyo	Russia	Tatarstan
United States	Aztlan	Russia	Tyva
United States	Ka Lahui/Hawaii	Serbia	Kosovo
United States	Lakotah	Serbia	Montenegro
United States	New Afrika	Ukraine	Crimea
		USSR	Armenia
Western Europe		USSR	Azerbaijan
		USSR	Belarus
Belgium	Flanders	USSR	Estonia
Belgium	Wallonie-France	USSR	Georgia
Belgium	Eupen-Malmedy	USSR	Kazakhstan
Cyprus	Northern Cyprus	USSR	Kyrgyzstan
Denmark	Faroe Islands	USSR	Latvia
Finland	Aland Islands	USSR	Lithuania
France	Alsace-Lorraine	USSR	Moldova
France	Bretagne	USSR	Tajikistan
France	Corsica	USSR	Turkmenistan
France	Catalunha/Catalonia	USSR	Ukraine
France	Euskadi (Basque)	USSR	Uzbekistan
France	Savoy	Yugoslavia	Bosnia
Italy	Val d'Aosta	Yugoslavia	Croatia
Italy	South Tyrol	Yugoslavia	Macedonia
Italy	Friuli	Yugoslavia	Slovenia
Italy	Sardinia		
Netherlands	Fryslan	***North Africa/Southwest Asia***	
Spain	Catalunya/Catalonia		
Spain	Euskadi (Basque)	Algeria	Kabylie
Spain	Galiza	Iran	Arabistan/Ahwazi/
United Kingdom	Northern Ireland		Khuzestan
United Kingdom	Scotland	Iran	Azerbaijan
United Kingdom	Cymru/Wales	Iran	Gilan
		Iran	Kurdistan
Central Eurasia/Eastern Europe		Iran	West Balochistan
		Iraq	Assyria
Albania	Northern Epirus	Iraq	Kurdistan
Azerbaijan	Lezgistan	Morocco	Western Sahara
Azerbaijan	Nagornyi Karabakh	Sudan	Darfur
Azerbaijan	Talysh-Mugan	Sudan	South Sudan
Bosnia	Herzeg-Bosna	Syria	West Kurdistan
Bosnia	Republika Srpska	Turkey	Armenia
Croatia	Krajina	Turkey	Kurdistan
Czechoslovakia	Slovakia		
Georgia	Abkhazia		

Sub-Saharan Africa

Angola	Cabinda
Cameroon	Ambazonia
Chad	Bornu/Kanowra
Chad	Logone Republic
Chad	Northern Chad
Chad	Wadai
Congo-Zaire	Katanga
Congo-Zaire	Kongo/Lower Congo
Congo-Zaire	South Kasai
Cote d'Ivoire	Anyiland
Equatorial Guinea	Bioko/Otcho
Ethiopia	Afar
Ethiopia	Eritrea
Ethiopia	Ogaadeen/Ogaden
Ethiopia	Oromiyaa/Oromia
Ghana	Asanteman
Ghana	Eweland/Togoland
Kenya	Somalia
Mali	Tamoust/Air-Azawad
Mauritania	Chemama
Mauritius	Rodrigues Island
Namibia	Caprivi
Niger	Tenere/Air-Azawad
Nigeria	Benin
Nigeria	Biafra
Nigeria	Bornu/Kanowra
Nigeria	Ibibioland
Nigeria	Niger Delta
Nigeria	Oduduwa Republic
Senegal	Casamance
South Africa	Kwazulu
South Africa	Volkstaat/Boer Republic
Tanzania	Zanzibar
Uganda	Ankole
Uganda	Buganda
Uganda	Bunyoro
Uganda	Rwenzururu
Zambia	Barotseland
Zimbabwe	Matabeleland

South and East Asia

Bangladesh	Banglabhumi/Kaderia
Bhutan	Sikkim
Cambodia	Champa
China	Chinese Islamic Republic
China	Eastern Turkestan
China	Southern Mongolia
China	Tibet
India	Assam
India	Bodoland/Dimasaland
India	Kargi Anglong
India	Kashmir
India	Khalistan
India	Ladakh
India	Manipur/Kangleipak
India	Nagaland
India	Tamil Nadu
India	Sikkim
India	Tripura
India	Zozam/Mizoram
Indonesia	Aceh
Indonesia	Bali
Indonesia	Timor Leste
Indonesia	Maluku/South Moluccas
Indonesia	South Sulawesi
Indonesia	Sulawesi
Indonesia	West Papua
Laos	Meoland
Malaysia	Sarawak
Malaysia	Singapore
Myanmar	Chinland/Zomi
Myanmar	Kachinland
Myanmar	Kawthoolei (Karen)
Myanmar	Karenni State/Kayah
Myanmar	Kukiland/Zozam
Myanmar	Monland
Myanmar	Nagalim
Myanmar	Rakhine State
Myanmar	Shan States
Myanmar	Wa State
Pakistan	Balochistan
Pakistan	Bangladesh
Pakistan	Sindhudesh
Pakistan	Pashtunistan/Waziristan
Philippines	Bangsamoro
Sri Lanka	Tamil Eelam
Thailand	Patani
Vietnam	Khmer-Kampuchea

Australia/Oceania

Papua New Guinea	Bougainville

population must have exceeded 300,000 at some time between 1945 and 2010. Thus, national-secession campaigns in mini-states and micro-states are hypothetically excluded, except there were no instances of such movements in the search of newspapers from 1945 to 2010.

Alternative Definitions of the Cases for Comparison

Compared to other compilations used to study secessionism, the list of 171 significant national-secession campaigns analyzed in this study permits a more comprehensive and more precise analysis of national-secession campaigns that have gained attention in major-power policy circles from 1945 to present. On one hand, it is more complete than other studies of secession, which tend to include only select case studies or casual references. For example, Alexis Heraclides lists only thirteen secessionist movements in the Third World from 1945 to 1990.[4] All of Heraclides's cases are included among the 100 "significant national-secession campaigns" of this study located in Africa and Asia. Yet most campaigns are missing from Heraclides's study, and he does not provide criteria to justify the exclusion of other African and Asian national-secession campaigns, such as Balochistan or Bougainville, Tibet or Timor. Similarly, in his seminal study, Lee C. Buchheit mentions in passing about three dozen secessionist campaigns and offers six case studies, but he does not intend this to be an exhaustive list.[5]

On the other hand, the list of 171 significant national-secession campaigns is more precisely focused on the phenomenon of national secession (as defined in chapter 2) than are lists of national self-determination movements. The latter set of lists brackets a heterogeneous variety of cases involving "the quest of national and indigenous peoples for self-governance," and many of these are neither nationalist nor secessionist. For example, Marshall and Gurr study 148 national self-determination conflicts from 1955 to 2002.[6] They do not intend to limit their study to conflicts over secession and so include such cases as a minority seeking a new segment-state or greater autonomy for an existing segment-state within a common-state (e.g., Russia's Yakuts and Yugoslavia's Hungarians), a minority seeking expanded cultural autonomy without formal statehood (e.g., many indigenous peoples in the Western Hemisphere), a regional-secession campaign without a distinct people (e.g., the Nevisians of St. Kitts-Nevis), and an independence campaign on behalf of an external colony or external occupied territory (e.g., Puerto Ricans and Palestinians).

Similarly, Minahan identifies 350 "nations still without states" in 2002, which constituted 575 campaigns against specific common-states.[7] By Minahan's definition, his movements qualify as nations because each exhibits self-identity and "outward trappings of national consciousness" (such as a flag) and supports "formation of a specific nationalist organization or political grouping that reflects its claim to self-determination." Nonetheless, he lists far more than national-secession campaigns, including autonomy campaigns for statehood within the existing common-state (such as a restored Volga German Republic), campaigns for nonterritorial forms of autonomy (such as the Baha'is), regional-secession campaigns (such as Texas), decolonization movements (such as Wallis and Futuna), and simply whimsical campaigns (such as the Principality of Seborga). Nonetheless, Minahan's exhaustive compilations serve as useful checks in the construction of a list of significant national-secession campaigns in that Minahan identifies cases that might otherwise be overlooked and truly sets the agenda for double-checking the list with additional searches in the news sources.

The cases associated with national secession overlap but are not conterminous with the cases identified in several recent studies of "national independence." Paul F. Diehl and Gary Goertz bracket both decolonization and separatism to identify 121 cases of successful national independence between 1816 and 1980.[8] Benjamin E. Goldsmith and Baogang He follow in this trajectory but relabel these all as cases of "decolonization." Goldsmith and He's list of 145 cases from 1900 to 1994 includes 122 cases in the time period studied in this book (1945–2010), and 20 of these are successful secessions such as the Soviet and Yugoslav republics.[9] These data sets select on successful independence, so they do not seek to include unsuccessful independence campaigns and provide no criteria for identifying such. This is not useful for the purposes of this book, for most of the 171 national-secession campaigns since 1945 have so far been unsuccessful. Philip G. Roeder identifies segment-states, both internal and external, as the most likely candidates for independence but preserves the distinction between secession and decolonization.[10] More importantly, the former category (internal segment-states) does not include all cases of unsuccessful but still significant national-secession campaigns. Bridget Coggins continues in this tradition of examining independence projects but relabels these all as "secessions" and introduces what I tend to think is an oxymoron—"anticolonial secessions"—in order to distinguish external from internal independence projects.[11] Ryan D. Griffiths follows on this trajectory.[12]

Of course, in empirical applications the seemingly crisp distinction between secession and decolonization becomes more ambiguous when the colonial power attempts to hold on to a colony threatening independence by reclassifying it as an overseas department or province. France designated Algeria as three overseas departments in the Fourth Republic, Portugal reclassified at least seven of its colonies (such as Angola or Portuguese India) as overseas provinces beginning in 1946, and Spain followed a similar strategy with two of its colonies in Africa beginning in 1958. In order to ensure that the results of this study addressing secessionism are not biased by the inclusion of cases of decolonization, the analysis excludes colonies-in-provincial-clothing.[13] Inclusion would yield significance levels about which this author could boast because all of these colonies-in-provincial-clothing developed significant independence campaigns pressing for independence and many had extreme values for variables used in this study such as geographic remoteness from the metropolitan capital or cultural separation from the rest of the common-state population.

Types of Violence

Intensity is measured by combining data from three sources: (1) data on civil wars from the UCDP/PRIO Armed Conflict Dataset, maintained by the Uppsala Conflict Data Program; (2) data on terrorism from the Global Terrorism Database (GTD), maintained by the National Consortium for the Study of Terrorism and Responses to Terrorism (START); and (3) data on violent protest from the Nonviolent and Violent Campaigns and Outcomes (NAVCO) Data Project, compiled by Erica Chenoweth and Orion A. Lewis.[14] The data on violence are limited to the thirty-seven years between 1970 and 2006 because of the limits imposed by combination of the three data sets: UCDP covers 1945 to present, START begins in 1970, and NAVCO ends in 2006. From these sources the intensity of individual campaigns is measured as campaign years in which there was

1. *high-intensity violence* (battle-related or domestic-terrorism–related deaths exceed 1,000 in a year)
2. *intense violence* (battle-related or domestic-terrorism–related deaths exceed 25 in a year)
3. **low-intensity violence** (terror-related deaths do not exceed 25 in a year)
4. **nonlethal violence** (violent actions such as terrorist attacks or violent protests with no fatalities)
5. *no violence*

Civil wars include violence by both sides; domestic terrorism includes both terrorist acts perpetrated by members of the campaign and pro-government terrorist attacks against the campaign. The index for each campaign includes only civil wars identified as territorial disputes over the homeland involving the specific campaign or involving leading organizations within the campaign. Similarly, the index includes only terrorist acts performed by actors or against actors identified as separatists associated with the specific campaign or a leading organization in that campaign.

The distinction among civil wars, terrorism, and violent protest is not precise, and this is reflected in significant overlap in the data sets from which this analysis draws. For example, most significant campaigns of terrorism between 1970 and 2010 coded in the Global Terrorism Database are also coded as civil wars in the UCDP/PRIO Armed Conflict Dataset. The correlation between the intensity of civil war in a year (measured as the battle-related deaths) and the logarithm of the number killed in terrorist acts is 0.74. In all campaign years in which the Global Terrorism Database records that the number killed in terrorist acts exceeded one thousand, the UCDP/PRIO Armed Conflict Dataset also records that battle-related deaths exceeded one thousand. In only twenty-nine campaign years (out of 6,152) did the number of deaths from terrorist acts exceed twenty-five, but the intensity of civil war was not coded as having twenty-five or more battle-related deaths. Of these twenty-nine instances (campaign years), fourteen years were simply discrepancies in coding the beginning or ending date of a civil war in that they preceded or followed by one year the beginning or end of an episode of civil war. Only five campaigns associated with twenty-five or more terrorism-related deaths in a single year were never coded as having had civil war: Armenia (USSR), East Turkestan (China), Miskitia (Nicaragua), Tamil Nadu (India), and West Balochistan (Iran).

Statistical Estimation of the Contribution of Violence to Independence

The statistical results reported in chapter 2 concerning the contribution of violence to independence derive from a logit estimate in which the dichotomous dependent variable indicates a year in which a campaign received independence. The cases are campaign years. The first independent variable is a measure of the recency of high-intensity violence—measured by the nearness in time since a civil war involving the parties to the secessionist dispute claimed at least one thousand battle-related deaths in a year.[15] The second term is a dichotomous indicator of multilateral peacekeeping against the status quo.[16] The results appear in table 2A.2.

TABLE 2A.2. Logit results: Impact of war on independence, 1945–2010

	COEFFICIENT	STANDARD ERROR
High-intensity war impact	0.786	0.818
Peacekeeping against the status quo	3.607	0.707***
Constant	−6.057	0.220
	N = 9,095	

Significance: *** < .001

Appendix to Chapter 5

Chapters 5 and 8 report statistical estimations of the probability that an ethnic group will serve as a platform population (or part of a platform population) for a national-secession campaign that becomes significant.

The Cases

The data set from which these probabilities are estimated comprises 3,741 cross-sectional observations on the ethnic groups within each independent common-state.[1] For example, one observation is Tamils in India from independence (1947) to 2010, and another is Indian Tamils in Sri Lanka from independence (1948) to 2010. These data cover 1,348 distinct ethnicities[2] in 169 countries covering the years of independence from 1945 to 2010.[3] The identification of ethnic groups in each country (not such an easy task as it might seem) is based on data collected by Solomon I. Bruk, a Soviet ethnographer who compiled population estimates for ethno-linguistic groups around the world for more than a quarter of a century and published these in several reference volumes, including *Atlas narodov mira* and *Naselenie mira: etnodemograficheskii spravochnik*.[4] The first of these provides estimates of the population of each group at midyear 1961, the second at midyear 1985.[5] Ethnographers sometimes diverge in their identifications of ethnic groups, and these definitions have been fluid in some parts of the world—notably in East Africa and Southeast Asia. The data set uses a consistent classification scheme, reconciling disagreements with the assistance of data from periodic editions of *Ethnologue,* the Joshua Project, and R. E. Asher and Christopher Moseley's *Atlas of the World's Languages.*[6] The data account for 96 percent of the world's population in 1961 and 99 percent in 1985. Ethnic groups that are not listed separately are typically so small that they are grouped together in amalgamated categories, such as the Pamiri groups along the Tajik-Afghan border or the Carib-speaking groups in the Caribbean region. These are instances in which ethnographic conventions are unclear: some would classify the larger aggregation as an ethnic group and the smaller groups as tribal subgroupings; others maintain that the smaller groupings should be counted separately as ethnic groups.

The objective in the statistical estimations reported in chapters 5 and 8 is to identify the most important cues and constraints that influence whether a national-secession campaign on the platform of the identified ethnic group becomes significant. Thus, unlike the Minorities at Risk (MAR) and Ethnic Political Relations (EPR) projects, this ethnic-group data set cannot identify the unit of analysis on the basis of the ethnic group's involvement in politics. In the EPR project, Andreas Wimmer, Lars-Erik Cederman, and Brian Min use "politically relevant ethnic groups" as their unit of analysis (observations). So whether a group is included in the data set and the identity and boundaries of each group are defined by politics: "if at least one significant political actor claims to represent the interests of that group in the national political arena, or if members of an ethnic category are systematically and intentionally discriminated against in the domain of public politics." In the EPR data set, "The list of politically relevant categories changes from one year to the next (either because certain categories ceased to be or became relevant for the first time, or because higher or lower levels of ethnic differentiation became salient)."[7] The list of "politically relevant ethnic groups" is similar to Ted Robert Gurr's list of ethno-political groups in the MAR data set. Gurr's groups are included in the MAR data set because they have come to international attention as objects of governmental discrimination or bases of mobilization for political action.[8] These other studies have defined their units of analysis to answer questions that are subsequent to the question put forward here. For the question asked in chapter 5, these earlier definitions would endogenize the definition of cases and would not permit us to investigate which groups achieved international attention as platforms for national-secession campaigns (and which groups did not).[9]

Thus, the ethnic-groups data set introduced here defines the unit of analysis in a way that is independent of the dependent variable. In the data set used in the statistical estimations reported in chapter 5 (and the analysis of campaign significance in chapter 8), ethnicities are defined primarily by cultural differences, such as language or religion. Political activism to promote independence is the dependent variable that the estimation seeks to explain. For example, there is no observation (case) called "Cabindans." Instead, the Cabinda secessionist project draws its primary support from the Bakongo people of Angola. They constitute an observation in the data set and are the platform population on which the significant Cabinda national-secession campaign has been constructed.

The Variables

The tests use the variables listed in table 5A.1.

TABLE 5A.1. Summary statistics: Variables included in tests of campaign significance

	ALL CASES				WITH HOMELAND			
	OBS	MEAN	MIN[a]	MAX[a]	OBS	MEAN	MIN[a]	MAX[a]
Dependent variable								
Campaign significance	3741	0.074	0	1	2119	0.130	0	1
Authenticity								
Distinct territory	3741	0.566	0	1	—	—	—	—
No alternative homeland	3741	0.658	0	1	2119	0.944	0	1
Realism								
Prior statehood	3741	0.027	0	1	2119	0.048	0	1
Platform population	3709	10.484	2.751	20.613	2119	11.373	2.751	20.613
Largest group	3741	0.039	0	1	2119	0.067	0	1
Ethno-linguistic coalition potential	3725	4.019	0	50.500	2118	5.024	0	50.500
Religious coalition potential	3730	0.052	0	0.499	2116	0.064	0	0.499
Costly defection								
Constitutional exclusion	3692	0.067	0	1	2087	0.044	0	1
Exclusion from governance	3692	0.877	0.000	1.000	2087	0.866	0.000	1.000
Home alone	3452	0.378	0.000	1.000	2020	0.604	0.000	1.000
Cultural grievance								
Muslim	3741	0.201	0	1	2119	0.216	0	1
Muslim minority in Christian state	3741	0.016	0	1	2119	0.015	0	1
Christian	3741	0.527	0	1	2119	0.465	0	1
Christian minority in Islamic state	3741	0.025	0	1	2119	0.009	0	1

(Continued)

TABLE 5A.1.   (Continued)

	ALL CASES			WITH HOMELAND			
	OBS	MEAN	MIN[a]	MAX[a]	OBS	MEAN	MIN[a]	MAX[a]
Economic grievance								
GDP per capita	3726	7.366	4.880	10.189	2108	6.799	4.880	10.189
Homeland development	1751	0.366	0	19.500	1750	0.366	0	19.500
Homeland urbanization	1749	0.055	0	3.119	1748	0.055	0	3.119
Relative homeland development	1751	1.575	0	410.526	1750	1.575	0	410.526
Economic greed								
Petroleum in homeland	1824	0.162	0	1	1823	0.162	0	1
Diamonds in homeland	1824	0.086	0	1	1823	0.086	0	1
Tactical opportunity								
Relative governing load	3739	3.644	1.554	7.580	2118	3.866	1.554	7.580
Democracy	3679	0.420	0.000	1.000	2093	0.318	0.000	1.000
Autocracy	3679	0.319	0.000	1.000	2093	0.376	0.000	1.000
Regime instability	3676	0.367	0.000	1.595	2090	0.422	0.000	1.595
OECD expatriates	3595	4.278	−6.908	12.113	2111	2.625	−6.908	12.113
Geographic exclave	3741	0.067	0	1	2119	0.114	0	1
Distance from national capital	1815	4.881	0	8.945	1814	4.879	0	8.945
Distance to international border	1815	2.410	0	7.753	1814	2.407	0	7.753
Adjacent homeland	3741	0.103	0	1	2119	0.154	0	1
Multiethnic project	3741	0.048	0	1	2119	0.084	0	1

[a] Min/max of 0/1 indicates a dichotomous variable; 0.000/1.000 indicates a continuous variable.

Dependent Variable: Significant National-Secession Campaign

This dichotomous variable indicates that the ethnic group is the platform population or part of the multiethnic platform population for one of the 171 significant national-secession campaigns identified in chapter 2.

Independent Variables: Programmatic Hypotheses

Distinct territory (a dichotomous variable) indicates that the ethnic group constitutes the dominant (plurality) population of some part of the territory of the common-state. This is operationalized from maps and descriptions of geographic settlement patterns of ethnic groups.[10]

No alternative homeland (a dichotomous variable) indicates that the ethnic group does not have an alternative, noncontiguous homeland (such as Norway for Norwegians in the United States) that might compete as a focal point. Ethnic groups with homelands that are adjacent to the common-state are identified by another variable (see "adjacent homeland," below).

Prior statehood (a dichotomous variable) indicates that the ethnic group had one of the following immediately prior to (or since) incorporation into the current common-state: an independent state prior to or since incorporation (but not earlier than World War I, e.g., Estonia), during a period of foreign occupation of the common-state (e.g., Slovakia), or during a period of civil war or revolution (e.g., Georgia); a separate protectorate or colony (e.g., Eritrea); or a proto-state (e.g., Wadaï).[11]

Platform population. The natural logarithm of each ethnic group's population is estimated at the midpoint year.[12] (For example, in common-states independent from 1945 to 2010 this midpoint year is 1978.)

Largest group (a dichotomous variable) indicates the largest ethnic group in each common-state.

Ethno-linguistic or *religious coalition potential.* Two variables estimate the potential for a larger platform based on a coalition of related ethnic groups. The first is the probability that in a random encounter within the common-state a member of the ethnic group will encounter another person who speaks either the same language or a closely related language within the same linguistic "group" (such as the Slavic or Tibeto-Burman language groups). The second is the probability of encountering another from the same religious civilization (such as Hindu or Islamic).[13]

Constitutional exclusion (a dichotomous variable) indicates that the common-state has declared a state religion or developed a particularly close identification with a religion (specifically, Christianity, Islam, Hinduism, or Buddhism) to which a majority of the ethnic group does not belong.[14]

Exclusion from governance measures the proportion of years in which the ethnic group did not participate in the ruling coalition (such as the cabinet or "government"), even though it was not constitutionally excluded (see the previous variable).[15]

Home alone measures the proportion of the global population of an ethnic group that resides within the observation-state in 1985. As this approaches 100 percent, fewer co-ethnics are abroad for migrants to join.[16]

Independent Variables: Hypotheses from Earlier Studies

Muslim and *Christian* (two dichotomous variables) indicate that members of the ethnic group are either predominantly Muslim or predominantly Christian.[17]

Muslim minority in Christian state and *Christian minority in Islamic state* (two dichotomous variables) indicate not simply "constitutional exclusion" (above) but the particular cultural content of that exclusion: Muslim ethnic minorities residing within states closely associated with a Christian church and Christian ethnic minorities residing in states with close association with Islam.

Common-state GDP per capita measures the common-state's development at the midpoint year expressed as the natural logarithm in constant dollars.[18]

Homeland development. This estimate of the development of the homeland itself (in 1992) uses GIS satellite measures of the nighttime light intensity for each pixel within the homeland divided by the population within that homeland.[19]

Homeland urbanization. This estimate of the urbanization of the homeland itself (in 1990) uses GIS satellite estimates of the proportion of the population residing in urban centers.[20]

Relative homeland development. This estimate of relative inequality is the ratio of the light intensity per capita within the homeland (see "homeland development," above) to the light intensity per capita for the country as a whole.

Petroleum in homeland (a dichotomous variable based on GIS data) indicates that oil or gas deposits are found within the homeland.[21]

Diamonds in homeland (a dichotomous variable based on GIS data) indicates that diamond deposits are found within the homeland.[22]

Relative governing load is the ratio of common-state governing load to state capacity—that is, the ratio of common-state area (natural logarithm) to common-state age (natural logarithm).[23]

Democracy and *Autocracy* measure, separately, the percentage of years that the common-state was a democracy or an autocracy. As either approaches 100 percent, this is an index of the stability and institutionalization of the regime.[24]

Regime instability measures the average annual change (average of the absolute value of the annual point changes) in the common-state's Polity score.

OECD expatriates. An indicator of a substantial, resourced diaspora is the population size (natural logarithm) of co-ethnics living in OECD countries in 1985.[25]

Geographic exclave (a dichotomous variable) indicates whether there is an exclave, such as Cabinda, or an island, such as Rapa Nui, on which at least 10 percent of the ethnic group's population resides and might constitute a base of operations against the common-state.

Distance from national capital. The distance in kilometers (plus one kilometer) from the common-state capital to the closest edge of the platform population's homeland (as identified in "distinct territory," above) is expressed as the natural logarithm.[26]

Distance to international border is the shortest distance in kilometers (plus one kilometer) between the outer edge of the platform population's homeland and an international border expressed as the natural logarithm.[27] This is estimated from GIS data.

Adjacent homeland (a dichotomous variable) indicates that the ethnic group constitutes the largest group in an adjacent independent state.[28]

Multiethnic project (a dichotomous variable) indicates that the platform population of the campaign consists of multiple ethnic groups.

Procedures

The estimation procedure is logit analysis, which permits estimation of the effect of each cue and constraint on the binary dependent variable. With additional calculation, logit analysis also provides estimates of the probability of a significant campaign when each independent variable takes on specific values. In the first model all ethnic groups are included (see table 5A.2, model 1) in a logit equation with clustering on the common-state. Because no ethnic groups without "distinct territory" within the respective common-state became platform populations for significant national-secession campaigns, these ethnic groups are dropped automatically by the logit analysis. Variables based on GIS data are unavailable for

TABLE 5A.2. Logit results: Ethnic groups that become platforms for significant national-secession campaigns (clustering on common-state)

	MODEL 1		MODEL 2	
	COEFFICIENT	STANDARD ERROR	COEFFICIENT	STANDARD ERROR
Authenticity				
Distinct territory	—[a]		—[a]	
No alternative homeland	1.9326	0.6060***	1.7737	0.5444***
Realism				
Prior statehood	4.7283	1.2766***	3.3219	0.6893***
Platform population	0.5081	0.0990***	0.5109	0.1077***
Largest group	−1.3336	0.5519*	−1.5250	0.5670**
Ethno-linguistic coalition	0.0253	0.0083**	0.0266	0.0089**
Religious coalition	0.0187	1.6565	0.5811	1.6221
Costly defection				
Constitutional exclusion	4.1052	1.0201***	3.8074	0.9503***
Exclusion from governance	1.7187	0.6277**	1.6587	0.6172**
Home alone	−0.3938	0.3263	−0.1765	0.3508

(Continued)

TABLE 5A.2. (Continued)

	MODEL 1		MODEL 2	
	COEFFICIENT	STANDARD ERROR	COEFFICIENT	STANDARD ERROR
Culture				
Muslim	1.1297	0.3746**	1.3287	0.3751***
Muslim minority in	1.7579	1.1610	1.6395	0.9586
Christian state				
Christian	1.3536	0.3426***	1.5721	0.3489***
Christian minority	−1.6377	1.4486	−1.6961	1.3048
in Muslim state				
Economic grievance				
Common-state	−0.0154	0.1481	−0.1112	0.1390
GDP per capita				
Homeland	—	—	0.1334	0.0695
development				
Homeland	—	—	0.8107	0.5812
urbanization				
Relative homeland	—	—	−0.0008	0.0052
development				
Economic greed				
Petroleum in	—	—	0.3216	0.2868
homeland				
Diamonds in	—	—	−0.3179	0.3790
homeland				
Tactical opportunity				
Relative governing	0.0889	0.1363	0.0519	0.1325
load				
Democracy	1.6891	0.9074	1.4467	0.7208*
Autocracy	1.7979	1.2580	1.5363	1.0156
Regime instability	0.2114	0.3705	0.0579	0.3657
Resourced	−0.0156	0.0673	−0.0473	0.0700
diaspora				
Geographic	0.9521	0.4786*	0.7889	0.5764
exclave				
Distance to	—	—	0.1118	0.0792
capital				
Distance to	—	—	−0.2038	0.0760**
border				
Adjacent	−0.5615	0.4005	−0.7868	0.3919*
homeland				
Constant	−14.4663	2.9848***	−13.6077	2.7190***
	N = 1,944		N = 1,610	
	Pseudo-R² = 0.367		Pseudo-R² = 0.324	

[a] Absence of distinct territory perfectly predicts no significant campaign. Ethnic groups without distinct territories were dropped from estimation.

Significance: *$p < .05$; **$p < .01$;***$p < .001$

some ethnic groups, so these variables are not included in this first model. In a second model the variables based on GIS data are included (see table 5A.2, model 2), but this results in a 17 percent decrease in the number of cases because of the limited coverage of the satellite data.

The presence of multiethnic projects in the data, such as the South Sudan or Eritrea projects, raises the suspicion that multiple observations on the same national-secession project may overweight the characteristics of these groups in the statistical estimation. One control for the interdependence among some cases appears in models 1 and 2 by inclusion of the coalition potential variable, but this does not resolve the problem. There is no conventional "fix" of such a confounding factor, so further tests use three alternative specifications of model 1 to see whether these change the statistical significance of estimates (see table 5A.3). First, a variable for multiethnic projects is added (model 1a). Second, only the largest ethnic group in each multiethnic project is included in the estimation (model 1b). And third, model 1 is estimated with clustering on linguistic phylum

TABLE 5A.3.   Reestimation of model 1 with controls for multiethnic projects

| | MODEL 1A | | MODEL 1B | | MODEL 1C | |
| | ADD VARIABLE | | DELETE CASES | | CLUSTER ON PHYLUM | |
	COEFFICIENT	STANDARD ERROR	COEFFICIENT	STANDARD ERROR	COEFFICIENT	STANDARD ERROR
Multiethnic project	3.6192	0.8376***	—		—	
No alternative homeland	2.1742	0.6195***	2.3836	0.8381**	1.9326	0.6524**
Prior statehood	3.9998	0.7651***	3.4389	0.6141***	4.7283	1.1231***
Platform population	0.6649	0.1111***	0.7054	0.1116***	0.5081	0.0860***
Largest group	−1.7124	0.6222**	−1.6831	0.6141**	−1.3336	0.6652*
Ethno-linguistic coalition	0.0240	0.0095*	0.0188	0.0099	0.0253	0.0082**
Religious coalition	0.0469	1.0911	−0.7312	1.0266	0.0187	1.2136
Constitutional exclusion	3.9469	0.9304***	3.4407	0.9522***	4.1052	0.9560***
Exclusion from governance	1.7383	0.5874**	2.2200	0.6067***	1.7187	0.7013*
Home alone	−0.9735	0.3867*	−0.7763	0.3759*	−0.3938	0.3562
Muslim	1.6862	0.4382***	1.3286	0.4268**	1.1297	0.3328***
Muslim minority in Christian state	1.0166	0.8957	1.1281	0.8431	1.7579	1.1326
Christian	1.9736	0.3427***	1.6491	0.3676***	1.3536	0.3066***
Christian minority in Islamic state	−2.8043	1.4278*	−1.6524	1.5208	−1.6377	1.5275

(Continued)

TABLE 5A.3. (Continued)

	MODEL 1A		MODEL 1B		MODEL 1C	
	ADD VARIABLE		DELETE CASES		CLUSTER ON PHYLUM	
	COEFFICIENT	STANDARD ERROR	COEFFICIENT	STANDARD ERROR	COEFFICIENT	STANDARD ERROR
GDP per capita	0.0760	0.1321	0.0337	0.1226	-0.0154	0.1419
Relative governing load	-0.0520	0.1189	-0.0064	0.0992	0.0889	0.1113
Democracy	1.2496	0.8448	1.4781	0.7340*	1.6891	0.8424*
Autocracy	1.4470	1.1078	1.2918	1.0507	1.7979	1.0709
Regime instability	0.1595	0.3467	-0.0757	0.3366	0.2114	0.3389
OECD diaspora	-0.0161	0.0689	-0.0099	0.0691	-0.0156	0.0658
Geographic exclave	0.4889	0.4257	0.5997	0.4835	0.9521	0.4876
Adjacent homeland	-0.7070	0.4394	-0.8776	0.4650	-0.5615	0.3743
Constant	-16.9226	2.4588***	-17.4790	2.3000***	-14.466	2.2362***
	N = 1,944		N = 1,808		N = 1,944	
	Pseudo-R^2 = 0.476		Pseudo-R^2 = 0.347		Pseudo-R^2 = 0.367	

Significance: *$p < .05$; **$p < .01$;***$p < .001$

within each country (model 1c). These three alternative specifications were also estimated for model 2 (not shown), with the same results. The programmatic variables remain strongly significant except for the coalition potential variable. As might be expected, this becomes less significant and drops below the .05 level of significance in one of the alternative specifications of model 1.

Models 1 and 2 are used to generate estimates of the effect of each variable on the probability that an ethnic group will be a platform population or part of a platform population for a significant national-secession campaign. These probabilities are calculated by the Clarify procedure developed by Gary King, Michael Tomz, and Jason Wittenberg.[29] In estimating first differences, all other variables are set to their means as the variable in question varies from minimum to maximum value. (Exceptions to this rule about setting other variables to their means are noted in the footnotes to the table of results.) These results are shown in table 5.1 in chapter 5.

Appendix to Chapter 7

The statistical results for protracted intense struggles reported in chapters 7 and 8 focus on the 171 significant national-secession campaigns identified in chapter 2. The statistical estimations use three data sets.[1] The first two measure the extent to which the national-secession campaigns were engaged in violence (including civil war, terrorism, and nonlethal violence) between 1970 and 2006. The first data set configures the data as cross-sectional observations for each campaign summarizing the entire period; the second configures this as panel data (pooled time-series cross section) with separate observations on individual years for each campaign. The third data set measures engagement of the campaigns in civil wars only (omitting terrorism and nonlethal violence) between 1945 and 2010 and is configured as panel observations for each year of each campaign.

Variables

The conflicts involve only wars or acts of terrorism and nonlethal violence in which the secessionists were parties. This focus on national secession violence diverges from the many fine, earlier studies that focus on "ethnic" civil wars—many of which do not involve national-secessionist goals.[2] The tests use the variables listed in table 7A.1. Several of the independent variables are identical to those described in the appendix to chapter 5, except that some platform populations are multiethnic groupings in the present data set, and the midpoint year refers to years of independence between 1970 and 2006 in the present data set.

TABLE 7A.1. Summary statistics: Variables included in estimation of protracted intensity

	CROSS-SECTION, 1970–2006				PANEL, 1945–2010			
	OBS	MEAN	MIN	MAX	OBS	MEAN	MIN	MAX
Dependent variable								
Protracted intensity	170	9.510	0	79.688				
Intense conflict					5566	0.112	0	1
Intense civil war					9095	0.091	0	1
Programmatic constraints								
Statehood	170	0.440	0	1	9095	0.383	0	1
Constitutional exclusion	170	0.082	0	1	9095	0.084	0	1
Governmental exclusion	170	0.749	0	1.000	9095	0.680	0	1
Exclusion from participation	168	0.257	0	1.000	9095	0.278	0	1
Democratic regime	170	0.352	0	1.000	9003	0.370	0	1
Platform size	170	13.593	6.654	18.070	9089	13.696	-8.207	18.146
Cultural grievances								
Linguistic distance	170	0.559	0	1				
Religious distance	170	0.453	0	1				
Civilization-cleft platform	170	0.324	0	1				
Linguistically divided platform	170	0.112	0	1				
Muslim	170	0.306	0	1				
Christian	170	0.524	0	1				
Economic grievances								
Homeland development	163	0.741	0	10.590				
Homeland urbanization	162	0.112	0	1.000				
Relative homeland development	163	2.584	0	79.843				
Common-state urbanization	169	38.184	6.1	93.800				
Common-state GDP per capita	167	7.728	6.240	9.618				
Economic growth					8271	0.023	-0.615	0.665

Tactical opportunities

Balance of coercive capacity	166	26.506	0.001	420.445	8638	35.541	0.000	3885.03
Weak common-state regime	170	0.210	0	1.000	9003	0.205	0	1
Petroleum in homeland	163	0.319	0	1				
Diamonds in homeland	163	0.117	0	1				
Distance between capitals	170	6.105	0	8.958				
Homeland exclave	170	0.118	0	1				
Distance to international border	163	1.767	0	7.772				
Adjacent homeland	170	0.153	0	1				
Mountainous terrain	170	276.506	0.723	1366.336				
Resourced expatriates	170	4.606	-1.152	11.067				
Other secessionist projects	170	3.999	0	13				
Sudan	170	0.006	0	1				
State violence	170	13.988	0	100				

Dependent Variables: Intensity and Protraction of Violence

Index of protracted intense conflict. This cross-sectional dependent variable is an index of protracted intensity that ranges from no violence to maximum intensity every year. This brings together data on civil wars from the UCDP/PRIO Armed Conflict Dataset, terrorist attacks from the Global Terrorism Database, and violent protests from the Nonviolent and Violent Campaigns and Outcomes Data Project (NAVCO) from 1970 to 2006.[3] In the computation of this index, first, each campaign year is scored zero to eight by the maximum intensity of violence reached in that campaign year according to the following scale:

8 = Highest-intensity violence. Battle-related or domestic-terrorism–related deaths exceed 1,000 in that year. Average deaths per year in this category = 2833.7; $ln(2833.7) = 7.95$.

5 = Intense violence. Battle-related or domestic terrorism-related deaths total between 25 and 1,000 in that year. Average deaths per year in this category = 144.8; $ln(144.8) = 4.98$.

2.5 = Low-intensity violence. Terror-related deaths do not exceed 25 in that year. Midpoint in this category = 12.5; $ln(12.5) = 2.53$.

1 = Least-intense violence. Terrorist attacks or violent protests produce no terror-related or battle-related deaths in that year.

The weights for the first three levels of the scale are the corresponding natural logarithms of the average number of deaths at that level. Second, in order to compute the total intensity of violence over the period, the year scores for each campaign are summed. Third, in order to calculate the annual average intensity (to control for the different numbers of years that each campaign is included in the data set), this sum is divided by the maximum score possible for that campaign. This is simply 8 (the maximum weight) times the number of years that the campaign is included in the data set (that is, since 1970 or since independence of the common-state within which the campaign is located and until 2006 or until achievement of independence by the secessionist campaign). This index of "protracted intense conflict" ranges from 0 to 100; the highest score represents highest-intensity violence associated with a campaign during every year that its common-state was independent and remained whole from 1970 to 2006. So the index of protracted intensity for each campaign is

$$\frac{100 \times \sum \text{Intensity}_t}{\text{Years} \times 8}$$

where Intensity_t is the maximum intensity of violence in year t
Years is the number of years that the campaign is in the data set.

Annual indicator of campaign violence. The first panel-data indicator of intensity is a dichotomous variable indicating that in this year the national-secession campaign was a party to violent conflict that brought at least 25 battle-related or terror-related deaths. Using the same sources as the previous index, these observations cover 170 campaigns from 1970 to 2006. (As in the cross-sectional index, Singapore is dropped because it became independent in 1965—prior to the first year of this data set.)

Annual indicator of civil war. The second panel-data indicator of intensity, permitting analysis of a longer historical period, is a dichotomous variable indicating that in this year the campaign was a party to a civil war that brought at least 25 battle-related civil war deaths. This indicator, covering all 171 campaigns from 1945 to 2010, uses only the data on civil wars.

There are two possible sources of measurement error in the dependent variables, so two dichotomous indicators are introduced in secondary reestimations of the equations. First, the terrorism measures distinguish deaths attributable to acts committed by the national-secession campaigns, but the estimates of death from battle in civil war do not distinguish the authors of casualties—that is, whether these were perpetrated by the national-secession campaign or the common-state government. In order to account for the deaths attributable to government violence, a secondary reestimation introduces a dichotomous indicator for years of intense common-state governmental violence against each campaign (described below). Second, the terrorism data permit focusing on violence attributable to secessionist campaigns, but the civil wars data do not permit separating out violence attributable to allies fighting alongside the secessionists but with different agendas. One campaign stands out, reporting substantially less terrorism (more than two standard deviations fewer than predicted by the intensity of civil war): South Sudan. This reflects the difficulty in classifying the military action of the South Sudan campaign, in which the leadership divided over competing objectives to transform Sudan or to secede as an independent South Sudan. (This division is described in chapter 2.) In a secondary reestimation, a dichotomous control variable is included for the South Sudan project. Alternatively, nine campaigns reported significantly more terrorism (more than two standard deviations more) than predicted from the civil wars data: East Turkestan (China), Euskadi (Spain), Ichkeria (Russia), Khalistan (India), Krajina (Croatia), Miskitia (Nicaragua), Niger Delta (Nigeria), Tamil Nadu (India), and Tamoust/Air and Azawad (Mali).[4]

Independent Variables: Cues to Programmatic Credibility

Statehood measures the proportion of years that the platform population and homeland were recognized by and within the jurisdiction of the common-state as a segment state (such as Tibet) or remained outside this jurisdiction as an unrecognized, de facto state (such as Transdniestria).[5] In the panel data, "statehood" is dichotomous and measured in each prior year (t-1).

Constitutional exclusion. This is described in the appendix to chapter 5. In the panel data this is dichotomous and measured in each prior year (t-1).

Governmental exclusion. This is described in the appendix to chapter 5. In the panel data this is dichotomous and measured in each prior year (t-1).

Exclusion from participation measures the proportion of years that the platform population confronted policies that "substantially restrict the group's political participation by comparison with other groups."[6] In the panel data this is dichotomous and measured in the prior year (t-1).

Democratic regime. This is described in the appendix to chapter 5. In the panel data this is dichotomous and measured in each prior year (t-1).

Platform size. This is described in the appendix to chapter 5. In the panel data this is measured in each prior year (t-1).

Independent Variables: Constraints Generating Motivations

Linguistic distance indicates that the platform population speaks a language that belongs to a different linguistic family (e.g., Slavic, Romance, or Germanic) than the language spoken by the largest ethnic group within the common-state.[7]

Religious distance indicates that the majority of the platform population belongs to a different civilization or religious sect (branch) than the largest ethnic group within the common-state. The data set identifies six civilizations (Western Christian, Orthodox Christian, Islam, Hinduism, Buddhism, and Ethnic) and eight sects (branches) within the first five civilizations: Catholicism and Protestantism, Eastern Orthodoxy and Oriental Orthodoxy, Shia Islam and Sunni Islam, Sikhism (within Hinduism), and Lamaism (within Buddhism).[8]

Linguistically divided platform indicates that the platform population comprises multiple ethno-linguistic groups (e.g., the South Sudan campaign) rather than a single titular ethnicity (e.g., the Estonia campaign).

Civilization-cleft platform indicates that the platform population is religiously diverse, including significant religious-civilization minorities.

Muslim or *Christian.* This is described in the appendix to chapter 5.

Homeland development. This is described in the appendix to chapter 5.

Homeland urbanization. This is described in the appendix to chapter 5.

Relative homeland development. This is described in the appendix to chapter 5.

Common-state urbanization is measured at the midpoint year.[9] In the panel data this is measured in each prior year (t-1).

Common-state GDP per capita is expressed as the natural logarithm and measured at the midpoint year.[10] In the panel data this is measured in each prior year (*t-1*).

Economic growth is measured by the percentage change in per capita gross domestic product in the prior year (change between year *t-2* and *t-1*).[11]

Independent Variables: Constraints on Coercive Contests

Balance of coercive capacity measures the balance between the mobilization potential of the platform population and the current common-state military capabilities. This is the ratio of the platform population to the armed forces of the common-state.[12] In the panel data this is measured in each prior year (*t-1*).

Weak common-state regime is the proportion of years that the common-state failed to establish a strong autocracy or strong democracy.[13] In the panel data this is dichotomous and measured in each prior year (*t-1*).

Petroleum in homeland. This is described in the appendix to chapter 5.

Diamonds in homeland. This is described in the appendix to chapter 5.

Distance between capitals is measured by the natural logarithm of the great circle distance (in kilometers) from the capital of the proposed secessionist state to the capital of the common-state.

Homeland exclave. This is described in the appendix to chapter 5.

Distance to international border. This is described in the appendix to chapter 5.

Adjacent homeland. This is described in the appendix to chapter 5.

Mountainous terrain is measured by the standard deviation of elevations within a 50 kilometer radius around the secessionist capital.[14]

Resourced expatriates is the natural logarithm of the number of co-ethnics (such as Armenians abroad) living in OECD countries in 1978.[15]

Other secessionist projects is the number of other significant national-secession projects within the same common-state.

Independent Variables: Control Variables for Measurement Error

South Sudan is a dummy variable for this one campaign because the violence data sources do not permit distinguishing violence that was secessionist from violence that was revolutionary (seeking to control Sudan's common-state government).

State violence against the platform population is the proportion of years that the common-state government engaged in military actions against identified platform populations.[16] This serves as a proxy for the multiple causes of the state violence that is also measured by the civil wars data.

Procedures

In the cross-sectional estimations the effect of the constraints identified in earlier hypotheses advanced by grievance and opportunities approaches are initially estimated in two different ways. First, they are estimated separately to assess their ability to explain protracted intense violence without the presence of the programmatic constraints. Second, all variables are included in a combined estimation. Table 7A.2 shows the results of these two approaches to initial estimations. The first two columns of numbers are the results from the separate estimations of each family of explanations, and the second two columns are the results from the combined estimation using all variables.

The variables that are significant at the .05 level in either of these initial estimations are then included in two reestimations shown in table 7A.3. (In these reestimations the "homeland urbanization" variable is dropped because so many observations are missing.) The last two columns of numbers include the variables to control for possible measurement error in the dependent variable. (In this second reestimation the "balance of coercive capacity" variable is dropped because it is not significant in the first reestimation and because so many observations are missing.)

The dependent variable in the cross-sectional estimation is not normally distributed—only 87 (51 percent) have nonzero scores. Moreover, variation of the dependent variable is limited between 0 and 100. In order to begin to address the estimation problems that might emerge from this, an alternative estimation of the equation uses a logit model. All variables from the equations in table 7A.3 are included in a panel (pooled time-series cross-sectional) estimation of the likelihood that in any year from 1970 to 2006 the campaign was party to a conflict that reported at least twenty-five terror-related or battle-related deaths (intense or highest-intensity violence). The first two columns of figures in table 7A.4 report the results of the estimations with robust standard errors controlling for clustering on the campaign. The second two columns in table 7A.4 show results when years of continuing intense violence are dropped. (That is, the second reestimation drops any year in which $Intense\ Violence_{t-1} = 1$. This second equation, which follows a procedure used in the study of the outbreak of civil war, is an estimate of the initiation of a new episode of intense violence—a slightly different question from the one addressed in chapter 7. The second reestimation, which removes years of continuing warfare, limits the problem of endogeneity in which war in year $t\text{-}1$ may affect independent variables such as democracy or exclusion from participation in year $t\text{-}1$. Nonetheless, this changes the question being addressed to the initiation of intense violence and does not address protraction.

TABLE 7A.2. Regression results: Estimation of alternative analytic approaches, 1970–2006 (cross-sectional OLS regression)

	SEPARATE ESTIMATIONS		COMBINED ESTIMATION	
	COEFFICIENT	STANDARD ERROR	COEFFICIENT	STANDARD ERROR
Equation 1: Grievances				
Linguistic distance	1.143	2.771	−2.049	2.566
Religious distance	2.697	2.797	−0.502	2.677
Linguistically divided platform	6.699	4.342	−0.412	4.211
Civilization-cleft platform	2.607	3.197	1.035	3.063
Muslim	0.711	3.091	2.444	2.936
Homeland development	−0.033	1.002	0.658	0.956
Homeland urbanization	−12.817	8.753	−16.070	7.741*
Relative homeland development	0.216	0.158	0.129	0.139
Common-state urbanization	−0.031	0.079	−0.032	0.076
Constant	7.744	4.224	—	—
	N = 161			
	R^2 = 0.086 (adjusted 0.032)			
Equation 2: Tactical opportunities				
Balance of coercive capacity	0.112	0.036**	0.041	0.036
Weak common-state regime	−9.565	6.407	−6.285	6.149
Petroleum in homeland	−3.791	3.064	−5.436	2.970
Diamonds in homeland	−6.229	4.359	0.915	4.084
Distance from capital	1.916	1.051	1.412	1.004
Homeland exclave	7.501	4.989	6.631	4.406
Distance to international border	−1.243	0.876	−0.706	0.765
Adjacent homeland	0.422	4.302	−0.791	3.869
Mountainous terrain	−0.001	0.005	−0.007	0.005
Resourced expatriates	0.077	0.724	0.319	0.697
Other secessionist projects	0.246	0.389	−0.024	0.381
Constant	−0.912	8.000	—	—
	N = 161			
	R^2 = 0.104 (adjusted 0.038)			
Equation 3: Programmatic constraints				
Statehood	6.447	2.345**	9.499	2.997**
Constitutional exclusion	19.804	4.378***	21.659	5.443***
Governmental exclusion	7.711	2.808**	8.291	3.467*
Exclusion from participation	22.654	2.934***	18.917	3.577***
Democratic regime	4.461	2.512	5.749	3.690
Platform size	1.669	0.648*	1.222	0.945
Constant	−30.438	9.548**	−28.384	12.641*
	N = 168		N = 157	
	R^2 = 0.406 (adjusted 0.384)		R^2 = 0.484 (adjusted 0.381)	

*Significance: *$p < .05$; **$p < .01$; ***$p < .001$*

TABLE 7A.3. Regression results: Alternative specifications of programmatic model, 1970–2006 (cross-sectional OLS regression)

	PROGRAMMATIC AND OTHER SIGNIFICANT CONSTRAINTS		PROGRAMMATIC AND CONTROL CONSTRAINTS	
	COEFFICIENT	STANDARD ERROR	COEFFICIENT	STANDARD ERROR
Statehood	6.872	2.430**	6.007	2.072**
Constitutional exclusion	20.105	4.657***	14.125	3.999***
Governmental exclusion	8.275	2.881**	7.386	2.479**
Exclusion from participation	22.365	3.066***	15.620	2.800***
Democratic regime	4.792	2.577	6.448	2.237**
Platform size	1.560	0.673*	1.077	0.578
Balance of coercive capacity	0.022	0.020	—	—
South Sudan	—	—	30.019	12.301*
State violence	—	—	0.208	0.033***
Constant	−30.136	9.763**	−23.539	8.490**
	N = 164		N = 168	
	R^2 = 0.402		R^2 = 0.543	
	(adjusted R^2 = 0.376)		(adjusted R^2 = 0.520)	

*Significance: *p < .05; **p < .01; ***p < .001*

TABLE 7A.4. Logit results: Initiation of intense violence, 1970–2006 (panel regression, clustering on campaign)

	YEARS OF INTENSE VIOLENCE		INITIATION OF INTENSE VIOLENCE EPISODE	
	COEFFICIENT	STANDARD ERROR	COEFFICIENT	STANDARD ERROR
Statehood (t-1)	1.0138	0.3580**	0.8644	0.3097**
Constitutional exclusion (t-1)	2.8777	0.6680***	1.9975	0.6372**
Governmental exclusion (t-1)	1.0942	0.5554*	0.3825	0.5231
Exclusion from participation (t-1)	2.3653	0.3897***	2.0053	0.2899***
Democratic regime (t-1)	0.5534	0.3582	−0.1460	0.2647
Platform size (t)	0.3899	0.1107***	0.2013	0.1098
Balance of coercive capacity (t-1)	−0.0089	0.0033**	−0.0034	0.0022
Constant	−10.3446	1.7726***	−7.9835	1.7827***
	N = 5,078		N = 4,655	
	R^2 = 0.273		R^2 = 0.159	

*Significance: *p < .05; **p < .01; ***p < .001*

In order to test the generalizability of these results to the whole period since World War II and to introduce the effect of variables that vary significantly over time (such as economic growth or regime weakness), a logit model uses the same variables as the previous equation, but just for civil wars (and so without terrorist violence) from 1945 to 2010. This equation also adds a variable for

TABLE 7A.5. Logit results: Initiation of civil wars, 1945–2010 (panel regression, clustering on campaign)

	COEFFICIENT	STANDARD ERROR
Statehood (t-1)	0.8654	0.3185**
Constitutional exclusion (t-1)	1.7950	0.7081*
Governmental exclusion (t-1)	0.5306	0.5676
Exclusion from political participation (t-1)	1.6909	0.2975***
Weak common-state regime (t-1)	0.6087	0.2949*
Platform size	0.1536	0.1092
Balance of coercive capacity (t-1)	−0.0045	0.0020*
Economic growth (t-2→t-1)	−2.1540	1.3254
Constant	−7.8381	1.7542***
N = 6,782		
R^2 = 0.107		

Significance: *$p < .05$; **$p < .01$; ***$p < .001$

"weak common-state regime" in the previous year (in place of democracy) and "economic growth" over the two previous years. This drops years of continuing violence. The two columns of figures in table 7A.5 report the results of this estimation with robust standard errors controlling for clustering on the campaign. The results in table 7A.5 permit estimation of the changing probabilities of initiating an episode of intense civil war in any year under varying constraints. As in chapter 5, these probabilities are estimated by the Clarify procedure.[17] The changes in these probabilities (first differences and percentage change) caused by variation of each variable from minimum to maximum values are shown in chapter 7 as table 7.3.

The strength of the findings in this study depends in part on the specifications of the estimation models. The residuals (the remainders after the actual value of a dependent variable for each case is subtracted from its predicted value) are both diagnostics and predictions. As diagnostics, the residuals may indicate two potential shortcomings in a model: whether the model employs a biased indicator of the dependent variable and whether the model omits important explanations from the independent variables. Correcting any bias or missing variables can improve the model in future reestimations. As predictions, these residuals point to "the dogs that didn't bark": campaigns that should have drawn international attention and significant campaigns that should have engaged in more protracted intense struggles but did not. These may be new hot spots in the future. No simple test is available to decide whether the residuals point to either a modeling problem or a real-world challenge; this can be addressed only by closer scrutiny.

The Model of Campaign Significance

The models of campaign significance analyzed in chapter 5 (based on the estimates presented in the appendix to that chapter) on first glance might raise questions about both dependent and independent variables. Yet post-estimation scrutiny supports confidence that these do not lead to systematic estimation errors that change the major conclusions of this book.

Bias in the Indicator of Campaign Significance

One obvious concern in the operationalization of campaign significance is the use of news sources located in Western Europe and North America, possibly leading to better coverage of projects where more correspondents and news bureaus are located and readers have greatest interest. For example, this may lead to over-reporting of campaigns closer to New York and London. This "overreporting" should appear in the residuals as underpredicted significance.

Theoretically, however, this may not be bias because the concept of significance being operationalized by this empirical indicator concerns getting attention in the capitals of the international community and particularly the capitals of the Western powers that play a disproportionate role as gatekeepers to the international community. Any overreporting and underreporting may reflect a fundamental reality in international politics: it may be much harder for national-secession campaigns to become significant—that is, to get on the international agenda—when they are isolated from Western observers. Any bias may be in the attention of the international community and not in this book's measurement of that attention.

The forty-seven cases shown in table 9A.1 stand out as "overreported" or substantially underpredicted by the model for campaign significance: these campaigns achieved significance even though the estimation model predicts that this was unlikely. Closer scrutiny reveals that only two are from the region where we might suspect overreporting—the German people's project for the Ostkantone in Belgium and the Dakota people's Lakotah project in the United States. The former campaign may have drawn attention not because it had achieved substantial programmatic coordination but because it touched the concern of Western powers about postwar borders immediately following World War II. Alternatively, the Lakotah campaign engaged in actions that were likely to achieve significance in any part of the world: through the American Indian Movement, the campaign organized highly visible protests in Washington, DC, occupation of a federal penitentiary on Alcatraz, petitions to foreign embassies for recognition, and a violent showdown at Wounded Knee, South Dakota. One additional case of overreporting may reflect a different type of source bias: the Rapa Nui project on Easter Island. Wide public interest in Easter Island's monuments may have been an opportunity that the Rapa Nui campaign used to gain attention that it might not otherwise have attracted. Nonetheless, prior to being a secessionist project (at a time that Easter Island was still an external territory), the Rapa Nui campaign was well enough coordinated to place its claims on the agenda of the Trusteeship Council of the United Nations.

Overreporting (or underpredicted significance) could be a consequence of national-secession campaigns piggybacking on international attention to

TABLE 9A.1. Projects that were more significant than predicted, 1945–2010 (analysis of residuals)

GROUP	UNDERPREDICTION	VIOLENCE	MULTIETHNIC	PROJECT
Fulani (Chad)	−0.997	X	X	North Chad
Buin (PapuaNG)	−0.990	X	X	Bougainville
Rapa Nui (Chile)	−0.980			Rapa Nui
Zaghawa (Chad)	−0.978	X	X	North Chad
Basubiya (Namibia)	−0.977			Caprivi
Nasioi (PapuaNG)	−0.973	X	X	Bougainville
Dakota (USA)	−0.972	X		Lakotah
Ladakhi (India)	−0.971			Ladakh
Bakonjo (Uganda)	−0.971	X		Ruwenzuru
Massa, Musgum (Chad)	−0.970		X	Logone Republic
Bambara (Mauritania)	−0.969		X	Chemama
Balozi (Zambia)	−0.965			Barotseland
Kayah (Myanmar)	−0.963	X		Karenni States
Ossetians (Georgia)	−0.954	X		South Ossetia
Greeks (Albania)	−0.950			North Epirus
Mikir (India)	−0.948	X		Karbi Anglong
Tigray (Ethiopia)	−0.947	X		Eritrea
Hausa (Chad)	−0.946	X	X	North Chad
Sara (Chad)	−0.944		X	Logone Republic
Wa (Myanmar)	−0.943	X		Wa State/Meng Vax
Sudanese Arabs (Chad)	−0.939	X	X	North Chad
Zulus (South Africa)	−0.938			KwaZulu
Tama (Chad)	−0.935	X	X	North Chad
Germans (Belgium)	−0.935			Eupen-Malmedy/Ostkantone
Baganda (Uganda)	−0.931			Buganda
Kresh (Sudan)	−0.929	X	X	North Chad
Serbs (Croatia)	−0.928	X		Krajina
Mizo (Myanmar)	−0.926			Kukiland/Zozam
Dadjo (Chad)	−0.926	X	X	North Chad
Kotoko (Chad)	−0.925		X	Logone Republic
Banyoro (Uganda)	−0.924			Bunyoro
Toubou (Chad)	−0.921	X	X	North Chad
Bosnians (Yugoslavia)	−0.921	X		Bosnia and Herzegovina
Afrikaaners (South Africa)	−0.921	X		Volkstaat/Orania/Boer Republic
Kacharis (India)	−0.918	X		Bodoland/Dimasaland
Abkhaz (Georgia)	−0.917	X		Abkhazia
Armenians (Turkey)	−0.917	X		Armenia
Russians (Moldova)	−0.916	X	X	Transdniestria
Miskito (Nicaragua)	−0.915	X		Miskitia
Galla (Ethiopia)	−0.915	X		Oromiyaa
Kanuri (Chad)	−0.913			Bornu/Kanowra
Mons (Myanmar)	−0.912	X		Monland
Khmer (Vietnam)	−0.912			Khmer-Kampuchea
Soninke (Mauritania)	−0.906		X	Chemama
Banyankole (Uganda)	−0.905			Ankole
Bakongo (Angola)	−0.905	X		Cabinda
Armenians (Azerbaijan)	−0.903	X		Armenia

Note: This list includes all ethnic groups associated with significant national-secession campaigns for which model 1 in table 5A.2 predicts a less than 10 percent probability of campaign significance.

nonsecessionist crises that concern the Western powers. For example, as shown in table 9A.1, almost a quarter of all cases of substantial underprediction are associated with two projects in Chad. One of these, the project for secession in North Chad, may have drawn attention in Western capitals more because of Libyan intervention than strong campaign coordination of a platform population around the nation-state project. The other, the Logone Republic project, was a shadowy campaign that drew the attention of the international media largely because it was one of the contending forces that battled for control of the national capital of N'Djamena. Whether this phenomenon should be treated as bias in the dependent variable or a missing independent variable is an issue for legitimate disagreement.

The obverse source of potential bias is underreporting by the press: projects in countries less well covered by Western media may have been missed by the operationalization of the dependent variable. These should appear as overpredicted cases in the estimation models. Table 9.1 shows the ten cases of greatest overprediction: these campaigns did not achieve significance, even though the estimation model predicts they should have. Yet the distribution of these cases does not suggest systematic bias in the dependent variable. The cases identified in table 9.1 as potential significant projects—Maharashtra, Sabah, Rumelia, and the northern Senegal Fulani-Toucouleur project—were not campaigns overlooked by the international press in major Western capitals. They are properly identified as cases with as-yet-unrealized potential to become significant campaigns.

The most fully developed of these campaigns is Sabah nationalism, yet this remained just below the radar of the international community throughout the 1945–2010 period. Competing projects, such as the project for Moro unity, have divided the Sabah platform, attracting many in the Sulu-Samal population away from a multiethnic Sabah campaign. The small core of enthusiasts for independence, drawing from Kadazans in particular, have been outmatched by a common-state (Malaysia) that has imposed strong centralization and assimilation pressures based on the "one language, one culture, one religion" policy, including a program of mass conversion to Malayaness and Islam. Malaysia has co-opted leading Sabah politicians into the coalition led by Barisan Nasional (National Front), which has governed Malaysia since 1973. Still, the relationship with Malaysia continues to be colored by periodic allegations that the political system developed in Peninsular Malaya and imposed on Sabah is distant from Sabah's own experience and has made it the victim of internal colonialism.[1] This is a project, given its location between Malaysia, Indonesia, and the Philippines and adjacent to the South China Sea, that has high potential for international mischief—if it grows into a significant campaign.

The secessionist potential of Marathi nationalism was contained in the 1945–2010 period. Marathi intellectuals divided between the celebration of the Maratha Empire and nation, forged in the seventeenth century by Chhatrapati Shivaji Maharaj, as the foundation of a contemporary sovereign state, on the one hand, and the ideology that this is the foundation for the broader Indian nation-state, on the other.[2] The former group emphasizes promotion of Marathi language and culture, xenophobic exclusion of other Indian peoples from the Marathi homeland, and pressure to expand the prerogatives of the Maharashtra state currently within India. Establishment of Maharashtra, carved from the former Bombay State in 1960, at first assuaged aspirations for greater statehood. Yet exclusionary pressures mounted. What began as attacks on Muslims and migrants from South India grew to attacks on migrants from throughout India. Nonetheless, the formal claim to independence for Maharashtra has taken second place in the public program of Marathi nationalism to the claim that the Marathi should play a larger role in defining the future of India.

The Rumelia campaign, based on Bulgarian Turks, is the weakest of these three and has failed to garner wide support or recognition. The totalitarian controls exercised by the Bulgarian Communist Party until 1989, which officially denied the existence of a Turkish minority, kept the issue from international attention. As the communist regime began to loosen its grip, Turkey opened its border, under pressure from the Todor Zhivkov government, and over the next four years more than 310,000 Turks fled Bulgaria. Postcommunist Bulgaria created a space for various movements and parties to press the rights of minorities, but the constitution prohibits ethnic or religious parties, and no major organization has openly championed secession.

Missing Explanations for Campaign Significance

Looking closer at the underpredicted cases in table 9A.1, three variables stand out on first glance as candidates for omitted variables in the estimation of campaign significance. These cases of underpredicted significance suggest that violence used to get on the international agenda has been omitted. More than three-fifths (61.7 percent) of the cases of underprediction were associated with campaigns that employed violence. By comparison, as noted in chapter 8, only 4.5 percent of all 3,741 ethnic groups were associated with such violence. As underscored in chapter 7, violence is one of the more powerful propaganda tools available to campaigns for programmatic coordination—and an excellent tactic to get a campaign's demands onto the international agenda. Including this variable is not as simple a solution as it might appear: as shown in the equations for protracted intensity, violence is collinear with the cues to campaign significance, making it a proxy or instrument for all the cues to campaign significance. In addition, we currently do not have data that permit attribution of violence in multiethnic campaigns to one constituent ethnic group or another.

Another candidate for an omitted variable that stands out on first glance concerns the phenomenon of multiethnic campaigns. The estimated model based on attributes of individual ethnic groups may not capture the qualities that permit multiethnic campaigns to get on the international agenda when they band together. This could lead to underprediction of these significant campaigns. Closer scrutiny highlights that multiethnicity is not unique to cases of underprediction: a third (34.0 percent) of the underpredicted cases were ethnic groups that formed parts of platforms for multiethnic projects such as Bougainville. Yet among all ethnic groups associated with significant campaigns, 43.1 percent were parts of platforms for multiethnic campaigns. The fact that multiethnic campaigns are less common among the underpredicted significant campaigns than among the predicted significant campaigns suggests that multiethnic platforms are not the source of underprediction. Moreover, independent variables to account for multiethnic coalitions are already included. For example, variables for "ethno-linguistic coalition" and "religious coalition" potential are already in the estimation models. (See table 5A.3, model 1a, in the appendix to chapter 5.)

A third candidate for an omitted explanatory variable that fails to bear up to closer inspection is spillover effects: it is plausible that campaigns with only limited programmatic coordination that would have left them insignificant in the eyes of the international community still gained international attention because they were seen as spillovers of more-substantial campaigns in adjacent countries. Yet only three of the cases of underpredicted significance in table 9A.1 might be considered spillovers. And only the Kukiland project in Myanmar and the Bornu project in Chad may have achieved attention primarily because of the attention drawn by the more-substantial ethnically linked projects in India and Nigeria, respectively. Alternatively, the third case of underpredicted campaign significance that might be caused by spillover (the Armenia campaign in Turkey) achieved significance by its own means (or that of its diaspora): its continued propaganda and extraordinary terrorist attacks against Turkish targets (particularly in West Germany) kept the Armenian claim against Turkey on the international agenda. It should be noted that among significant campaigns not singled out by the residuals as underpredicted, ethnically linked conflicts are fairly common, including Air and Azawad in Mali and Niger, Azerbaijan in Iran and the USSR, Balochistan in Iran and Pakistan, Cabinda/Kongo in Angola and Congo/Zaire, Catalunya in France and Spain, Collasuyo in Bolivia and Peru, Croatia/

Bosna-Herzog in Yugoslavia and Bosnia, Euskadi in France and Spain, Kurdistan in four countries, Nagaland in India and Myanmar, Republika Srpska/Krajina in Bosnia and Croatia, and Tamil Eelam/Tamil Nadu in Sri Lanka and India. Yet these were not instances of spillover significance; they constituted separate campaigns within their respective common-states that achieved significance by their own programmatic coordination.

Improving the Models of Protracted Intensity

The models of protracted intensity analyzed in chapter 7 (based on the estimations presented in the appendix to that chapter) on first glance might also raise questions about bias in the dependent variable and omitted explanatory variables. Yet closer scrutiny of the patterns of underpredicted violence shown in table 9A.2 and overpredicted violence in table 9.2 appear to confirm the analysis of the strategy of programmatic coordination.

Bias in the Index of Protracted Intensity

Close scrutiny of the dependent variable, reported in chapter 2, shows the high correlation between the measures of civil war and terrorism intensity. This gives greater confidence in the validity of each measure but does not rule out

TABLE 9A.2. Campaigns that were more violent than predicted, 1970–2006 (analysis of residuals)

NATIONAL-SECESSION CAMPAIGN	EXCESS YEARS[a]	COMMON-STATE
Eritrea	7.70	Ethiopia
Kurdistan	7.06	Iraq
Euskadi	4.93	Spain
Ichkeria/Chechnya	4.82	Russia
Timor Leste	4.62	Indonesia
Northern Ireland	4.36	United Kingdom
Kawthoolei/Karen State	4.35	Myanmar
South Sudan	4.18	Sudan
Bangsamoro	3.74	Philippines
Kurdistan	3.64	Turkey
Manipur/Kangleipak	3.12	India
Shan States	3.06	Myanmar

Note: This list includes all campaigns that reported at least three years more highest-intensity violence than is predicted by model 2 in table 7A.2.

[a] The number of years of highest-intensity violence above the prediction.

coincident systematic bias. If there is systematic bias in the data, it is common to these two major data sources.

The geographic distribution of cases of underpredicted and overpredicted violence does not suggest a systematic bias towards Western countries but may suggest underreporting of events in those countries that are inaccessible to Western news agencies. The twelve cases of underpredicted (and possibly over-reported) violence are distributed across all continents except the Americas, and many occurred in countries with difficult access for the Western media. Nonetheless, the cases of unrealized potential for protracted intense violence (overprediction) noted in table 9.2 do indicate the possibility of underreporting events in the most tightly controlled societies, such as the USSR or China, that deny access by Western observers to parts of their territories. For example, we learned of violence in the Caucasus region—such as Abkhazian demonstrations and violence—that had taken place during more-restrictive Soviet periods only later during perestroika under Gorbachev and during the Yeltsin years. Yet even during the Stalin years, news of Ukrainian, Estonian, Latvian, and Lithuanian resistance wars reached the West through private or covert channels.

Missing Explanations for Protracted Intensity

Turning to omitted explanatory variables, it is worth noting that many of the twelve campaigns in table 9A.2 with substantially more violence than predicted by the model are the exemplary cases used throughout this study to illustrate the most extensive programmatic coordination. This suggests that the authenticity and realism cues in the models tap only a part of the programmatic cues that lead to coordination success. There may be specific elements of ideological-organization work, prescribed by the strategy of programmatic coordination, that additional variables should capture in future reestimations of the model. These were highlighted in this study's narrative accounts but not fully captured in the statistical models.

As shown in table 9.2, six campaigns topped the list of unrealized potential for more protracted intense violence in the years 1970–2006. Closer scrutiny does not reveal any common explanation for this unrealized potential that has been omitted from the estimations. The one exception to this is the ability of totalitarian regimes to keep the lid on violence until they begin to liberalize and open up. Throughout much of the 1970–2006 period, the party-states of China and the USSR kept a tight lid on opposition. Loosening totalitarian controls might have provided an opportunity for greater violence in the USSR, but the Moldovan campaign achieved independence within three years of the introduction of perestroika. Alternatively, the Tibetan campaign apparently remains a potential source for substantially greater long-term violence, except that the Beijing regime has shown little inclination to loosen common-state controls there.

Similarly, overwhelming state suppression may account for the limited capacity of the Chemama campaign to undertake a protracted intense struggle in the 1970–2006 period. Brutal suppression backed near-totalitarian control over many Africans through enslavement, turning many black Africans into chattel dependents and making protracted intense struggle difficult to organize. Approximately 60,000 black Africans fled Mauritania for Senegal and Mali in 1989, including many who "were rounded up in their villages, stripped of their identity card, and shipped across the river to Senegal."[3] Policies to end slavery and repatriate the refugees and a general easing of repression may afford opportunities for campaign coordination that will sustain a more protracted intense struggle in the future.

Alternatively, the time for a protracted intense struggle by the Assyrians may have passed. Although Assyrians have a history of military prowess, which the British mandate authorities used to suppress Kurdish and Arab nationalists in Mesopotamia, Iraqi suppression of the Assyrians since independence has limited Assyrian violence. As early as the Simele Massacre of 1933, successive Iraqi regimes undertook preemptive military action to disperse and assimilate the Assyrian population. Destruction of traditional villages forced many people to go to the major cities or abroad, dissipating the homeland movement. The Western protectorate, with a no-fly zone above the 36th parallel and Operation Provide Comfort, relieved some of this repression but also constrained the Assyrians' military action. The dispersal of the Assyrians, small size, and complicated relationship with the Kurdish Regional Government and international protectors may limit the scale of their violence in the future. The intrusion by ISIS, which brought further dispersal and genocide, may have finally broken the Assyrian national-secession campaign within its homeland.

The Afar campaign may also remain quiet for reasons of international politics. The Afar insurgency against the Ethiopian common-state that began under the Afar Liberation Front in 1975 was divided by the fight for Eritrean independence. After 1993 the successor group—the Afar Revolutionary Democratic Unity Front—gradually made peace with the Ethiopian common-state government as it came to see Eritrean cross-border raids as a greater threat to the security of Afar towns and the existence of an independent Eritrea as a greater obstacle to the future unification of Afars in Djibouti, Eritrea, and Ethiopia.[4] As long as this special relationship with the Ethiopian common-state government continues, the violence is likely to remain subdued.

The return to violence by the Mon campaign seems to hang on the outcome of an internal debate on whether armed struggle will create the best conditions for programmatic coordination. The Mon cease-fire of June 1995 in Myanmar came after reversals on the battlefield and, as Ashley South notes, once "it was clear that only a negotiated settlement with Rangoon would allow the [New Mon State Party] to retain control over its remaining liberated zones." Yet this produced only a fragile peace, and increasing numbers of veterans of the armed struggle returned to guerilla warfare. Even though this "would almost inevitably lead to military defeat, a further deterioration of the human rights situation in Mon State, and another acute phase in the refugee crisis along the border," some enthusiasts, with the ready support of expressionists, saw a return to war as essential to keep alive the campaign for independence against the temptations of collaboration.[5]

Notes

1. THREE QUESTIONS ABOUT NATIONAL SECESSION

1. On various consequences of citizenship and statehood, see Aasland and Fløtten 2001; Barrington 1995; Bloom 2008; Brubaker 1992; Howard 2006; Kolstø 2000; Weil 2001.

2. New, uncommon, or contested terms appear in bold type, are defined in the text, and also appear in the Glossary.

3. The precise percentages were 15.5, 39.2, and 50.6, respectively. These are calculated from 1971 data in US Bureau of the Census 2006 and Maddison 2011.

4. That is, 800 + 7,200 − 200 = 7,800; Gellner 1983, 44–45.

5. Wilson 2009.

6. Pool 2001, 157.

7. The US Department of the Army's (2007, 3) *Counterinsurgency Field Manual* identifies secession as one of the two major goals of insurgencies in recent years. The other goal is overthrow of the central government.

8. Calculations of battle-related deaths are based on "best estimates" reported in the UCDP/PRIO Armed Conflict Dataset. This total refers to "deaths caused by the warring parties that can be directly related to combat" (Uppsala Conflict Data Program 2011). Calculations for terrorism are based on the Global Terrorism Database (National Consortium for the Study of Terrorism and Responses to Terrorism 2013).

9. Pool 2001, 157.

10. Walter 2009b, 4.

11. Even many revolutionary movements may be constrained by operational weakness and engage in strategic opportunism. Adam B. Ulam (1965, 314) writes that the Bolsheviks in the Russian Revolution of 1917 "did not seize power.... They picked it up." Hannah Arendt argues that this is common to revolutions (see LeJeune 2014).

12. The former is a major consideration in Jenne 2007.

13. Smith 1996, 597.

14. Bovingdon 2010, 92–93.

15. Bovingdon 2010, 91.

16. See table 2.3. Of course, these voting results may not accurately reflect public sentiment, for these referenda may be accompanied by coercion. However, the results do reflect the relative power of each campaign to mobilize support.

17. Connor 1984, 56–57.

18. Kalyvas and Balcells 2010, 420–21.

19. Sterling 1981, 150–71; Clark 1984, 233–34; Romano 2006, 70; Pool 2001, 82–83; O'Ballance 1989, 12, 15.

20. See, for example, the white-supremacist and secessionist Northwest Front in the United States: northwestfront.org/about/the-butler-plan-the-homeland.

21. Lenin 1899 [1972], 224.

22. Quoted in Paret and Shy 1962, 21. See also Leites and Wolfe 1970, 154; Kalyvas and Balcells 2010, 420–21.

23. The structure of a national-secession program resembles what used to be described as a revolutionary ideology; see Brzezinski 1960, 384. For the diverse meanings now given to the term *ideology,* see, for example, Costalli and Ruggeri 2017.

24. Roeder 2007, 12. This draws on the broader philosophical claim, expressed crisply by Max Weber, that a "nation is a community of sentiment which would adequately manifest itself in a state of its own. . . ." (quoted in Gerth and Mills 1958, 176); see also Kohn 1944 [2005], 19; Kedourie 1960.

25. Bunce 2005, 412.

26. US Department of the Army 2007, 25.

27. Compare Kydd and Walter 2006.

28. Lenin 1906 [1972], 222; italics original.

29. According to a T-shirt popular among my ROTC students years ago, "When you have them by the b*lls, their hearts and minds will follow."

30. Hoffer 1951, 3, 9.

31. Mao 1938a [1965], 143.

32. For example, see Benford and Snow 2000; Diani 1992, 1–2; McCarthy and Zald 1987, 20; Tilly and Wood 2009, 3–4.

33. The experience of having seen national-secession campaigns reemerge within the collapsing Soviet Union, and some of these reemerging after decades of no public discussion of their continuing relevance, leads me to be cautious about claiming that unsuccessful campaigns have died. Many of these campaigns had survived underground in face-to-face exchanges.

34. See Nussio 2017; Kübler-Ross 1973.

35. Popkin 1994, 216.

36. Rapoport 1961, 273. See also Meadwell 1993, 215.

37. Compare Whitmeyer 2002.

38. See, for example, US Department of the Army 2007, 1.

2. STRATEGIC CONSTRAINTS

1. This is different from saying, as I do in Roeder (2007), that only campaigns with segment-states become sovereign states.

2. Dominique Mosbergen, "Texas Secession Petition Racks Up More Than 80,000 Signatures, Qualifies for White House Response," Huffington Post Politics, November 14, 2012.

3. Goode 2011, 23, 24, 25, 27. In classifications of actual cases there is, of course, an element of professional judgment because regionalists understand that they can give special legitimacy to their campaigns if they can "ethnify" and "nationalize" their populations. For example, the Padania movement in northern Italy, which J. Paul Goode uses as a model of regionalism, has inspired a small circle of intellectuals to try to invent a separate cultural history for the Padanian population, hinting at a distinct ancestry and seeking to elevate it to a nation to legitimate the claim to statehood. The judgment in this borderline case, drawing on that of experts such as John A. Agnew (2002), is to see the coterie of Padanian nationalists as peripheral to the secession campaign and classify it as a case of regional-secessionism. Similarly, California's secessionists in the Calexit campaign claimed that Californians constitute a nation, but few took seriously the claim that Californians are not Americans.

4. For empirical analysis of patterns actually observed in the period of this study, it is also important to avoid two temptations—to substitute our suspicions of what goals may truly lurk in the hearts of autonomists or to substitute our predictions about their goals in the future.

5. Anderson, von der Mehden, and Young 1967, 74. See also Scott 2009.

6. By similar logic, occupied territories not formally annexed to the metropole (such as Palestine's relationship to Israel) are considered external territories. Occupied territories formally annexed to the metropole (such as Sahara's relationship to Morocco) are

considered part of the metropole. For different treatments of the distinction between secession and decolonization, see the discussion in the appendix to this chapter. For an excellent study of anticolonial mobilization, see Lawrence 2013.

7. United Nations General Assembly Resolution 2625(XXV), 1970.

8. United Nations General Assembly Resolution 1514(XV), 1960.

9. See, for example, Griffiths 2016.

10. In these tabulations of countries and campaigns, the successor state and rump state (e.g., USSR and Russia) or key constituent and amalgamated state (North Yemen and Yemen) are treated as one continuous case. Secessionist campaigns (e.g., Kosovo) in a successor state (Serbia) are not counted separately if they also appear in the pre-breakup or pre-amalgamation state (e.g., Yugoslavia).

11. Zaheer 1994, 177.

12. Zaheer 1994, 184; Raghavan 2013, 267.

13. For a discussion of the relationship between the campaign for Kosovo independence and the more-moderate members of the Kosovar leadership, see Jenne 2007, 169–77.

14. Phillips 2012, 89, see also pp. 92, 110. See also Perritt 2008, 130–51.

15. Ker-Lindsay 2009, 13.

16. Ker-Lindsay 2009, 16.

17. Burg and Shoup 1999, 318, 334–35, 352. See also Burg and Shoup 1999, 93, 96, 100, 205, 287, 289, 291, 295, 316, and 317; Lampe 1996, 354–56; Bennett 1995, 186; Tanner 2001, 274. Based on the decision of the European arbitration commission under the French jurist Robert Badinter, the European Community foreign ministers invited applications for recognition only from the republics and rejected applications from smaller breakaway regions.

18. Kingsbury 2009, 68.

19. Le Riche and Arnold 2012, 138; see also p. 135.

20. Pool 2001, 133.

21. Iyob 1995, 125, 134–35.

22. Whether the campaign actually changed voters' positions on independence in the final stretch is unclear: the 55–45 split in the final vote for independence in 2006 is identical to the split identified in surveys taken in March 2001 but substantially more favorable than the 33–67 split reported in surveys prior to 1999. Under these conditions, mobilization of a surge of supporters to the polls was critically important to the success of the campaign's effort to demonstrate programmatic preemption.

23. Morrison 2009, 191; see also pp. 182–220; Huszka 2003, 44–45; Pavlovič 2003.

24. Keith 2005.

25. Ongkili 1985, 181–90.

26. Bunce 1999, 97–98, 124.

27. Rychlik 2000, 62. See also Heimann 2009, 307–20.

28. Private communication from Valerie Bunce, October 9, 2015.

29. Bennett 1995, 138, 139, 154–60. See also Lampe 1996, 351–52; Tanner 2001, 249.

30. Lampe 1996, 352; Tanner 2001, 227, 250, 273–74, 279; Bennett 1995, 165–72.

31. Lampe 1996, 353; Ramet 1992, 256–57; Kim and Migdalovitz 1993.

32. Eduard Kondratov, "News Hotline: Moldova Will Not Sign the Union Treaty," *Izvestiia*, August 9, 1991.

33. Wilson 2009, 161–62; see also Motyl 1993, 23–24; Zaprudnik 1993, 145–65.

34. More precisely, this is 87 campaigns or 51.2 percent of the 170. These data are described in the appendix to this chapter.

35. More precisely, 56 campaigns or 32.9 percent, and 27 campaigns or 15.9 percent, respectively.

36. Using percentage of campaign years controls for the number of years that each campaign was part of the specific common-state.

37. The gap in intensity is not caused solely by foreign involvement. The gap narrows only a little even if years of substantial foreign involvement are excluded. For other civil wars, excluding autonomist wars, 30.7 percent of years at war without significant foreign involvement (Type ≠ 4) reached one thousand battle-related deaths; for nationalist-secessionist conflicts, this was 21.1 percent of years at war without significant foreign involvement.

38. Lacina 2006, 279.

39. Intervention in Bosnia came in response to the secessionist conflicts with the Republika Srpska and Herzeg-Bosnia, but this intervention backed up Bosnia's claim to sovereign statehood.

40. For example, see Kilcullen 2009.

41. Cases of significant foreign involvement are identified by the variable "Conflict-Type = 4" in the UCDP (2011) data set.

3. ORGANIZATION AND MOBILIZATION IN CAMPAIGN DEVELOPMENT

1. Chester I. Barnard (1962) labels these activities "organizational maintenance." For Barnard, as James Q. Wilson (1995, 30) summarizes, organizational "maintenance includes not only survival, but also . . . producing and sustaining cooperative effort." Barnard defines the concept of an organization broadly and abstractly "as a system of consciously coordinated activities or forces of two or more persons," so his analysis embraces problems of coordination well beyond those found within formal groups that we commonly label organizations.

2. Meyer 1984, 36–42.

3. For example, Selznick 1960; Gamson 1975; Tarrow 1994; Paret and Shy 1962; US Department of the Army 2007.

4. Guevara 1961, chapter 1, sections 1 and 2.

5. Lenin (1920a [1974], 1920b [1974]) hints that in national and colonial struggles it may be necessary to reach out to other classes such as the peasantry and national bourgeoisie, but he does not envision substituting a national program for the revolution's class program.

6. Lenin 1899 [1972], 1902b [1973]; Mao 1937 [1961], 1938a [1965]; Barnard 1962; Wilson 1995.

7. This focus on nationalist leaders also follows the lead of such diverse scholars of nationalism as Benedict Anderson (1991, 47–65), who analyzes the critical role of colonial bureaucrats ("Creole pioneers") in the definition of Latin American nation-state projects; Paul R. Brass (1991, 44), who highlights the role of Pakistani elites seeking an economic or political advantage by emphasizing national distinctiveness; and Liah Greenfeld (1992), who explores the anomie of elites in the emergence of European nationalisms.

8. Hroch 2000, 23.

9. Mary Heimann's (2009, 14) elegant description of the origins of Czech and Slovak nationalisms within the Habsburg Empire highlights the choice among options made by the leaders of these campaigns: "To be a Czech or Slovak patriot in the late nineteenth century and early decades of the twentieth century was still a political choice, not a fluke of birth. It means adopting the posture of a Slav patriot: reading the right newspapers and books; donating to the right causes; supporting the right cultural events; joining the right university societies and belonging to the right political party." Still later, many of the leaders of these campaigns, such as Tomáš Masaryk and Jozef Tiso, were born of mixed parentage, raised in other cultural traditions, or supporters of alternative projects earlier in

their careers, but, among these many options open to them, they finally chose campaigns for nation-state independence.

10. Barnard 1962, 73.

11. *Oxford English Dictionary* 2000, meaning 5b.

12. Sterling 1981, 7–8, 13–16, 286–297; Romerstein 1986. See the discussion and sources cited in Kalyvas and Balcells 2010, 420–21.

13. Clark 1984, 233–34.

14. Kingsbury 2009.

15. Pool 2001, 82–83.

16. Sterling 1981, 150–71.

17. Romano 2006, 70ff.

18. Staff Researcher 2013.

19. O'Ballance 1989, 12, 15.

20. As Ted Robert Gurr and Jack A. Goldstone (1991, 335) note, these principles also provided strategic guidance in building decolonization/national-liberation movements and completing successful revolutions in Vietnam, Cambodia, Zimbabwe, Nicaragua, Angola, Mozambique, Guinea-Bissau, Cape Verde, and Namibia.

21. O'Ballance 1989, 67.

22. Chamberlain 2007, 20, 33, 53; Kingsbury 2009, 43. See also Hill 2002, 43–46, 49–51.

23. Quoted in Chamberlain 2007, 127.

24. Hill 2002, 52.

25. Hill 2002, 77.

26. Hill 2002, 69; Kingsbury 2009, 43–50. For a similar story about the disarray in the early Eritrean independence campaign, see Erlich 1983, 5–6; Markakis 1987, 67–68; Iyob 1995, 61–81.

27. Kingsbury 2009, 51; see also p. 53.

28. Kingsbury 2009, 58.

29. Quoted in DeVotta 2004, 99.

30. US Joint Chiefs of Staff 2009, II-14.

31. Senn 1990, 7.

32. Hoffer 1951, 146; see also pp. 40, 137. See also Meadwell 1993, 212.

33. Lieven 1993, 224. See also Senn 1990, 2, 58; Krickus 1997, 50–51; Trapans 1991, 30–32.

34. Clark 1984, 96; Sullivan 1988, 163–65.

35. Lenin 1904 [1974], as quoted in Central Committee of the C. P. S. U. (B.) 1939, 48.

36. Hoffer 1951, 118.

37. See Roeder 2007, 117–23, for examples at the end of the Russian Empire.

38. Lieven 1993, 227; Taagepera 1993, 112–35.

39. On the South Sudan campaign up to 1972, see Markakis 1987, 146–68.

40. LeRiche and Arnold 2012, 55. They note (p. 24) with some sense of irony that "while the referendum may have been the long-sought realization of self-determination— that is, with an inherent bias towards secession—it was achieved by an insurgent movement that had officially fought for a 'New Sudan': unified but secular, democratic and with devolved governance."

41. Zaheer 1994, 125–26, 163–66.

42. Kilcullen 2009, 35–36.

43. Lenin 1901 [1973], 23.

44. Leites and Wolf 1970, 154–55.

45. See, for example, Clark 1984, 211; Parkinson 2013.

46. Díez Medrano 1995, 136.

47. Pool 2001, 81. See also Johnson 1962, 151.
48. Markakis 1987, 113.
49. Pool 2001, 61, 112.
50. Schurmann 1971, 416; Blaufarb 1977, 3; US Department of the Army 2007, 22.
51. Quoted in English 2006, 402.
52. O'Ballance 1989, 119.
53. Sullivan 1988, 12. See also Mees 2004, 318–21.
54. Clark 1984, 34.
55. Clark 1984, 61; Sullivan 1988, 53, 127.
56. Sullivan 1988, 208–09.
57. Sullivan 1988, 28–33, 209–10, 238–41.
58. Sullivan 1988, 241. See also Díez Medrano 1995, 145–49.
59. Lecours 2012, 273.
60. Clark 1984, 32, 97.

4. PROGRAMMATIC COORDINATION IN CAMPAIGNS

1. Pool 2001, 36–37, 47–49; Erlich 1983, 31–32; Iyob 1995, 98–107.
2. Markakis 1987, 114; Pool 2001, 55, 142; Iyob 1995, 108–17.
3. Erlich 1983, 85.
4. Iyob 1995, 119.
5. Erlich 1983, 96. See also Iyob 1995, 119–20.
6. Markakis 1987, 134.
7. Markakis 1987, 144.
8. Pool 2001, 83–85, 90; Markakis 1987, 143.
9. Pool 2001, 55. See also Erlich 1983, 118–19.
10. Markakis 1987, 143.
11. Iyob 1995, 123; see also pp. 120–21.
12. Lenin 1902a [1974], 246.
13. Giap 1961, 33.
14. Hroch 2000, 185–86. See also Dion 1996; Lecours 2012, 279–81; Meadwell 1993, 225.
15. Wilson 1995, 34; see also pp. ix–xi.
16. The literature on selective material incentives is extensively developed in the political economy tradition. Seminal works on selective material incentives and collective action, rebellion, and nationalism include Olson 1965; Popkin 1979; and Rogowski 1985.
17. The diversity of incentives is similar to Ashutosh Varshney's (2003) distinction among different bases of social action. See also Weinstein 2007, 7–16; Zürcher 2007, 3.
18. Morrison 2009, 206–07; Huszka 2003.
19. US Joint Chiefs of Staff 2009, II-11.
20. Wilson 1995, 27.
21. Lenin 1902a [1974]; Johnson 1962, 77, 89.
22. Lenin 1902b [1973], 409–10. See also Lenin 1920a [1974], 1920b [1974]; Moshiri 1991, 8; Central Committee of the C. P. S. U. (B.) 1939, 37, 46; Meadwell 1993, 215; Rapoport 1961, 273; Yu 1950.
23. Meyer 1984, 39.
24. Irish Republic Army, General Headquarters 1956 [1985], chapter 6.
25. Mao 1938a [1965], 155.
26. Johnson 1962, 3–5.
27. Pool 2001, 89–90, 105; see also pp. 99–101.
28. Quoted in English 2006, 418.
29. Lenin 1909 [1973], 254; Central Committee of the C. P. S. U. (B.) 1939, 191; Paret and Shy 1962, 26; Kilcullen 2009, 34; Perritt 2008, 25–35.

30. Kaufman 2011, 953.

31. Persuasion through argumentation is more limited and rational than the process of "framing," which can be transformative as it shapes "culture and meaning." William A. Gamson and Andre Modigliani (1987) define a frame as "a central organizing idea or story line that provides meaning to an unfolding strip of events. . . ." Unlike framing, persuasion does not try to change worldviews through deep psychological processes but to draw out the logical connections between the program and individual worldviews. For examples of the application of the concept of framing to the study of a secessionist movement, see Romano 2006, 15, 99. Anatol Rapoport (1961, 273) writes that, similar to framing, debates are attempts "to induce the opponent to adopt another image."

32. Goldstone 1991, 44, 45. See also Gurr and Goldstone 1991, 336; US Department of the Army 2007, 25.

33. Central Committee of the C. P. S. U. (B.) 1939, 17.

34. Romano 2006, 74.

35. Lieven 1993, 234.

36. Meadwell 1993, 225.

37. US Department of the Army 2007, 17.

38. Trapans 1991, 26.

39. Quoted in Paret and Shy 1962, 21; see also pp. 8, 19.

40. Central Committee of the C. P. S. U. (B.) 1939, 143–44. See also Schurmann 1971, 104–08.

41. Paret and Shy 1962, 27; see also pp. 21–24.

42. Kenny 2010, 536. See also case studies of the role of ideology in communist insurgencies in Oppenheim et al., 2015; Ron 2001; Thaler 2012.

43. Irish Republican Army, General Headquarters 1956 [1985], chapter 5.

44. Clark 1984, 158.

45. See also Kaufman 2011, 943.

46. The additional information that independence is now possible in the short term may touch off a cascade of participation similar to that closely analyzed by Susanne Lohmann (1994). Yet this information is relevant only if the campaign has prepared members of the platform population with the expectation that independence will be beneficial to them.

47. That is, the pragmatists cannot know the leaders' true types, and they also know that even cynical leaders may find it advantageous to pose as enthusiasts. Even those leaders who were enthusiasts in the past may not have irrevocably tied their hands so that they cannot defect in the future. Pragmatists may look for signs of costly commitments by leaders such as a life of deprivation for the cause that reveals their true type or audacious and unforgivable acts of violence against the common-state that elicit vocal commitments from the common-state government never to compromise with these secessionist leaders.

48. Hoffer 1951, 110.

49. Skitka and Bauman 2008, 31–33.

50. Wilson 1995, 195–97.

51. Lenin 1910 [1974], 370–71; Lenin 1902b [1973], 452.

52. Lenin 1919 [1974], 91.

53. Lenin 1910 [1974], 363.

54. Lenin, 1902b [1973], 440–43. In *What Is to Be Done?* Lenin rails against "amateurism" in staffers, which leaves the movement exposed to police penetration, arrest, and disruption.

55. Gall and de Waal 1998, 277, 105.

56. Erlich 1983, 119.

57. Quoted in Pool 2001, 126.

58. Mao 1938b [1965], 202. See also Johnson 1962, 71.

59. Hroch 2000, 14.

60. Hill 2002, 109; see also pp. 106, 132 33, 182 83. See also Johnson 1962, 87; Pool 2001, 110.

61. In Eritrea, David Pool (2001, 106) emphasizes that "the underlying pattern was one of centralized control and guidance balanced by considerable scope for initiative on the part of EPLF cadres."

62. Wilson 1995, 48, 295.

63. Gellner 1964, 167.

64. Hroch 2000, 134. See also Meadwell 1993, 212–13.

65. To counter these claims, the common-state government in London issued reports that independence would be costly for the Scots, who would need to create new administrative organs and currency, negotiate division of the North Sea oil revenues, and petition for separate membership in the European Union, which might be vetoed by member-governments that feared secession in their own common-states. See "Scottish Independence: Salmond Outlines Vision," *Scotsman,* May 25, 2014; "UK Finance Ministry Warns on Scottish Independence Costs," Reuters, May 25, 2014; "Scots Are Divided over Independence, and Its Economic Costs," *New York Times,* June 2, 2014. As reported in the last article, these instrumental arguments had little influence on true believers, such as Ms. Elrick, who was convinced that she and her husband were British.

66. Meadwell 1993, 212; see also p. 225. See also Thomas D. Lancaster's (1987, 573–74) description of the distribution of reasons given by Basque respondents for their attitudes about the proper relationship with their respective common-states.

67. Young 1999, 9–10, 40, 47. The PQ did not succeed at recruiting broadly within the Francophone business community, which feared that independence and even the threat of secession would lead to economic decline in Montreal and the surrounding region.

68. Hill 2002, 109, 183.

69. Hoffer 1951, 13. See also Central Committee of the C. P. S. U. (B.) 1939, 142, 143.

70. US Department of the Army 2007, 23.

71. For a description of machines in Russian segment-states, see Roeder 2007, 81–160.

72. Alexander A. Schuessler (2000, ix) describes one form of expressive activities "in which individuals express and reaffirm, to others and to themselves, who they are." For expressionists, participation is "not a form of investment, but a form of consumption, as the participant derives value from participation itself" (p. 46). Elisabeth Jean Wood (2003, 18–19, 234–37) describes one form of expressive behavior: the "pleasure of agency," which is "the positive affect associated with self-determination, autonomy, self-esteem, efficacy, and pride that come from the successful assertion of intention." This is not instrumental and is undiminished if unsuccessful.

73. Sullivan 1988, 74, 92. See also Clark 1984, 49.

74. Sullivan 1988, 248.

75. Clark 1984, 103.

76. Sullivan 1988, 246–47.

77. English 2006, 382.

78. Sullivan 1988, 157; see also pp. 62, 66, 115–16, 149–50, 153–54, 198. See also Clark 1984, 69–70.

79. Sullivan 1988, 120, 131.

80. Kingsbury 2009, 55–56, 58.

81. Schelling 1963, 70; see also pp. 58, 68.

82. Romano 2006, 27, 37, 66.

83. Whitmeyer 2002, 334.

84. Posted on the website of the Northwest Front: northwestfront.org/about/the-butler-plan-the-homeland.

85. Bovingdon 2010, 148; see also pp. 13, 24, 28, 36, 81–82, 139, 140, 152.

86. Compare Esteban and Ray 2008.

87. Sullivan 1988, 275. On the original ideology of nationalism that shaped the Basque Nationalist Party, see Flynn 2000, 148–50. See also Flynn's (2000, 188–92) more general discussion of ideological pluralism within nationalist campaigns.

88. Illustrative of this division was the profusion of Kurdish political parties, which included the Kurdistan Conservative Party (KCP), Kurdistan Islamic Union (PIK), Turkish Kurdish Socialist Party (TSKP), Kurdistan Freedom Party (PKK/RIZGARI), and Kurdistan Proletarian Union (KAWA). See Romano 2006, 70.

89. Entessar 1992, 90, 94–95; Romano 2006, 131; see also pp. 136, 142.

90. See, for example, Lee 2008.

91. Connor 1970, 93; see also Smith 1986, 18; Robinson 1979 [2000], 177, 201.

92. Petersen 2002, 24–25; Greenfeld 1992; Hechter 1975 [1998], 10, 39. See also Nairn 2003; Wimmer 2002, 42, 104.

93. Collier 2000a, 12, 13; Collier 2000b, 839; Collier and Hoeffler 1998, 564; Gellner 1964, 167, 169. See also Alesina and Spolaore 1997, 1028, 1037; Wittman 1991, 126.

94. Hobsbawm 1983. Platform populations identified in political programs can become identities in their own right; see Green, Palmquist, and Schickler 2002.

95. Kedourie 1960, 67.

96. McAdam, Tarrow, and Tilly 2001, 5, 6, 120. Contrast Beissinger 2002; particularly see 107, 141, 164, 165.

97. Fearon and Laitin 2003, 75.

5. SIGNIFICANT CAMPAIGNS

1. During the breakup of the Soviet Union, several Mordvin scholars advanced arguments that their people are not one nation but two—Moksha and Erzyan—and that the Mordvinian (A)SSR should be divided in two states. If the reader has not previously read of Mordvins, Erzyans, or Mokshas, this may be one illustration of the widespread failure of projects to come to the attention of even highly informed publics.

2. Solchanyk 1994, 48, 60; Kubicek 2000, 276.

3. The validity of the referendum results is contested, but validity is typically less important to a campaign than the corroboration of its ability to demonstrate programmatic preemption and the relative inefficacy of alternative campaigns. See Eduard Kondratov and Viktor Filippov, "Political Map: The Crimean Peninsula," *Izvestiia,* October 16, 1991, in *Current Digest of the Soviet Press* (hereafter *CDSP*) 43, no. 42 (1991): 9; Konstantin Parishkura, "Elections: The First Crimean President Is Ready to Join the CIS," *Segodnia,* February 1, 1994, in *CDSP* 46, no. 5 (1994): 6; "NEGA Reports: Crimea," *Nezavisimaia gazeta,* April 1, 1994, in *CDSP* 46, no. 13 (1994): 8; Sasse 2007, 129–73; David M. Herszenhorn, "Crimea Votes to Secede from Ukraine as Russian Troops Keep Watch," *New York Times,* March 17, 2014; Stephen Lee Myers and Peter Baker, "Putin Says Crimea Now Independent, Defying the West," *New York Times,* March 18, 2014.

4. Neil MacFarquhar, "For Russia, Negatives Seem to Outweigh Positives of an Invasion," *New York Times,* April 27, 2014; David M. Herszenhorn, "Away from Show of Diplomacy in Geneva, Putin Puts On a Show of His Own," *New York Times,* April 18, 2014.

5. Andrew E. Kramer, "Separatist Cadre Hopes for a Reprise in Ukraine," *New York Times,* August 4, 2014.

6. Andrew Higgins, "'Idea' of a Pro-Russian Country, but Little Else," *New York Times,* April 20, 2014. See also C. J. Chivers and Noah Sneider, "Behind the Masks in Ukraine, Many Faces of Rebellion," *New York Times,* May 4, 2014; Sabrina Tavernise and David M. Herszenhorn, "Patchwork Makeup of Rebels Fighting Ukraine Makes Peace Talks Elusive," *New York Times,* July 10, 2014.

7. Carlotta Gall, "In Ruins of Ukrainian Town, Residents Crave Food, Water and Peace," *New York Times,* September 21, 2014; Andrew E. Kramer, "Workers Quiet Unrest in Cities in Eastern Ukraine," *New York Times,* May 16, 2014.

8. Andrew E. Kramer, "Fears of Impending Change Darken Normally Lighthearted Odessa," *New York Times,* March 10, 2014; David M. Herszenhorn, "Crimea Votes to Secede from Ukraine as Russian Troops Keep Watch," *New York Times,* March 17, 2014; David M. Herszenhorn, "In East Ukraine, Protestors Seek Russian Troops," *New York Times,* April 8, 2014; Andrew E. Kramer, "Rebel-Backed Elections to Cement Status Quo in Ukraine," *New York Times,* November 3, 2014.

9. E. Kondratov, "Hearing One Another: How Moldavia Is Solving the 'Language Problem,'" *Izvestiia,* January 31, 1989, in *CDSP* 41, no. 7 (1989): 1. See also "In the Moldavian Communist Party Central Committee," *Sovetskaia Moldaviia,* January 27, 1989, in *CDSP* 41, no. 7 (1989): 5–6.

10. G. Ovcharenko, "Moldavia Today: Twenty-Four Hours for a Decision," *Pravda,* August 28, 1989, in *CDSP* 41, no. 35 (1989): 5; "We Report the Details: According to Unstable Recipes," *Pravda,* August 29, 1989, in *CDSP* 41, no. 35 (1989): 6.

11. E. Kondratov, "Moldova: The Alignment of Forces Today," *Izvestiia,* January 21, 1991, in *CDSP* 43, no. 3 (1991): 27; Aleksandr Tago, "Moldova: Struggle for Independence Intensifies—The Opposing Sides Each Have Their Own Understanding of This Word," *Nezavisimaia gazeta,* January 14, 1993, in *CDSP* 45, no. 3 (1993): 23–24.

12. Dmitry Zhdannikov, "Moldova: A Preplanned Victory—Which Turned Out to Be Essentially Useless," *Segodnia,* March 11, 1994, in *CDSP* 46, no. 10 (1994): 26. See also King 1994.

13. Laitin 1994, 2007; Schelling 1978, 213–43; Schelling 1963, 57–58, 68.

14. See the discussion in Roeder 2007, 121–23.

15. The multiplication of different identities that divide populations in diverse ways—each specific to particular situations—is noted by Anderson, von der Mehden, and Young 1967, 60–67. Psychological experiments highlight how identities are situation-specific and how new identities can be created with just a little cuing. Studies on the change of identities by situational cues manipulated by experimenters include Billig and Tajfel 1973; Brewer 1979; Kurzban, Tooby, and Cosmides 2001; Levine and Campbell 1972; Locksley, Ortiz and Hepburn 1980; Sherif et al. 1961; Tajfel et al. 1971; and Tajfel 1978.

16. The concept of an "imagined community" is introduced by Benedict Anderson (1991).

17. The dependent variable is a dichotomous indicator so that, for example, the Naga of India, who became the platform for the Nagaland national-secession campaign that claims the attention of the international print media, are coded as 1. Alternatively, the Navajo of the United States, who did not become the platform of a national-secession campaign that claimed international media attention, despite efforts of those who have pushed a Dinétah project, are coded as 0.

18. Wimmer, Cederman, and Min 2009; Gurr 2000.

19. Hobsbawm 1983. See also Hale 2008, 33–56, for a discussion of "uncertainty reduction."

20. Brass 1991, 74.

21. This focus on authenticity among enthusiasts is closely tied to the idea of legitimacy. Compare Toft 2002/3, 88.

22. Norman 1999, 38. See also Sorens 2005, 317, 319.

23. William Yardley, "Dreams of a Unified Northwest Are Halted at the Border," *New York Times,* February 27, 2010. The Cascadia project represents a substantially different political program from the Northwest Territorial Imperative.

24. Connor 1978.

25. Wimmer 2013a, 90.

26. The Connor-Kohn argument is part of a larger conceptual problem in the analysis of nationalism: the conflation of the concepts of ethnic groups and nations. See Cobban 1944, 48; Kymlicka 1995, 11, 18; Wimmer 2013a, 7–8.

27. Weber 1922 [1968], I:389; Gerth and Mills 1958, 176. See also Chandra and Wilkinson 2008, 520, 523.

28. Chris Buckley, "China Convicts and Sentences 20 Accused of Militant Separatism in Restive Region," *New York Times,* March 28, 2013; Edward Wong, "To Quell Unrest, Beijing Moves to Scatter Uighurs Across China," *New York Times,* November 9, 2014.

29. Huntington 2004, 186–87.

30. Barrington, Herron, and Silver 2003, 297.

31. The presence of an adjacent homeland was also negatively associated with the likelihood of a significant campaign, but this is a substantially smaller effect and shows statistical significance (at the .05 level) in only one of the two models.

32. Smith 1986, 64–65.

33. Sullivan 1988, 22.

34. Erlich 1983, 11.

35. Markakis 1987, 66; Iyob 1995, 67.

36. Walter 2009b, 113. See also Sorens 2012, 62.

37. Hechter and Levi 1979, 264.

38. Saideman, Dougherty, and Jenne 2005, 609, 616.

39. Buhaug 2006, 692, 694.

40. The probability of a significant campaign for ethnic groups with potential coalitions constituting 50 percent was 43.6, but for ethnic groups with coalitions constituting only 10 percent, this probability was 21.9.

41. See the results in table 5A.2 for "religious coalition."

42. McGarry 1999, 215.

43. Kilcullen 2009, 213. See also Bartkus 1999, 21.

44. Almond and Verba 1965, 204.

45. Wimmer, Cederman, and Min 2009, 321, 329, 332–33. See also Wimmer 2013a, 176–77, 196.

46. See the "home alone" variable in table 5A.2. Two confounding factors may make this variable an ambiguous index of the exit option. First, smaller expatriate communities may be associated with ethnic groups that are less socially mobilized (such as groups in the Amazon). Second, large expatriate communities may be the source of intellectual, financial, and logistical support for campaigns. Variables indicating these separate effects ("homeland development," "homeland urbanization," and "resourced diaspora") are not collinear with "home alone," and when they are included, this variable does not become significant.

47. This suggests that the exit effect swamps the tactical-logistical effect (described in chapter 8) when proximate exits are available.

6. INTRACTABLE DISPUTES

1. See also Goddard 2006, 35, 36–37.

2. Svante E. Cornell (2002, 246) contends that "central governments are nevertheless almost universally reluctant to accede to demands for autonomy. . . ." See also Joshua Keating, "The U.S. Likes the World Map the Way It Is," *New York Times,* September 24, 2017.

3. See also Mooney and Schuldt 2008.

4. Romano 2006, 145.

5. Wilson 1995, xi, 47.

6. Rapoport 1961, 10–11.

7. Wilson 1995, 286–77. See also US Joint Chiefs of Staff 2009, 11-4.

8. Schelling 1966, 135–36, italics added.

9. The bargaining model adopted in international relations theory was influenced by the earlier literature on labor-management negotiations. Industrial strikes, the presumed parallel to war, enter this model by raising the costs to management of holding out rather than conceding to labor's demands; see Watson and McKersie 1991, 30–41.

10. In 2006, Kolstø (2006, 726) also identified Somaliland, Tamil Eelam, and the Turkish Republic of Northern Cyprus as surviving quasi-states and Biafra, Eritrea, Katanga, Republika Srpska, and Republika Srpska Krajina as former quasi-states. See also Caspersen 2012; Coggins 2014; Pegg 1998.

11. For overviews of the politics in these de facto states, see Hale 2014; von Steinsdorff 2012. For overviews of the individual conflicts, see King 2001; Roeder 2007. For the international importance of nation- and state-building strategies, see Pegg 1998.

12. For Georgia, see ICG 2005a, 8–9; Middel 2005; Matveeva 2004. See also Saakashvili's "Road Map for a Comprehensive, Peaceful, Political Settlement of the Conflict in Abkhazia," described in ICG 2007, 7. For Azerbaijan, see ICG 2005c, 13; Cornell 2001, 122.

13. On Georgia, see ICG 2004c, 2; ICG 2007, 4; Vaux 2003, 16. On Azerbaijan, see ICG 2005b, 16–23. On the diverging pronouncements of the government and parliament in Moldova, see ICG 2006a, 11, fn 79, 19.

14. Blaustein and Flanz 2006, Georgia. The Georgian government was not even willing to restore South Ossetia as an administrative jurisdiction after dissolving this in the redrawing of provincial lines. Even in its NATO Individual Partnership Action Plan (IPAP), Georgia demonstrates an unwillingness to commit to the existence of a South Ossetia when it notes that the "frozen conflicts in Abkhazia and the Tskhinvali Region (South Ossetia) hinder the stable development of the country." See Middel 2005.

15. Vaux and Barrett 2003, 12, 15; ICG 2004b, 1, 9–11; Council of Europe 2002, 2004. See also King 2000, 209–23; Blaustein and Flanz 2006, Moldova, iv; Matveeva 2004.

16. Nevertheless, there is little doubt that belief in the authenticity of the program for independence cultivated by the campaign remained strong and that if given a moderate likelihood of success (realism), many Chechens would once again try to walk away with independence. And the Chechen leaders appear to be consolidating the type of exclusive control within the Republic of Chechnya that will enable them to demonstrate programmatic preemption for independence should an opportunity unfold in a future common-state crisis.

17. For overviews of the wars of the 1990s, see Zürcher 2007; O'Ballance 1997.

18. See also Rutland 1994, 843. To clarify nomenclature: "Nagorno-" is the adverbial form of the adjective "Nagornyi," used in this instance because Karabakh is an adjective, modifying "oblast." That is probably more Russian grammar than most readers care to know.

19. For example, David M. Herszenhorn, "Clashes Intensify between Armenia and Azerbaijan over Coveted Land," *New York Times,* February 1, 2015; Andrew E. Kramer, "Ethnic Tinderbox Flares in Nagorno-Karabakh," *New York Times,* April 3, 2016.

20. "Nagorno-Karabakh: A Mountainous Conflict," *Economist,* September 6, 2014, www.economist.com.

21. Kolstø and Blakkisrud 2008, 500–02.

22. Shnirelman 2001, 149–86.

23. National Statistical Service of the Nagorno-Karabakh Republic, "The Results of 2005 Census of the Nagorno-Karabakh Republic," table 5.1, census.stat-nkr.am.

24. ICG 2005b, 26.

25. Although contested, these elections did not result in a true turnover in power: at the end of the terms of Robert Kocharyan (1994–97) and Arkadi Ghukasyan (1997–2007), the inside candidate from the president's administration won handily. (Leonard Petrosyan filled the last six months of Kocharyan's term.) Dmitrii Zhdannikov, "Election: President Elected in Nagorno-Karabakh," *Segodnia,* December 24, 1994, in *Current Digest of the [Post-]Soviet Press* (hereafter *CDSP*) 46, no. 51 (1994): 25–26; Leonid Gankin and Gennadii Sysoev, "Karabakh Gets a Leader," *Kommersant-Daily,* September 3, 1997, in *CDSP* 49, no. 35 (1997): 17–18. In the July 19, 2007, presidential election, Bako Saakyan won with 85 percent of the vote, and on July 19, 2012, he won reelection with 66.7 percent: "Former Security Chief Wins Nagorno-Karabakh Vote," Radio Free Europe/Radio Liberty (hereafter RFE/RL), July 20, 2007; "Incumbent President Wins Nagorno-Karabakh Presidential Poll," RIA-Novosti, July 20, 2012, 12:04.

26. Shnirelman 2001, 201–350. See also Hewitt 1996. Abkhazia's first president, Vladislav Ardzinba, was a scholar of Hittite civilization, and the minister of foreign affairs, Viacheslav Chirikba, was a linguist of Caucasian languages; together they authored the introduction to a new history textbook, *History of Abkhazia,* published for the 1993 school year. See also the historical articles available on the Abkhaz World website that document Abkhaz historical claims, particularly claims of victimization by the Georgians.

27. O'Loughlin, Kolossov, and Toal 2011, 23, 25.

28. "The Population of Abkhazia Stands at 240,705," Abkhaz World, December 29, 2011.

29. RIA Novosti, February 16, 2010.

30. ICG 2013, 20.

31. Anaid Gogoryan, "High Expectations Placed on Abkhazia's New Leader," Institute for War and Peace Reporting, September 12, 2014.

32. ICG 2010a.

33. "Constitution of the Republic of Abkhazia (Apsny)," Abkhaz World, downloaded August 15, 2014.

34. For a sobering view of the successes of these undertakings, see Lynch 2004, 44–45, 47.

35. When Sergei Bagapsh died in May 2011, snap presidential elections were called in August 2011 and confirmed that Aleksandr Ankvab would serve out the remainder of Bagapsh's term.

36. Apsnypress press release, August 25, 2014, 12:07.

37. For press coverage, see Anaid Gogoryan, "High Expectations Placed on Abkhazia's New Leader," Institute for War and Peace Reporting, September 12, 2014; Giorgi Lomsadze, "Abkhazia: The Post-Soviet Revolution the World Blinked and Missed," Eurasianet/NewEast Network, *Guardian Today,* June 9, 2014; Polina Devitt and Jason Bush, "Abkhazia Elects Opposition Leader as President," Reuters, August 25, 2014.

38. ICG 2006b.

39. Soon after this declaration, a reported two hundred busloads of Georgian activists flooded into the oblast's capital, Tskhinvali, followed by Georgian troops, and for the next two months a small civil war raged in the region. Intervention by troops of the USSR police (MVD and KGB) forced the Georgians to retreat. For an in-depth study of the South Ossetian conflict, see Birch 1996.

40. See also Nelson and Amonashvili 1992.

41. If the South Ossetian population stands at only ten to twenty thousand, it would not take a particularly large influx of Georgians to claim numerical predominance. For a visual image of the destruction, use Goggle Earth to take an aerial flight from Tskhinvali, which is well repaired, eastward and northward over the nearby villages that were previously inhabited by Georgians.

42. Official website of the President of Republic of South Ossetia: prezidentruo.org.

43. Shnirelman 2001, 353–80. See also the documents on the genocide on the RES website: cominf.org.

44. ICG 2010b, 1, 11.

45. Alexander Skakov, "South Ossetia: Aftermath and Outlook," Carnegie Moscow Center, Black Sea Peacebuilding Network, Russian Expert Group, Report No. 2011/1.

46. "South Ossetians Vote for Independence," *Guardian,* November 13, 2006.

47. ICG 2010b, 13.

48. Liz Fuller, "South Ossetian Opposition Calls for Referendum on Unification," RFE/RL, January 8, 2014.

49. Nonetheless, South Ossetian elections were less democratic and even more tumultuous than those in Abkhazia. The republic's first president, Liudvig Chibirov, elevated to the presidency from his post of Supreme Soviet chairman, won reelection in 1996 but came in third in the next election. The 2001 election of Edward Kokoity gave his followers a decade to establish control over the administrative apparatus, but in the 2011 elections an opposition candidate seemed poised to claim victory. Pressed by the Kokoity machine, the Supreme Court, citing electoral violations, declared the election void and disqualified the candidates from running again. New elections in early 2012 resulted in the victory of Leonid Tibilov on April 8. See "The CEC of South Ossetia Has Announced the Final Results of the Election and the Referendum," RES/Information Agency of the Republic of South Ossetia, November 17, 2011, 15:20; "The Court Has Confirmed the Decision on Recognition of Presidential Election in the RSO the Void [*sic*]," RES, December 7, 2011, 11:53; "Leonid Tibilov Has Been Announced the Elected President of South Ossetia," RES, April 9, 2012, 15:01.

50. "Oglasheny predvaritel'nye itogi pridnistrovskoi perepisi naseleniia," Ol'via-press.

51. Quoted in Matsuzato 2008, 115.

52. Stefan Wolff, *The Transnistrian Issue: Moving Beyond the Status Quo,* report to the European Parliament, October 2012.

53. Protsyk 2009, 276.

54. Prior to the annexation of the right-bank Bessarabia/Moldavia to the USSR at the beginning of World War II, the left bank from 1924 to 1940 constituted the Moldavian ASSR.

55. After two decades of stultifying monopolization of power by Smirnov, the 2011 elections offered important opposition to the incumbent following a split within his elite coalition over issues of corruption and economic opportunities. In the runoff, Shevchuk won against Moscow's preferred candidate, Anatolii Kaminskii. See *Freedom in the World,* 2014, Transnistria, freedomhouse.org.

56. Protsyk 2009, 278–79.

57. Evangelista 2002; Gall and de Waal 1998; Lieven 1998.

58. Moscow's candidate, Akhmad Kadyrov, won handily, but terrorists assassinated Kadyrov seven months later, and new presidential elections had to be held in August 2004.

59. *Moscow Times,* August 16, 2005; Reuters Foundation, AlertNet, November 8, 2005.

60. German 2003, 76–111.

61. Ali Kazikhanov, "Supreme Soviet Announces Self-Dissolution," *Izvestiia,* September 16, 1991, in *CDSP* 43, no. 37 (1991): 33–34; Ali Kazikhanov, "Opposition Tries to Seize Power," *Izvestiia,* April 1, 1992, in *CDSP* 44, no. 13 (1992): 22.

62. Maria Eismont, "Chechen Opposition Prepares for Fall of the Dudaev Regime," *Segodnia,* May 12, 1994, in *CDSP* 46, no. 19 (1994): 12; Natalia Pachegina, "All Power Transferred to Provisional Council," *Nezavisimaia gazeta,* June 8, 1994, in *CDSP* 46, no. 23 (1994): 12.

63. Cornell 2001, 213–14; Zürcher 2007, 85–92; German 2003, 59–60; Maria Eismont, "Four Main Contenders for the Presidency," *Segodnia,* January 25, 1997, in *CDSP* 49, no.

4 (1997): 1–2; Dmitrii Alyoshin, "Maskhadov Is Officially Declared Winner," *Segodnia,* February 3, 1997, in *CDSP* 49, no. 5 (1997): 6–7.

64. Quoted in Evangelista 2002, 28.

65. ICG 2010a, 14.

66. Lynch 2007, 485–87.

67. See also Cornell 2001, 44–45.

68. ICG 2007, 7.

69. Quoted in Evangelista 2002, 25.

70. Lieven 1998, 69.

71. Evangelista 2002, 56–57.

72. Interviewed in P. Mirkadyrov, "Evropa Davno Perestala Byt' Chisto Beloi I Khristianskoi," *Zerkalo,* 2004, www.consortium-initiative.org. See also Vaux and Goodhand 2002, 19.

73. Quoted in de Waal 2003, 260.

74. ICG 2009, 4.

75. Vaux and Goodhand 2002, 12.

76. Quoted in Cornell 2001, 189.

77. "Viacheslav Chirikba: Abkhazia Will Never Renounce Its Independence," abkhaz world.com.

78. "At Geneva International Discussions, OSCE Chair's Special Representative Calls for Maintaining Substantive Dialogue," June 18, 2014, osce.org/cio.

79. ICG 2004c, 5.

80. ICG 2004a, 8, 13.

81. "Memorandum on the Principles of Settlement of Relations" and "Bases for Normalization of Relations Between the Republic of Moldova and Transdniestria."

82. "Agreement on the Basis of Relations Between the Republic of Moldova and Transdniestria."

83. ICG 2003, 9.

84. ICG 2006a, 2.

85. Stefan Wolff, "Progress Stalls on Moldova-Transnistria Conflict," *World Politics Review,* March 18, 2013, worldpoliticsreview.com; Dmitri Trenin, "Transnistria: A Gathering Storm," Carnegie Moscow Center, April 7, 2014, carnegie.ru; "OSCE Hopes That a New Round of Negotiations on Transnistrian Conflict Will Take Place in May," Teleradio Moldova, April 15, 2014, 9:31, trm.md; "OSCE Calls for Preserving 5+2 Format for Negotiations on Transdniestria," *Kyiv Post,* August 30, 2014, kyivpost.com.

86. Quoted in Gall and de Waal 1998, 169; see also p. 118. See also Evangelista 2002, 23–25, 27; Lieven 1998, 68.

87. ICG 2003, 10; ICG 2004a, 24.

88. Cornell 2001, 114.

89. Itar-TASS.com, April 18, 2009. See also "Minsk Group Meeting with Azerbaijani President on Karabakh," RFE/RL, May 29, 2009.

90. Ali Abasov and Haroutiun Khachatrian, *The Karabakh Conflict—Variants of Settlement: Concepts and Reality,* 3rd ed. (Baku and Yerevan: Areat-Noyan Tappan, 2006), www.ca-c.org; Cornell 2001; Goble 1992; Laitin and Suny 1999; Maresca 1994.

91. Cornell 2001, 192.

92. For analysis of the options in the South Ossetian conflict, see Birch 1996, 182–89.

93. ICG 2005c, 11.

94. Cornell 2001, 118–19.

95. ICG 2009, 7.

96. "At Geneva International Discussions, OSCE Chair's Special Representative Calls for Maintaining Substantive Dialogue," June 18, 2014, osce.org/cio.

97. ICG 2013, 13.

98. Kolstø and Blakkisrud 2008, 507.

99. Other circumstances, such as segment-statehood, can aid programmatic coordination, but without external support and de facto independence, campaigns must work harder to achieve and sustain programmatic preemption in the face of a determined common-state government. For a description of political machines in segment-states, see Roeder 2007.

100. O'Loughlin, Kolossov, and Toal 2011, 4. The frustration among Abkhazian and South Ossetian leaders that their struggle was not seen in the same light as Kosovo's struggle for liberation from Serbia is a recurring theme in their appeals to the international community. They argued that the European and American characterization of their struggles did as much violence to reality as characterizing Kosovo's struggle as simply an American-Serbian war.

101. "State Strategy on the Occupied Territories: Engagement through Cooperation," civil.ge/files/files/SMR-Strategy-en.pdf.

102. Fearon 1995b, 390.

7. PROTRACTED INTENSE STRUGGLES

1. Based on data in Uppsala Conflict Data Program (UCDP) 2011. External wars—whether interstate or colonial wars—are excluded from these calculations.

2. Based on data in National Consortium for the Study of Terrorism and Responses to Terrorism (START) 2013. More commonly, terrorism was associated with religious and class campaigns, such as Islamism or communism.

3. National-secession civil wars averaged 5.1 years per episode compared to 4.2 years for all other civil wars, calculated from UCDP 2011. See also Walter 2009b, 4.

4. Sullivan 1988, 1–2, 16–21; National Consortium for the Study of Terrorism and Responses to Terrorism 2013.

5. Compare Kydd and Walter 2006.

6. See also Toft 2003, 2–3. Compare Lawrence 2010; Tilly 1978, 216.

7. Lenin 1906 [1972], 11:214. See also Mao 1938a [1965].

8. See, for example, Byman 1998.

9. Sullivan 1988, 45, 135. See also Clark 1984, 41.

10. Sullivan 1988, 74.

11. Sullivan 1988, 36, 113, 139. See also Clark 1984, 35–37.

12. Clark 1984, 51–52.

13. For a generalization of this observation, see Leites and Wolfe 1970, 61–62; US Joint Chiefs of Staff 2009, II-2. See the application of this strategy by the Kosovo Liberation Army in Perritt 2008, 62–73.

14. US Joint Chiefs of Staff 2009, II-1, 2. See also Fearon and Laitin 2000.

15. Fearon and Laitin 2000, 856–57.

16. Crenshaw 1981; Fromkin 1975; Price 1977; Thornton 1964.

17. Kingsbury 2009, 51–52.

18. Romano 2006, 160.

19. Kingsbury 2009, 51–52.

20. Sullivan 1988, 72; Clark 1984, 51.

21. Romano 2006, 87.

22. Romano 2006, 75.

23. Romano 2006, 88–89.

24. Paret and Shy 1962, 19.

25. Mao 1937 [1961], 43, italics added.

26. Quoted in Paret and Shy 1962, 8, 21.

27. Sullivan 1988, 187; Clark 1984, 77–81, 93; Wilson 1995, 288–89.

28. Sullivan (1988, 277–78), writing in the mid-1980s, argues that within the Basque platform population some "moderate members of the nationalist community, whether businessmen, priests, or professional people," saw ETA's activists "as, at worst, mistaken" and excused "someone who had been convicted for monstrous crimes . . . as a well meaning if impetuous patriot." On subsequent developments, see Ahedo 2005, 182–83, 185. Compare Lyall, Blair, and Imai 2013.

29. Sullivan 1988, 272.

30. Clark 1984, 34, 43.

31. Sullivan 1988, 62, 69–70, 138.

32. Quoted in English 2006, 388.

33. Quoted in English 2003, 343.

34. English 2006, 372, 380, 382, 399, 404, 409.

35. A segment-state is a jurisdiction within a common-state designated as the homeland of a specific titular nation, such as the Ukrainian SSR for the Ukrainians within the Soviet Union (Roeder 2007). For a discussion of the relationship of segment-states to violence, see the exchange in Hoddie and Hartzell 2014.

36. See also Toft 2002/3, 103; Toft 2006; Cohen 1997; and Walter 2006. Contrast Fearon 1995a.

37. See Lecours 2012, 274–75.

38. It is common to note that the independent effect of current statehood is difficult to measure because ethnic groups with well-developed nationalism are more likely to get segment-states. Nevertheless, this does not challenge the major point made here: even if current statehood had no independent effect on programmatic coordination, it would still be a good indicator.

39. Smith 1996, 655.

40. This is central to the classic Maoist strategy of creating base areas—the Yenan way. See Johnson 1962, 97, 100.

41. Pool 2001, 100.

42. O'Ballance 1989, 71–72.

43. See also Buhaug, Cederman, and Rød (2008); Ellingsen 2000. Contrast Cunningham 2013b.

44. The logarithmic transformation of the platform population shown in figure 7.2 represents the best fit. Nonlogarithmic, polynomial, and dichotomous (smallest or small versus the rest) specifications failed to achieve statistical significance.

45. See also Bwy 1968, 51; Toft 2003. Contrast Fearon and Laitin 2003, 79.

46. See also Wimmer, Cederman, and Min 2009, 317; Wimmer and Min 2006; Cederman, Wimmer, and Min 2010; Walter 2006; and Cohen 1997.

47. See also Hegre et al. 2001; Collier 2000a; and Vreeland 2008. Contrast Ellingsen 2000; Gurr 2000; Hibbs 1973; Lacina 2006; Mansfield and Snyder 2002; and Muller and Weede 1990.

48. Compare Buhaug 2006, 700; Sorens 2012, 129; Walter 2009b, 82.

8. COMPLEMENTARY EXPLANATIONS

1. Kalyvas 2003, 486.

2. See Lenin's (1902b [1973]) discussion of spontaneity and consciousness.

3. Collier 2000a, 13.

4. Aspinall 2007, 968.

5. Bwy 1968, 17.

6. Gurr 1970, 210. See also Davies 1962; Tanter and Midlarsky 1967, 270–71; US Joint Chiefs of Staff 2009, II-8.

7. Kaufman 2006, 47, 51.

8. Breuilly 1994; Seton Watson 1977.

9. Hutchinson 1987, 33. See also Smith 1981.

10. Cottam and Cottam 2001, 95.

11. Gurr 2000, 67. See also Conversi 1997, 162–86; Lancaster 1987; Linz 1980.

12. Tajfel 1970. See also Cottam et al. 2010, 201; Cuhadar and Dayton 2011; Hale 2008; Petersen 2002. Contrast Laitin 2007, 15–18.

13. Connor 1994, 82, 84. See also Huntington 1996, 130, 253; Vanhanen 1999, 59.

14. Pye 1966, 136. See also the extension to ethno-demographic (fragmentation and polarization) hypotheses in Blimes 2006; Buhaug 2006; Collier 2000a; Collier and Hoeffler 2004; Ellingsen 2000; Fearon and Laitin 2003; Hegre and Sambanis 2006; Hegre et al. 2001; Hibbs 1973; Lacina 2006; Laitin 2007; Montalvo and Reynal-Querol 2005; Reynal-Querol 2002; Sambanis 2001.

15. Robinson 1979 [2000], 177, 201. See also Huntington 1996, 183, 263–64; Toft 2007, 104, 113.

16. The variables "Christian minority in an Islamic state" and "Muslim minority in a Christian state" are set to zero in these estimates of probabilities.

17. See Hastings 1997.

18. Lecours 2012.

19. See also Jenne 2006; Lacina 2006.

20. Fishman 1999, 445. See also Fishman 1973, 52–55; Vanhanen 1999, 59.

21. Huntington 1996, 137, 254. See also Roeder 2003; Toft 2007.

22. Horowitz 1985, 267. Contrast Cunningham 2013a.

23. Contrast Cunningham 2014.

24. Hroch 2000, 165.

25. Compare Brubaker 1996, 108; Ellingsen 2000, 234.

26. Anderson, von der Mehden, and Young 1967, 72. See also Bovingdon 2010, 109; Horowitz 1985, 235; Sorens 2012, 60–62; Walter 2009b, 115.

27. Hechter 1975 [1998], 39–43. See also Nairn 2003, 322–29. On general political violence, see Blattman and Miguel 2010, 4; Flanigan and Fogelman 1970; Walter 2009a, 244.

28. Gourevitch 1979; Roeder 1991. See also Cederman, Weidman, and Gleditsch 2011.

29. Ross 2004, 41. See also Buhaug 2006, 697; Le Billon 2001, 574. Contrast Walter 2009b, 116.

30. Hroch 2000, 161. See also Clark 1984, 147; Jenne 2006.

31. "Common-state GDP per capita" and "common-state urbanization" are substituted for each other in alternative estimations because they are collinear. See also Zürcher 2007, 220–21. On general political violence, see Bwy 1968; Davies 1962, 7; Feierabend, Feierabend, and Nesvold 1969; Hibbs 1973.

32. Petersen 2002, 2. See also Glaeser 2005; Scott 1976; Tanter and Midlarsky 1967. On general political violence, see Boix 2008; Collier 2000a; Mitchell 1968, 423; Nagel 1974, 454, 459–60; Paranzino 1972, 577–78; Russett 1964, 449.

33. Deutsch 1961, 493.

34. Hroch 2000, 158, 172.

35. Hibbs 1973, 71, 175, 191. See also Wimmer 2002, 4.

36. Greenfeld 1992, 15. See also Coleman 1968; Deutsch 1961, 1966; Eckstein 1988, 796–97; Hibbs 1973; Huntington 1968; Olson 1963.

37. On general political violence, see Blattman and Miguel 2010; Bwy 1968; Fearon and Laitin 2003; Flanigan and Fogelman 1970; Hegre and Sambanis 2006; Hibbs 1973, 37–40, 52–53. See also Cornelius 1969; Nelson 1969.

38. For example, see Averch, Koehler, and Denton 1971; Leites and Wolfe 1970.

39. Fearon and Laitin 2003, 75. See also Laitin 2007.

40. Collier, Hoeffler, and Söderbom 2008, 464. See also Blattman and Miguel 2010; Collier and Hoeffler 1998.

41. Mason, Weingarten, and Fett 1999. See also Wagner 1993.

42. Fearon 1995a; de Rouen and Sobek 2004, 304; Toft 2003, 21; Toft 2006. See also Cunningham 2006; Cunningham 2014; Walter 2009b.

43. Fearon 1995b; Walter 2002.

44. Collier and Hoeffler 1998, 564.

45. Clark 1984, 224, 227.

46. Mao 1938a [1965], 136–37; US Department of the Army 2007, 11–12.

47. Grievance theories complicate the analysis of the relationship of the coercive capabilities of the common-state to the use of violence by nationalist-secessionists: rising common-state capabilities fuel growing resentment among secessionists. See Gurr 1970, 251. Contrast Bwy 1968; Hibbs 1973.

48. Wimmer 2013b, 136.

49. See also Walter 2009b, 118. Compare Bartkus 1999, 10; Buhaug 2006, 694.

50. Filson and Werner 2002, 831. See also Collier and Hoeffler 1998; Lacina 2006; Wagner 1993. Contrast Cunningham 2013b; Cunningham 2014; Walter 2009b.

51. Laitin 2007, 21–22. See also Cohen 1997; Fearon and Laitin 2003; Hegre et al. 2001; Mansfield and Snyder 2002.

52. "Common-state weakness," when substituted for "democratic regime" in other equations, is not significant and does less well as a predictor of protracted intensity.

53. Contrast Anderson, von der Mehden, and Young 1967, 70; Wimmer 2013b, 153.

54. Connor 1984, 221.

55. Donald Horowitz (1985, 230) adds a third competing consideration in these calculations: "A group that might otherwise be disposed to separatism will not be so disposed if its secession is likely to lead, not to independence, but to incorporation in a neighboring state, membership in which is viewed as even less desirable than membership in the existing state."

56. See also Jenne 2006; Walter 2009b, 116. Contrast Brubaker 1996, 5; Marshall and Gurr 2003.

57. See also Lacina 2006, 281–82; US Department of the Army 2007, 28.

58. See also Zürcher 2007, 221–23. On general political violence, see Averch and Koehler 1970, 17; Averch, Koehler, and Denton 1971; Collier, Hoeffler, and Söderbom 2008; Fearon and Laitin 2003, 80–81, 85; Lacina 2006; Laitin 2007; Mitchell 1968, 430; Mitchell 1969, 1170; Montalvo and Reynal-Querol 2005, 805; Paige 1970, 36; Paranzino 1972; Paret and Shy 1962, 32.

59. Bovingdon 2010, 137.

60. Mirak 1997, 402, 408. See also Collier 2000a, 14; Sheffer 2003, 155; Walter 2009a, 248.

61. Collier 2000a, 2, 4, 6, 10. See also Collier and Hoeffler 1998; Le Billon 2001; Ross 2004; Wimmer, Cederman, and Min 2009.

62. See also Sorens 2012; Walter 2009b.

63. See, for example, Fair 2005; Pool 2001, 129, 142–43; Romano 2006, 58–59.

64. Ross 2004, 47. See also Sorens 2012, 129.

65. Toft 2002/3, 103. See also Ross 2004, 60–61.

66. Ellingsen 2000, 234, 243; Fearon and Laitin 2003; Walter 2006, 123. See also Cederman et al. 2013; Cunningham 2013b; Cunningham 2014.

9. LOOKING FORWARD

1. Compare Pettee 1966, 15–18. The terms *coup* and *revolution* may also be used to refer to the means employed or the outcome, including unintended outcomes, of those means. The distinction here concerns only the objectives of the leaders.

2. Bankowicz 2012, 55.

3. Skocpol 1979, 4–5.

4. Page 1959.

5. Grossman 1991, 1999.

6. See Fabry 2010; Griffiths 2016.

7. See, for just one example, Roeder 2007.

8. See Goldstone et al. 2010.

9. See World Bank 2011, chapter 2; US Joint Chiefs of Staff 2013.

10. Wintrobe 2006, 169.

11. Summers 1982, 5–6; Davis and Kohn 1971.

12. Clausewitz 1976, 87, 89. In revolutionary circles this was challenged by Che Guevara (1961), who substituted military for political leadership and saw the military as the primary tool for rallying the population.

13. In this context the purpose of outsiders' development assistance and brute force is to convince the platform population that they want to be members of the common-nation and common-state—not allies of an outside power. This is in sharp contrast with the preoccupation with winning friends for America in Afghanistan and Iraq villages; see, e.g., Kaplan 2013, 246–48, 325–27, 343. The analysis of the strategy of programmatic coordination suggests that there may be greater strategic vision in the policy that has been disparagingly labeled "leading from behind" by its critics. From the perspective of the interventionists' military, arm's-length involvement may free them to do what they do best without becoming directly involved in the implementation of development missions.

APPENDIX TO CHAPTER 2

1. The statistical data analyzed in this book are available in two groups of data sets posted at http://pages.ucsd.edu/~proeder/data.htm.

2. The search terms were "secession*," "declaration of independence," "separatis*," and "autonomy."

3. Minahan 1996, 2002; Marshall and Gurr 2003. Wikipedia's copious lists include "active autonomist and secessionist movements," "historical autonomist and secessionist movements," "states with limited recognition," and "historical unrecognized countries." The most comprehensive website lists with links to specific secessionist organizations include "active autonomist and secessionist movements," which appears on the website of the American Secession Project at www.secessionist.us, and the members of the Unrepresented Nations and Peoples Organization at www.unpo.org.

4. Heraclides (1990, 344) identifies the Kurdish Republic of Mahabad in Iran, East Turkestan Republic in China, Hyderabad in India, Moluccans in Indonesia, Nagas in India, Karens in Burma, Katanga, Biafra, Bangladesh, South Sudan, Iraqi Kurdistan, Eritrea, and Moros in the Philippines.

5. Buchheit 1978.

6. Marshall and Gurr 2003, 57–64.

7. Minahan 2002, xi–xii. Some "nations" confronted multiple states, as the Kurds confront Iran, Iraq, Syria, and Turkey, and each of these constitutes a separate campaign.

8. Diehl and Goertz 1991. See also Goertz and Diehl 1992 on "territorial changes." See also Sambanis 2004 on the distinction between "civil" versus "extra-systemic" wars.

9. Goldsmith and He 2008. There are two curious but minor omissions here: Bangladesh and Slovakia.

10. Roeder 2007.

11. Coggins 2011, 442.

12. Griffiths 2016.

13. Alternatively, Fearon (2004, 278, fn 6) includes in his count of civil wars those anti-colonial wars such as Algeria or Angola as "civil wars under the jurisdiction of the metropole." Another class of ambiguous cases that are excluded include the realms of the crown that are not formally part of the metropole—holdovers from pre-democratic dynastic authority. In the relationship of the Kingdom of the Netherlands to its constituent countries, which includes the Netherlands proper, the other constituent countries are outside

the Netherlands and its representative institutions but are part of the kingdom and its government. Similarly, the British Crown Dependencies (Isle of Man and the Channel Islands) are subject to the Crown but are not parts of the United Kingdom.

14. Uppsala Conflict Data Program 2011; National Consortium for the Study of Terrorism and Responses to Terrorism (START) 2013; Chenoweth and Lewis 2013.

15. Specifically, this is calculated as $1/n$, where n is the number of years since the end of war. It is 1 during years of war and the first year of peace but asymptotically approaches 0 with more years of peace. The data on wars are from UCDP 2011.

16. The data on multilateral interventions are from Fortna 2004; "List of Peacekeeping Operations 1948–2013," www.un.org/en/peacekeeping/documents/operationslist.pdf; and UCDP 2011.

APPENDIX TO CHAPTER 5

1. The statistical data analyzed in this book are available in two groups of data sets posted at http://pages.ucsd.edu/~proeder/data.htm.

2. An ethnicity such as the Tamils or Kurds may reside in multiple countries and be counted as a different ethnic group in each country. This total of 1,348 ethnicities does not count an amalgamation such as Arabs as a separate ethnicity when individual ethnicities such as Iraqi Arabs are in the data set. Nonetheless, in some countries amalgamations rather than individual groups are recorded.

3. To avoid duplication in cases when common-states such as the USSR are divided, ethnic groups are counted in the successor states unless their secessionism was directed specifically at the initial common-state. Thus, Jews appear as an ethnic group in many Soviet successor states but not in the USSR; Georgians appear as an ethnic group in the USSR but not in Georgia. For amalgamated states such as Vietnam, ethnic groups appear in the amalgamated state; ethnic groups in the predecessor states such as North and South Vietnam appear if their secessionism was directed only at the predecessor state. Thus, the total number of countries is only 169; three predecessor states that appear in the count in table 2.2 are dropped here.

4. Bruk and Apenchenko 1964; Bruk 1986.

5. For countries that became independent after 1985, the data set uses national censuses to identify ethnic groups and to estimate their populations. Because these tend to be postcommunist states, they tend to use ethnic categories and counts that are close, if not identical, to those in Bruk and Apenchenko 1964 and Bruk 1986.

6. SIL International various years; Joshua Project 2012; Asher and Moseley 2007. Kanchan Chandra and Steven Wilkinson (2008, 517) note that cultural identities and practices can separate individuals on multiple dimensions, including race, language, or religion and that the dimensions which become activated in politics vary. Although the definition of ethnic groups used here relies on conventional ethnographic categories, the data collected for each group measure these multiple dimensions that may unite or divide individual ethnic groups and may link them with or separate them from other ethnic groups within their common-state or in other common-states.

7. Wimmer, Cederman, and Min 2009, 325–26.

8. Gurr 2000, 5, 7.

9. See also Hug 2013.

10. The maps appear in Bruk and Apenchenko 1964; the descriptions of settlement patterns appear in Bruk 1986.

11. These data are compiled from annual editions of *Statesman's Yearbook*.

12. Estimates are interpolated from population data in Bruk and Apenchenko 1964; Bruk 1986; and national censuses.

13. These estimates are calculated from data in Bruk and Apenchenko 1964; Bruk 1986; Joshua Project 2012; Barrett, Kurian, and Johnson 2001; and Barrett 1982.

14. Data on constitutional status are derived from Barrett, Kurian, and Johnson 2001 and Barrett 1982. The religious affiliation of the platform population is from Bruk 1986 and Joshua Project 2012.

15. This relies on data in Cederman, Min, and Wimmer 2009 but adds data for ethnic groups not coded in EPR and extends the data to 2009. Although some minor recodings are made so that the variable more precisely indicates exclusion from the executive organ (e.g., the government or Politburo), for cases found in both data sets the governmental exclusion variable correlates with the proportion of years that ERP indicates an ethnic group was not "monopolistic" or "dominant" nearly perfectly (r = 0.97; n = 5,158).

16. Calculated from data in Bruk 1986.

17. Sources of data: Bruk 1986 and Joshua Project 2012.

18. Source of data: Maddison 2011. In an alternative specification of the equation, urbanization of the common-state at the midpoint year was used in place of the GDP per capita. Urbanization is calculated from data in United Nations 2001. Urbanization is highly correlated with GDP per capita (r = .87) and so was used as an alternative measure of development. It was even less significant as a predictor of campaign significance.

19. Sources of data: United States Defense Meteorological Satellite Program 2011 and Center for International Earth Science Information Network 2005. I am grateful to Konstantin Ash, who actually calculated these variables for me. On this and other methods using satellite sensing, see Sendhil Mullainathan, "A Dark Sky at Night Tells No Economic Lies," *New York Times*, April 3, 2016.

20. The definition of the area included in urban centers is based on data in Schneider, Friedl, and Potere 2009.

21. Source of data: Lujala, Rød, and Thieme 2007.

22. Source of data: Gilmore et al. 2005.

23. On state size as a measure of governing load, see Wimmer, Cederman, and Min 2009, 323; Alesina and Spolaore 2003; Collier and Hoeffler 1998, 564. On state age as an indicator of capacity, see Gurr 2000, 163; Wimmer, Cederman, and Min 2009, 317.

24. Source of data: Marshall, Gurr, and Jaggers 2010, using 6 as the lowest Polity score for democracies and –6 as the highest Polity score for autocracies.

25. Calculated from data in Bruk 1986.

26. Based on Tollefsen, Strand, and Buhaug 2012. See also Buhaug 2006, 697; Anderson, von der Mehden, and Young 1967, 71.

27. Based on Tollefsen, Strand, and Buhaug 2012.

28. Based on population data in Bruk and Apenchenko 1964 and Bruk 1986.

29. King, Tomz, and Wittenberg 2000.

APPENDIX TO CHAPTER 7

1. The statistical data are available at http://pages.ucsd.edu/~proeder/data.htm.

2. Kaufmann 1996; Sambanis 2001; Fearon and Laitin 2003. For example, the label "ethnic wars" includes intercommunal violence (for example, the Kyrgyz-Uzbek conflict over lands in the Fergana and Osh valleys) and ethnic revolutions (for example, the Hutu-Tutsi conflict to control the government of Rwanda).

3. Data sources are Uppsala Conflict Data Program 2011; National Consortium for the Study of Terrorism and Responses to Terrorism 2013; and Chenoweth and Lewis 2013.

4. In addition, seventeen campaigns reported no years of even low-intensity civil war but minor instances of terrorism with fewer than twenty-five deaths: Armenia (Turkey), Bretagne (France), Catalunya (Spain), Corsica (France), Euskadi (France), Galiza (Spain), Georgia (USSR), Karbi Anglong (India), Lakotah (USA), Matabeleland (Zimbabwe), New Afrika (USA), Quebec (Canada), Rwenzururu (Uganda), Sindhudesh (Pakistan), Somalia (Kenya), Volkstaat (South Africa), and Zozam (India).

5. Data on segment-states are from Roeder 2007, 355–64, updated to 2010. Data on de facto states are from *Statesman's Yearbook* 1945–2010; Kolstø 2006, 726; and Caspersen and Stansfield 2011, 4. The list of de facto states used in this analysis is consistent with the latter two sources, except that it also includes Eastern Turkestan (1945–49), Herzeg-Bosna (1992–94), Iranian Azerbaijan (1945–46), Iranian Kurdistan (1945–46), South Kasai (1960–61), Southern Mongolia (1945–46), and Tibet (1945–50).

6. This is based on the Minorities at Risk's political discrimination index (recoding 3 and 4 = 1; otherwise = 0) with updating to bring this variable through 2009; see Minorities at Risk 2009.

7. Source of data: Bruk 1986.

8. Sources of data: Bruk 1986 and Joshua Project 2012.

9. Data on urbanization are interpolated from United Nations 2001.

10. Data on GDP per capita are from Maddison 2011. These are highly correlated (r = .93) with "urbanization," so the two variables are used in alternative specifications of the statistical model.

11. This is computed from data in Maddison 2011.

12. Source of armed forces data: Banks 2011. Population estimates are based on Bruk and Apenchenko 1964 and Bruk 1986 and, for states created after 1985, on census reports. Because most of the latter are postcommunist states, their census definitions of ethnic groups correspond closely with those in Bruk and Apenchenko 1964 and Bruk 1986.

13. Data are calculated from Marshall, Gurr, and Jaggers 2010, where "weak common-state regime" is the proportion of years that the regime was an anocracy (a Polity score from –5 to +5), in constitutional transition (–88), or in political turmoil (–77).

14. These are estimated from GTOPO digital elevation data, yielding about 8,000 elevation measures around each secessionist capital. The source of the raw data is United States Geological Survey 2005. These GIS estimates of topography were calculated by Tricia Toomey.

15. Source of data: Bruk 1986.

16. Source of data: Genocide Prevention Advisory Network 2015. These include only the episodes identified by Gregory Stanton at Genocide Watch as "genocides, politicides, and other mass murder" perpetrated against separatists by governments.

17. King, Tomz, and Wittenberg 2000.

APPENDIX TO CHAPTER 9

1. Yusoff 2006, 206–322; Dambul, Omar, and Osman 2010, 35–55, 103–18; Chen 2012, 118–20; Barlocco 2014, 54.

2. Benei 2008, 166–67.

3. World Directory of Minorities and Indigenous Peoples: Mauritania, available on the website of the Minority Rights Group International: www.minorityrights.org.

4. Ethiopia's Afar Region January 18, 2012, available on the website of the BBC: www.bbc.com. See also United States, Library of Congress, Federal Research Division 1991, 248.

5. South 2003, 219, 316, 337.

Glossary

action plan. Part of a program that outlines operational objectives and tactics to bring about the strategic goal described in the program's doctrine (such as its nation-state project).

activation phases. See longueur and surge.

association stage. The third developmental stage of a campaign, in which cadres cultivate a participatory reserve and coordinate expectations among reservists and the larger platform population about the authenticity and realism of the program.

authenticity. Assessment by members of a platform population that a program's goal (such as its nation-state project) will bring coordination among its members regarding its core claims about the identity of its platform population and its rights (such as the claim that the platform population constitutes a nation with a right to sovereign statehood).

autonomy campaign. A peoplehood and statehood campaign that seeks creation of a new segment-state or expansion of the prerogatives of an existing segment-state within its common-state, but not sovereignty outside the common-state.

campaign. A coordinated course of action designed to shape public opinion throughout a platform population for or against some political object (strategic goal).

capacitation stage. The second developmental stage of a campaign, in which leaders recruit and educate a campaign staff, which includes cadres and activists, to carry out the tasks of programmatic coordination within the platform population.

championship. An exchange between campaign and common-state leaders in which the objective is not to influence the other's behavior but to persuade bystanders (or audience) by arguments and deeds.

common-state. The jurisdiction that is currently recognized by the international community as the sovereign authority over the secessionists' nation and homeland (even if the secessionists have a segment-state or de facto state of their own) and over the rump state that would be left behind if the secessionists achieved independence.

debate. An exchange between campaign and common-state leaders in which the objective is to influence the other party's behavior by changing the other party's worldview.

developmental stages. See establishment stage, capacitation stage, and association stage.

establishment stage. The initial developmental stage of a campaign, in which founders coordinate on a strategic goal, draft a program, and establish campaign leadership.

expressive incentives/expressionists. Opportunities created by the campaign for cathartic release of personal emotions such as anger or rage or to indulge in the sport of protesting and mayhem where the act is an end in itself; the type of person attracted by such opportunities.

forecast uncertainty. One of the strategic constraints on campaigns by which they cannot influence the timing of opportunities to demonstrate programmatic preemption or forecast the timing and nature of those opportunities with certainty.

game. An exchange between campaign and common-state leaders in which each attempts to influence the other's behavior by influencing their expectation of payoff from different options.

high-intensity violence. A level of intensity in which battle- or terrorism-related deaths exceed 1,000 in a year.

indeterminacy. The quality of a causal factor, such as an identified personal, parochial, or particularistic motivation, that predicts action but not coordination of action in pursuit of a common goal; hence, the motive is not a determinate (sufficient) cause of coordinated action in pursuit of the goal.

intense violence. A level of intensity in which the total number of battle- or terrorism-related deaths is between 25 and 1,000 in a year.

intensity. A measure of the costs inflicted on the other side by the tactics employed by a campaign.

intractability. The inability of the parties to a dispute (e.g., a campaign and a common-state government) to reach agreement on the substantive issue that divides them (such as independence for the platform population's homeland).

longueur. An activation phase when there are few opportunities for surges and the strategic goal of the campaign (such as independence) is not within sight.

low-intensity violence. A level of intensity in which battle- and terrorism-related deaths do not exceed 25 in a year.

material incentives/pragmatists. Tangible and intangible rewards such as money and power for which the strategic goal of the campaign is only an instrumental means; the type of persons motivated by expectation of such payoff.

motivational heterogeneity. The diversity of types (enthusiasts, expressionists, and pragmatists) and motivations (cultural identity; economic, social, and cultural grievance; and greed) that divides a platform population but must be drawn together behind the common strategic goal (such as independence).

national secessionism. The claim that a population residing inside the metropolitan territory of another sovereign state constitutes a nation that has a right to its own sovereign state, which should control the part of the common-state's territory that the nation considers its homeland.

nonlethal violence. A level of intensity in which armed attacks or violent protests bring no battle- or terrorism-related deaths in that year.

operational objective. The goal that a campaign sets for its own actions (such as programmatic preemption) that in interaction with the operational choices of other key actors (such as the common-state government and international community) is expected to result in the desired strategic outcome.

operational weakness. A strategic constraint on a campaign that is too weak to expect to be able to impose its strategic goal on the common-state (such as seize independence over the resistance of the common-state government).

peoplehood campaign. A campaign claiming that its platform population constitutes a distinctive people with a right to make political claims, which may include nonstatehood protections, segment-statehood within the common-state, or sovereign independence outside the common-state.

platform population. The individuals that a program identifies as a group, the expected support base of the campaign, and the source of its claims (such as a nation with a right to a sovereign state of its own).

program. An analysis of the status quo, that links a doctrine (such as a nation-state project), which analyzes the source of current inadequacies and prescribes an idealized future, to an action plan outlining methods for achieving the idealized future.

programmatic preemption. An operational objective, represented by coordination of a platform population around a strategic goal (such as independence), so members of the platform will not accept compromises or see alternative strategic goals as viable options.

protraction. The length of time that significance, intractability, or intensity persists.

purposive incentives/enthusiasts. Intangible rewards that derive from the satisfaction of having contributed to a campaign for a specific strategic goal; the type of persons motivated by such rewards.

realism. The assessment by members of the platform population that other members will see the strategic goal of a campaign (such as an independent nation-state) as a practical possibility and the action plan (means) to this end proposed by the campaign as feasible.

regional-secession campaign. A subset of statehood projects seeking independence from a common-state based on the claim that the region, rather than a people, should be sovereign.

remoteness. The quality of a causal factor (such as tactical-logistical opportunities) constraining operational objectives (such as attempting battlefield victory over the common-state government) that are not currently being considered by an actor.

secession campaign. A statehood project, based either on a region or on a people plus homeland, that seeks sovereignty.

segment-state. A political-territorial jurisdiction set aside for a titular platform population within a common-state.

significance (campaign). Success in gaining attention of major powers in the international community to the strategic goal of a campaign.

statehood campaign. A project to create or elevate a region or the homeland of a platform population as a political jurisdiction either inside a common-state (such as a segment-state) or outside as a sovereign state.

stateless autonomy campaign. A project to exclude more policy domains affecting a platform population from the jurisdiction of a common-state either as an ungoverned or self-governing community.

strategic constraints. See operational weakness, strategic opportunism, and forecast uncertainty.

strategic goal. The outcome (such as independence) sought by a campaign that emerges through interaction between achievement of its operational objective and the actions of other key actors (such as the common-state government and international community).

strategic opportunism. A strategic response to operational weakness by which a campaign awaits opportunities to receive or "pick up" its strategic goal (such as independence) because the campaign cannot by its own means create these opportunities.

strategy of programmatic coordination. The strategy first made formal by Vladimir Lenin to achieve programmatic preemption within a platform population.

substitutability. The quality of a causal factor, such as a personal, parochial, or particularistic motivation, that bears no unique (necessary) relationship to the strategic goal (e.g., national secessionism) so that other motivations may be substituted.

surge. An activation phase characterized by increased activity by the staff and the participatory reserve of a campaign.

tactics. Specific engagements of personnel and other resources (such as in an electoral campaign, protest, or armed assault) to advance a campaign towards its operational objective.

References

Aasland, Aadne, and Toone Fløtten. 2001. "Ethnicity and Social Exclusion in Estonia and Latvia." *Europe and Asia Studies* 53 (November), 1023–49.

Agnew, John A. 2002. *Place and Politics in Modern Italy*. Chicago: University of Chicago Press.

Ahedo, Igor. 2005. "Political Parties in the Basque Autonomous Community." In *Basque Society: Structures, Institutions, and Contemporary Life,* ed. Gabriel Gatti, Ignacio Irazuzta, and Iñaki Martínez de Albeniz, 176–87. Reno: University of Nevada, Center for Basque Studies.

Alesina, Alberto, and Enrico Spolaore. 1997. "On the Number and Size of Nations." *Quarterly Journal of Economics* 112 (November), 1027–56.

Alesina, Alberto, and Enrico Spolaore. 2003. *The Size of Nations*. Cambridge: MIT Press.

Almond, Gabriel A., and Sidney Verba. 1965. *The Civic Culture: Political Attitudes and Democracy in Five Nations*. Boston: Little, Brown.

Anderson, Benedict. 1991. *Imagined Communities: Reflections on the Origin and Spread of Nationalism,* rev. ed. New York: Verso.

Anderson, Charles W., Fred R. von der Mehden, and Crawford Young. 1967. *Issues of Political Development*. Englewood Cliffs, NJ: Prentice-Hall.

Asher, R. E., and Christopher Moseley. 2007. *Atlas of the World's Languages,* 2nd ed. New York: Routledge.

Aspinall, Edward. 2007. "The Construction of Grievance: Natural Resource and Identity in a Separatist Conflict." *Journal of Conflict Resolution* 51 (December), 950–72.

Averch, Harvey A., and John E. Koehler. 1970. *The Huk Rebellion in the Philippines: Quantitative Approaches*. RAND Memorandum RM-6254-APRA, August 1970. Santa Monica: RAND.

Averch, Harvey A., John E. Koehler, and Frank H. Denton. 1971. *The Matrix of Policy in the Philippines*. Princeton: Princeton University Press.

Bankowicz, Marek. 2012. *Coup d'État: A Critical Theoretical Synthesis*. Frankfurt: Peter Lang.

Banks, Arthur S. 2011. The Cross-National Time-Series Data Archive. www.cntsdata.com.

Barlocco, Fausto. 2014. *Identity and the State in Malaysia*. New York: Routledge.

Barnard, Chester I. 1962. *The Functions of the Executive*. Cambridge: Harvard University Press.

Barrett, David B., ed. 1982. *World Christian Encyclopedia: A Comparative Study of Churches and Religions in the Modern World*. New York: Oxford University Press.

Barrett, David B., George T. Kurian, and Todd M. Johnson, eds. 2001. *World Christian Encyclopedia: A Comparative Study of Churches and Religions in the Modern World,* 2nd ed. New York: Oxford University Press.

Barrington, Lowell. 1995. "The Domestic and International Consequences of Citizenship in the Soviet Successor States." *Europe-Asia Studies* 5 (July), 731–63.

Barrington, Lowell, Erik S. Herron, and Brian D. Silver. 2003. "The Motherland Calling: Views of Homeland among Russians in the Near Abroad." *World Politics* 55 (January), 290–313.

Bartkus, Viva Ona. 1999. *The Dynamic of Secession*. Cambridge: Cambridge University Press.

Beissinger, Mark R. 2002. *Nationalist Mobilization and the Collapse of the Soviet State*. New York: Cambridge University Press.

Benei, Véronique. 2008. *Schooling Passions: Nation, History, and Language in Contemporary Western India*. Stanford: Stanford University Press.

Benford, Robert D., and David A. Snow. 2000. "Framing Processes and Social Movements: An Overview and Assessment." *Annual Review of Sociology* 26, 611–39.

Bennett, Christopher. 1995. *Yugoslavia's Bloody Collapse: Causes, Course and Consequences*. New York: New York University Press.

Billig, Michael, and Henri Tajfel. 1973. "Social Categorization and Similarity in Intergroup Behavior." *European Journal of Social Psychology* 3 (January-March), 27–52.

Birch, Julian. 1996. "The Georgian/South Ossetian Territorial and Boundary Dispute." In *Transcaucasian Boundaries*, ed. John F. R. Wright, Suzanne Goldenberg, and Richard Schofield, 151–89. New York: St. Martin's.

Blattman, Christopher, and Edward Miguel. 2010. "Civil War." *Journal of Economic Literature* 48 (March), 3–57.

Blaufarb, Douglas S. 1977. *The Counterinsurgency Era: U.S. Doctrine and Performance, 1950 to the Present*. New York: Free Press.

Blaustein, Albert P., and Gisbert H. Flanz. 2006. *Constitutions of the Countries of the World*, 20 vols. Dobbs Ferry, NY: Oceana.

Blimes, Randall J. 2006. "The Indirect Effect of Ethnic Heterogeneity on the Likelihood of Civil War Onset." *Journal of Conflict Resolution* 50 (August), 536–47.

Bloom, Stephen. 2008. "Which Minority Is Appeased? Coalition Potential and Redistribution in Latvia and Ukraine." *Europe-Asia Studies* 60 (November), 1575–1600.

Boix, Carles. 2008. "Economic Roots of Civil Wars and Revolutions in the Contemporary World." *World Politics* 60 (April 2008), 390–437.

Bovingdon, Gardner. 2010. *The Uyghurs: Strangers in Their Own Land*. New York: Columbia University Press.

Brass, Paul R. 1991. *Ethnicity and Nationalism: Theory and Comparison*. New Delhi: Sage.

Breuilly, John. 1994. *Nationalism and the State*, 2nd ed. Chicago: University of Chicago Press.

Brewer, Marilynn B. 1979. "In-Group Bias in the Minimal Intergroup Situation: A Cognitive-Motivational Analysis." *Psychological Bulletin* 86 (2), 307–24.

Brubaker, Rogers. 1992. *Citizenship and Nationhood in France and Germany*. Cambridge: Harvard University Press.

Brubaker, Rogers. 1996. *Nationalism Reframed: Nationhood and the National Question in the New Europe*. Cambridge: Cambridge University Press.

Bruk, S[olomon] I. 1986. *Naselenie Mira: Etnodemograficheskii Spravochnik*, 2nd ed. Moscow: Izdatel'stvo Nauka.

Bruk, S[olomon] I., and V. S. Apenchenko, eds. 1964. *Atlas Narodov Mira*. Moscow: Glavnoe Upravlenie Geodezii I Kartografii Gosudarstvennogo Geologicheskogo Komiteta SSSR and Institut Etnografii im. N. N. Miklukho-Maklaia Akademii Nauk SSSR.

Brzezinski, Zbigniew K. 1960. *The Soviet Bloc: Unity and Conflict*. Cambridge: Harvard University Press.

Buchheit, Lee C. 1978. *Secession: The Legitimacy of Self-Determination*. New Haven: Yale University Press.

Buhaug, Halvard. 2006. "Relative Capability and Rebel Objective in Civil War." *Journal of Peace Research* 43 (November), 691–708.

Buhaug, Halvard, Lars-Erik Cederman, and Jan Ketil Rød. 2008. "Disaggregating Ethnic Conflict: A Dyadic Model of Exclusion Theory." *International Organization* 62 (July), 531–51.

Bunce, Valerie. 1999. *Subversive Institutions: The Design and the Destruction of Socialism and the State*. New York: Cambridge University Press.

Bunce, Valerie. 2005. "The National Idea: Imperial Legacies and Post-Communist Pathways in Eastern Europe." *East European Politics and Societies* 19 (Summer), 406–42.

Burg, Steven L., and Paul S. Shoup. 1999. *The War in Bosnia-Herzegovina: Ethnic Conflict and International Intervention*. Armonk, NY: M. E. Sharpe.

Bwy, D[ouglas] P. 1968. "Political Instability in Latin America: The Cross-Cultural Test of a Causal Model." *Latin American Research Review* 3 (Spring), 17–66.

Byman, Daniel. 1998. "The Logic of Ethnic Terrorism." *Studies in Conflict and Terrorism* 21 (2), 149–69.

Caspersen, Nina. 2012. *Unrecognized States: The Struggle for Sovereignty in the Modern International System*. Cambridge, UK: Polity.

Caspersen, Nina, and Garth Stansfield, eds. 2011. *Unrecognized States in the International System*. New York: Routledge.

Cederman, Lars-Erik, Kristian Skrede Gleditsch, Idean Salehyan, and Julian Wucherpfennig. 2013. "Transborder Ethnic Kin and Civil War." *International Organization* 67 (April), 389–410.

Cederman, Lars-Erik, Brian Min, and Andreas Wimmer. 2009. *Ethnic Power Relations Dataset*. https://icr.ethz.ch/data/epr.

Cederman, Lars-Erik, Nils B. Weidman, and Kristian Skrede Gleditsch. 2011. "Horizontal Inequalities and Ethnonationalist Civil War: A Global Comparison." *American Political Science Review* 105 (August), 478–95.

Cederman, Lars-Erik, Andreas Wimmer, and Brian Min. 2010. "Why Do Ethnic Groups Rebel? New Data and Analysis." *World Politics* 62 (January), 87–119.

Center for International Earth Science Information Network/Columbia University and Centro Internacional de Agricultura Tropical. 2005. Gridded Population of the World, Version 3: Population Density Grid. Palisades, NY: NASA Socioeconomic Data and Applications Center. http://sedac.ciesin.columbia/edu/data/set/gpw-v3-population-density.

Central Committee of the C. P. S. U. (B.). 1939. *History of the Communist Party of the Soviet Union (Bolsheviks), Short Course*. New York: International.

Chamberlain, Ernest. 2007. *Faltering Steps: Independence Movements in East Timor—1940s to the early 1970s*. Point Lonsdale, Victoria, Australia: Ernest Chamberlain.

Chandra, Kanchan, and Steven Wilkinson. 2008. "Measuring the Effect of 'Ethnicity.'" *Comparative Political Studies* 41 (April/May), 515–63.

Chen, James. 2012. "Forced to the Periphery: Recent Chinese Politics in East Malaysia." In *Malaysian Chinese: Recent Developments and Prospects*, ed. Lee Hock Guan and Leo Suradinata, 109–21. Singapore: Institute of Southeast Asian Studies.

Chenoweth, Erica, and Orion A. Lewis. 2013. "Unpacking Nonviolent Campaigns: Introducing the NAVCO 2.0 Dataset." *Journal of Peace Research* 50 (May), 415–23.

Clark, Robert P. 1984. *The Basque Insurgents: ETA 1952–1980*. Madison: University of Wisconsin Press.

Clausewitz, Carl von. 1976. *On War,* ed. Michael Howard and Peter Paret. Princeton: Princeton University Press.

Cobban, Alfred. 1944. *National Self-Determination.* Chicago: University of Chicago Press.

Coggins, Bridget. 2011. "Friends in High Places: International Politics and the Emergence of States from Secessionism." *International Organization* 65 (July), 433–67.

Coggins, Bridget. 2014. *Power Politics and State Formation in the Twentieth Century: The Dynamics of Recognition.* New York: Cambridge University Press.

Cohen, Frank S. 1997. "Proportional versus Majoritarian Ethnic Conflict Management in Democracies." *Comparative Political Studies* 30 (October), 607–30.

Coleman, James S., ed. 1968. *Education and Political Development.* Princeton: Princeton University Press.

Collier, Paul. 2000a. "Economic Causes of Civil Conflict and Their Implications for Policy." Washington, DC: World Bank.

Collier, Paul. 2000b. "Rebellion as a Quasi-criminal Activity." *Journal of Conflict Resolution,* 44 (December), 839–53.

Collier, Paul, and Anke Hoeffler. 1998. "On Economic Causes of Civil War." *Oxford Economic Papers* 50 (October), 563–73.

Collier, Paul, and Anke Hoeffler. 2004. "Greed and Grievance in Civil War." *Oxford Economic Papers* 56 (October), 563–95.

Collier, Paul, Anke Hoeffler, and Måns Söderbom. 2008. "Post-conflict Risks." *Journal of Peace Research* 45 (July), 461–78.

Connor, Walker. 1970. "Ethnic Nationalism as a Political Force." *World Affairs* 133 (September), 91–97.

Connor, Walker. 1978. "A Nation Is a Nation, Is a State, Is an Ethnic Group, Is a. . . ." *Ethnic and Racial Studies* 1 (October), 379–88.

Connor, Walker. 1984. *The National Question in Marxist-Leninist Theory and Strategy.* Princeton: Princeton University Press.

Connor, Walker. 1994. *Ethnonationalism: The Quest for Understanding.* Princeton: Princeton University Press.

Conversi, Daniele. 1997. *The Basques, the Catalans, and Spain: Alternative Routes to Nationalist Mobilisation.* Reno: University of Nevada Press.

Cornelius, Wayne A., Jr. 1969. "Urbanization as an Agent in Latin American Political Instability: The Case of Mexico." *American Political Science Review* 63 (September), 833–57.

Cornell, Svante E. 2001. *Small Nations and Great Powers: A Study of Ethnopolitical Conflict in the Caucasus.* London: Routledge Curzon.

Cornell, Svante E. 2002. "Autonomy as a Source of Conflict: Caucasian Conflicts in Theoretical Perspective." *World Politics* 54 (January), 245–76.

Costalli, Stefano, and Andrea Ruggeri, eds. 2017. "Policy Symposium: Emotions, Ideologies, and Violent Political Mobilization." *PS* 50 (October), 923–51.

Cottam, Martha L., and Richard W. Cottam. 2001. *Nationalism and Politics: The Political Behavior of Nation States.* Boulder, CO: Lynne Reiner.

Cottam, Martha L., Beth Dietz-Uhler, Elena Mastors, and Thomas Preston. 2010. *Introduction to Political Psychology,* 2nd ed. New York: Psychology Press.

Council of Europe. 2002. Commission for Democracy through Law [COECDL]. *Opinion on the Law on Modification and Addition in the Constitution of the Republic of Moldova in Particular concerning the Status of Gagauzia.* Adopted at its 50th Plenary Session, Venice, March 8–9. www.venice.coe.int.

Council of Europe. 2004. Commission for Democracy through Law [COECDL]. *Opinion on the Draft Constitutional Law of Georgia on the Status of the Autonomous Republic of Adjara.* Adopted at its 59th Plenary Session, Venice, June 18–19. www.venice.coe.int.

Crenshaw, Martha. 1981. "The Causes of Terrorism." *Comparative Politics* 13 (July), 379–99.

Cuhadar, Esra, and Bruce Dayton. 2011. "The Social Psychology of Identity and Inter-group Conflict: From Theory to Practice." *International Studies Perspectives* 12 (August), 273–93.

Cunningham, David E. 2006. "Veto Players and Civil War Duration." *American Journal of Political Science* 50 (October), 875–92.

Cunningham, Kathleen Gallagher. 2013a. "Actor Fragmentation and Civil War Bargaining: How Internal Divisions Generate Civil Conflict." *American Journal of Political Science* 57 (July), 659–72.

Cunningham, Kathleen Gallagher. 2013b. "Understanding Strategic Choice: The Determinants of Civil War and Nonviolent Campaign in Self-Determination Disputes." *Journal of Peace Research* 50 (May), 291–304.

Cunningham, Kathleen Gallagher. 2014. *Inside the Politics of Self-Determination.* New York: Oxford University Press.

Current Digest of the Soviet Press [later, *Current Digest of the Post-Soviet Press*]. Various years. Columbus, OH: Current Digest of the Soviet Press.

Dambul, Ramzah, Marja Azlima Omar, and Sabihah Osman, eds. 2010. *Sabah Priority Issues: Setting the Course for Change.* Kota Kinabalu: Universiti Malaysia Sabah.

Davies, James C. 1962. "Toward a Theory of Revolution." *American Sociological Review* 27 (February), 5–19.

Davis, Donald E., and Walter S. G. Kohn. 1971. "Lenin as Disciple of Clausewitz." *Military Review* 51 (September), 49–55.

de Rouen, Karl R., Jr., and David Sobek. 2004. "The Dynamics of Civil War Duration and Outcome." *Journal of Peace Research* 41 (May), 303–20.

de Waal, Thomas. 2003. *Black Garden: Armenia and Azerbaijan through Peace and War.* New York: New York University Press.

Deutsch, Karl W. 1961. "Social Mobilization and Political Development." *American Political Science Review* 55 (September), 493–514.

Deutsch, Karl W. 1966. *Nationalism and Social Communication: An Inquiry into the Foundations of Nationality,* 2nd ed. Cambridge: MIT Press.

DeVotta, Neil. 2004. *Blowback: Linguistic Nationalism, Institutional Decay, and Ethnic Conflict in Sri Lanka.* Stanford: Stanford University Press.

Diani, Mario. 1992. "The Concept of a Social Movement." *Sociological Review* 40 (February), 1–25.

Diehl, Paul F., and Gary Goertz. 1991. "Entering International Society: Military Conflict and National Independence, 1816–1980." *Comparative Political Studies* 23 (January), 497–518.

Díez Medrano, Juan. 1995. *Divided Nations: Class, Politics, and Nationalism in the Basque Country and Catalonia.* Ithaca: Cornell University Press.

Dion, Stéphane. 1996. "Why Is Secession Difficult in Well-Established Democracies? Lessons from Quebec." *British Journal of Political Science* 26 (April), 269–83.

Eckstein, Harry. 1988. "A Culturalist Theory of Political Change." *American Political Science Review* 82 (September), 789–804.

Ellingsen, Tanja. 2000. "Colorful Communities or Ethnic Witches Brew? Multiethnicity and Domestic Conflict during and after the Cold War." *Journal of Conflict Resolution* 44 (April), 228–49.

English, Richard. 2003. *Armed Struggle: The History of the IRA.* New York: Oxford University Press.

English, Richard. 2006. *Irish Freedom: The History of Nationalism in Ireland.* London: Pan.

Entessar, Nader. 1992. *Kurdish Ethnonationalism.* Boulder, CO: Lynne Reiner.

Erlich, Haggai. 1983. *The Struggle over Eritrea, 1962–1978: War and Revolution in the Horn of Africa.* Stanford, CA: Hoover Institution Press.

Esteban, Joan, and Debraj Ray. 2008. "On the Salience of Ethnic Conflict." *American Economic Review* 98 (December), 2185–202.

Evangelista, Matthew. 2002. *The Chechen Wars: Will Russia Go the Way of the Soviet Union?* Washington, DC: Brookings Institution.

Fabry, Mikulas. 2010. *Recognizing States: International Society and the Establishment of New States.* New York: Oxford University Press.

Fair, C. Christine. 2005. "Diaspora Involvement in Insurgencies: Insights from the Khalistan and Tamil Eelam Movements." *Nationalism and Ethnic Politics* 11 (1), 125–56.

Fearon, James D. 1995a. "Commitment Problems and the Spread of Ethnic Conflict." In *The International Spread of Ethnic Conflict: Fear, Diffusion, and Escalation,* ed. David A. Lake and Donald Rothchild, 107–26. Princeton: Princeton University Press.

Fearon, James D. 1995b. "Rationalist Explanations for War." *International Organization* 49 (June), 379–414.

Fearon, James D. 2004. "Why Do Some Civil Wars Last So Much Longer Than Others?" *Journal of Peace Research* 41 (May), 275–301.

Fearon, James D., and David D. Laitin. 2000. "Violence and the Social Construction of Ethnic Identity." *International Organization* 54 (September), 845–77.

Fearon, James D., and David D. Laitin. 2003. "Ethnicity, Insurgency, and Civil War." *American Political Science Review* 97 (February), 75–90.

Feierabend, Ivo D., Rosalind L. Feierabend, and Betty Nesvold. 1969. "Social Change and Political Violence: Cross-National Patterns." In *Violence in America: Historical and Comparative Perspectives,* rev. ed., ed. Hugh Davis Graham and Ted Robert Gurr, 632–87. New York: Bantam.

Filson, Darren, and Suzanne Werner. 2002. "A Bargaining Model of War and Peace: Anticipating the Onset, Duration, and Outcome of War." *American Journal of Political Science* 46 (October), 819–38.

Fishman, Joshua A. 1973. *Language and Nationalism: Two Integrative Essays.* Rowley, MA: Newbury House.

Fishman, Joshua A., ed. 1999. "Concluding Comments." In *Handbook of Language and Ethnic Identity,* ed. Joshua A. Fishman, 444–54. New York: Oxford University Press.

Flanigan, William H., and Edwin Fogelman. 1970. "Patterns of Political Violence in Comparative Historical Perspective." *Comparative Politics* 3 (October), 1–20.

Flynn, M. K. 2000. *Ideology, Mobilization and the Nation: The Rise of Irish, Basque and Carlist Nationalist Movements in the Nineteenth and Early Twentieth Centuries.* New York: St. Martin's.

Fortna, Virginia Page. 2004. "Does Peacekeeping Keep Peace? International Intervention and the Duration of Peace after Civil War." *International Studies Quarterly* 48 (June), 269–92.

Fromkin, David. 1975. "The Strategy of Terrorism." *Foreign Affairs* 53 (July), 683–98.

Gall, Carlotta, and Thomas de Waal. 1998. *Chechnya: Calamity in the Caucasus.* New York: New York University Press.

Gamson, William. 1975. *The Strategy of Social Protest.* Homewood, IL: Dorsey.

Gamson, William A., and Andre Modigliani. 1987. "The Changing Culture of Affirmative Action." In *Research in Political Sociology,* ed. R. G. Braungart and M. M. Braungart, 3:137–77. Greenwich, CT: JAI.

Gellner, Ernest. 1964. *Thought and Change.* Chicago: University of Chicago Press.

Gellner, Ernest. 1983. *Nations and Nationalism*. Ithaca: Cornell University Press.

Genocide Prevention Advisory Network. 2015. "Genocides, Politicides, and Other Mass Murder since 1945." www.gpanet.org.

German, Tracey C. 2003. *Russia's Chechen War*. New York: Routledge Curzon.

Gerth, H. H., and C. Wright Mills, eds. 1958. *From Max Weber: Essays in Sociology*. London: Routledge & Kegan Paul.

Giap, Vo Nguyen. 1961. *People's War, People's Army*. Hanoi: Foreign Language Publishing House.

Gilmore, Elisabeth, Nils Petter Gleditsch, Päivi Lujala, and Jan Ketil Rød. 2005. "Conflict Diamonds: A New Dataset." *Conflict Management and Peace Science* 22 (July), 257–92.

Glaeser, Edward L. 2005. "The Political Economy of Hatred." *Quarterly Journal of Economics* 120 (February), 45–86.

Goble, Paul. 1992. "Coping with the Nagorno-Karabakh Crisis." *Fletcher Forum of World Affairs* 16 (Summer), 19–26.

Goddard, Stacie F. 2006. "Uncommon Ground: Indivisible Territory and the Politics of Legitimacy." *International Organization* 60 (Winter), 35–68.

Goertz, Gary, and Paul F. Diehl. 1992. *Territorial Changes and International Conflict*. New York: Routledge.

Goldsmith, Benjamin E., and Baogang He. 2008. "Letting Go without a Fight: Decolonization, Democracy, and War, 1900–94." *Journal of Peace Research* 45 (September), 587–611.

Goldstone, Jack A. 1991. "An Analytical Framework." In *Revolutions of the Late Twentieth Century*, ed. Jack A. Gladstone, Ted Robert Gurr, and Farrokh Moshiri, 37–51. Boulder, CO: Westview.

Goldstone, Jack A. et al. 2010. "A Global Model for Forecasting Political Instability." *American Journal of Political Science* 54 (January), 190–208.

Goode, J. Paul. 2011. *The Decline of Regionalism in Putin's Russia*. New York: Routledge.

Gourevitch, Peter Alexis. 1979. "The Reemergence of 'Peripheral Nationalisms': Some Comparative Speculations on the Spatial Distribution of Political Leadership and Economic Growth." *Comparative Studies in Society and History* 21 (July), 303–22.

Green, Donald, Bradley Palmquist, and Eric Schickler. 2002. *Partisan Hearts and Minds: Political Parties and Social Identities of Voters*. New Haven: Yale University Press.

Greenfeld, Liah. 1992. *Nationalism: Five Roads to Modernity*. Cambridge: Harvard University Press.

Griffiths, Ryan D. 2016. *Age of Secession: The International and Domestic Determinants of State Birth*. New York: Cambridge University Press.

Grossman, Herschel I. 1991. "A General Equilibrium Model of Insurrections." *American Economic Review* 81 (September), 912–21.

Grossman, Herschel I. 1999. "Kleptocracy and Revolution." *Oxford Economic Papers* 51 (April), 267–83.

Guevara, Ernesto Che. 1961. *Guerrilla Warfare*.

Gurr, Ted Robert. 1970. *Why Men Rebel*. Princeton: Princeton University Press.

Gurr, Ted Robert. 2000. *Peoples versus States: Minorities at Risk in the New Century*. Washington, DC: United States Institute of Peace.

Gurr, Ted Robert, and Jack A. Goldstone. 1991. "Comparisons and Policy Implications." In *Revolutions of the Late Twentieth Century*, ed. Jack A. Gladstone, Ted Robert Gurr, and Farrokh Moshiri, 324–52. Boulder, CO: Westview.

Hale, Henry. 2008. *The Foundations of Ethnic Politics: Separatism of States and Nations in Eurasia and the World.* New York: Cambridge University Press.

Hale, Henry. 2014. *Patronal Politics: Eurasian Regime Dynamics in Comparative Perspective.* New York: Cambridge University Press.

Hastings, Adrian. 1997. *The Construction of Nationhood: Ethnicity, Religion, and Nationalism.* New York: Cambridge.

Hechter, Michael. 1975 [1998]. *Internal Colonialism: The Celtic Fringe in British National Development.* Berkeley: University of California Press.

Hechter, Michael, and Margaret Levi. 1979. "The Comparative Analysis of Ethnoregional Movements." *Ethnic and Racial Studies* 2 (July), 262–74.

Hegre, Håvard, Tanja Ellingsen, Scott Gates, and Nils Petter Gleditsch. 2001. "Toward a Democratic Civil Peace? Democracy, Political Change, and Civil War, 1816–1992." *American Political Science Review* 95 (March), 33–48.

Hegre, Håvard, and Nicholas Sambanis. 2006. "Sensitivity Analysis of Empirical Results on Civil War Onset." *Journal of Conflict Resolution* 50 (August), 508–35.

Heimann, Mary. 2009. *Czechoslovakia: The State That Failed.* New Haven: Yale University Press.

Heraclides, Alexis. 1990. "Secessionist Minorities and External Involvement." *International Organization* 44 (Summer), 341–78.

Hewitt, B. G. 1996. "Abkhazia: A Problem of Identity and Ownership." In *Transcaucasian Boundaries,* ed. John F. R. Wright, Suzanne Goldenberg, and Richard Schofield, 190–225. New York: St. Martin's.

Hibbs, Douglas A., Jr., 1973. *Mass Political Violence: A Cross-National Causal Analysis.* New York: Wiley.

Hill, Helen M. 2002. *Stirrings of Nationalism in East Timor: Fretilin 1974–78: The Origins, Ideologies and Strategies of a Nationalist Movement.* Otford, New South Wales, Australia: Otford.

Hobsbawm, Eric. 1983. "Introduction: Inventing Traditions." In *The Invention of Tradition,* ed. Eric Hobsbawm and Terrence Ranger, 1–14. New York: Cambridge University Press.

Hoddie, Matthew, and Caroline A. Hartzell. 2014. "Segment States in the Developing World: Conflict's Cause or Cure?" *Ethnopolitics* 13 (January), 1–104.

Hoffer, Eric. 1951. *The True Believer: Thoughts on the Nature of Mass Movements.* New York: Harper & Row.

Horowitz, Donald. 1985. *Ethnic Groups in Conflict.* Berkeley: University of California Press.

Howard, Marc Morje. 2006. "Comparative Citizenship: An Agenda for Cross-National Research." *Perspectives on Politics* 4 (September), 443–55.

Hroch, Miroslav. 2000. *Social Preconditions of National Revival in Europe: A Comparative Analysis of the Social Composition of Patriotic Groups among the Smaller European Nations.* New York: Columbia University Press.

Hug, Simon. 2013. "The Use and Misuse of the 'Minorities at Risk' Project." *Annual Review of Political Science* 16, 191–208.

Huntington, Samuel P. 1968. *Political Order in Changing Societies.* New Haven: Yale University Press.

Huntington, Samuel P. 1996. *The Clash of Civilizations and the Remaking of World Order.* New York: Simon and Schuster.

Huntington, Samuel P. 2004. *Who Are We? The Challenges to America's National Identity.* New York: Simon and Schuster.

Huszka, Beáta. 2003. "The Dispute over Montenegrin Independence." In *Montenegro in Transition: Problems of Identity and Statehood,* ed. Florian Bieber, 43–62. Baden-Baden: Nomos Verlagsgesellschaft.

Hutchinson, John. 1987. *The Dynamics of Cultural Nationalism*. London: Allen and Unwin.

International Crisis Group [ICG]. 2003. "Moldova: No Quick Fix." Europe Report No. 147. Chisinau/Brussels, August 12.

International Crisis Group [ICG]. 2004a. "Moldova: Regional Tensions over Transdniestria." Europe Report No. 157. Chisinau/Brussels, June 17.

International Crisis Group [ICG]. 2004b. "Saakashvili's Ajara Success: Repeatable Elsewhere in Georgia?" Europe Briefing. Tbilisi/Brussels, August 18.

International Crisis Group [ICG]. 2004c. "Georgia: Avoiding War in South Ossetia." Europe Report No. 159. Tbilisi/Brussels, November 26.

International Crisis Group [ICG]. 2005a. "Georgia-South Ossetia: Refugee Return the Path to Peace." Europe Briefing No. 38. Tbilisi/Brussels, April 19.

International Crisis Group [ICG]. 2005b. "Nagorno-Karabakh: Viewing the Conflict From the Ground." Europe Report No. 166. Tbilisi/Brussels, September 14.

International Crisis Group [ICG]. 2005c. "Nagorno-Karabakh: A Plan for Peace." Europe Report No. 167. Tbilisi/Brussels, October 11.

International Crisis Group [ICG]. 2006a. "Moldova's Uncertain Future." Europe Report No. 175. Chisinau/Brussels, August 17.

International Crisis Group [ICG]. 2006b. "Abkhazia Today." Europe Report No. 176. Tbilisi/Brussels, September 15.

International Crisis Group [ICG]. 2007. "Abkhazia: Ways Forward." Europe Report No. 179. Tbilisi/Brussels, January 18.

International Crisis Group [ICG]. 2009. "Nagorno-Karabakh: Getting to a Breakthrough." European Briefing No. 55. October 7.

International Crisis Group [ICG]. 2010a. "Abkhazia: Deepening Dependence." Europe Report No. 202. February 26.

International Crisis Group [ICG]. 2010b. "South Ossetia: The Burden of Recognition." Europe Report No. 205. Tbilisi/Brussels, June 7.

International Crisis Group [ICG]. 2013. "Abkhazia: The Long Road to Reconciliation." Europe Report No. 224. Tbilisi/Brussels, April 10.

Irish Republican Army. General Headquarters. 1956 [1985]. *Handbook for Volunteers of the Irish Republican Army*. Boulder, CO: Paladin.

Iyob, Ruth. 1995. *The Eritrean Struggle for Independence: Domination, Resistance, Nationalism, 1941–1993*. New York: Cambridge University Press.

Jenne, Erin K. 2006. "National Self-Determination: A Deadly Mobilizing Device." In *Negotiating Self-Determination*, ed. Hurst Hannum and Eileen F. Babbitt, 7–36. Lanham, MD: Lexington.

Jenne, Erin K. 2007. *Ethnic Bargaining: The Paradox of Minority Empowerment*. Ithaca: Cornell University Press.

Johnson, Chalmers A. 1962. *Peasant Nationalism and Communist Power: The Emergence of Revolutionary China 1937–1945*. Stanford: Stanford University Press.

Joshua Project. 2012. www.joshuaproject.net.

Kalyvas, Stathis N. 2003. "The Ontology of 'Political Violence': Action and Identity in Civil Wars." *Perspectives on Politics* 1 (September), 475–94.

Kalyvas, Stathis N., and Laia Balcells. 2010. "International System and Technologies of Rebellion: How the End of the Cold War Shaped Internal Conflict." *American Political Science Review* 104 (August), 415–29.

Kaplan, Fred. 2013. *The Insurgents: David Petraeus and the Plot to Change the American Way of War*. New York: Simon and Schuster.

Kaufman, Stuart J. 2006. "Symbolic Politics or Rational Choice? Testing Theories of Extreme Ethnic Violence." *International Security* 30 (Spring), 45–86.

Kaufman, Stuart J. 2011. "Symbols, Frames, and Violence: Studying Ethnic War in the Philippines." *International Studies Quarterly* 55 (December), 937–58.

Kaufmann, Chaim. 1996. "Possible and Impossible Solutions to Ethnic Civil Wars." *International Security* 20 (Spring), 136–75.

Kedourie, Elie. 1960. *Nationalism*. London: Hutchinson.

Keesing's Contemporary Archives. Farmington Hills, MI: Keesing's Worldwide.

Keith, Patrick. 2005. *Ousted! An Insider's Story of the Ties That Failed to Bind*. Singapore: Media Masters.

Kenny, Paul D. 2010. "Structural Integrity and Cohesion in Insurgent Organizations: Evidence from Protracted Conflicts in Ireland and Burma." *International Studies Review* 12 (December), 533–55.

Ker-Lindsay, James. 2009. *Kosovo: The Path to Contested Statehood in the Balkans*. London: I. B. Tauris.

Kilcullen, David. 2009. *The Accidental Guerrilla: Fighting Small Wars in the Midst of a Big One*. New York: Oxford University Press.

Kim, Julie, and Carol Migdalovitz. 1993. *Macedonia (Skopje): Recognition and Conflict Prevention*. CRS-1993-FND-0024. Washington, DC: Library of Congress, January 11.

King, Charles. 1994. "Moldovan Identity and the Politics of Pan-Romanianism." *Slavic Review* 53 (Summer), 345–68.

King, Charles. 2000. *The Moldovans: Romania, Russia, and the Politics of Culture*. Stanford: Hoover Institution Press.

King, Charles. 2001. "The Benefits of Ethnic War: Understanding Eurasia's Unrecognized States." *World Politics* 53 (July), 524–52.

King, Gary, Michael Tomz, and Jason Wittenberg. 2000. "Making the Most of Statistical Analyses: Improving Interpretation and Presentation." *American Journal of Political Science* 44 (April), 347–61.

Kingsbury, Damien. 2009. *East Timor: The Price of Liberty*. New York: Palgrave Macmillan.

Kohn, Hans. 1944 [2005]. *The Idea of Nationalism: A Study in Its Origins and Background*. New Brunswick: Transaction.

Kolstø, Pål. 2000. *Political Construction Sites: Nation-Building in Russia and the Post-Soviet States*. Boulder, CO: Westview.

Kolstø, Pål. 2006. "The Sustainability and Future of Unrecognized Quasi-states." *Journal of Peace Research*, 43 (November), 723–40.

Kolstø, Pål, and Helge Blakkisrud. 2008. "Living with Non-recognition: State- and Nation-Building in South Caucasian Quasi-states." *Europe-Asia Studies*, 60 (May), 483–509.

Krickus, Richard J. 1997. *Showdown: The Lithuanian Rebellion and the Breakup of the Soviet Empire*. Washington, DC: Brassey's.

Kubicek, Paul. 2000. "Regional Polarization in Ukraine: Public Opinion, Voting, and Legislative Behavior." *Europe-Asia Studies* 52 (March), 273–94.

Kübler-Ross, Elisabeth. 1973. *On Death and Dying*. New York: Routledge.

Kurzban, Robert, John Tooby, and Ledia Cosmides. 2001. "Can Race Be Erased? Coalitional Computation and Social Categorization." *PNAS* 98 (December 18), 15387–92.

Kydd, Andrew H., and Barbara F. Walter. 2006. "The Strategies of Terrorism." *International Security* 31 (Summer), 49–80.

Kymlicka, Will. 1995. *Multicultural Citizenship: A Liberal Theory of Minority Rights*. Oxford: Clarendon.

Lacina, Bethany. 2006. "Explaining the Severity of Civil Wars." *Journal of Conflict Resolution* 50 (April), 276–89.

Laitin, David D. 1994. "The Tower of Babel as a Coordination Game: Political Linguistics in Ghana." *American Political Science Review* 88 (September), 622–34.

Laitin, David D. 2007. *Nations, States, and Violence*. Oxford: Oxford University Press.

Laitin, David, and Ronald Suny. 1999. "Armenia and Azerbaijan: Thinking a Way out of Karabakh." *Middle East Policy* 7 (October), 145–76.

Lampe, John R. 1996. *Yugoslavia as History: Twice There Was a Country*. Cambridge: Cambridge University Press.

Lancaster, Thomas D. 1987. "Comparative Nationalism: The Basques in Spain and France." *European Journal of Political Research* 15 (September), 561–90.

Lawrence, Adria K. 2010. "Triggering Nationalist Violence: Competition and Conflict in Uprisings against Colonial Rulers." *International Security* 35 (Fall), 88–122.

Lawrence, Adria K. 2013. *Imperial Rule and the Politics of Nationalism: Anti-colonial Protest in the French Empire*. New York: Cambridge University Press.

Le Billon, Philippe. 2001. "The Political Ecology of War: Natural Resources and Armed Conflicts." *Political Geography* 20 (June), 561–84.

Lecours, André. 2012. "Sub-state Nationalism in the Western World: Explaining Continued Appeal." *Ethnopolitics* 11 (3), 268–86.

Lee, Taeku. 2008. "Race, Immigration, and the Identity-to-Politics Link." *Annual Review of Political Science* 11, 457–78.

Leites, Nathan, and Charles Wolfe, Jr. 1970. *Rebellion and Authority: An Analytic Essay on Insurgent Conflicts*. Chicago: Markham.

LeJeune, John Louis. 2014. *Hannah Arendt and the Problem of Revolution*. Doctoral dissertation. La Jolla, University of California, San Diego.

Lenin, Vladimir I. 1899 [1972]. "An Urgent Question," *Rabochaia Gazeta*. In *Collected Works*, 4:221–26. Moscow: Progress Publishers.

Lenin, Vladimir I. 1901 [1973]. "Where to Begin." *Iskra*, May 1901. In *Collected Works*, 5:17–24. Moscow: Progress Publishers.

Lenin, Vladimir I. 1902a [1974]. "A Letter to a Comrade on Our Organisational Tasks." In *Collected Works*, 6:229–50. Moscow: Progress Publishers.

Lenin, Vladimir I. 1902b [1973]. *What Is to Be Done? Burning Questions of Our Movement*. In *Collected Works*, 5:347–567. Moscow: Progress Publishers.

Lenin, Vladimir I. 1904 [1974]. "One Step Forward, Two Steps Back (The Crisis in Our Party)." In *Collected Works*, 7:201–423. Moscow: Progress Publishers.

Lenin, Vladimir I. 1906 [1972]. "Guerrilla Warfare." *Proletary*, September 30, 1906. In *Collected Works*, 11:213–23. Moscow: Progress Publishers.

Lenin, Vladimir I. 1909 [1973]. "On the Road." In *Collected Works*, 15:345–55. Moscow: Progress Publishers.

Lenin, Vladimir I. 1910 [1974]. "Ivan Vasilyevich Babushkin—an Obituary." In *Collected Works*, 16:361–64. Moscow: Progress Publishers.

Lenin, Vladimir I. 1919 [1974]. "A Speech in Memory of Y. M. Sverdlov at a Special Session of the All-Russia Central Executive Committee, March 18, 1919." In *Collected Works*, 29:89–94. Moscow: Progress Publishers.

Lenin, Vladimir I. 1920a [1974]. "Draft Theses on National and Colonial Questions for the Second Congress of the Communist International." In *Collected Works*, 31:144–51. Moscow: Progress Publishers.

Lenin, Vladimir I. 1920b [1974]. "Report of the Commission on the National and the Colonial Questions [Second Congress of the Communist International]." In *Collected Works*, 31:240–45. Moscow: Progress Publishers.

LeRiche, Matthew, and Matthew Arnold. 2012. *South Sudan: From Revolution to Independence*. New York: Columbia University Press.

Levine, Robert A., and Donald T. Campbell. 1972. *Ethnocentrism: Theories of Conflict, Ethnic Attitudes, and Group Behavior*. New York: Wiley.

Lieven, Anatol. 1993. *The Baltic Revolution: Estonia, Latvia, and Lithuania and the Path to Independence*. New Haven: Yale University Press.

Lieven, Anatol. 1998. *Chechnya: Tombstone of Russian Power*. New Haven: Yale University Press.

Linz, Juan J. 1980. "The Basque in Spain: National and Political Conflict in a New Democracy." In *Resolving Nationality Conflicts: The Role of Public Opinion Research*, ed. W. Phillips Davison and Leon Gordenker, 11–52. New York: Praeger.

Locksley, Anne, Vilma Ortiz, and Christine Hepburn. 1980. "Social Categorization and Discriminatory Behavior: Extinguishing the Minimal Intergroup Discrimination Effect." *Journal of Personality and Social Psychology* 39 (November), 773–83.

Lohmann, Susanne. 1994. "The Dynamics of Informational Cascades: The Monday Demonstrations in Leipzig, East Germany, 1989–91." *World Politics* 47 (October), 42–101.

Lujala, Päivi, Jan Ketil Rød, and Nadia Thieme. 2007. "Fighting over Oil: Introducing a New Dataset." *Conflict Management and Peace Science*, 24 (July), 239–56.

Lyall, Jason, Grame Blair, and Kosuke Imai. 2013. "Explaining Support for Combatants During Wartime: A Survey Experiment in Afghanistan." *American Political Science Review* 107 (November), 679–705.

Lynch, Dov. 2004. *Engaging Eurasia's Separatist States: Unresolved Conflicts and De Facto States*. Washington, DC: United States Institute of Peace.

Lynch, Dov. 2007. "De Facto 'States' around the Black Sea: The Importance of Fear." *Southeast European and Black Sea Studies* 7 (3), 483–96.

Maddison, Angus. 2011. *Statistics on World Population, GDP, and Per Capita GDP, 1–2008 AD*. www.ggde.net/Maddison/oriindex.htm.

Mansfield, Edward D., and Jack Snyder. 2002. "Democratic Transitions, Institutional Strength, and War." *International Organization* 56 (Spring), 297–337.

Mao Zedong. 1937 [1961]. "On Guerrilla Warfare," trans. Samuel B. Griffith. New York: Praeger.

Mao Zedong. 1938a [1965]. "On Protracted War." In *Selected Works of Mao Tse-tung*, 2:113–94. Peking: Foreign Languages Press.

Mao Zedong. 1938b [1965]. "The Role of the Chinese Communist Party in the National War." In *Selected Works of Mao Tse-tung*, 2:195–211. Peking: Foreign Languages Press.

Maresca, John J. 1994. "A Proposal for Settlement of the Conflict over Nagorno-Karabakh." Special Report No. 9. Washington, DC: United States Institute for Peace, August.

Markakis, John. 1987. *National and Class Conflict in the Horn of Africa*. New York: Cambridge University Press.

Marshall, Monty G., and Ted Robert Gurr. 2003. *Peace and Conflict 2003: A Global Survey of Armed Conflicts, Self-Determination Movements, and Democracy*. College Park: University of Maryland, Center for International Development and Conflict Management.

Marshall, Monty G., Ted Robert Gurr, and Keith Jaggers. 2010. *Polity IV Project*. www.systemicpeace.org/inscrdata.html.

Mason, T. David, Joseph P. Weingarten, Jr., and Patrick J. Fett. 1999. "Win, Lose, or Draw: Predicting the Outcomes of Civil Wars." *Political Research Quarterly* 52 (June), 239–68.

Matsuzato, Kimitaka. 2008. "From Belligerent to Multi-ethnic Democracy: Domestic Politics in Unrecognized States after the Ceasefires." *Eurasian Review* 1 (November), 95–119.

Matveeva, Anna. 2004. "Minorities in the South Caucasus." Sub-regional Seminar, Minority Rights: Cultural Diversity and Development in Central Asia, Bishkek, October 2004. New York: United Nations Office of the High Commissioner for Human Rights.

McAdam, Doug, Sidney Tarrow, and Charles Tilly. 2001. *Dynamics of Contention.* New York: Cambridge University Press.

McCarthy, John D., and Mayer N. Zald. 1987. "Resource Mobilization and Social Movements: A Partial Theory." In *Social Movements in an Organizational Society,* ed. Mayer N. Zald and John D. McCarthy, 15–41. New Brunswick, NJ: Transaction.

McGarry, John. 1999. "'Orphans of Secession': National Pluralism in Secessionist Regions and Post-secession States." In *National Self-Determination and Secession,* ed. Margaret Moore, 215–32. Oxford: Oxford University Press.

Meadwell, Hudson. 1993. "The Politics of Nationalism in Quebec." *World Politics* 45 (January), 203–41.

Mees, Ludger. 2004. "Politics, Economy, or Culture? The Rise and Development of Basque Nationalism in the Light of Social Movement Theory." *Theory and Society* 33 (June-August), 311–31.

Meyer, Alfred G. 1984. *Communism,* 4th ed. New York: Random House.

Middel, Bert. 2005. "Minorities in the South Caucasus: Factor of Instability?" NATO Parliamentary Assembly.

Minahan, James. 1996. *Nations without States: A Historical Dictionary of Contemporary National Movements.* Westport, CT: Greenwood.

Minahan, James. 2002. *Encyclopedia of the Stateless Nations: Ethnic and National Groups around the World.* Westport, CT: Greenwood.

Minorities at Risk. 2009. *Minorities at Risk Dataset.* www.cidcm.umd.edu/mar.

Mirak, Robert. 1997. "The Armenians in America." In *The Armenian People from Ancient to Modern Times,* ed. Richard G. Hovannisian, 2:389–411. New York: St. Martin's.

Mitchell, Edward J. 1968. "Inequality and Insurgency: A Statistical Study of South Vietnam." *World Politics* 20 (April), 421–38.

Mitchell, Edward J. 1969. "Some Econometrics of the Huk Rebellion." *American Political Science Review* 63 (December), 1159–71.

Montalvo, Jose G., and Marta Reynal-Querol. 2005. "Ethnic Polarization, Potential Conflict, and Civil Wars." *American Economic Review* 95 (June), 796–816.

Mooney, Christopher Z., and Richard G. Schuldt. 2008. "Does Morality Policy Exist? Testing a Basic Assumption." *Policy Studies Journal* 36 (2), 199–218.

Morrison, Kenneth. 2009. *Montenegro: A Modern History.* London: I. B. Taurus.

Moshiri, Farrokh. 1991. "Revolutionary Conflict Theory in an Evolutionary Perspective." In *Revolutions of the Late Twentieth Century,* ed. Jack A. Gladstone, Ted Robert Gurr, and Farrokh Moshiri, 4–36. Boulder, CO: Westview.

Motyl, Alexander J. 1993. *Dilemmas of Independence: Ukraine after Totalitarianism.* New York: Council of Foreign Relations Press.

Muller, Edward N., and Erich Weede. 1990. "Cross-national Variation in Political Violence: A Rational Action Approach." *Journal of Conflict Resolution* 34, 624–51.

Nagel, Jack. 1974. "Inequality and Discontent: A Nonlinear Hypothesis." *World Politics* 26 (July), 453–72.

Nairn, Tom. 2003. *The Break-Up of Britain: Crisis and Neo-Nationalism,* 3rd ed. Altona, Victoria, Australia: Common Ground.

National Consortium for the Study of Terrorism and Responses to Terrorism (START). 2013. Global Terrorism Database. http://www.start.umd.edu/gtd.

Nelson, Joan M. 1969. *Migrants, Urban Poverty, and Instability in Developing Nations.* Occasional Papers in International Affairs, No. 22. Harvard University, Center for International Affairs.

Nelson, Lynn D., and Paata Amonashvili. 1992. "Voting and Political Attitudes in Soviet Georgia." *Soviet Studies* 44, 687–97.

Norman, Wayne. 1999. "The Ethics of Secession as the Regulation of Secessionist Politics." In *National Self-Determination and Secession,* ed. Margaret Moore, 34–61. Oxford: Oxford University Press.

Nussio, Enzo. 2017. "How Ideology Channels Indeterminate Emotions into Armed Mobilization." *PS* 50 (October), 928–31.

O'Ballance, Edgar. 1989. *The Cyanide War: Tamil Insurrection in Sri Lanka 1973–88.* London: Brassey's.

O'Ballance, Edgar. 1997. *Wars in the Caucasus, 1990–1995.* New York: New York University Press.

O'Loughlin, John, Vladimir Kolossov, and Gerard Toal. 2011. "Inside Abkhazia: Survey of Attitudes in a De Facto State." *Post-Soviet Affairs* 27 (1), 1–36.

Olson, Mancur, Jr. 1963. "Rapid Growth as a Destabilizing Force." *Journal of Economic History* 23 (December), 529–52.

Olson, Mancur, Jr. 1965. *The Logic of Collective Action: Public Goods and the Theory of Groups.* Cambridge: Harvard University Press.

Ongkili, James P. 1985. *Nation-Building in Malaysia 1946–1974.* Singapore: Oxford University Press.

Oppenheim, Ben, Abbey Steele, Juan F. Vargas, and Michael Weintraub. 2015. "True Believers, Deserters, and Traitors: Who Leaves Insurgent Groups and Why." *Journal of Conflict Resolution* 59 (August), 794–823.

Page, Stanley W. 1959. *Lenin and World Revolution.* New York: New York University Press.

Paige, Jeffrey M. 1970. "Inequality and Insurgency in Vietnam: A Re-analysis." *World Politics* 23 (October), 24–37.

Paranzino, Dennis. 1972. "Inequality and Insurgency in Vietnam: A Further Re-analysis." *World Politics* 24 (July), 565–78.

Paret, Peter, and John W. Shy. 1962. *Guerrillas in the 1960's.* New York: Praeger.

Parkinson, Sarah Elizabeth. 2013. "Organizing Rebellion: Rethinking High-Risk Mobilization and Social Networks in War." *American Political Science Review* 107 (August), 418–32.

Pavlović, Srđa. 2003. "Who Are Montenegrins? Statehood, Identity, and Civic Society." In *Montenegro in Transition: Problems of Identity and Statehood,* ed. Florian Bieber, 83–106. Baden-Baden: Nomos Verlagsgesellschaft.

Pegg, Scott. 1998. *International Society and the De Facto State.* Brookfield: Ashgate.

Perritt, Henry H., Jr. 2008. *Kosovo Liberation Army: The Inside Story of an Insurgency.* Urbana: University of Illinois Press.

Petersen, Roger D. 2002. *Understanding Ethnic Violence: Fear, Hatred, and Resentment in Twentieth-Century Eastern Europe.* Cambridge: Cambridge University Press.

Pettee, George. 1966. "Revolution—Typology and Process." In *Revolution* [Nomos VIII], ed. Carl J. Friedirch, 10–33. New York: Atherton.

Phillips, David L. 2012. *Liberating Kosovo: Coercive Diplomacy and U.S. Intervention.* Cambridge: MIT Press.

Pool, David. 2001. *From Guerrillas to Government: The Eritrean People's Liberation Front.* Athens: Ohio University Press.

Popkin, Samuel L. 1979. *The Rational Peasant: The Political Economy of Rural Society in Vietnam.* Berkeley: University of California Press.

Popkin, Samuel L. 1994. *The Reasoning Voter: Communication and Persuasion in Presidential Campaigns,* 2nd ed. Chicago: University of Chicago Press.

Price, H. Edward, Jr. 1977. "The Strategy and Tactics of Revolutionary Terrorism." *Comparative Studies in Society and History* 19 (January), 52–66.

Protsyk, Oleh. 2009. "Representation and Democracy in Eurasia's Unrecognized States: The Case of Transnistria." *Post-Soviet Affairs* 25 (3), 257–81.

Pye, Lucian W. 1966. *Aspects of Political Development.* Boston: Little, Brown.

Raghavan, Srinath. 2013. *1971: A Global History of the Creation of Bangladesh.* Cambridge, MA: Harvard University Press.

Ramet, Sabrina P. 1992. *Nationalism and Federation in Yugoslavia, 1962–1991,* 2nd ed. Bloomington: Indiana University Press.

Rapoport, Anatol. 1961. *Fights, Games, and Debates.* Ann Arbor: University of Michigan Press.

Reynal-Querol, Marta. 2002. "Ethnicity, Political Systems and Civil Wars." *Journal of Conflict Resolution* 46 (February), 29–54.

Robinson, Francis. 1979 [2000]. *Islam and Muslim History in South Asia.* Oxford: Oxford University Press.

Roeder, Philip G. 1991. "Soviet Federalism and Ethnic Mobilization." *World Politics* 43 (January), 196–232.

Roeder, Philip G. 2003. "Clash of Civilizations and the Escalation of Ethnopolitical Conflicts." *Comparative Political Studies* 36 (June), 509–40.

Roeder, Philip G. 2007. *Where Nation-States Come from: Institutional Change in the Age of Nationalism.* Princeton: Princeton University Press.

Rogowski, Ronald. 1985. "Causes and Varieties of Nationalism: A Rationalist Account." In *New Nationalisms of the Developed World: Toward Explanation,* ed. Edward A. Tiryakian and Ronald Rogowski, 87–107. Boston: Allen and Unwin.

Romano, David. 2006. *The Kurdish Nationalist Movement: Opportunity, Mobilization, and Identity.* Cambridge: Cambridge University Press.

Romerstein, Herbert. 1986. "Political Doctrine and Apparatus." In *The Hydra of Carnage: The International Linkages of Terrorism and Other Low-Intensity Operations,* ed. Uri Ra'anan et al., 59–75. Lexington, MA: Lexington.

Ron, James. 2001. "Ideology in Context: Explaining Sendero Luminoso's Tactical Escalation." *Journal of Peace Research* 38 (September), 569–92.

Ross, Michael L. 2004. "How Do Natural Resources Influence Civil War: Evidence from Thirteen Cases." *International Organization* 58 (Winter), 35–67.

Russett, Bruce M. 1964. "Inequality and Instability: The Relation of Land Tenure to Politics." *World Politics* 16 (April), 442–54.

Rutland, Peter. 1994. "Democracy and Nationalism in Armenia." *Europe-Asia Studies* 46 (5), 839–61.

Rychlik, Jan. 2000. "The Possibilities for Czech-Slovak Compromise, 1989–1992." In *Irreconcilable Differences? Explaining Czechoslovakia's Dissolution,* ed. and trans. Michael Kraus and Allison Stranger, 49–66. Lanham, MD: Rowman & Littlefield.

Saideman, Stephen M., Beth K. Dougherty, and Erin K. Jenne. 2005. "Dilemmas of Divorce: How Secessionist Identities Cut Both Ways." *Security Studies* 14 (October-December), 607–36.

Sambanis, Nicholas. 2001. "Do Ethnic and Nonethnic Civil Wars Have the Same Causes?" *Journal of Conflict Resolution* 45 (June), 259–82.

Sambanis, Nicholas. 2004. "What Is Civil War? Conceptual and Empirical Complexities of an Operational Definition." *Journal of Conflict Resolution* 48 (December), 814–58.

Sasse, Gwendolyn. 2007. *The Crimea Question: Identity, Transition, and Conflict*. Cambridge: Harvard University Press.

Schelling, Thomas C. 1963. *The Strategy of Conflict*. New York: Oxford University Press.

Schelling, Thomas C. 1966. *Arms and Influence*. New Haven: Yale University Press.

Schelling, Thomas C. 1978. *Micromotives and Macrobehavior*. New York: Norton.

Schneider, A., M. A. Friedl, and D. Potere. 2009. "A New Map of Global Urban Extent from MODIS Data." *Environmental Research Letters*, 4 (October-December), article 044003.

Schuessler, Alexander A. 2000. *The Logic of Expressive Choice*. Princeton: Princeton University Press.

Schurmann, Franz. 1971. *Ideology and Organization in Communist China*, enlarged edition. Berkeley: University of California Press.

Scott, James C. 1976. *The Moral Economy of the Peasant: Rebellion and Subsistence in Southeast Asia*. New Haven: Yale University Press.

Scott, James C. 2009. *The Art of Not Being Governed: An Anarchist History of Upland Southeast Asia*. New Haven: Yale University Press.

Selznick, Philip. 1960. *The Organizational Weapon: A Study of Bolshevik Strategy and Tactics*. Glencoe, IL: Free Press.

Senn, Alfred Erich. 1990. *Lithuania Awakening*. Berkeley: University of California Press.

Seton Watson, Hugh. 1977. *Nations and States: An Enquiry into the Origins of Nations and the Politics of Nationalism*. London: Methuen.

Sheffer, Gabriel. 2003. *Diaspora Politics: At Home Abroad*. New York: Cambridge University Press.

Sherif, Muzafer, O. J. Harvey, B. Jack White, William R. Hood, and Carolyn W. Sherif. 1961. *Intergroup Conflict and Cooperation: The Robbers Cave Experiment*. Norman: University of Oklahoma Book Exchange.

Shnirelman, Victor A. 2001. *The Value of the Past: Myths, Identity, and Politics in Transcaucasia*. Senri Ethnological Studies no. 57. Osaka: National Museum of Ethnology.

SIL [Summer Institute of Linguistics] International. Various years. *Ethnologue*. Dallas, TX: SIL International.

Skitka, Linda J., and Christopher W. Bauman. 2008. "Moral Conviction and Political Engagement." *Political Psychology* 29 (February), 29–54.

Skocpol, Theda. 1979. *States and Social Revolutions: A Comparative Analysis of France, Russia, and China*. Cambridge: Cambridge University Press.

Smith, Anthony D. 1981. *The Ethnic Revival*. Cambridge: Cambridge University Press.

Smith, Anthony D. 1986. *The Ethnic Origins of Nations*. Cambridge: Blackwell.

Smith, Warren W., Jr. 1996. *Tibetan Nation: A History of Tibetan Nationalism and Sino-Tibetan Relations*. Boulder, CO: Westview.

Solchanyk, Roman. 1994. "The Politics of State Building: Centre-Periphery Relations in Post-Soviet Ukraine." *Europe-Asia Studies* 46 (1), 47–68.

Sorens, Jason. 2005. "The Cross-sectional Determinants of Secessionism in Advanced Democracies." *Comparative Political Studies* 38 (April), 304–26.

Sorens, Jason. 2012. *Secessionism: Identity, Interest, and Strategy*. Montreal: McGill-Queen's University Press.

South, Ashley. 2003. *Mon Nationalism and Civil War in Burma: The Golden Sheldrake*. New York: Routledge Curzon.

Staff Researcher. 2013. *War and Insurgency in the Western Sahara*. Carlisle, PA: Strategic Studies Institute and U.S. War College Press.

Statesman's Yearbook. Various years. New York: St. Martin's.

Sterling, Claire. 1981. *The Terror Network: The Secret War of International Terrorism*. New York: Holt, Rinehart, and Winston.

Sullivan, John. 1988. *ETA and Basque Nationalism: The Fight for Euskadi 1890–1986*. New York: Routledge.

Summers, Harry G., Jr. 1982. *On Strategy: A Critical Analysis of the Vietnam War*. Novato, CA: Presidio.

Taagepera. Rein. 1993. *Estonia: Return to Independence*. Boulder, CO: Westview.

Tajfel, Henri. 1970. "Experiments in Intergroup Discrimination." *Scientific American* 223 (November), 96–102.

Tajfel, Henri. 1978. *Differentiation between Social Groups: Studies in the Social Psychology of Intergroup Relations*. New York: Academic Press.

Tajfel, Henri, M. G. Billig, R. P. Bundy, and Claude Flament. 1971. "Social Categorization and Intergroup Behavior." *European Journal of Social Psychology* 1 (April-June), 149–78.

Tanner, Marcus. 2001. *Croatia: A Nation Forged in War,* 2nd ed. New Haven: Yale University Press.

Tanter, Raymond, and Manus Midlarsky. 1967. "A Theory of Revolution." *Journal of Conflict Resolution* 11 (September), 264–80.

Tarrow, Sidney G. 1994. *Power in Movement: Social Movements, Collective Action, and Politics*. New York: Cambridge University Press.

Thaler, Kai M. 2012. "Ideology and Violence in Civil Wars: Theory and Evidence from Mozambique and Angola." *Civil Wars* 14, 546–67.

Thornton, Thomas Perry. 1964. "Terror as a Weapon of Political Agitation." In *Internal War*, ed. Harry Eckstein, 71–99. Glencoe, IL: Free Press.

Tilly, Charles. 1978. *From Mobilization to Revolution*. Reading, MA: Addison-Wesley.

Tilly, Charles, and Lesley J. Wood. 2009. *Social Movements, 1768–2008,* 2nd ed. Boulder, CO: Paradigm.

Toft, Monica Duffy. 2002/3. "Indivisible Territory, Geographic Concentration, and Ethnic War." *Security Studies* 12 (Winter), 82–119.

Toft, Monica Duffy. 2003. *The Geography of Ethnic Violence: Identity, Interests, and the Indivisibility of Territory*. Princeton: Princeton University Press.

Toft, Monica Duffy. 2006. "Issue Indivisibility and Time Horizons as Rationalist Explanations for War." *Security Studies* 15 (January–March), 34–69.

Toft, Monica Duffy. 2007. "Getting Religion? The Puzzling Case of Islam and Civil War." *International Security* 31 (Spring), 97–131.

Tollefsen, Andreas Forø, Håvard Strand, and Halvard Buhaug. 2012. "PRIO-GRID: A Unified Spatial Data Structure." *Journal of Peace Research* 49 (March), 363–74.

Trapans, Jan Arveds. 1991. "The Sources of Latvia's Popular Movement." In *Toward Independence: The Baltic Popular Movements,* ed. Jan Arveds Trapans, 25–41. Boulder, CO: Westview.

Ulam, Adam B. 1965. *The Bolsheviks: The Intellectual, Personal, and Political History of the Triumph of Communism in Russia*. New York: Collier.

United Nations. 2001. Secretariat. Department of Economic and Social Affairs. Population Division. *World Urbanization Prospects: 1999 Revision*. New York: United Nations.

United States. Bureau of the Census. 2006. World Population Estimates. International Database. www.census.gov/population/international/data/idb/informationgate way.php.

United States. Defense Meteorological Satellite Program. 2011. "Nightime Lights." http://www.ngdc.noaa.gov/dmsp/downloadV4composites.html.

United States. Department of the Army. 2007. *The U.S. Army/Marine Corps Counterinsurgency Field Manual.* Chicago: University of Chicago Press.

United States. Geological Survey. 2005. Eros Data Center Distributed Active Archive Center. Global Digital Elevation Model (GTOPO30).

United States. Joint Chiefs of Staff. 2009. *Counterinsurgency Operations.* Jt. Pub 3–24. Washington, DC: JCS.

United States. Joint Chiefs of Staff. 2013. *Counterinsurgency.* Jt. Pub 3–24. Washington, DC: JCS.

United States. Library of Congress. Federal Research Division. 1991. *Ethiopia: A Country Study,* 4th ed. Thomas P. Ofcansky and LaVerle Berry, contributors. Washington, DC: Government Printing Office.

Uppsala Conflict Data Program. 2011. *UCDP/PRIO Armed Conflict Dataset.* http://www.pcr.uu.se/research/ucdp/datasets/ucdp_prio_armed_conflict_dataset.

Vanhanen, Tatu. 1999. "Domestic Ethnic Conflict and Ethnic Nepotism: A Comparative Analysis." *Journal of Peace Research* 36 (January), 55–73.

Varshney, Ashutosh. 2003. "Nationalism, Ethnic Conflict, and Rationality." *Perspectives on Politics* 1 (March), 85–99.

Vaux, Tony. 2003. "Strategic Conflict Assessment: Georgia." Report for the Global Conflict Prevention Pool, UK Government. London: Humanitarian Initiatives, July.

Vaux, Tony, and Jan Barrett. 2003. "Conflict Interests: Moldova and the Impact of Transdniestria." London: Humanitarian Initiatives, January.

Vaux, Tony, and Jonathan Goodhand. 2002. "War and Peace in the Southern Caucasus: A Strategic Conflict Assessment of the Armenia-Azerbaijan Conflict." London: Humanitarian Initiatives.

von Steinsdorff, Silvia, ed. 2012. "In Search of Legitimacy: Post-Soviet De Facto States between Institutional Stabilization and Political Transformation." *Communist and Post-Communist Studies* 45 (June), 117–206.

Vreeland, James Raymond. 2008. "The Effect of Political Regime on Civil War: Unpacking Anocracy." *Journal of Conflict Resolution* 52 (June), 401–25.

Wagner, Robert Harrison. 1993. "The Causes of Peace." In *Stopping the Killing: How Civil Wars End,* ed. Roy Licklider, 235–68. New York: New York University Press.

Walter, Barbara F. 2002. *Committing to Peace: The Successful Settlement of Civil Wars.* Princeton: Princeton University Press.

Walter, Barbara F. 2006. "Information, Uncertainty, and the Decision to Secede." *International Organization* 60 (Winter), 105–35.

Walter, Barbara F. 2009a. "Bargaining Failures and Civil War." *Annual Review of Political Science* 12, 243–61.

Walter, Barbara F. 2009b. *Reputation and Civil War.* Cambridge: Cambridge University Press.

Watson, Richard E., and Robert B. McKersie. 1991. *A Behavioral Theory of Labor Negotiations: An Analysis of a Social Interaction System,* 2nd ed. Ithaca, NY: ILR Press.

Weber, Max. 1922 [1968]. *Economy and Society: An Outline of Interpretive Sociology.* Berkeley: University of California Press.

Weil, Patrick. 2001. "Access to Citizenship: A Comparison of Twenty-Five Nationality Laws." In *Citizenship Today: Global Perspectives and Practices,* ed. Alexander Aleinikoff and Douglass Blusmeyer, 17–35. Washington DC: Carnegie Endowment for International Peace.

Weinstein, Jeremy M. 2007. *Inside Rebellion: The Politics of Insurgent Violence.* New York: Cambridge University Press.

Whitmeyer, Joseph M. 2002. "Elites and Popular Nationalism." *British Journal of Sociology* 53 (September), 321–41.

Wilson, Andrew. 2009. *The Ukrainians: Unexpected Nation,* 3rd ed. New Haven: Yale University Press.

Wilson, James Q. 1995. *Political Organizations.* Princeton: Princeton University Press.

Wimmer, Andreas. 2002. *Nationalist Exclusion and Ethnic Conflict: Shadows of Modernity.* Cambridge: Cambridge University Press.

Wimmer, Andreas. 2013a. *Ethnic Boundary Making: Institutions, Power, Networks.* New York: Oxford University Press.

Wimmer, Andreas. 2013b. *Waves of War: Nationalism, State Formation, and Ethnic Exclusion in the Modern World.* New York: Cambridge University Press.

Wimmer, Andreas, Lars-Erik Cederman, and Brian Min. 2009. "Ethnic Politics and Armed Conflict: A Configurational Analysis of a New Global Data Set." *American Sociological Review* 74 (April), 316–37.

Wimmer, Andreas, and Brian Min. 2006. "From Empire to Nation-State: Explaining Wars in the Modern World, 1816–2001." *American Sociological Review* 71 (December), 867–97.

Wintrobe, Ronald. 2006. "Extremism, Suicide Terror, and Authoritarianism." *Public Choice* 128 (July), 169–95.

Wittman, Donald. 1991. "Nations and States: Mergers and Acquisitions; Dissolutions and Divorce." *American Economic Review* 81 (May), 126–29.

Wood, Elisabeth Jean. 2003. *Insurgent Collective Action and Civil War in El Salvador.* Cambridge: Cambridge University Press.

World Bank. 2011. *World Development Report 2011: Conflict, Security, and Development.* Washington, DC: World Bank.

Young, Robert A. 1999. *The Struggle for Quebec: From Referendum to Referendum?* Montreal: McGill-Queen's University Press.

Yu Huai. 1950. "The National Bourgeoisie in the Chinese Revolution." *People's China* (January).

Yusoff, Mohammad Agus. 2006. *Malaysian Federalism: Conflict or Consensus.* Bangi: Penerbit Universiti Kebangsaan Malaysia.

Zaheer, Hasan. 1994. *The Separation of East Pakistan: The Rise and Realization of Bengali Muslim Nationalism.* New York: Oxford University Press.

Zaprudnik, Jan. 1993. *Belarus: At a Crossroads in History.* Boulder, CO: Westview.

Zürcher, Christoph. 2007. *The Post-Soviet Wars: Rebellion, Ethnic Conflict, and Nationhood in the Caucasus.* New York: New York University Press.

Index

Page numbers in *italics* refer to figures and tables.

Minahan, James, 199, 202–3
minorities, 176–77. *See also* ethnic groups
Minorities at Risk (MAR), 208
Minsk Group, 140–41
mobilization, 46–51; coordination and, 63–66; demobilization, 62; phases, 54–63; programmatic preemption and, 91; social, 179; in Timor Leste campaign, 51–53; violence and, 153–54
Modigliani, Andre, 245n31
Moksha project, 92, 100, 247n1
Moldova, 38, 82, *93*, 194, 236; intractable disputes, 122–24, 132–35, *133*, 139, 142, 143–44, 147; significance and, *93*–94, 96–97
Moldovan Popular Front (MPF), 38, 96
Mon/Monland, 194, 237–38
Montenegro, 22, 34, 37, 70–71
moral hazard, 81
Mordvins, 247n1
Moro National Liberation Front, 75
Moro unity, 232
Moscow Agreement (1992), 132, 141
Moseley, Christopher, 208
motivational heterogeneity, 16–17, 67; coordination of, 9–10, 70–73, 77–79; defined, 71. *See also* enthusiasts; expressionists; pragmatists
motivations, 13, 196–97; cultural, 171–77; economic, 171–72, 177–80. *See also* expressive incentives; incentives; material incentives; purposive incentives
Mozambique, 243n20
Mujibir Rahman (Mujib), 30, 58
multiethnic coalitions, 111, 234
Muslims, 99, 114, 176, 191. *See also* ISIS; Islamists
Myanmar/Burma, 27, 41, 44, 77, 150, 163, 234, 238

Nagaland, 235, 248n17
Nagornyi Karabakh, 3, 39, 41, 122–23, *125*, 125–26, 139–41, 144–47
Nakhchuo, 135
Namibia, 243n20
National Consortium for the Study of Terrorism and Responses to Terrorism (START), 204, 254n2
National Council of the Common-People's (Maubere) Resistance (CNRM), 53
nationalism, 48, 184; as elite phenomenon, 16; human differences and, 90–91; indigenous, 88–89; as popular ("mass") phenomenon, 16; propagation and, 75

national-secession campaigns: analytic model of, 12–19; death of, 14, 240n33; defined, 23, 191; failed projects, 88–89, 92, 94–95; goals of, 1–2, 9, 48–49, 67, 189; identifying, 23–28, 199–205; as revolutionary activity, 1–2; significant (since 1945), 26–28 (*see also* significant campaigns); successful (*see* secessions, successful)
national-secession civil wars, 149, 254n3. *See also* civil wars; protracted intensity
National Union of Timorese Students (UNETIM), 52
National Union of Timorese Workers, 52
nations: defined, 106; idea of, 175–76; as inventions, 104
nation-state project, defined, 9
NATO, 32
Navajo, 248n17
Navarrese intellectuals, 56
negotiations, 117–18, 138–48; as propaganda, 119, 148; pseudo-bargaining, 143–45. *See also* bargaining; deadlock; intractability
neologisms, 99, 111
Nicaragua, 243n20
Nigeria, 25, 28, 234
Nonviolent and Violent Campaigns and Outcomes Data Project (NAVCO), 204, 220
Norman, Wayne, 105
North Africa, 42
North Atlantic world, 169, 175, 176, 184
Northern Cyprus, 3, 43, 164, 250n10
Northern Ireland, 7, 44, 77, 86–87, 159–60. *See also* Irish Republican Army (IRA)
North Ossetia, 131, 141
Northwest Territorial Imperative, 89, 248n23
Norway, 4, 33
Novorossiia (New Russia), 2, *93*, 93–95, 99–100
Nuer, 111

O'Ballance, Edgar, 50, 62
Obama, Barack, 24
occupied territories, 25–26, 240n6
Oceania, 27–28
Odessa, 94–95
Ogaadeen, 41
O'Loughlin, John, 127
operational objectives, 45; defined, 9; of successful campaigns, 22–23; violence and, 10–11, 155–56, 169
operational weakness, 45, 91, 180, 189; defined, 5; of revolutionary movements, 239n11

United States, 23–25, 32–34, 147, 230, 248n17
unsuccessful campaigns. *See* failed projects
Uppsala Conflict Data Program (UCDP),
    204, 254n1
USSR. *See* Soviet Union
Uzbekistan, 22, 39

Varshney, Ashutosh, 244n17
Vaux, Tony, 141
Velvet Divorce, 35
Verba, Sidney, 114
Vietcong, 180
Vietnam, 243n20
violence, 3–5; authenticity and, 161, 164–69;
    bargaining and, 18, 181–82, 250n9;
    campaign leaders' information on, 43–45;
    in civil wars, 204–5; constraints on, 151,
    153–54, 157–60, 167–69; cues for, 151, 156;
    as cue to authenticity and realism, 156;
    as expressive incentive, 85–87; grievances
    and, 170; high-intensity, 40–43, 204–5;
    independence and, 42–43, 120–21, 205;
    intense, 3, 40, 204; low-intensity, 204;
    mobilization and, 153–54; nonlethal, 204;
    operational objectives and, 10–11, 155–56,
    169; organization and, 153–54; platform
    populations and, 161; pragmatists and,
    156–57; programmatic coordination and,
    152–60; programmatic preemption and, 11,
    91, 154–55; as propaganda, 152, 170, 233;
    realism and, 156, 161, 164–69; secessions,
    successful and, 40–43; tactical-logistical
    opportunities and, 170; types of, 190–92,
    204–5. *See also* civil wars; collaborationism;
    compromise; intensity; protracted intensity

Vojvodina (Magyar), 25, 37
Volga German Republic, 24
Volkova, Anna, 134
Volskii, Arkadii, 80
von der Mehden, Fred R., 25, 178, 248n15

Walter, Barbara F., 110, 187
Weber, Max, 106, 240n24
Weingarten, Joseph P., Jr., 181
Western Papua, 111
Western powers, 33–34, 36, 230–33
Whitmeyer, Joseph M., 88
Wilkinson, Steven, 259n6
Wilson, Andrew, 39
Wilson, James Q., 49, 70, 119–20, 242n1
Wimmer, Andreas, 105, 114, 183, 208
Wintrobe, Ronald, 195
Wittenberg, Jason, 216
Wolf, Charles, Jr., 60
Wolff, Stefan, 134
Wood, Elisabeth Jean, 246n72

Xi Jinping, 107
Xinjiang, 6, 89, 107, 186

Yandarbiev, Zelimkhan, 80, 140
Yanukovych, Yurii, 95
Yeltsin, Boris, 39, 135, 140, 143, 236
Young, Crawford, 25, 178, 248n15
Yugoslavia, 2–3, 27–28, 32, 36–37, 42, 50, 58
Yugoslav National Army (JNA), 36

Zavgaev, Doku, 136–37
Zhivkov, Todor, 233
Zimbabwe, 243n20

CPSIA information can be obtained
at www.ICGtesting.com
Printed in the USA
BVHW08*0727020918
526118BV00001B/11/P

9 781501 725982